"DOERS OF THE WORD"

"DOERS OF THE WORD"

African-American Women Speakers
and Writers in the North
(1830–1880)

CARLA L. PETERSON

Rutgers University Press
New Brunswick, New Jersey, and London

First published in cloth by Oxford University Press, Inc., 1995

First published in paperback by Rutgers University Press,
New Brunswick, New Jersey, 1998

Library of Congress Cataloging-in-Publication Data

Peterson, Carla L., 1944–   .
    Doers of the word : African-American women speakers and writers in
the North (1830–1880) / Carla L. Peterson.
        p.   cm.
    Originally published: New York : Oxford University Press, 1995.
    Includes bibliographical references and index.
    ISBN 0-8135-2514-4 (pbk. : alk. paper)
    1. American prose literature—Afro-American authors—History and
criticism.   2. American prose literature—Northeastern States—
History and criticism.   3. American prose literature—Women
authors—History and criticism.   4. American prose literature—19th
century—History and criticism.   5. Women and literature—United
States—History—19th century.   6. Afro-American women social
reformers—Northeastern States.   7. Social problems—United
States—History—19th century.   8. Afro-Americans—Social
conditions—19th century.   9. Social problems in
literature.   10. Afro-Americans in literature.   11. Race in
literature.   I. Title.
    [PS153.N5P443   1998]
    810.9′9287′08996073—dc21   97-41838
                                                                      CIP

British Library Cataloguing in Publication Data is available.

Manufactured in the United States of America

For my mother
Vera Joseph Peterson

and in memory of my grandmother
Rhoda Jane Delisser

Acknowledgments

This book took shape slowly over a number of years. The idea of writing it came to me after reading Dorothy Sterling's *We Are Your Sisters*, which led to my desire to investigate the more literary aspects of the oratory and writing of some of the women whose lives she so vividly evokes. I started work on the project during a fellowship year at the Center for Advanced Study in the Behavioral Sciences at Stanford in 1987–88. I owe a particular debt to two of my Center colleagues: Kitty Sklar, who pointed out to me that "defining my population" was my first and most difficult task, and Carol Stack, whose work on the black family opened up to me the possibilities of a broad cultural perspective.

Several other fellowships provided me with additional time off for research and writing: a University of Maryland Graduate Research Board Award as well as American Council of Learned Societies and American Association of University Women fellowships. My research was greatly facilitated by the holdings of several libraries and the help of their staffs: the Library of Congress, the Antiquarian Society, the Pennsylvania Historical Society, the Library Company of Philadelphia, where I was assisted by Denise Larrabee and Philip Lapsansky, and the Moorland-Spingarn Library at Howard University, where Esme Bahn and Janet Sims-Wood were always ready to help me.

Along the way I was supported by many colleagues, students, and friends. At the University of Maryland my graduate students stimulated me to hone and refine my arguments, and my group of Sister Scholars was always available to provide me with moral and intellectual encouragement. Specifically, I would like to thank Nellie McKay, who patiently listened to many conference papers in which I tried out arguments for the first time; Claudia Tate, who read and commented on the entire manuscript; Ira Berlin, who did his best to ensure the accuracy of my historical analyses; and my two graduate assistants, Lisa Koch and Sujata Moorti, who helped me with footnotes and bibliography. I owe the largest debt of gratitude to Shelley Fisher Fishkin for critiquing the manuscript with painstaking acuity and care. Finally, I wish to thank my family—my husband,

David, and my daughters, Sarah and Julia—for their willingness to allow these nineteenth-century black women to enter their lives and sit with them at the dinner table for a number of years. I am especially grateful to David who not only gave me support and editorial assistance during the writing process but more significantly located Cumberworth's statue at the Louvre.

A different version of chapter 6 appeared as "Capitalism, Black (Under)-development, and the Production of the African American Novel in the 1850s," *American Literary History* 4 (Winter 1992): 559–83. Material from chapters 1, 3, 4, and 6 appeared in my essay "'Doers of the Word': Theorizing African-American Women Writers in the Antebellum North," in *The (Other) American Traditions: Nineteenth-Century American Women Writers*, ed. Joyce Warren (New Brunswick, N.J.: Rutgers University Press, 1993), 183–202. Reprinted by permission of Rutgers University Press.

In chapter 2 I wish to call the readers' attention to Nell Irvin Painter's fine essay, "Representing Truth: Sojourner Truth's Knowing and Becoming Known," *Journal of American History* 81 (September 1994): 461–92, which appeared after this book went to press.

Finally, I would like to honor the memory of Stanley George, my editor at Oxford University Press, who provided friendly advice and encouragement when I most needed it. He will be missed.

Contents

"DOERS OF THE WORD"

1

"Doers of the Word": Theorizing African-American Women Speakers and Writers in the Antebellum North

Throughout the nineteenth century a number of black women traveled in the northeastern, mid-Atlantic, and midwestern states, insisting on their right to preach the gospel, to lecture, and to write on such topics as religious evangelicism, abolitionism, moral reform, temperance, and women's rights. Adapting a verse from the Epistle of James to describe their self-appointed cultural mission, they thought of themselves as "doers of the word."[1] In invoking themselves as such, these women recognized the extent to which their efforts to "elevate the race" and achieve "racial uplift" lay not only in their engagement in specific political and social activities but also in their faith in the performative power of the word—both spoken and written. For these and other activists—Sojourner Truth, Maria Stewart, Jarena Lee, Nancy Prince, Mary Ann Shadd Cary, Frances Ellen Watkins Harper, Sarah Parker Remond, Harriet A. Jacobs, Harriet E. Wilson, and Charlotte Forten—speaking and writing constituted a form of doing, of social action continuous with their social, political, and cultural work.

Doers of the Word is an attempt to understand the cultural work of these black women activists. As such, it forms part of the recovery work currently being undertaken by literary critics and historians alike to rediscover and reinterpret the complexities of nineteenth-century African-American culture and in the process shed new light on our present historical moment. More specifically, it takes its place alongside such exemplary scholarship as Dorothy Sterling's *We Are Your Sisters*, Angela Davis's *Women, Race, and Class*, Hazel Carby's *Reconstructing Womanhood*, Joanne Braxton's *Black Women Writing Autobiography*, Claudia Tate's *Domestic Allegories of Political Desire*, and Frances Smith Foster's *Written by Herself*. Its point of departure lies in the premise that resistant "civil rights movements" are not a modern phenomenon but can be traced at least as far back as the early nineteenth century, and that investigations of African-American culture in the "free" North provide an important counterweight to the more numerous histories of Southern slavery, where power relations between blacks and whites took on a highly specific and codified configuration. In particular, the study seeks to recover from scholarly neglect the contributions made by black women to racial uplift efforts in the North from the antebellum era through Reconstruction, to analyze the role of gender (as well as class and religion) in the construction of ideologies of black cultural nationalism during this period. Its goal is to enlarge our historical understanding of nineteenth-century black resistance movements by supplementing the existing scholarship on Frederick Douglass, David Walker, Henry Highland Garnet, Martin Delany, and other male figures with an examination of the role of black women in these movements.[2]

To analyze the cultural production of these women, I emphasize at the outset the need to ground literary scholarship in historical specificity. I would argue that since so much of our history has yet to be recovered, we are not yet in a position to theorize in a totalizing fashion about black literary production, either by constructing a literary canon of masterpiece texts; by formulating a black aesthetic based on the cultural matrix of the blues, the vernacular, or folk expression; or, more narrowly, by insisting upon the existence of a transhistorical black feminist aesthetic. Such theorizing tends to elide historical difference and to underestimate the complexity of African-American experience, thus promoting notions of an essential or authentic racial blackness that misunderstands the ways in which African Americans have been marked not only by the social category of race but also by gender, class, religion, and region.

Historical specificity does not imply, however, a mere devotion to the accumulation and recording of facts for, as Abdul R. JanMohamed and David Lloyd have insisted, the "theoretical and archival work of minority culture must always be concurrent and mutually reinforcing," so that if "archival work is essential to the critical articulation of minority discourse, at the same time . . . theoretical reflection cannot be dispensed with."[3] Archival work enables us to recover the details of a particular period of African-American history—to apprehend the specific circumstances under which African Americans experienced daily life and to reconstruct the various modes of social action and cultural expression through which they sought to counter oppression and empower themselves and their communities. On the basis of such recovery work, we can then attempt to interpret the nature, meaning, and implications of such action and expression—in short, to theorize their significance. Theory is, finally, embedded in archival work from the start since "history" is recoverable only through written texts and artifacts that themselves require interpretation. History is always already constructed and enmeshed in theory.

I begin my study in the early 1830s at the moment when a substantial body of writing by black women first emerged; and I trace this writing through the Reconstruction period in order to examine these women's reactions to the ever-shifting political and social landscape of race and gender relations after the Civil War as well as their expectations of the widened roles they hoped to play in both their communities and the nation at large. To analyze their writings, I have needed to historicize notions of literature and broaden literary study into a larger field of cultural investigation. Indeed, the dominant trend in literary scholarship has been to privilege the slave narrative as *the* African-American literary form of the antebellum period, focusing in particular on Frederick Douglass's 1845 *Narrative* and Harriet Jacobs's 1861 *Incidents in the Life of a Slave Girl.* In such a reconstruction, the slave narrative becomes the metonym for nineteenth-century African-American literary production. As a result, literary criticism of the late twentieth century has come dangerously close to replicating the historical situation of the early nineteenth century in its valorization of those African-American texts produced under the direction of white sponsors for the consumption of a white readership, while marginalizing and even occluding those other forms of narrative writing produced specifically for the black community.

Rather than privilege any one literary form over others and reify early African-American texts into a monolithic literary canon or tradition, I have followed nineteenth-century African-American definitions of what constitutes a literary text. At the end of a chapter entitled "Afro-American Literature" in *The Work of the Afro-American Woman* (1894), Mrs. N. F. Mossell appended a list of publications that juxtaposes slave narratives to sociological texts, fiction, journalism, history, religious studies, poetry, and spiritual autobiographies.[4] This list includes—as does my own study—genres and texts that would be considered either "nonliterary" by modernist criteria, and thus more appropriate to the fields of history or sociology, or "minor" by historical standards, and thus unworthy of serious attention. Mossell's inclusions thus sharply underscore the political significance of modernist disciplinary/aesthetic exclusion: the erasure from scholarly investigation of "minority" texts considered insufficiently "important" or "beautiful" by dominant cultural standards. Further extending this reevaluation of the African-American literary text, I suggest that literary analysis can no longer merely focus on texts as pure objects but must examine how these were shaped both by a politics of publication (for example, access to mainstream publishing houses, self-publication, white abolitionist patronage) and by a politics of reception (for example, negotiation of multiple audiences, audience constraints).

Such revised notions of textuality have led me finally to question the validity of dividing historical event from literary account as separate objects of scholarly investigation, the one pertaining to fields within the social sciences, the other to literary criticism. In my work I seek to bridge the disciplines of history, literary criticism, and anthropology by building upon Foucault's interdisciplinary model of discourse. For Foucault, discourse is above all a practical strategy designed to overcome the distinction between idea and action in historical study. It represents, quite generally, a means of constituting and producing social knowledge. Following his own formulation, it is a field of knowledge "made up of the totality of all effective statements (whether spoken or written), in their dispersion as events and the occurrence that is proper to them."[5] Discourses, then, are not simply verbal utterances but are constituted by social practices that themselves include institutions, their sites and modes of operation, forms of subjectivity, and power relations, as well as their enunciation.

Working with such notions from an explicitly feminist perspective, my study seeks to define and analyze the discourse of Northern African-American women from approximately 1830 to 1880 as generated both from within their culture and as a response to the dominant discourses of racism and sexism. In so doing I remain fully aware of the constructed nature of my narrative, that my attempts at historical reconstruction are grounded, in Donna Haraway's terms, in a "partial perspective" offering "situated knowledges."[6] My "partial perspective" is revealed from the outset in the initial series of questions that I ask about these African-American women and their literary production: What empowered them to act, to speak out, and to write? From what particular site(s) did they carry out such activities? What are the different power relations embedded in the different modes of acting, speaking, and writing, and how did these black women negotiate these relations? How might one distinguish between their social action and its literary representation?

From my "situated" location, I have been struck first of all by the limitations of current theory and its vocabulary to analyze the cultural production of black women. If indeed "all the women are white, all the blacks are men, but some of us are brave," how can the "brave" be conceptualized and with what terminology?[7] To answer this question we need, on the one hand, to examine the working relationship between black men and women, to analyze the ways in which they were on many occasions mutually supportive in their racial uplift efforts yet antagonistic on others. On the other hand, we must also assess the degree to which, given their racial difference, communication was possible between black and white women, and to which, even in the absence of direct contact, these women might have shared similar cultural values. To talk about the "brave" remains a complex task, however, for the very use of the term opens onto indefiniteness and multiplicity rather than neat categorization, and points toward an idea of "selfhood" that can be articulated only with difficulty. Accompanied by neither noun nor adjective that would specify it, the term *brave* forces us to recognize the extent to which sociological categories have reified notions of subjectivity and to rethink the ways in which these might be utilized, in the process dismantling binary modes of thought and throwing traditional systems of difference into crisis. Following Nancy Hewitt, we might instead think of the subject as a *compound* "composed of elements that are chemically bonded to each other, the composition of each being transformed so that the original components can no longer be separated from each other."[8]

I suggest at the outset that the "brave" who form the subject of this book worked and wrote from positions of marginality, from social, psychological, and geographic sites that were peripheral to the dominant culture and, very often, to their own. This notion of marginality is, however, as problematic as that of the brave, for, if positions at the center tend to be fixed, such is not the case for locations on the periphery, which can move and slide along the circumference. Indeed, the black women I study repeatedly shifted approaches, strategies, and venues as they sought to achieve their goals of racial uplift. Furthermore, we must be wary of constructing a fixed binary that opposes and hierarchizes center and margins, for such positionings are conceptualized, to return to Haraway's terms, only from "partial" and "situated" perspectives. Finally, we must be careful not to fetishize positions on the margins as "pure" spaces of "radical openness and possibility" but must recognize that "margins have been both sites of repression and sites of resistance."[9] Indeed, margins are often uncomfortable places; as the lives of African-American women, past and present, exemplify, they can be sources of horrifying pain, generators of unspeakable terrors, particularly in their exploitation of the black female body.

AFRICAN-AMERICAN LOCAL PLACE IN THE ANTEBELLUM NORTH

How can we begin, then, to conceptualize African-American culture in the antebellum North? We have long recognized the ways in which dominated peoples have often found their national history distorted, hidden, or even abrogated by imperialist-colonial forces and have needed to disrupt hegemonic notions of history and their place in them in order to initiate historical reconstruction from their own perspective. The line "time broadens into space" by the Australian poet Les Murray further suggests the extent to which such peoples have not been able to take place for granted and how, in fact, conditions of colonization, both internal and external, have equally foregrounded the category of space.[10] In the process, geography becomes of central importance, and what Edward Said has asserted as paradigmatic for externally colonized peoples is equally pertinent to the history of African Americans:

> [What] radically distinguishes the imagination of anti-imperialism . . . is the primacy of the geographical in it. Imperialism after all is an act of geographical violence through which virtually every space in the world is explored, charted, and finally brought under control. For the native, the history of his/her colonial servitude is inaugurated by the loss to an outsider of the local place, whose concrete geographical identity must thereafter be searched for and somehow restored . . . historically and abductively from the deprivations of the present."[11]

If the local place is initially recoverable only through the imagination, the natives' ultimate goal is, of course, its actual restoration.

For nineteenth-century African Americans, this local space was double. It was, on the one hand, that place in Africa, before the Middle Passage, from which they or their forebears had been kidnapped but to which they for the most part did not wish to return, except perhaps through imaginative speculation. On the other hand, it was also that place in the United States—South or North—which functioned as what Foucault has called a "disciplinary partitioning" within a "carceral continuum," an enclosed panoptic space by means of which the dominant U.S. culture marked the exclusion of African Americans (as well as other racial and ethnic minorities) in order to keep them under constant surveillance, discipline them, and produce "docile bodies."[12]

If, from the point of view of those in power, such a panoptic space was designed to subjugate and police the Other, from the point of view of this Other it eventually came to constitute "home." Foucault's vision of modern disciplinary society is presented mainly from the perspective of those in positions of authority. My study asks whether it is possible to imagine a scenario whereby the incarcerated could escape, and perhaps even return, the gaze of their wardens; undo the dominant culture's definitions of such binary oppositions as order/disorder, normal/abnormal, harmless/dangerous; break down those boundaries separating the one from the Other; and in the process create a space that they could call home. In seeking to answer this question, I remain mindful of the fact that home is never natural or safe; it is always grounded in a material situation that is subject to change and involves a complicated working out of the relationship between personal identity, family, and community that challenges the very notion of these entities as "coherent, historically continuous, stable."[13]

The panoptic space allotted to nineteenth-century African Americans in the free North was anything but mechanistically organized. The vast majority lived in urban environments—cities like Philadelphia, Boston, New York, Salem, and Rochester—which, under pressure from emerging Jacksonian commercial and manufacturing capitalism, had been reduced to near chaos. Social and economic mobility, foreign immigration, religious upheavals all contributed to an unprecedented degree of transience and fragmentation within, and between, cities. While their African-American inhabitants constituted a distinct social entity determinedly seeking to recreate a local place for themselves, they nonetheless remained a heterogeneous and shifting group, as did their experiences; such diversity undermines any essentialist notions of blackness that we might be tempted to construct.

In analyzing this African-American population I identify four social spheres through which it carried out its activities: the domestic, ethnic community, ethnic public, and national public spheres.[14] The heterogeneity of the black community manifested itself in a number of ways, for example, in a division between freeborn and slave-born inhabitants, persons of Northern and Southern origins, dark- and light-skinned individuals. Such divisions tended ultimately to sort themselves out along class lines. The elite, exemplified by Sarah Parker Remond, Charlotte Forten, and even Frances Ellen Watkins Harper, was generally composed of a freeborn, Northern-rooted, and light-skinned population, who had achieved a high degree of literacy. Its men found steady employment as small business owners and craftsmen, or, less frequently, as professionals, principally ministers (Richard Allen, Daniel Payne), teachers (William Watkins), and doctors (William Wells Brown, Martin Delany); some were even independent businessmen (Paul Cuffe, James Forten, John Remond). As James Horton has shown, these men aspired—often unrealistically—to incorporate the dominant culture's ideology of true womanhood into its social code and thereby privatize its women. As the century progressed, this elite increasingly withdrew from participation in Baptist and Methodist religious practices in order to affiliate with the more sedate black Episcopalian and Presbyterian churches. In contrast, the black subaltern class, of which Sojourner Truth and Jarena Lee were members, was composed primarily of unskilled laborers, the men employed as sailors, waiters, or mechanics, the women as domestics and laundresses. Less literate, this group was rooted in oral and folk culture and formed the bedrock of Methodist and Baptist churches.[15]

While such internal stratification was real enough, African-American elite and subaltern classes nonetheless formed a loosely knit cultural group; as Gary Nash has noted, "the lines that separated [their] cultural expressions . . . were never tightly drawn."[16] In fact, these black urban communities represented what Stallybrass and White have called a "hybrid place" in which categories usually kept separate—high and low, native and foreign, polite and savage, sacred and profane—commingle and result in cultural forms perceived as grotesque by the dominant culture.[17] Hybridity may be evidenced in the very notion of a black elite; for while its members did achieve high social positions as well-respected leaders of their community, their economic and occupational status was often disproportionately lower. Furthermore, many religious and cultural practices, which were themselves adaptations of Africanisms to North American black urban life, could on occasion to bring together elite and subaltern classes—the antiphonal choral singing of religious worship, variants of the John Kunering ritual and the Congo dance, the parades of kings and governors on election day, the preparation and consumption of stews and other foods.[18]

If the principles of hybridity upon which these black urban communities were based were inexplicable to the dominant culture in their disruption of fixed hierarchies and binary oppositions, to their own members they were readily comprehensible as necessary strategies for self-empowerment, community building, and the construction of home. African Americans needed to resist, and to adapt themselves, not only to the forces of white racism but also to a growing capitalist economy in which wealth was increasingly concentrated in the hands of a small number of manufacturers who controlled the wage labor of an urban workforce composed of native whites, European immigrants, and blacks. At the very bottom of this workforce, black men and women strove to transform their marginal status into a source of strength, to achieve social and economic autonomy by circumventing capitalist structures and holding on to precapitalist forms of behavior. Urban blacks thus sought to engage in skilled crafts and trades in which in-house production or self-employment would be possible, in the process offering service to the black community rather than a white clientele.[19] Outside of work, community members came together in voluntary benevolent associations—mutual aid societies, orphanages, almshouses—designed to succor those in need.[20] In the domestic sphere, finally, living arrangements reflected an adaptation of African family patterns; households were based not primarily on nuclear family structures but rather on larger domestic networks that often included nonkin members, for example, boarders who were gradually incorporated into the household and contributed to its maintenance.

Within this black urban population, however, the elite did separate itself out to some degree, working, speaking, and writing from within the ethnic public sphere—a set of broader institutions designed to provide intellectual and political leadership to the African-American population as a whole. Although these institutions were located primarily in the North, they were conceived as national since they were dedicated to the national interest of all African Americans. One such institution was black Masonry, founded in 1784 with the opening of Boston's African Lodge No. 459 under the direction of Prince Hall, who insisted that the Masonic principles of charity be extended among blacks to encompass both local community service and broader antislavery work.[21] Of equal importance was the church, in particular the African Methodist Episcopal (AME) Church formed as a separate black discipline by Richard Allen in 1816 as an outgrowth of the Free African Society that had been organized in 1787 after he and Absalom Jones quit Philadelphia's Saint George's Methodist Church in protest over its discriminatory practices.[22] In 1831 Richard Allen was also instrumental in initiating the convention movement through which African Americans came together annually to debate public civic issues of critical importance to their welfare—for example, the abolition of slavery, the petitioning for civil rights, the establishment of vocational and other schools, strategies to combat job discrimination, the desirability of emigration. Rivaling the convention movement was the American Moral Reform Society that brought together the New York and Philadelphia leadership between 1835 and 1842.[23]

At about the same time that the black leadership began organizing its annual conventions, William Lloyd Garrison's antislavery movement was gaining momentum. Integrated from the outset, it included black men like Charlotte Forten's uncle, Robert Purvis, and Shadd Cary's father, Abraham Shadd, both of whom took part in the formation of the American Anti-Slavery Society in December 1833. Black men were also active members of many of the society's affiliates, the Massachusetts, New York, and Pennsylvania Anti-Slavery Societies, for example; in addition, several women's auxiliaries, such as the Philadelphia and the Boston Female Anti-Slavery Societies, were also organized around these male societies. The existence of such affiliate groups gave impetus throughout the 1830s to the formation of all-black antislavery societies in many smaller communities, Rochester and Geneva, New York; Troy, Michigan; and Lexington, Massachusetts, for example; yet these never converged to form a separate national organization.[24] Finally, but by no means least important as a vehicle for self-representation, the African-American press was inaugurated with the publication of Samuel Cornish and John Russwurm's *Freedom's Journal* in 1827, followed, among others, by the *Colored American*, Douglass's *North Star, Frederick Douglass' Paper,* and *Douglass' Monthly*, Shadd Cary's *Provincial Freeman*, and, on the eve of the Civil War, the first black monthly magazine, Thomas Hamilton's *Anglo-African Magazine*, which was eventually superseded by the *Weekly Anglo-African.*

Returning to Foucault's notion of discourse, what must be emphasized here is the centrality of these institutions—in particular the national institutions—to the reproduction of African-American social, cultural, and literary knowledge in the nineteenth century. In his analysis of antebellum American society, Alexis de Tocqueville had already pointed to the great significance of "associations" in U.S. democratic life. Later twentieth-century critics such as Antonio Gramsci and Benedict Anderson have further underscored the importance of institutions in the struggle of subaltern classes to resist hegemonic control and of emerging nationalist movements to forge national consciousness. Although institutions are frequently viewed as cumbersome bureaucracies that stifle individual initiative and inhibit social change, they have often provided subordinated groups with a means to power: they create organized consent among their members by means of specific cultural, social, and intellectual activities; they work to promote the welfare of the population as a whole over that of specific individuals or groups; they encourage the careful planning of resistance strategies; they make public and thus more effective hitherto privately held sentiments. In particular, both de Tocqueville and Anderson emphasize the importance of the newspaper as an institution that connects people by articulating a sameness of purpose and providing a common means of executing designs. Thus, the newspaper, and other cultural forms as well, helps create "imagined community." For, if it is impossible for each member of the nation to know all the other members, these vehicles now make possible that "in the minds of each lives the image of their communion," a communion "conceived as a deep horizontal comradeship."[25]

AFRICAN-AMERICAN DISCOURSE IN THE ANTEBELLUM NORTH

I would argue that nineteenth-century African-American literary production—both spoken and written—had its origins not only in the white abolitionist movement that underwrote the publication of slave narratives but also in the national institutions of the black elite that addressed a specifically black audience. Through these organizations, the elite worked to construct a program of "racial uplift" that sought to raise the masses to its own social and cultural level as well as to theorize issues of black nationality. It came to conceptualize local place in terms of both the black community itself and the nation as a whole, demanding equal

11

civil and political rights for all African Americans. Some social historians have argued that this agenda was threatened from the outset by divisions within the black elite as well as by its social ideology that sought merely to replicate the values of the hegemony and assimilate into white middle-class culture.[26] Indeed, this racial uplift program encouraged the elite self-consciously to assert its social distance both from the "degraded" Northern subaltern class of unskilled and illiterate laborers and from Southern slaves, to articulate its aspirations to middle-class status by means of improved education and acceptance of Euro-American standards of civilization, and to proclaim its adherence to the dominant culture's ethic of hard work, self-help, and moral purity.

Yet to critique this ideology of racial uplift as bourgeois or conservative is to misunderstand the dynamics of social change under conditions of internal (or external) colonization. Frantz Fanon, for example, has written of the need for a "revolutionary elite who have come up from the people" to acknowledge its estrangement from the masses before joining with them to undertake their political education, "opening their minds, awakening them, and allowing the birth of their intelligence."[27] Moreover, not only did the black elite seek to uplift the subaltern class, it also recognized the imperative need for racial solidarity: "Identified with a people over whom weary ages of degradation have passed," wrote Watkins Harper in 1857, "whatever concerns them, as a race, concerns me."[28] Finally, if this elite's assimilationist ideology was on one level complicitous with the dominant culture, on another level it sought to subvert this culture, condemning its failure to uphold its stated ideals and asserting the African American's right to both political freedom and cultural distinctiveness. Indeed, W. E. B. Du Bois was later to characterize such racial uplift work as a "determined effort at self-realization and self-development despite environing opinion," and to argue that these early leaders had in fact inaugurated a new period in African-American history in which "the assertion of the manhood rights of the Negro by himself was the main reliance" and the single most important goal "ultimate assimilation *through* self-assertion, and on no other terms."[29]

Given the fact of internal colonization and of the irretrievable loss of local place in the Old World, these early African-American leaders were only too well aware of their deracination and of the consequent need to come to terms with their Americanness and incorporate it into their lives. We can again turn to Fanon for an acute analysis of the problematics of defining a national culture once the impossibility of returning to a utopic precolonized condition and of claiming an originary folk culture has been acknowledged: "We must not therefore be content with delving into the past of a people in order to find coherent elements which will counteract colonialism's attempts to falsify and harm. . . . A national culture is not a folklore, nor an abstract populism that believes it can discover the people's true nature. . . . A national culture is the whole body of efforts made by a people in the sphere of thought to describe, justify, and praise the action through which that people has created itself and keeps itself in existence."[30]

12

Such notions of cultural hybridity were already fully articulated in the writings of Maria Stewart. As early as 1831, she openly lamented the fall of "poor, despised Africa" once "the seat, if not the parent of science, . . . the resort of sages and legislators of other nations," praised the rise of American civilization, and urged its imitation by African Americans: "I see [the American people] thriving in arts, and sciences, and in polite literature. Their highest aim is to excel in political, moral, and religious improvement. . . . The Americans have practiced nothing but head-work these 200 years, and we have done their drudgery. And is it not high time for us to imitate their examples, and practice head-work too, and keep what we have got, and get what we can?" Yet at the same time her writings exude a strong revolutionary note as she repeatedly invoked the Old Testament rhetoric of prophecy to chastise America for its oppression of blacks, envisaging its destruction at the hands of God and predicting the resurrection of the African race as recorded in Psalm 68: "'Ethiopia shall again stretch forth her hands unto God.'"[31]

Literary production like that of Maria Stewart may thus be seen as an important part of the self-empowerment and community-building strategies of the African-American elite. Yet if black leaders strove through writing to implement the stated objective of *Freedom's Journal*—"We wish to plead our own cause"— they also discovered that writing gave rise to complex problems of commodification. Indeed, the very act of authorship could at times separate black writers from their broader community, constituting them as a distinct class that sought to speak not only for itself but also for the subaltern, and thereby working to some extent against community cohesiveness. Furthermore, these writers often found it difficult to depend on a black readership and patronage exclusively and were consequently obliged to write under the aegis of white sponsors and to accede to the inevitable constraining presence of a white audience that might be indifferent or even unsympathetic to their needs. Finally, African-American literary production was vastly complicated by the dominant culture's market economy, which sought to regulate the production and dissemination of literary texts. Although the history of African-American publication in the antebellum period is difficult to reconstruct, available information suggests that the primary venues for publishing were self-publication, publication by a white abolitionist press (in particular that of Garrison's *Liberator*), publication in Britain, and lastly, publication by mainstream U.S. houses that generally remained reluctant to place black authors on their lists.

Given this disruptive potential of writing, what kind of literary discourse could nineteenth-century African-American writers invent for themselves in their efforts to write racial uplift? One common eighteenth-century myth held that enslaved blacks were but "talking apes" whose ability to speak had become the very cause of their enslavement, in contrast to those left behind in the jungle who had "refrain[ed] from speaking in order to avoid being made slaves."[32] But nineteenth-century African-American literary discourse cannot be dismissed as a mere aping of the dominant discourse that inevitably leads to enslavement to the values of the hegemony. Neither was it simply a version of Foucauldian "counter-discourse" designed to counter the dominant discourse by maintaining while reversing and redeploying the terms, categories, and values of the hegemony.

Aware of the necessity of becoming "producers" rather than remaining "merely, as now, consumers,"[33] African-American writers constructed a productive discourse generated from within the community that borrows the vocabulary and categories of the dominant discourse only to dislocate them from their privileged position of authority and adapt them to the local place.[34] This discourse constitutes, then, a particular form of Stallybrass and White's cultural hybridity, one that, as Homi Bhabha has suggested in another context, effectively deconstructs the dichotomy embedded in the assumption that colonial power manifests itself either in "the noisy command of colonialist authority or the silent repression of native traditions." Indeed, while this African-American discourse appears merely to reiterate the dominant discourse, it in fact disrupts it and "challenges its boundaries" by inscribing both presence and absence in its texts. On the one hand, it introduces what Bhabha has called "denied knowledges" from the native culture into the dominant discourse so as to "estrange" the latter's "basis of . . . authority."[35] On the other hand, it may also configure a silence around the gaps that open up between the "inter/faces of the 'official language' of the text and the cultural difference brought to it" by native tradition.[36] Counteracting the text's tendency toward cultural complicity, such presences and absences work to subvert literary commodification; they constitute, in fact, imaginative recreations of local place and function as cultural sites of resistance. As Henry Louis Gates has suggested, black texts embody a "black double-voicedness," or "signify," as they repeat texts of the Western literary tradition but with a "signal difference" that resides in the author's evocation of "black" cultural forms.[37] Finally, if such a hybrid discourse is designed to negotiate multiple audiences, it also suggests the possibility of African-American authors' address to an "imagined community" beyond their immediate readership, a community preoccupied with the central task of forging a political and cultural nationality.

The Social Spheres of African-American Women

Within this general context of nineteenth-century African-American discursive practices, how can black women's culture and writing be specified? We need first of all to locate the particular position(s) of black women within Northern urban communities—to examine the different spaces they inhabited, to look at how they crossed social and geographic boundaries and negotiated "private" and "public" spheres. In so doing we must emphasize spatial plurality by remaining attentive to the ways in which the categories of race, gender, class, and culture complicated the politics of location of nineteenth-century black women. From such a perspec-

tive of heterogeneity, general paradigms break down; the private-public dichotomy must be adapted to specific historical circumstance. As we shall see, the
discourse of these black women constitutes a particular form of hybridity in its
disruption not only of the discourse of the dominant culture but also of that of the
black male elite.

Historians of the dominant culture have typically located nineteenth-century
women within the "private" sphere as opposed to the "public," which remained
the province of men. More recently, however, scholars have insisted that this
private-public dichotomy is too reductive and needs to be reconceptualized. They
point out, first of all, that the private sphere is everywhere infiltrated by the public.
Women's duties as laborers in the household, as procreators, and as socializers of
children are all carried out in the name of the public interest; they may more
properly be termed "domestic" rather than "private." Moreover, in antebellum
America the Southern slave household itself defied the ideology of separate
spheres as it contained within it aspects of both productive and reproductive
relations, regulating both the labor and sexual relations of master and slave
classes.[38] Finally, black men in the North obviously could not participate in
activities in the national public sphere to the same extent as men from the
dominant culture given the limitations imposed on their civil and political rights.
Such a constraint helped minimize although it did not eradicate the domestic-
public dichotomy in Northern black communities.

Like white women, black women saw "domestic economy" as an empowering
cultural model. Yet the domestic sphere of black society cannot be conceptualized
in the same way as that of the dominant culture. Indeed, given the economic
system that undergirded Northern black communities, as well as the demographic
situation of black women—greater percentage than men, low fertility and
birthrate—African-American familial life cannot be construed in the same terms
as the white middle-class family.[39] We cannot make assumptions about the primacy of the nuclear family nor of women as wives and mothers; we need to think
instead in terms of broader domestic networks, both kin and nonkin. In fact,
almost all the women studied in this book followed the "anomalous" pattern of
late marriage or early widowhood and consequently bore no, or few, children.
They were thus freed from many of the domestic obligations that burdened most
women, black and white. But, ever aware of the importance of preserving the
integrity of black family life and its domestic networks, these black women sought
to make of the family a site of cultural resistance. They constitute striking examples of how, to quote Mina Caulfield, "families, generally under the leadership of
women, have fought back, defending subsistence production as it becomes more
precarious, cementing family bonds and building new networks of mutual support
as the old ones come under attack, consolidating and developing cultures of
resistance—cultures which, like the role of women and family life itself, have
been devalued under imperialist ideology."[40] Thus, Stewart, Prince, and Watkins
Harper insisted that black women dedicate themselves to proper household

maintenance, child rearing, gardening, diet, and hygiene. Still other women, like Sarah Mapps Douglass, spoke out on issues of women's physiology and anatomy, underscoring the need for black women to care for their bodies.[41]

Furthermore, the activities of black women, like those of black men, extended beyond the family into the ethnic community sphere. Black women joined in female benevolent associations that coexisted alongside similar men's organizations in order to take care of others in the community and, in particular, of each other. They involved themselves in what we could call the politics of domestic economy, which provided a solid base for cooperative community action. Stewart, Prince, Watkins Harper, and Jacobs, for example, devoted themselves to moral reform activities, creating "asylums" to shelter destitute young women, organizing mutual aid societies to succor the needy, or participating in the free produce and temperance movements. Stewart and Forten joined literary societies—the former Boston's Afric-American Female Intelligence Society in 1832, the latter a Philadelphia women's society in 1858—designed to enhance the intellectual and moral quality of black women's lives.[42] Black men, who were themselves deeply engaged in moral reform work, encouraged these benevolent activities, which they saw as necessary to the success of racial uplift. This community sphere thus functioned as an intermediate sphere situated somewhere between the domestic/private and the public. It can be viewed as "public" as it is located outside the "home" and remains preoccupied with the welfare of the general population, but it is also "domestic" in that it represents an extension of the values of "home" into the community; and it is "private" insofar as it is able to remain hidden, abstracted from the gaze of the dominant culture. For nineteenth-century African Americans, this sphere was vital to the preservation of both the bodily integrity and the psychic security of families and individuals.

Finally, many of these black women—Truth, Lee, Stewart, Prince, and Watkins Harper, for example—entered the national public sphere as workers, principally domestics or seamstresses. In this unprotected public sphere, black women suffered indignities and assaults not experienced by their white counterparts. In an autobiographical essay, Remond enumerated the many different places from which black women (and men) were likely to be expelled on account of racial prejudice: "They are excluded from public hotels, . . . omnibus[es], . . . steam-boats . . . places of amusements."[43] As public workers black women gained little prestige but did achieve economic independence as well as the geographic mobility and physical freedom that would enable them to take part in the public work of evangelicism, abolitionism, temperance, and women's rights. In the postbellum period such activity was expanded to include increased participation in the temperance and women's rights movements as well as vocal support for the Fifteenth Amendment, collaboration with the educational institutions of the Freedmen's Bureau, and, in the case of Truth, lobbying for the granting of western territory to the freed people.

Importantly, however, significant limits *were* placed on black women's activities beyond the community level, in the ethnic public sphere of black national institutions dominated by men of the elite. It is true that several of the women studied here did form close personal friendships with men of this elite who, impressed by the women's extraordinary talent, disregarded the cultural constraints imposed on women's public activities to act as their mentors. Thus, David Walker became Stewart's role model; after his death she praised him as one who "has distinguished himself in these modern days by acting wholly in the defense of African rights and liberty";[44] as bishop of the AME Church, Richard Allen offered Jarena Lee an unofficial preaching role in Philadelphia's churches; Martin Delany was instrumental in helping Shadd Cary shape her ideas concerning political nationhood; Charles Lenox Remond encouraged his sister Sarah's activities as an antislavery lecturer; and, finally, William Watkins proposed a framework of Christian social justice that would later be that of his niece Watkins Harper as well. Nevertheless, these women were officially excluded from those black national institutions mentioned earlier through which men of the elite came together to promote public civic debate on practical issues of racial uplift as well as those more theoretical considerations of black nationality.[45] For example, in the first several years of its existence women were denied membership in the American Moral Reform Society; moreover, women were neither allowed to attain leadership positions in the AME Church nor permitted to voice their opinions at the annual national conventions; finally, considerable opposition was mounted within the black community against Shadd Cary's editorship of the *Provincial Freeman.* In thus restricting the role of black women in the articulation of racial uplift programs, the black male leadership strove, in what it believed were the best interests of the community, to contain heterogeneity, silence difference, and gender blackness as male.

Black Women and Liminality

How, then, could black women enter into the arena of public civic debate? I suggest that they did so by "achieving" an additional "oppression," by consciously adopting a self-marginalization that became superimposed upon the already ascribed oppressions of race and gender and that paradoxically allowed empowerment.[46] In so doing, these women entered into a state of liminality defined, following Victor Turner, as that moment and place in which an individual, separated from society, comes to be "betwixt and between the positions assigned and arrayed by law, custom, convention and ceremonial," and in which the creation of *communitas* becomes possible: *"Communitas* emerges where social structure is not. . . . [I]t transgresses or dissolves the norms that govern structured and institutionalized relationships and is accompanied by experiences of unprecedented potency."[47] From the perspective of the black women studied in this book, these liminal spaces came to function, however temporarily, as their "center," offering them greater possibilities of self-expression as well as the potential to effect social change. Yet even in their marginal positions these women were not purely "outside of" but remained "a part of"; as such they were never fully free from, but remained in tension with, the fixed social and economic male-dominated hierarchies that structured Northern urban life.

For the older generation of women, Truth and Lee, for example, the liminal space they chose to enter was the clearing, the site of religious evangelical activities that had been unleashed by the Second Great Awakening and drew the powerless—women, blacks, rural folk, and all those dislocated by the economic upheaval of the Jacksonian market revolution—to religion as a source of power. In such places social hierarchies of race, class, and gender are overturned and deconstructed as the congregants merge in varying degrees of religious ecstasy with the Godhead. For the somewhat younger women, Stewart, Watkins Harper, Remond, and Shadd Cary, their liminal place became that of the public platform from which they lectured to "promiscuous assemblies," audiences composed of both men and women. As oratory was deemed to be a specifically masculine genre and public speaking an activity proper only to men, these women were charged with unsexing themselves through an unseemly exposure of the female body. White women—Frances Wright, Angelina Grimké, Abby Kelley, Lucretia Mott, to name a few—were also engaged in public lecturing during this period and were equally vulnerable to public scorn and hostility.[48] But these women generally found themselves cushioned by their race, class affiliation, family ties, and secure economic status. In contrast, public speaking often led to greater social and economic uncertainty for black women. In making the decision to engage in such activities, they often left their employment as teachers, seamstresses, or domestics to live on their own, separated from family and community; public lecturing became their chief means of livelihood, frequently rendering them dependent on the generosity of their audiences and hosts. Finally, for almost all the women studied, marginality was engendered by the act of travel in which the mere fact of geographic displacement (as with Lee) or the journey away from "home" to another location (the frontier of Canada for Shadd Cary, the swamps of the South Carolina Sea Islands for Forten) could open up new sites of empowerment or simply challenge the very notion of a stable home for African Americans.

It is important to note, however, that these women often entered the liminal space of *communitas* alone and could remain isolated within it despite the fact that their activities were designed to enhance community welfare. Indeed, these women did not always become part of the *communitas* but rather held an ambiguous insider/outsider status in relation to it. Moreover, if the absence of social structure made *communitas* possible for these women, it was its very existence that enabled black men to organize themselves in the ethnic public sphere. The elite's exclusion of black women from its national organizations, coupled with the women's lack of public power to create similar formal institutions, prevented black women leaders from joining together to form a national political community of their own in the antebellum period.

As Ann Boylan has noted, black women eagerly joined the broad racially mixed antislavery movement, participating "in many Female Anti-Slavery Societies, and in the three Anti-Slavery Conventions of American Women held between 1837 and 1839."[49] Furthermore, a number of the black women under study here were clearly cognizant of each other's cultural work, and their paths did sometimes cross. An 1854 article by Shadd Cary entitled "The Humbug of Reform" contains a reference to a speech given by Sojourner Truth.[50] Given Truth's widespread reputation, most of the other women probably also knew of her public activities; and Truth and Jacobs undoubtedly collaborated in their activities with the Freedmen's Bureau in Virginia during the Civil War. In addition, we know that Stewart and Prince both worshiped at the First African Baptist Church in Boston while Thomas Paul was still pastor there. Watkins Harper and Shadd Cary clearly knew of one another through the intermediary of William Still, met in the late 1850s and probably again in the 1890s at the foundation of the National Association of Colored Women. A mentor-protégé relationship brought Remond and Forten together from approximately 1854 to 1858. Finally, as a leading member of post-Reconstruction Washington D.C. black society, Forten, who by then had married the well-known Presbyterian minister Francis Grimké, was undoubtedly acquainted with Watkins Harper, Jacobs, and Shadd Cary. Watkins Harper mentions Forten in an essay written in the mid 1870s and corresponded with Francis Grimké during the 1890s; Grimké also wrote a moving tribute to Jacobs on the occasion of her death; finally, both Forten Grimké and Shadd Cary attended meetings of the Bethel Literary and Historical Association in the 1880s and 1890s.

As noted earlier, antebellum black women did come together in significant numbers to create their own local organizations—principally literary, antislavery, and mutual aid societies—designed to take care of family and community needs. It is impossible to underestimate the importance of such local associations in helping the development of black women's organizational skills, encouraging self and community empowerment, and validating practical work as an essential component of nation building. Yet in the final analysis the creation of a national network of black women leaders that would allow them as a group to enter into the arena of public civic debate and engage in sustained written production did not occur in the antebellum period. It was not until the Reconstruction period that black women joined the national organizations of black men and white women in significant numbers; and it was not until the early 1880s that they were able to create national organizations of their own that would come to function as their own "home places."

If such liminal spaces functioned as centers of empowerment, however, they also remained sites of oppression, separating the women from their "homes" and "native" communities, forcing an unfeminine exposure of the body, and thus further reminding them of their difference. Indeed, nineteenth-century black women were conceptualized by the dominant culture chiefly in bodily terms, in contrast to middle-class white women whose femininity, as defined by the cult of true womanhood, cohered around notions of the self-effacing body. According to this ideology, white women were to be hidden in the privacy of the domestic sphere, where they were encouraged to develop purity of mind and soul, impose complete emotional restraint on their physical movements through stringent rules of etiquette, and veil their already pale and delicate bodies in clothes that, following the sentimental ideal of transparency, would translate inner purity into outward form.[51] In contrast, the black woman's body was always envisioned as public and exposed. If in Europe this exposed body was caged and subjected to minute scientific inquiry, in the United States it was perceived, at least initially, as an uninhibited laboring body that was masculinized.[52] In descriptions in *Journey in the Seaboard Slave States*, for example, Frederick Law Olmsted emphasized the exposure of the female slave's body: "The dress of most of them was . . . reefed up . . . at the hips, so as to show their heavy legs, wrapped round with a piece of old blanket, in lieu of leggings or stockings. Most of them worked with bare arms, but wore strong shoes on the feet, and handkerchiefs on their heads." Olmsted further noted that no distinction appears to have been made between the "muscular" field work of male and female slaves: "The women . . . were engaged at exactly the same labor as the men; driving the carts, loading them with dirt, and dumping them upon the road; cutting down trees, and drawing wood by hand, to lay across the miry places; hoeing, and shoveling."[53]

Intimately linked in the white imagination to this masculine labor of slave women were those more feminine forms of work—the reproductive labor of childbirth, the obligation to fulfill the sexual pleasure of slave masters, and the nurturing of the latter's children. In Fanny Kemble's *Journal*, descriptions of the bodily suffering of slave women repeatedly associate the vicissitudes of "hard field work" with those of childbearing, emphasizing in particular "the terrible hardships the women underwent in being thus driven to labor before they had recovered from childbearing"; and an 1861 report commissioned by the federal government and reprinted by Remond noted that "cases occurred where the negress was overtaken by the pains of labour, and gave birth to her child in the field." Much less sympathetic, but perhaps more typical, was Olmsted's conflation of labor and sexuality in his depiction of the sensuality of slave women engaged in field work: "Clumsy, awkward, gross, elephantine in all their movements; pouting, grinning, and leering at us; sly, sensual, and shameless, in all their expressions and demeanor; I never before had witnessed, I thought, anything more revolting."[54] Feminine attributes and functions of the black female body were thus commonly represented in degraded terms as abnormal excessive sexual activity; and, when superimposed on masculine ones, led to the creation of a complexly ambiguous portrait of the nineteenth-century black woman. As a result, the public exposure of black women cultural workers on the margins could only be perceived by the dominant culture, and by a segment of the black male elite as well, as a form of social disorder that confirmed notions of the black female body as unruly, grotesque, carnivalesque.[55] In her 1846 *Memoirs*, for example, Zilpha Elaw recounts a conversation with a minister's wife who "assuming the theologian, reprobated female preaching as . . . disorderly and improper."[56]

Such cultural constructions could quite possibly result in the transformation of the black female subject into an "abject creature" who internalizes the images of herself as dirty, disorderly, and grotesque.[57] Although the writings by, and about, the women studied in this book may at times suggest racial insecurity, they are much more frequently pervaded by portraits of a sick and debilitated body. Indeed, almost all these women were plagued throughout their lives by illnesses that often remained undiagnosed but whose symptoms were headaches, fevers, coughs, chills, cramps, or simply extreme fatigue. In such instances illness may quite possibly have occurred as a consequence of the bodily degradation to which these women were subjected or as a psychosomatic strategy for negotiating such degradation. In either case the black female body might well have functioned as what Elaine Scarry has called the "body in pain," whereby the powerless become voiceless bodies subject to pain and dominated by the bodiless voices of those in power. In her book Scarry enumerates different mechanisms through which the voiceless body of pain can be transformed into a bodiless voice of power: most generally, the human subject seeks to alleviate pain by giving it a place in the world through verbal articulation; in the Judeo-Christian tradition, God authorizes man to divest himself of his body and seek power through the making of material artifacts, including language; in Christian interpretations of death, finally, the resurrection of the soul privileges the verbal category over the material by endowing man with an immortal voice.[58] Similarly, for Kristeva, abjection may be spiritualized by means of the Christian ritual of communion in which "all corporeality is elevated, spiritualized, and sublimated"; but, most importantly, it is "the Word . . . [that] purifies from the abject."[59]

How, then, did nineteenth-century black women social activists conciliate these differing interpretations of the black female body as empowered, on the one hand, and disordered on the other? The need to negotiate between these two extremes was particularly urgent for black female public speakers who offered themselves so vulnerably to the public gaze. In her *Memoirs*, for example, Zilpha Elaw recollected with pain how "the people were collecting from every quarter, to gaze at the unexampled prodigy of a coloured female preacher. . . . I observed, with very painful emotions, the crowd outside, pointing with their fingers at me, and saying, 'that's her,' 'that's her.'"[60] Audience response to Watkins Harper's public lecturing was even more telling, however, in its grotesque evocation of the black woman speaker as variably masculine and painted: "I don't know but that you would laugh if you were to hear some of the remarks which my lectures call forth," she wrote in a letter to William Still. "'She is a man,' again 'She is not

21

colored, she is painted.'"[61] In this comment the black woman speaker is predictably masculinized, and she is also racialized as "painted." Yet the term "painted" also resexualizes her, and dangerously so, as an actress, and perhaps even a prostitute. In fact, these women lecturers needed in some sense to become actresses in order to negotiate their public exposure in front of "promiscuous assemblies"; and, as we shall see, their acting strategies ranged from deliberate attempts to call attention to the materiality of the black female body in both its productive and reproductive functions in order then to subvert the dominant culture's construction of it (Truth), to efforts to decorporealize the body from the outset and present the self as a disembodied voice (Watkins Harper).

I would argue that from their dislocated and liminal positions these black women ultimately turned to the *literary representation* of self-marginalization—to the writing of self, spirituality, and travel, the reprinting of public lectures, and the creation of fictional worlds—in an attempt to veil the body while continuing their racial uplift activities in the public sphere. In particular, they turned to writing in reaction to, and in tension with, their exclusion from black national institutions. Striving to achieve an empowering narrative authority, they hoped that their writing would both challenge the power of those institutions to which they had been barred access *and* compel these institutions to legitimate their social activism in the public sphere.

My study of African-American women in the nineteenth century is loosely organized around the liminal sites I identified earlier—religious evangelicism, travel, public speaking—as well as the writing of fiction. The discussion of each woman begins with an attempt to narrativize and interpret those important social and biographical facts that might help us better to appreciate her cultural production. It then turns to an analysis of the cultural production itself, whether the speech in its printed form which, although never ascertainable, often sustains the fiction of the actual social exchange, or the written text. Taken together, my analyses suggest the possibility of tracing significant shifts in the use of literary discourses and generic conventions.

I argue that these black women appropriated many different cultural discourses ranging from a reliance on Africanisms to the adoption of standard literary conventions in order to become producers rather than mere consumers of literary expression. In her role as an itinerant lecturer, Truth was not only a Christian "doer of the word" but also a participant in the African belief in *Nommo,* or the Word as the productive life force that brings about generation and change. In addition, Truth employed Africanisms, folk proverbs and sayings, and African-American idioms in her lectures, creating what the dominant culture regarded as a quaint idiosyncratic speech; in fact, however, Truth's speech constitutes a serious political discourse through which she sought to define the specific positionality of nineteenth-century black women.[62] To prophesy the future of both black and white races in America and the role of black women in its making, Lee and Stewart grounded their sermons and spiritual writings in biblical discourse—particularly that of the Old Testament Prophets and the New Testament book of Revelation—producing powerful texts that their readers and audiences, however, often interpreted as mere emotional outbursts filled with undecipherable meanings. Watkins Harper, Forten, and Jacobs appropriated the sentimental discourse that had entered and permeated white women's culture by way of the eighteenth-century European cult of sensibility in order to invoke figures of sentimentality—the African-American slave (man, woman, child, or family), the drunkard husband or father, the seduced woman, the child dying of hunger—that would excite the readers' compassion and move them not to emotional consumption but to productive action. Given the particular social and cultural construction of black women's lives, such writing differed in significant ways from that of black men in its ability to imagine cultural possibilities specifically engendered by women's space and women's work. Finally, in the postbellum period black women sought to take advantage of the expansion and institutionalization of literary culture; and in becoming increasingly involved in the already existing national organizations of black men and white women while gradually creating institutions of their own, they hoped to appropriate new forms of social discourse that would help them further their cultural work.

As these black women narrated their thoughts and experiences, the location and perspective of the narrating *I* in relation to that which is narrated gained particular importance as evidenced by their careful manipulation of point of view, thus demanding from us a critical consideration of genre. Indeed, for these women the question of genre was not so much a choice of literary convention as an epistemological issue: how to represent the relationship of the self to the self and the Other. The only woman unable to author her own life story, Truth was obliged to confide its telling to white women abolitionists whose ethnobiographies construct her as irrecoverably Other. In asserting their desire and ability to narrate their own life stories themselves, Lee, Prince, Jacobs, and Forten wrote spiritual and secular autobiographies as well as journals in which the *I* seeks to narrate itself from its own constructed point of view. In composing travel accounts and ethnographies, Prince and Shadd Cary sought to deflect the public's gaze from themselves in order to represent the Other. Finally, in turning to more explicitly fictional modes and techniques in the 1850s, Wilson, Watkins Harper, and Jacobs created fictionalized versions of both self and Other from multiple perspectives, thereby striving to escape the scrutiny of the dominant culture and achieve perspectives of omniscience denied them in their actual historical moment and place.

2

"A Sign unto This Nation": Sojourner Truth, History, Orature, and Modernity

Of all the women studied in this book Sojourner Truth is undoubtedly the best known, having achieved, along with Harriet Tubman, almost legendary status. Yet the fact remains that much of Truth's life and work is clouded in historical uncertainty, leaving us unable to answer many questions about her with any real assurance. If knowledge of a historical figure comes to us mediated by the perceptions of contemporaries and later historians, this is especially true of Truth. Given her illiteracy, meant here the inability to read and write, Truth has not left us with any writing of her own; moreover, facts and interpretations of events in her life have often been multiple, contradictory, and sometimes unverifiable. Such written documentation has ensured Truth's continued presence in the historical record, yet it has also meant that she has in a sense become an overdetermined historical figure. My organization of this chapter deliberately reflects this sense of overdetermination—of the degree to which Truth comes to us as always already interpreted by others from their own situated and partial perspectives. Thus, I start by examining the written record surrounding Truth and then later proceed to speculate about those aspects of her life that lie beyond writing, including, of course, her speeches.

What we know of Truth suggests that her adult life was marked by a relative isolation from the black community. If Truth, like other black women of this period, was locked out of the social institutions of the black male leadership, it also appears that she was never an integral member of black society. After her emancipation from slavery, she affiliated with several white-dominated communitarian societies in what seems to have been an attempt to constitute a social group for herself denied by the experience of slavery. Subsequent to their failure, Truth appears to have moved largely in white abolitionist and feminist circles, giving two white women permission to write the story of her life. Given her inability to read and write, we may well wonder whether Truth's illiteracy was not in some sense the source of her dependence on white reformers. These dependent relationships were, however, extremely complex, centering on issues of control over self-representation. Indeed, although Truth appears to have been locked out of the economy of "writing," she nonetheless emphatically insisted throughout her life on her own historical agency expressed in different modes of "writing" as well as in other cultural forms rooted in African and African-American traditions. Misunderstood by the dominant culture, these latter forms were often dismissed as merely quaint. And yet Truth's engagement with her contemporary culture, with its technological developments in particular, was such that she may be marked as truly modern.

Much of our information about Sojourner Truth's life derives from the 1850 biography, *Narrative of Sojourner Truth,* written by Olive Gilbert, a rather inconspicuous member of white abolitionist circles and a friend of William Lloyd Garrison. In the 1870s it was slightly revised and considerably enlarged by Frances Titus, whom Truth had met in the 1860s while both women were working to resettle the freed slaves, to include Truth's activities during the 1850s, the Civil War, and Reconstruction.[1] Truth was born Isabella Bomefree in Ulster County, New York, in 1797, to James and Betsey (or Mau-mau Bett) Bomefree, who were the slaves of a Dutch man, Colonel Hardenbergh. In the late eighteenth century, New York State could not yet lay claim to being "free" territory but in fact relied on slave labor in its urban and, even more prominently, rural industries. Thus, the Bomefrees engaged in forms of field work not altogether dissimilar from those described by Olmsted in his travel accounts of seaboard-state slavery. Moreover, as Margaret Washington has noted, Dutch slaveowners tended to be strong defenders of slavery, harsh in their treatment of their slaves and reluctant to pass manumission laws in the wake of American independence.[2] Isabella's parents were believed to have been of unmixed African ancestry, her mother in particular of pure Guinea Coast blood. If this supposition is accurate, James and Mau-mau Bett might well have been part of the re-Africanization of Northern slavery that occurred between 1740 and 1770 due to a temporary shortage of indentured white labor from Europe; in any event, it was most certainly they who were responsible for imparting to Isabella those elements of African culture that are evident in her speech patterns, belief system, and behavior.

While still a young child, Isabella was separated from her parents and sold at a slave auction. After yet a further sale, she was bought in 1817 by a John J. Dumont, with whom she resided until 1826. During this time she was married (not legally, of course, and not altogether happily) to an older slave named Thomas by whom she had several children. According to Gilbert's *Narrative,* Dumont had promised Isabella that "if she would do well" he would manumit her one year before legal emancipation set for July 4, 1827, but when the time came he reneged on his promise, reluctant to "give up the profits of his faithful Bell"

(39). With a determination that was to become characteristic of her, Isabella "concluded to take her freedom into her own hands, and seek her fortune in some other place" (41); in her escape she left her children with her husband, whom she felt was in a better position to provide for them. Her departure led her to the nearby Van Wagenen family, where she remained long enough to recover her son, Peter, who had been illegally sold into slavery in the South. With Peter she then struck out on her own in the hope—"of course . . . not in her power" according to Gilbert—"to make to herself a home, around whose sacred hearthstone she could collect her family, as they gradually emerged from their prison-house of bondage" (71).

Isabella's search for "home" led her first to New York City, where she lived an isolated and uncertain life emblematic of the difficulties facing unskilled African Americans who had been excluded from the economic expansion sweeping the North and for whom the meaning of freedom thus remained undefined. Gilbert's account of Isabella's life in New York at that time is remarkably similar to Harriet Jacobs's later autobiographical narration of her years there. Like Jacobs, Isabella served as a domestic in the home of a wealthy family, the Latourettes: "She worked for them, and they generously gave her a home while she labored for others, and in their kindness made her as one of their own" (86). Despite, or perhaps because of, this kindness, Isabella found herself isolated from the African-American community, worshiping at a white Methodist church and unable to supervise the upbringing of her son, who eventually fell prey to the temptations of the city. Her troubles gradually resolved themselves once her son agreed to become a seaman, thus following an occupational pattern common to young black men of this period who found themselves at the bottom of the urban workforce.[3] And her isolation decreased when she agreed to accompany Mrs. Latourette on her visits to the Magdalene Asylum, an early association composed primarily of white women moral reformers devoted to the rehabilitation of New York prostitutes.[4] Finally, around this same time Isabella left the white church in order to join the African-American Zion's Church; it was at this church that she unknowingly sat beside a sister from whom she had been separated by slavery, leading her to lament when later informed of this fact: "'Oh Lord, . . . what is this slavery, that it can do such dreadful things? what evil can it not do?'" (81).

Such a lament reflects Isabella's acute sense of loneliness and suggests her longing to experience some semblance of family life denied her by slavery. This longing, I would argue, finds outward expression in Isabella's repeated efforts to become part of a communal society whose values are based on notions of collectivity and mutual sharing.[5] If such a hunger for community constituted for Isabella an attempt to overcome the fragmentation of family life engendered by slavery, it might also have been due to her inability successfully to compete in the capitalist economy brought about by the Jacksonian market revolution in the urban Northeast. Just as importantly, finally, it might also have been indicative of a desire—however unconscious—to reconstitute some form of African social life, centered on the compound and on a commitment to the collectivity rather than to the individual household, that might have come to Isabella through her elders.[6] Indeed, in the 1830s and 1840s Isabella came to participate in two very different communal experiments that flourished briefly in the Northeast, the kingdom Matthias in New York and the Northampton Association in Massachusetts; in the late 1850s she became part of the spiritualist community of Harmonia located near Battle Creek, Michigan; finally, in the aftermath of the Civil War one of Isabella's chief projects was to relocate the freed slaves in self-contained communities on land set aside for them in the West by the federal government.

The kingdom Matthias was an enthusiastic religious movement that emerged briefly in New York during the early 1830s. Claiming to be a Jew, a man by the name of Robert Matthews had renamed himself Matthias and fashioned himself rather eccentrically as an Old Testament prophet in dress, behavior, and speech. While nonbelievers dismissed him as a fanatic and "grotesque" (90), Isabella, who like many other illiterate slaves had memorized large portions of the Bible, seems to have been able readily to fit him into the traditions of Old and New Testament prophecy. Thus, according to Gilbert, at her first sight of him, Isabella's "early impression of seeing Jesus in the flesh rushed to her mind" (90). Moreover, Matthias's oratorical style, which was grounded like that of many slave preachers in the oral traditions of the Old Testament, undoubtedly resonated with familiarity in Isabella's ears. Finally, the prophecies themselves, which pronounced "vengeance on the land, and that the law of God was the only rule of government" (89), differed little in style or content from the jeremiads delivered by such radical antebellum African-American leaders as David Walker in the 1820s and 1830s. Yet events were gradually to reveal a dark underside to Matthias's kingdom not unlike the later sexual practices of John Humphrey Noyes's Oneida community. The kingdom broke up in 1835 under charges of adulterous practices that encouraged "match spirits" freely to cohabit with one another regardless of marital status and after the discovery of the fatal poisoning of one of its members, Mr. Pierson. Despite her implication in this scandal and the consequent negative publicity, Isabella appears never to have become embittered against Matthias; in fact, her self-naming shortly thereafter as "Sojourner Truth" may well have constituted an indirect tribute to Matthias, who referred to himself variously as a "traveller" and the "Spirit of Truth."

Truth's other early experiment with communal living was with the Northampton Association, where she resided from 1843 to 1846. An outgrowth of the transcendentalist movement, the Northampton Association drew to it many white abolitionists, including William Lloyd Garrison's brother-in-law George Benson, and adopted as its primary goal the achievement of social and economic equality. Opposed to the capitalist system that encouraged class divisions and hierarchies, fostered competition among individuals, and degraded labor in favor of "speculative pursuits," it established itself as an organization that made no distinction "on account of color, . . . [or] between the strong and the weak, the skilful and unskilful, . . . the rich and the poor," and that sought to restore dignity to labor.[7] Operating a silkmill and a sawmill, the association was initially controlled by two companies, an industrial community and a stock company, but shortly before Truth's arrival decided to do away with this double arrangement to make the decision-making process of its affairs more communal: "Last year labour and capital held joint sway. This year, as an experiment, labour has exclusive control."[8] Few specific facts are known about Truth's years there, but it appears that she was thoroughly at home in this Fourierist community and was devastated when the association broke up.

Indeed, like the kingdom Matthias, the Northampton Association eventually foundered and once again left Truth without a home. After the dissolution of the kingdom Matthias in 1835, Truth had temporarily abandoned the idea of acquiring a home. Adopting the name Sojourner Truth, thereby emphasizing the importance of travel in the telling of truth, and maintaining, perhaps in a tacit acknowledgment of Matthias's continuing power over her, that "'the Spirit calls me there, and I must go'" (100), Truth became an itinerant preacher, exhorting in particular the Millerites, followers of a millenarian movement that predicted the end of the world in 1843. In 1846, after the demise of the Northampton Association, Truth decided to return to her earlier itinerant ministry. She struck out on her own, crisscrossed the Northeast, and penetrated into Ohio and Indiana, following her call "to 'lecture,' . . . [and] 'testifying of the hope that was in her'" (101) by speaking to large audiences composed primarily of religious devotees of the Second Great Awakening and participants in the temperance movement. Given the frenetic pace of her travels, it is not surprising that, according to Gilbert, her worried children's "imaginations painted her as a wandering maniac" (109).

The facts of Truth's biography thus suggest a tension in her life between active participation in communitarian experiments and the solitary stance of the lone traveler. If on the one hand Truth longed to be enfolded within the warmth of family and community, on the other hand she was to discover that she could best achieve the leadership position to which she aspired in antebellum evangelical and antislavery movements by positioning herself as an isolated figure on the margins. Yet both these spaces of travel and communal experiment must be viewed as liminal ones. First of all, the very fact of itinerancy constitutes a form of self-marginalization in its dislocation of home and disruption of quotidian habits. Second, Truth's travels in the 1830s and 1840s took her into those marginal spaces of the Second Great Awakening in which hierarchies between rich and poor, black and white, male and female, urban and rural break down in the face of a collective religious experience. Finally, the two established communal experiments in which Truth participated may be seen as reflective of Turner's notion of liminal *communitas,* which exists "in contrast . . . to social structure, as an alternative and more 'liberated' way of being socially human, a way both of being detached from social structure . . . and also more attached to *other* disengaged persons."[9] Moreover, since both these communities were predominantly white, Truth could only occupy a marginal and ambiguous position within them; here too, she found herself, ultimately, alone.

Truth was to occupy this same ambiguous position in the two organized movements with which she became affiliated in the 1850s—the Garrisonian antislavery movement at whose behest she lectured in the company of such abolitionists as Garrison, Putnam, the Britisher George Thompson (and Frederick Douglass early on), and the women's rights movement led by Elizabeth Cady Stanton and Susan B. Anthony. Indeed, it would seem that the black urban elite that constituted the vanguard of the community's abolitionist and racial uplift movements viewed Truth's refusal to conform to middle-class social conventions and her determination to flaunt her subaltern origins with a great deal of uneasiness. For example, in a retrospective account of his first meeting with Truth in the 1840s, Douglass described her as "a genuine specimen of the uncultured negro . . . [who] cared very little for elegance of speech or refinement of manners . . . [and] seemed to feel it her duty to trip me up in my speeches and to ridicule my efforts to speak and act like a person of cultivation and refinement."[10] It is difficult to ascertain whether it was Truth's adamant nonconformism or the elite's disdain, or a combination of both, that separated her from the community of black social activists.

In striking contrast, whites, as Nell Painter has noted, appear to have been quite comfortable with Truth, as her demeanor seemed to conform nicely to their image of the black woman.[11] In their perception of her, Truth was alternatively and overdeterminedly constructed as either invisible or visible, constituting either lack or surplus. In the kingdom Matthias, for example, Truth's blackness enabled her to witness events and conversations hidden to others: "To this object, even her color assisted [given] the manner in which the colored people, and especially slaves, are treated; they are scarcely regarded as being present" (91). But as a woman lecturer, Truth was fully exposed to the public gaze and perceived as unruly and excessive. It is this form of visibility, of course, rather than Truth's invisibility, that is reproduced in the many contemporary published accounts of her, forging a reputation that would last well beyond her death in 1883. Thus, in Gilbert's *Narrative* Truth's views are termed "curious and original" (101), her style "peculiar" (110), her "modes of expression" "singular and sometimes uncouth" (114), her "figures" "the most original and expressive" (114); finally her voice is rendered as "powerful and sonorous" (119). All these traits converge to suggest an unruliness and excess of body and speech that make of Truth an "entertainer" (119) who attracts the curious gaze of the public. In their narratives Gilbert and Titus invite their contemporary readership to just such a form of gazing.

Unlike the other women studied in this book, Truth did not possess the requisite skills to represent herself in writing. While the exact status of her literacy is currently undergoing reevaluation by certain historians, it remains clear that Truth never engaged in any sustained act of literary self-representation.[12] Freely acknowledging her subaltern status, she permitted two white women writers to tell her life story so that she could sell it at a profit after her lectures and thereby support herself. Truth had in fact already had early experience with the difficulties of attempting black testimonial. At the two trials that marked the demise of the kingdom Matthias in which Pierson's death and the adulterous relationships of the match spirits were investigated, Truth was forbidden to take the stand to testify either in her own defense or on behalf of others; instead, the court relied exclusively on the testimony of the kingdom's white members. It was only at the end of the Civil War that Truth was finally able to give legal testimony and win a trial that would result in the integration of streetcars in Washington, D.C. (187). For the African-American subject, white testimony was of course often problematic and suspect; indeed, the pamphlet literature engendered by the two kingdom Matthias trials foregrounds the unreliabilty of white representations and interpretations of blackness especially when these concern issues of black female power and sexuality. On the one hand, Truth's very blackness led the journalist William Stone to view her as a witch. Editor of the New York *Commercial Advertiser,* Stone spoke out on many of the controversial issues of the day, agitating against women's rights and suffrage, mediating between Masons and anti-Masonic forces, advocating both the emancipation and colonization of slaves, and exposing impostors such as Matthias. Incriminating Truth in the blackberry poisoning of Mr. Pierson, Stone referred to her as "the most wicked of the wicked." On the other hand, this same racial difference led Gilbert Vale, a less well known journalist and editor of *Citizen of the World,* to claim that, because of the lack of an appropriate match spirit, Truth, in contrast to the white women in the kingdom, had not engaged in any sexual relations and was consequently chaste.[13]

To define their role as white amanuenses offering a testimonial of Truth's life, both Olive Gilbert and Frances Titus chose to portray themselves as women who have "achieved" Culture writing on behalf of a child of Nature whose attributes are chiefly physical and thus "ascribed." In his preface to Gilbert's 1850 *Narrative,* Garrison had largely averted his gaze from Truth, relegating her to the frame of his text while focusing his discussion on the ways in which other nations currently gaze in disgust at slaveholding America. In contrast, in her preface to the 1878 edition Titus relied on a series of natural images, first temporal and then geographic, to explain Truth's perdurance. If Truth is as old as the U.S. Century (1776–1876), if she has experienced a physical rejuvenation since the end of the Civil War, it is because she is a natural object able to withstand the ravages of time: by means of analogy, her body becomes the palms of Africa, her blood its rivers fed by tropical fires, her life the sun itself. If African Americans, as children of Nature, are admitted to have the potential of achieving Culture, this potential remains future; they stand yet "on the Pisgah of freedom, looking into the promised land, where the culture which has so long been denied them can, by their own efforts, be obtained" (vii).

Titus's very use of language in the preface, much like the language of the narratives themselves, reinforces the dichotomy between ascribed Nature and achieved Culture. For, Titus as narrator relies heavily on the established discourse of the King James Bible while rendering Truth's speech and biblical quotations in an African-American idiom. As John Wideman has pointed out, such a dichotomy between white literary frame and black dialect is prevalent in much nineteenth-century writing—white and black—and works to hierarchize speech usage. The white literary frame is seen as a "matured mode of literate expression," while black dialect appears "infantile" and thus "inferior"; yet the white frame is necessary because it contains what is otherwise chaotic, renders respectable that which it places inside it.[14]

Undertaking a testimonial of Truth's life, Gilbert and Titus composed what I will call, following Philippe Lejeune, an "ethnobiography," defined as the "autobiography of those who do not write."[15] Interestingly, neither woman signed her narrative. It is possible, of course, to interpret this lack of signature as an index of narrative self-authorization such that the life story is seen to narrate itself. Yet both Gilbert's and Titus's self-perception was as essentially private women; in an 1870 letter to Truth Gilbert, for example, described herself as "not so public a personage as yourself. . . . [M]ine is a very quiet mark compared to yours" (277, 276). Thus, literary anonymity here seems to point to questions of public authorship faced by nineteenth-century women writers. If a written signature implies the actual nonpresence of the signer, it also marks, as Derrida has noted, his or her "having-been-present in a past now" and suggests a "transcendental form of nowness (*maintenance*)" that is inscribed not only in the signature's singularity but in its iterability and reproducibility as well.[16] It is this lack of transcendental nowness that is denied to the woman writer who dares not sign her text but can only leave the trace of a continued nonpresence.

The complexity of female authorship is further reinforced here by the printer's notation "Published for the author," which inscribes a certain ambiguity in the term "author": is the author Sojourner Truth, the author of her own life, or Gilbert/Titus, the author of the narrative of the life of Sojourner Truth? If this notation seems to confuse the identity of the author, suggesting some form of authorial collaboration and the presence of a "floating writing" in the narrative, the text itself dispels such speculations as it firmly establishes the separate existence of, and gap between, author and ethnographic subject. For, Gilbert's and Titus's ethnobiographies focus on a cultural subject who has been excluded from writing and curiously inquire "What is on the other side of writing?" Establishing itself as a written text composed by those who can write for those who can read, this ethnobiography isolates the subject and her culture, turning her into a commodity, exploiting and reifying her by means of various constructed images, including that of Harriet Beecher Stowe's "Libyan Sibyl."[17]

If there is no signature that explicitly reveals the authorship of the ethnobiographies, the structure and style of Gilbert's and Titus's narratives themselves suggest authorial presence and control such that writing itself becomes a form of signature. Indeed, the differences between the two writers' use of narrative conventions, stances, and strategies indicate a particularized textual construction that is related not only to the individual personality of each author but to the historical moment of narrative composition as well. Though written in the third person, Gilbert's 1850 *Narrative* relies heavily—yet with interesting modifications—on the conventions of the slave narrative and the spiritual autobiography that typified African-American writing in the antebellum period. In its focus on a single heroic individual, Gilbert's text, like the slave narrative, underscores the uniqueness of its subject; but, unlike the slave narrative, it does not emphasize her representativeness. Moreover, as we shall see, uniqueness here is located in the peculiar forms of Truth's oral speech rather than the ex-slave's acquisition of literacy and consequent ability to write. Like the slave narrative, too, Gilbert's ethnobiography is a chronological account that attends foremost to the moral growth of its subject, tracing Truth's increasing awareness of the evils of slavery (underscored here, as in the slave narrative, in a separate chapter on slave horrors), her determination to resist slavery and finally to escape it. These conventions of the slave narrative are doubled by those of the spiritual autobiography that record Truth's spiritual growth and conversion in a discourse that echoes Bunyan's *Pilgrim's Progress* and insists that the subject has a soul and is worthy of biographical notice. What is perhaps most significant is that in its focus on Truth's individuality Gilbert's narrative (and Titus's as well) refuses to foreground Truth's search for community but focuses instead on those events that isolate her and mark her as extraordinary.

In contrast, Titus's ethnobiographical narrative eschews chronological progression to ground itself in the conventions of documentary writing, reproducing in its latter part approximately fifty pages of newspaper columns culled from the abolitionist, feminist, and mainstream press and another fifty pages of private and public correspondence. Carleton Mabee has suggested that such a narrative method is indicative of Titus's relative lack of education and literary sophistication.[18] If indeed the case, this very lack sharply counteracts the ideological function of the naturalizing images that structure Titus's preface as well as Stowe's inserted essay, "The Libyan Sibyl." Indeed, in her narrative Titus relied on some of the more notable journalistic trends that were developing in mid-nineteenth-century America: the democratization of news whose focus is now broadened to include all social spheres, the increasing emphasis of news on elements of human interest, and finally the belief that news can provide objective, value-free, and impartial reportage.[19]

Gilbert's, and to a lesser extent Titus's, ethnobiographies both make explicit the mediating function of the narrator. Gilbert grounds her narrative authority to interpret and generalize in her frequent claim to having been an eyewitness to the practices of slavery: "And the writer of this knows, from personal observation, that . . ." (34). She freely offers editorial comments on various events in Truth's life, even transforming narrative description into commentary. Thus, her portrait of the old James Bomefree ("His hair was white like wool—he was almost blind— and his gait was more a creep than a walk") resonates with mythological over- tones and endows him with a dignity that makes the account of his death par- ticularly brutal: "[T]his faithful slave, this deserted wreck of humanity, was found on his miserable pallet, frozen and stiff in death" (22, 25). Finally, Gilbert manipulates narrative language by self-consciously setting limits to the express- ible. At certain textual moments she insists that the intensity of Truth's emotions are beyond expression—"'Ah!' she says, with emphasis that cannot be written" (39). At others she shifts from an ethnobiographical mode of narration grounded in facts to the more fictional discourse of sentimentality in order to raise what Margaret Washington has called the "indelicate subject" of black female sexu- ality.[20] As in Harriet Jacobs's later autobiography, sentimental conventions are invoked here to determine what in a black woman's life is, and is not, appro- priately expressible: "From this source arose a long series of trials in the life of our heroine, which we must pass over in silence; some from motives of delicacy, and others, because the relation of them might inflict undeserved pain on some now living . . ." (30).

If Gilbert's and Titus's ethnobiographies confirm the authors' control over the writing process, they also reveal the degree to which Truth herself was aware of both the power of written language to authorize and interpret experience and her exclusion from this arena of power. In her narrative Gilbert gives an account of Truth's conviction that God is a "great man" whose omniscience is manifested in his ability to write and in his written record of human activity: "She believed he not only saw, but noted down all her actions in a great book. . . ." By analogy, however, such omniscience is equally that of the white man since God writes "even as her master kept a record of whatever he wished not to forget" (59). The power, but also danger, of "man's" written texts, Truth perspicaciously intuited, derives from the fact that subjective interpretations—"ideas and suppositions"— are always embedded in the written "records . . . of truth" (109), and that the reading of any written record is itself invariably accompanied by interpretation.

Truth's distrust of written texts, particularly insofar as they concerned her, is nowhere more evident than in her dismissal of Stowe's lengthy description of her in her article "The Libyan Sibyl," first published in the April 1863 issue of the *Atlantic Monthly* and then reprinted in Titus's narrative: "She would never listen to Mrs. Stowe's 'Libyan Sibyl.' 'Oh!' she would say, 'I don't want to hear about that old symbol; read me something that is going on *now*, something about this great war'" (174). Truth's attributed use of the term "symbol" is clearly deroga- tory and suggests her awareness of the dangers of analogy-making by means of figurative language. In his immensely popular *Lectures on Rhetoric and Belles- Lettres,* first published in 1783, the British rhetorician Hugh Blair began his chapter on the origin and nature of figurative language by insisting on the natural-ness of figures of speech, on the impossibility that any user of language can speak or write without resorting to them. Yet the rest of Blair's chapter carefully pro-ceeds to attend to the constructed nature of figures, analyzing both their structure and their effect on the listener/reader. Figures of speech are designed "to illus-trate a subject, or to throw light upon it"; they are interpretive. If one of the advantages of the figure is its ability to present two objects together to our view without confusion instead of just one, even more significantly the figure may "often strike the imagination more than the principal idea itself"; at the extreme, it may even erase the idea in its own favor. Such an erasure is possible because figures, unlike "simple expression," are bodies: "As the figure, or shape of one body, distinguishes it from another, so these forms of Speech have, each of them, a cast or turn peculiar to itself." If Blair explicitly asserts that the creation of such figurative or bodied language is most characteristic of primitive peoples, of "sav-age tribes of men . . . much given to wonder and astonishment," his discussion implicitly suggests that it is just as, perhaps even more, characteristic of civilized persons, of rhetoricians seeking to enrich, dignify, and illustrate their discourse. And Stowe's essay underscores just how easily bodied language may be put to use not only by savage tribes of men but by polite peoples writing *about* "savage tribes of men."[21]

Truth's attributed use of the term "symbol" to refer to Stowe's "Libyan Sibyl" is instructive, for it points to her awareness of the nature and function of figurative language, of the extent to which such language is inherently interpretive and can thus be used against that which it is meant to illustrate. As a figure, the symbol is one of the most bodied forms of language, in which a visible object is made to stand for or suggest something less visible and tangible. And, indeed, Stowe's use of figures in her essay to represent Truth emphasizes above all the material. Significantly, Stowe's text is framed at its beginning and end by bodies—by the verbal portraits of two pieces of sculpture to which Truth is analogized. In her introductory section Stowe describes how Truth reminds her so forcefully of "Cumberworth's celebrated statuette of the Negro Woman at the Fountain" (151). But this brief allusion to Cumberworth's statue is then over-shadowed by Stowe's later reference to William Wetmore Story's *Libyan Sibyl* that concludes the essay. Here Stowe informs the reader that it was an earlier conversation with Story about Truth that served as the genesis of Story's statue, which in turn provided her essay with its title.

Story's *Libyan Sibyl* is a massive female figure sculpted out of pure white marble. She is seated, the upper part of her body, which is nude, leans forward slightly; the lower part is covered by loose drapery. Her right leg is crossed over the left, and her right elbow rests on her knee while the palm of her right hand gently cups her chin. Her headdress is elaborate as is the pendant around her head; according to Jean Fagan Yellin, to Story's audience their designs of two interlocking triangles would have suggested the Seal of Solomon. In her analysis of the statue Yellin argues that the Sibyl's pose is similar to that of Judea Capta, a figure representing the Jews in Babylonian captivity that also functioned as a type symbolizing "desolation" for both New England Puritans and nineteenth-century abolitionists. Yellin concludes that: "Story posed his sibyl in an attitude commonly assigned to defeated barbarians in Roman art [inviting] the viewer to consider parallels between the American enslavement of Africans and the Roman enslavement of defeated peoples—including the inhabitants of Britain and Jerusalem."[22]

In a letter to Charles Sumner reprinted in Henry James's *William Wetmore Story and His Friends*, Story himself offers an interpretation of his *Libyan Sibyl*. Significantly, even as he attends to the African woman's body, Story sanitizes her. She is conceptualized as "Libyan Africa of course, not Congo." Even more importantly, however, Story's description of his sibyl adheres closely to the dominant culture's view of the black woman by envisioning her doubly as masculine and feminine. For if her nude torso presents her as "large-bosomed," the sibyl is also a "very massive figure, big-shouldered, . . . with nothing of the Venus in it." In his narrative commentary, finally, James offers us yet another interpretive paradigm through which to view the sibyl. Defining Story as "frankly and forcibly romantic," he argues that the artist sought in his work to offer "the observer a spectacle and, as nearly as possible, a scene" out of subjects "already consecrated to the imagination—by history, poetry, legend—and so offered them with all their signs and tokens, their features and enhancements."[23] To view the *Libyan Sibyl* as a representation of Truth, then, spectators needed to attend to such "signs and token" and thus engage in multi-layered typological interpretation.

Stowe ends her essay with a lengthy commentary on the *Libyan Sibyl* and its reception by the British press, and she of course gave her essay that title. Such an emphasis invites the reader to think of Truth in terms of Story's statue alone and to overlook Stowe's earlier comment that analogizes Truth to Cumberworth's statue. Indeed, at the beginning of her essay Stowe recalled how in their first meeting Truth "gave the impression of a physical development which in her early youth must have been as fine a specimen of the torrid zone as Cumberworth's celebrated statuette of the Negro Woman at the Fountain. Indeed, she so strongly reminded me of that figure, that, when I recall the events of her life, as she narrated them to me, I imagine her as a living, breathing impersonation of that work of art" (151).

My research into the work of the relatively obscure French/British sculptor Charles Cumberworth (1811–52) has led me to conclude that this statue of the Negro Woman at the Fountain might well be one of the artist's renderings of Marie, the female slave character in Bernardin de Saint-Pierre's *Paul et Virginie*, executed in the mid 1840s and exhibited at the Paris Salon of 1846. Unremarkable perhaps in its own right, Cumberworth's Marie à la Fontaine is remarkable in its contrast to Story's *Sibyl*. *Marie* is a full-standing bronze figure. She is fully clothed, although the bodice of her dress falls off her left shoulder to expose her

Charles Cumberworth. *Marie à la Fontaine* (1840s). Cliché des Musées Nationaux, Paris. ©RMN.

William Wetmore Story. *The Libyan Sibyl* (1861).
The Metropolitan Museum of Art, Gift of the Erving Wolf Foundation, 1979.
(1979. 266)

left breast. Her left hand is placed akimbo while her right arm bends at the elbow in order to allow her right hand to hold aloft a large vase out of which protrudes what appears to be a profusion of vegetation. The left side of her dress is slightly raised and her feet are bare. Most significantly, in contrast to Story's *Libyan Sibyl* Cumberworth's *Marie* is "Congo African"; her features are more markedly Negroid, her coloring is bronze, and a turban covers her head. As a representation of Truth, the statue is obviously mediated in its explicit reference to Saint-Pierre's fictional character. Unlike Story's *Libyan Sibyl*, however, it does not require multiple levels of interpretation in order for the viewer to read Truth through it. But given the *Libyan Sibyl's* peculiar representation of the African woman and greater fame, this statue undoubtedly better suited both Stowe's ideological purposes and her *Atlantic Monthly* readership than did Cumberworth's *Marie.*

Indeed, Yellin suggests that in her essay Stowe turned back to Story's statue to construct Truth not only as mysterious but also as passive and inhuman. I would likewise emphasize the degree to which Stowe's verbal description of Truth does indeed adapt iself to Story's marble portraiture but in somewhat different ways from those suggested by Yellin: a focus on the black woman's body that materializes her but also, in reinventing her through the imagination, dehistoricizes her. In the first part of her essay Stowe reproduces in quotation marks (and in dialect, of course) Truth's narration of her own life. But if Truth insists on positioning herself as a subject in history, Stowe's later comments about her both materialize and dehistoricize her. Truth's bodied nature is emphasized throughout in Stowe's depiction of her, along with her grandson ("the fattest, jolliest woolly-headed little specimen of Africa that one can imagine," 152), as an "entertainer" to be gazed upon, a singer whose voice is intimately connected to her bodily energy (161). Stowe's description does not masculinize her as Frances Gage's would shortly do. But, much like Titus in her preface, Stowe repeatedly invokes nature images to analogize Truth's body to exotic African landscapes.[24] Thus, Truth's "African nature" is imaged as "those unexplored depths of being and feeling, mighty and dark as the gigantic depths of tropical forests, mysterious as the hidden rivers and mines of that burning continent whose life-history is yet to be" (170). What is especially signficant about these metaphoric and symbolic representations of Truth is the degree to which they privilege geography—first the geography of continent, then that of the body—over history, ultimately tending toward a dehistoricization of Truth herself. Stowe's use of landscape images resituates Truth in an African continent that has no history—"whose life-history is yet to be"—and is marked by a timeless materiality that comes to inhabit Truth's body: she is indifferently "calm and erect, as one of her own native palmtrees waving alone in the desert," or as quoted earlier, "mighty and dark as the gigantic depths of tropical forests," "mysterious as the hidden rivers and mines of that burning continent" (153, 170).

Dismissing such attempts to portray her in a bodied language as a dehistoricized symbol, Truth insisted instead on relocating all representations of her in history and proposed herself as a sign possessing historical agency: "'The Lord has made me a sign unto this nation, an' I go round a' testifyin,' an' showin' on em' their sins agin my people'" (152). In so doing she refused to embody any abstract symbolic value but worked instead to inform herself about contemporary political events that she could then reinterpret to the people: "'. . . read me something that is going on *now,* something about this great war'" (174); "I can't read a book, but I can read de people'" (216).

As a sign, Truth sought a platform from which she could become a "doer of the word" and claim that right to give testimony on the state of the nation that had been denied her by the New York courts of law. Before turning to the issue of Truth's orature, her participation in oral rather than written literary traditions, however, we may want to question whether Truth, while herself not a writer, was not able in some way to take advantage of writing. I would like to suggest not only that Truth was able to make use of various technologies of writing but that it was her very lack of literacy that made possible her appropriation of different modes of "writing" and enabled her to enter "modernity"; no longer "primitive," she must be marked as "modern."

During the Civil War Truth devised a highly interesting strategy through which she could in some sense engage in the process of narrative writing. Titus entitled her narrative of Truth "Book of Life," taking this title from a series of notebooks in which Truth had collected the autographs of friends in public life—William Lloyd and Helen Garrison, Amy Post, Wendell Phillips, Samuel and Abby May, Charles Sumner, Frederick Douglass—in the process attaching great significance to the written signature: "'To all calling upon her, she asks the question, "Don't you want to write your name in de Book of Life?" to which query, the counter one in relation to the same "Book of Life," is generally put, and Sojourner is usually gratified by the chirography of her visitor . . .'" (232–33). On the most immediate level the signature functions here as a form of the documentary, testifying to the historical importance of the signers on the stage of national events. In addition, the signature points back self-referentially to the signer's own public authority and power, to what Derrida has called his or her transcendental nowness or *maintenance.* Even more significantly, however, Truth's "Book of Life," whose very title echoes biblical beliefs in God's omnipotence, underscores the degree to which the signer's signature confers power on the signatee—Truth—as well. First, the signatee's very existence is necessary in order for the signer to write and sign his or her writing. Second, the signatee inevitably comes to shape the form this writing takes, making the signer in a sense dependent on the signatee. Indeed, one could say that at the moment of writing the signer comes into existence only in relation to the signatee; thus, as they signed their autograph in her "Book of Life," Truth's friends and acquaintances received definition primarily in terms of their relationship to her. Third, the signatee can put the signer's signature to his or her own particular use. Most

39

especially, we have seen how the signature, while singular, is of necessity also iterable, reproducible, and thus detachable; it may, in fact, come to function as a quotation. Thus, in her "Book of Life" Truth compiled the signatures as a series of quotations, providing her own frame for them and, in a sense, creating her own written text. And finally, by allowing Titus to publish the signatures in her narrative, she chose to give them a public existence.

In 1863, at about the same time that she became interested in collecting the signatures of friends in public life, Truth also agreed to have photographs made of herself, which she sold after her lectures much as she had sold copies of Gilbert's *Narrative* in the 1850s. The photograph thus came to function for Truth as a form of autobiography, of recorded testimony, of a signature both singular and reproducible, through which she once again hoped in some measure to enter the culture of writing. The photographs of Truth that remain in the historical record suggest an interesting ambiguity of cultural form that is again indicative of the problematics of self-representation faced by nineteenth-century black women in relationship to the dominant culture.

As Dan Schiller has noted, the new technology of daguerreotypy reinforced mid-nineteenth-century American ideologies of realism that asserted that artistic representation should, and could, be objective and true to nature. Photography thus became an important instrument of realism as the photograph was perceived to be strictly truthful, a nonsymbolic reflection of the objective world revealing Nature herself; in fact, its objectivity was believed to transform history itself into nature.[25] Despite such pronouncements about artistic naturalness, however, the photograph was, of course, a technological invention, a cultural artifact. The origins and development of the *carte de visite* photograph (a photograph mounted on a 2$^1/_2$-by-4-inch calling card) as well as the later cabinet photograph (mounted on a somewhat larger card measuring 4$^1/_4$-by-6$^1/_2$ inches), both of which were favored by Truth, point to the cultural foundations of photography and suggest interesting social complexities. Created by the duke of Parma in 1857 as an innovative improvement on the more conventional calling card, the *carte de visite* was initially designed for an elite defined by its leisure-time social activities; but, transported to the United States, it was soon popularized and made democratic, becoming in the words of a contemporary photographer "the social currency, the sentimental 'green-backs' of civilization."[26] At the height of its popularity, the *carte de visite* became an instrument of mass culture, a vehicle facilitating the accession of the private into the public sphere. For, just as private citizens could now transform themselves into writers and readily publish their views in newspapers in the form of letters to the editor, so now they could publicize themselves by means of the photograph.[27] In particular, the *carte de visite* and cabinet photograph became an inexpensive and easily available vehicle of publicity, a means of keeping oneself constantly in the public eye, for celebrities of all kinds— entertainers, politicians, military men, and professionals.[28]

Truth's use of the *carte de visite* and cabinet photograph suggests a willingness on her part to take advantage of this modern technological art form; and her appropriation of it once again points to its very ambiguity as a cultural artifact. One prevailing argument contends that the photograph can only be a commodity in a capitalist consumer society; it constitutes a consumable object whose relationship to the world is impersonal and open to exploitation by society. Yet if the social construction of the photograph implies commodification, it may also intimate resistance to commodification. In agreeing to have photographic images made of herself, Truth insisted on maintaining control over them by having them copyrighted in her own name and selling them on her own terms at profit. In a letter written to Oliver Johnson early in 1864 that she requested be published in the *National Anti-Slavery Standard,* Truth announced "that now I am about to have a new, and, I hope much better photograph taken of me, which a friend here is going to have copy-righted for my benefit; and when this is done I shall have letters written in answer to all those who have been sent, and enclose the required photographs." In a private letter sent shortly after to her friend Mary Gale, Truth expressed her concern about the quality of her photographic images: "I wanted to send you the best. I enclose you three all in different positions—they say here that they are much better than my old ones"; and she also explained her need to increase their cost to one dollar for three photographs, or thirty-five cents for one, due to the cost of paper, envelopes, and stamps.[29]

Moreover, if the photograph constitutes a commodified object to be bought and sold on the marketplace, at the same time it produces a subjective reality and may function as a more personal means of communication, as a form of writing. In other words, if the photograph is denotative, it is also connotative. An examination of some of Truth's photographic images suggests the extent to which they float between these two poles of denotation and connotation, creating a kind of ambiguity that impedes any reified categorization of Truth.

Truth's photographic consumers consisted in large part of those antebellum white abolitionists who continued to remain active in the fight for the civil rights of African Americans during and after the Civil War. In her photographs Truth appears not as a child of Nature but as a historical being who inhabits the realm of Culture, thus returning us to a consideration of the cultural form and content of photography. For if on the one hand the photograph seems to be a flat image, a mere mask, on the other it is a sign indicative of a historical reality; similarly, if it appears as an isolated fragment, a decontextualized quotation, it also takes its place within a cultural field as a culturally constructed image.[30] In the present instance we have no way of knowing who was responsible for Truth's cultural presentation in her photographs, although we do know that she willingly agreed to their retouching. Examining her photographic images as a form of writing, however, we may nevertheless attempt to specify their cultural field and representation of the figure of the black woman.

The dozen or so photographs that we possess of Truth take pains to emphasize her femininity; indeed, several depict Truth knitting or present her against a

Sojourner Truth. Cabinet Card, 1864. Courtesy Sophia Smith Collection, Smith College, Northhamption, MA.

background of feminizing elements taken from a domestic interior: a vase of flowers, a cloth-covered table, a mantelpiece, a carpet.[31] In most of the photographs Truth is dressed in plain Quaker garb—a dark dress, covered by a white shawl, with a white bonnet on her head. Such a presentation accords fully with contemporary accounts of Truth's mode of dress, suggesting that she made no attempt here to appear different from her daily custom. Yet it does contrast in one detail with two well-known descriptions of her by white abolitionist women. In Stowe's essay Truth is said to be wearing "a bright Madras handkerchief, arranged as a turban, after the manner of her race" (152), and Frances Gage's later account of Truth's appearance at a women's rights convention claims that "an uncouth sun-bonnet" covered her white turban.[32]

Sojourner Truth. Courtesy of the State University of New York at New Paltz, Sojourner Truth Library.

In at least two photographs, however, Truth's appearance is more "folk" and more in accordance with Stowe's and Gage's conception of her: her vest, jacket, and skirt are of a plaid or striped material, a wooden walking stick is in one hand, a plaid bag hangs over the other arm. We have no way of knowing how much control Truth had over her choice of dress, whether it was dictated by her friends, the photographer, or Truth herself. Nor do we know what style of dress Truth might have preferred; is the supposedly better photograph alluded to in the letter to Oliver Johnson one in which Truth is dressed in folk clothes or one in which she is in Quaker garb and the trappings of conventional femininity are the most evident? This latter representational image was obviously designed to suggest both Truth's feminine nature and her evangelical mission; I would argue that it is meant to indicate acceptable class status as well. Yet if Truth does not appear in these photographs as one of the folk, neither does she, with her shawl, bonnet, and even glasses and knitting, reflect the genteel middle-class demeanor so evident in contemporaneous photographs of Watkins Harper, Shadd Cary, or Sarah Parker Remond. The effect of these photographs is to present Truth to the observer as a hybrid, to endow her with a social and cultural ambiguity that defies categorization and perhaps allowed her to challenge commodification.

There is yet a final ambiguity embedded in Truth's photographs that constitutes, I think, another form of resistance to commodification. It resides in the caption that accompanied them: "I sell the shadow to support the substance"— the shadow meaning the photographic image, the substance Truth's actual bodily self as well as the social causes to which she had committed herself. Yet it is also possible to reinterpret these two terms such that it is the absent person who becomes the shadow by virtue of her nonpresence, and the present photographic object that is now the substance. By substantiating herself in her photographs as an image for consumption by her white abolitionist audiences, Truth could remain a shadow elusive to everyone but herself.

Truth's request to Oliver Johnson that he publish her letter in the *Standard* indicates, finally, the extent to which she sought to appropriate, and manipulate, the newspaper as a modern technological instrument designed to gather and disseminate general information and, more particularly, to generate personal publicity. An 1864 letter dictated on her behalf to Rowland Johnson finds Truth asking for copies of the *Standard* so that the contrabands of Freedmen's Village might be informed of events of national importance. In the same letter she requested that Johnson "'publish my whereabouts, and anything in this letter you think would interest the friends of Freedom, Justice, and Truth, in the *Standard* and *Anglo-African,* and any other paper you may see fit'" (180). Similarly, an 1871 letter to the *New York Tribune* suggests that information about Truth published in the newspaper has become the catalyst for the provision of yet more news: "'Seeing an item in your paper about me, I thought I would give you the particulars of what I am trying to do, in hopes that you would print a letter about it and so help on the good cause'" (239). Thus, from the 1850s on Truth appropriated the newspaper to fashion it into a nexus of information by, and about, her. Beyond that, as we shall see, she also endeavored to forge it into an instrument that would help her to reach out to those from whom she had become isolated in an act of imagining community.

Our analysis of Gilbert's and Titus's ethnobiographies of "one who does not write" forces us to come to terms with the difficulty of recognizing and naming that which lies on the other side of writing. In an effort to open up our vision of the unwritten, I suggest that we speculate upon some of the ways in which Truth's life explodes beyond the narrative plots of the dominant culture, beyond writing itself, acknowledging at the same time the degree to which our knowledge of Truth's life is always already enmeshed in writing. What we discover is that elements of this life belonging to a culture beyond writing may be traced to African and African-American oral cultures. Yet while these are in fact present in the narratives written about Truth, they are not always explicitly named. For example, Truth's desire to overcome isolation and participate in communal social arrangements may be interpreted, as I suggested earlier, as an undefined yearning to return to an African social past that emphasizes commitment not to the individual or the nuclear family but to the collectivity that congregates in a compound where space is not bounded.

Along with Margaret Washington and Gloria Joseph, I would argue that Truth's epistemological worldview, ritualistic practices, and spiritual experiences contain residues of African oral culture.[33] Margaret Washington has shown that Truth's participation in Pinkster festivals, which merged Pentecostal rituals with African forms of entertainment, indicates the degree to which African traditions were immediately available to her. I would further suggest that Truth's conviction that God manifests himself in material objects such as the moon and the stars echoes James Gronniosaw's earlier account of the African belief that "there was no power but the sun, moon, and stars; that they made all our country."[34] These statements reflect an African perspective that holds that no distinction exists between spiritual and material worlds, but that animate and inanimate objects, spirit and matter, are bound together in one system ordered by God. Washington has also demonstrated that many of Truth's spiritual experiences, including her conversion in which she was visited by the Holy Wind, are not only Pentecostal but are grounded in Africanisms. It might thus even be possible to interpret Truth's affiliation with Spiritualism in the late 1850s as a natural extension of African religious beliefs that emphasize spirit communication and possession. Finally, Truth's belief in the primacy of the oral in the world at large, and more particularly in the religious world, which allowed her to converse freely with God in "her rural sanctuary" (60), corresponds to the African notion that the world is primarily one of sound in which speech can make the past present, vision a reality. The concept of words as "doing" is not only Christian but African as well.[35]

Gilbert's and Titus's recording in their narratives of selected speeches by

Truth may be interpreted as an effort to neutralize the opposition between the one who writes and the one who does not.[36] Yet I would argue that it also opens the way for verbal Africanisms and African-Americanisms beyond the black dialect constructed by the dominant culture to infiltrate the narratives. Further, it intimates the presence of a double discourse addressed to a double audience, an immediate audience composed primarily of whites and, as I shall later suggest, a larger "absent" audience composed of her own people. An African-Americanism is already present in Truth's aspiration to transform herself into a "sign unto this nation." Indeed, to the African-American slave the world was filled with signs that were not only to be read but functioned primarily as "calls to action."[37] Thus, Truth hoped that as a "sign" the nation would heed her "testifyin', an' showin' on 'em their sins agin my people" and be moved to action. As with all other public speakers—male or female, white or black—Truth needed carefully to assess the rhetorical context of her lecturing and to negotiate the complex relationship between self, situation, subject, and audience, a task particularly problematic, as we have seen, for black women. Indeed, the question facing Truth was whether it was possible for her to gain an audience, make herself heard, and maintain her authority while resisting commodification by the public gaze according to the terms and categories set up by the dominant culture.

As we have seen thus far, the dominant culture's perceptions and representations of Truth were foremost as an unruly material body. In accounts of her public speaking, most especially, emphasis was frequently placed on Truth's grotesque appearance and behavior: "She is a crazy, ignorant, repelling negress, and her guardians would do a Christian act to restrict her entirely to private life" (204). More often than not, Truth's grotesqueness is attributable to the dominant culture's masculinization of the black female body, already intimated in Story's commentary on his Libyan Sibyl and explicitly voiced by Olmsted in his description of slave women. In her narrative, for example, Gilbert records how to her owner, Dumont, Truth was above all a masculine laboring body: "*'that* wench . . . is better to me than a *man*—for she will do a good family's washing in the night, and be ready in the morning to go into the field'" (33). Most significantly, however, this social construction of Truth's body as masculine because laboring is often displaced by a biological one that results in a presumption of generic and/or sexual ambiguity. In Gilbert's narrative we are told that a lawyer to whom Truth had appealed for help in recovering her son from slavery "looked at her a few moments, as if to ascertain if he were contemplating a new variety of the genus homo" (51). Even more dramatic was the reported incident at the 1858 antislavery meeting in Silver Lake, Indiana, where a Dr. Strain accused Truth of masquerading her essential biological masculinity as femininity: "A rumor was immediately circulated that Sojourner was an imposter; that she was, indeed, a man disguised in women's clothing." And as her oratory was perceived to issue directly from her body, Truth's voice was equally perceived as bodied and hence also masculine: "'your voice is not the voice of a woman, it is the voice of a man, and we believe you are a man'" (138). To remove such doubts about her body, Truth reportedly gave bodily testimony by revealing her breasts to the audience.

Kristeva would contend that given such cultural constructions Truth could only become an abject creature for whom writing "alone purifies from the abject."[38] Yet I would respond that Truth resisted, and even exploited, abjection by appropriating the act of public speaking and by subverting the dominant culture's constructions of black womanhood while seeming to accept them. In so doing Truth exhibited no fear of exposing her body to the public gaze. For just as she rewrote the relationship between signer and signatee to allow the latter manipulative power over the written signature, so she strove in her public lecturing to reconfigure the relationship between audience and speaker in order to control the audience's gaze. If, as Stowe wrote in her "Libyan Sibyl" essay, the Beechers wished to gaze upon her as an "entertainer," Truth in turn insisted on reversing the power relationship embedded in this gaze: "'Well, honey, de Lord bless ye! I jes' thought I'd like to come an' have a look at ye'" (152). As an entertainer Truth adopted the stance taken, in Turner's formulation, by those who are weak and of low status (the court jester, for example) in order to embody the moral values of *communitas,* to insist on the need for an "open" rather than a "closed" morality, and thus acquire power.[39] Truth brought her open moral sense to bear on the historical problems of slavery, racism, women's rights, and, in particular, the need to reconceptualize contemporary notions of the "brave." For Truth these issues were further complicated in the postbellum period as African Americans sought to claim a place for themselves within the political economy of the nation and as gender relations between men and women within the black community became increasingly problematic.[40]

Our knowledge of the form and content of Truth's speeches is constrained by our exclusive dependence on the written record, on our access to those speeches alone that were selectively chosen by the reporter, transcribed according to his or her linguistic preferences, and reprinted in the newspapers of the period, in Gilbert's and Titus' narratives, or in Stanton and Anthony's *History of Woman Suffrage.* Working with this written record left to us by history and acknowledging its corruption, I would suggest that it is still worth examining some of Truth's speeches to look for traces of the "native" culture, to place them within the context of both contemporary American oratorical traditions and African and African-American orature, to examine them as hybrid discourse.[41] Kenneth Cmiel has argued that by midcentury antebellum American eloquence was dominated by a "middling culture" that mixed high and low styles, allowing classical rhetoric to be penetrated by such expressive modes as folk dialects, slang, plain speaking, jargon, bombast, and/or euphemism. While prominent public figures as diverse as Henry Ward Beecher and Abraham Lincoln freely resorted to this "democratic idiom," pressure remained on the few women speakers of the period to continue employing a refined style. Truth refused to accede to this pressure, relying instead on dialect, folk expressions, and plain speaking to persuade her audiences. As a consequence, Cmiel interprets Truth's speaking style as part of this evolution of American oratory, comparing it to "the rustic dignity of Abraham Lincoln"; in the process, however, he neglects to consider the ways in which Truth's speech might well have been affiliated with other "native" oral traditions familiar to her from her childhood.[42]

Truth's links to African and African-American oral cultures may be located, as we have suggested, in her belief in the primacy of the spoken word, its importance as a mode of action rather than simply an articulation of thought, its magical power to create events, to make the past present, and vision reality.[43] Moreover, in such cultures the oral word does not exist simply in a verbal context but in a larger human one that involves bodily presence. The voice is directly and intimately connected to bodily activity, giving rise to what Ong has called a "verbomotor lifestyle" and what I have characterized as Truth's "bodied voice." And, as Ong has remarked, verbomotor cultures readily lend themselves to highly rhythmic speech as they link bodily functions—breathing, gesture—to oral speech patterns.[44] Rhythmic discourse may in fact evolve into song. In an important chapter in his book, Carleton Mabee has emphasized the importance of song in Truth's speaking repertoire and has suggested her probable familiarity with "Juba," an "African-American dance, accompanied by singing, clapping, patting the hands on the thighs, and patting the feet on the ground." Finally, rhythmic discourse may lead to an alternation of song and speech characteristic of African oral culture and present in many of Truth's performances.[45] A postbellum review in a Kansas newspaper, for example, commented that in her public speaking Truth demonstrated that "she has a poetic element in her nature, and has several times given forth her thought in spontaneous rhyme."[46]

Specific idiosyncracies of speech also suggest Truth's close ties to African and African-American oral traditions. On the most general level we may note orature's general stylistic inclination toward verbal accumulation and redundancy. Other devices reflect both the personal and communal tendencies of African oral narrative. On the one hand, the speaker may seek to affirm his or her own personal authority by "resort[ing] to a story that recapitulates his experience of coming to know: how he acquired his knowledge, when, from whom, whether any further evidence is available."[47]On the other hand, he or she may also employ verbal structures designed to cement community values. Call-and-response, for example, functions to involve the entire community in the performance and thus bring it together; proverbs work to reinforce the social values of the community, often allowing the speaker to position him- or herself as a teacher whose goal it is to bridge any gap that might have opened between different members or constituencies within the community.[48] Finally, African-American folk culture is characterized by the use of a deflationary form of humor designed to turn the social world, in particular black-white relations, on its head.[49]

In their reprinting, Truth's speeches were invariably contextualized by editorial commentaries that could only comprehend her language usage as "quaint," "peculiar," "singular," or "original." In so doing they failed to recognize the presence in these speeches of an other/native cultural background. Those who ridiculed her bodily movements were unable to connect them to the verbomotor lifestyle of oral culture. Those who noted her penchant for "spontaneous rhyme" could neither understand how it related to her speech nor appreciate the cultural context that invited the conjunction of song and speech: "Her speaking is disjointed. . . . In fact, she talks in public just as she does all the time. There is not much connection, but she just drifts along."[50]

Such assessments of Truth's public speaking leave us with a series of unanswered questions. Was Truth indeed the naive child of Nature that her biographers and reviewers believed her to be? Or did she deliberately manipulate this naive persona as the most effective rhetorical stance available to her to speak to white audiences even though she was, according to Fred Tomkins, "able to speak in correct and beautiful English"?[51] Did she knowingly invent a double discourse that would allow her to reach beyond her white audiences to speak to those of her own race, particularly its women, thereby imagining community and working toward the creation of an African-American local place? Finally, did she suspect that the cultivation of such speech, in striking contrast to that of other black public lecturers of the period, could in fact function as yet another sign of modernity, that it could become what Werner Sollors has labeled a marker of ethnicity that relies on modern traditionalisms in order to insist on the cultural distinctiveness of the ethnic group?[52] In the remainder of this chapter I offer a reading—speculative rather than definitive—of several of Truth's 1850s speeches in the hopes of enlarging our contemporary vision not only of Truth's oratory but more generally of the antebellum African-American culture that lay on the other side of writing.

Several of Truth's antebellum speeches address the issue of Southern slavery and Northern discrimination against free blacks, in the process seeking to redefine the place of African Americans in the political economy of the nation. In one lecture, delivered to a religious meeting around 1852 and reprinted in the *National Anti-Slavery Standard* and then again in Titus's narrative, Truth attacked the Constitution as a document that has failed to protect the rights of African Americans. In a pattern reflective of African oral traditions and belief systems, Truth began her speech with a personal account that, in affirming the primacy of the spoken word and the presence of God in the material world, also offered incontrovertible proof of the rightness of her own political position. Going out into "de fields and de woods," she examines a sheaf of wheat and asks God what is the matter with it. His response, "'Sojourner, dere is a little weasel in it,'" allows Truth to analogize the ailing Constitution to the weevil-infested wheat: "Den I says, God, what ails *dis* Constitution? He says to me, "'Sojourner, dere is a little weasel in it'" (147). Truth's (conscious or unconscious) use of malapropism here most probably worked to undercut the seriousness of her message to her audience. Yet her metaphoric evocation of the weevil in the wheat, a common saying among African-American slaves warning of the presence of an informer within the community, functioned as a vigorous reminder of the resourcefulness of slave culture and undoubtedly resonated powerfully in the ear of an African American audience or readership.

In two other speeches, one reported in the December 10, 1853 issue of the *National Anti-Slavery Standard* and the other in the July 14, 1854 issue of the *Liberator,* Truth vehemently assailed the economic discrimination against free blacks in the North and the exploitation of slave labor in the South. To accomplish her ideological ends Truth made use of the African-American verbal device that allowed her humorously to reverse the hierarchies of the social world while masking the aggressiveness of her satiric intent. She was thus able successfully to demonstrate how whites, convinced of their own racial superiority, in fact displace and abuse blacks economically, betraying in the process their own moral and spiritual inferiority. Although the 1854 speech appears quite disjointed, it in fact quite logically argues the case against white superiority in the moral, economic, and spiritual realms. It demonstrates how slaves have been able to care for themselves "better than the white people had brought them up," how whites owe blacks so much for their labor that "if they paid it all back, they wouldn't have any thing left for seed," how, given their many tribulations on earth, God has reserved the rewards of heaven for blacks, not whites.

In her 1853 speech in which she specifically addressed a black audience, Truth focused her attention on economic issues, enumerating the many menial occupations from which urban blacks were excluded—as waiters, bootblacks, street cleaners, coachmen, and barbers. Rather than merely complain about such economic discrimination, however, Truth proceeded to point out the current deterioration of such services in urban centers and consequently to argue the case for the inferiority of white labor. Broadening her argument, finally, she sought to reposition African-American workers within the national political economy, contending, along much the same lines as Shadd Cary and Watkins Harper, that blacks stand a better chance of achieving economic independence in agrarian rather than urban occupations: "I was lately lecturing out in Pennsylvania, the farmers wanted good men and women to work their farms on shares for them. Why can't you go out there?—and depend upon it, in the course of time you will get to be independent."

Two other antebellum speeches of Truth's that have entered into the written record focus on the issue of women's rights and were delivered at the 1851 Woman's Rights Convention in Akron, Ohio, and the 1853 Broadway Tabernacle Convention, respectively, to primarily white female audiences. These speeches are important statements in Truth's broad-based efforts to redefine the specific position of the black woman, the "brave" who can claim privilege on the basis of neither whiteness nor maleness. As she grappled with such redefinition, Truth needed to situate the black woman vis-à-vis the dominant culture's central construction of true womanhood as well as the feminist-abolitionists' more marginal reconceptualizations of femininity. Truth's contempt for, and rejection of, the cult of true womanhood is suggested in Titus's account of the 1858 antislavery meeting in Silver Lake, Indiana, in which her femininity was reportedly at issue. Whereas many of the white women present felt shame at Truth's public exposure of her "private" sexual organs, Truth apparently felt none. In her speech she reportedly redefined her breasts not as emblems of an essential femininity but as a sign of her public labor power, the socially enforced labor that had ensured the well-being of her masters' children and that thus differentiated her from white women: ". . . her breasts had suckled many a white babe, to the exclusion of her own offspring . . ." (139).

Truth needed, in addition, to redefine the black woman in relation to the feminist-abolitionists' construction of her. In her *Appeal to the Christian Women of the South* concerning the terrible condition of slaves, Angelina Grimké had spoken sympathetically of their plight and promised to "be faithful in pleading the cause of the oppressed" while urging "submission on the[ir] part" as the wisest policy. Both of Grimké's *Appeals* were, in fact, addressed specifically and exclusively to white women—South and North—suggesting that she was far more interested in rethinking the parameters of white women's culture than in forging a space for the "brave" to emerge into autonomous womanhood. Both Angelina and her sister Sarah, moreover, resorted to the analogy of "the slavery of sex" to define the obstacles that stood in the way of the full liberation of white women. Once again we are alerted here to the dangers that may inhere in the use of figurative language. The analogy of white women's lack of rights to slavery is valid to a certain extent: white women have no legal existence and cannot bring legal action, they cannot hold property but are themselves property, they have no control over their children, and so on. Nevertheless, there are ways in which this analogy is clearly invalid: the (white) *feme sole* possesses legal rights denied to the (white) *feme covert*, white women have the legal right of petition as well as education, those of middle-class status are maintained in a protected private sphere, their families are not customarily broken up, and so forth. Finally, it is important to note that in the construction of this analogy the slave is initially ungendered. As the analogy is expanded upon, this slave is most often gendered as male and the historical specificity of the female slave is thereby erased; if her special condition is addressed, she is invariably envisioned as victim.[53]

Truth's two antebellum women's rights speeches may be found in Stanton and Anthony's *History of Woman Suffrage*, but the 1851 speech (the famous "A'n't I a Woman" speech) has a longer and more complex publishing history. As Mabee has noted, at least four accounts of the speech were reported in newspapers shortly after the close of the convention, one in the June 6 issue of the *New York Daily Tribune*, another in the June 13 issue of the *Liberator,* still another in the June 14 issue of Jane Swisshelm's *Saturday Visiter,* and the longest in the June 21 issue of the *Anti-Slavery Bugle.* Frances D. Gage's "reminiscences" of the speech were not written until years later, when the essay appeared in the April 23, 1863 issue of the *Independent;* it was then reprinted in both Titus's narrative and Stanton and Anthony's *History.* Mabee has quite astutely questioned the accuracy of Gage's version of the speech as well as the veracity of some of the factual details provided in her editorial comments and has suggested that the 1851 *Anti-Slavery Bugle* version is probably a closer approximation of the speech that Truth actually gave.[54] We simply have no way of ascertaining what Truth actually said. What I propose to do is read Gage's reminiscences of Truth as a representation of a black woman by a white woman, and then compare them with the earlier 1851 *Bugle* speech.

As printed in the *History of Woman Suffrage,* Truth's 1851 and 1853 speeches are both contextualized by editorial narratives designed to place them in the proper historical and social context in which they were given. Both editorial narratives underscore the double burden of "color and sex" that Truth, and all black women, must bear (1:567). In particular, in her introductory comments to the 1851 speech, Gage relates the disgust felt by many of the women present that a "darkey" is to be allowed to speak: "'Woman's rights and niggers! . . . Don't let her speak!'" (1:115). In contrast, Gage emphasizes her own rejection of the irreconcilable contradiction between the concept of "woman" and that of "nigger," seeking instead to define Truth's specificity as a black woman. Yet Gage's use of bodied symbols here to portray Truth—"the Lybian Statue [sic]," "this almost Amazon form"—once again results in a dehistoricization of the black woman (1:115–16).

Truth's speech is an argument in favor of the equality of "woman." While it might give the appearance of disjointedness, as recorded by Gage it is in fact quite logically organized. Revising somewhat the African-American system of antiphony, it improvisationally but systematically "responds" to the "call" of male superiority made earlier by some ministers present at the convention. To their claim of man's superior intellect, Truth replies, from a position of open morality that relies on the wisdom of folk sayings, that men have the obligation to aid women in their acquisition of knowledge: "'If my cup won't hold but a pint, and yourn holds a quart, wouldn't ye be mean not to let me have my little half-measure full?'" To their argument that men are superior because of the manhood of Christ, Truth retorts that Christ originated not from a man but from God and a woman. And to the "theological view of the sin of our first mother," Truth responds that Eve "'was strong enough to turn de world upside down all alone'" (1:115, 116).

Yet the thrust of Truth's argument lies in the first part of her speech in which she debunks the cult of true womanhood whereby "dat man ober dar say dat womin needs to be helped into carriages, and lifted ober ditches" in order to assert the worth and equality of black womanhood. In a series of statements she affirms her masculine strength based on her ability to perform strenuous physical labor: "I have ploughed, and planted, and gathered into barns, and no man could head me." But in a second series of rhetorical questions she pleads her identity as a woman—"'and a'n't I a woman?'"—an identity that remains incontrovertible given the fact of her motherhood: "I have borne thirteen chilern, and seen 'em mos' all sold off to slavery, and when I cried out with my mother's grief, none but Jesus heard me!" (1:116). Although at first glance it might appear that Truth here has adopted a paradigm similar to that of Frances Gage or Dr. Strain, in fact her construction of her own identity derives specifically, as Jean Fagin Yellin has noted, from her historical experience as a slave whose productive and reproductive labor has been owned and exploited by slaveholders. Indeed, the extent of Truth's difference from Gage may be measured in Gage's concluding editorial comment, "She had taken us up in her strong arms and carried us safely over the slough of difficulty turning the whole tide in our favor" (1:116–17). Yellin's observation that Gage here "cast the black woman as a powerful rescuer and herself and the other white women at the convention as powerless rescued female victims" must be further refined to emphasize that Gage has in fact placed black women in the same structural position as those men who help white women into carriages and lift them over ditches.[55]

As personal "reminiscences," Gage's account is constrained not only by her own social ideology but also by her memory and by the moment of narration itself. An exploration of this narrative moment indicates that Gage wrote her account shortly after the appearance of Stowe's "Libyan Sibyl" essay and while living on the South Carolina Sea Islands, where she had joined women like Charlotte Forten to work on behalf of the newly freed people. I would suggest that Gage's reminiscences were in fact highly influenced by these events such that the historical figure of Truth is overshadowed by other, contradictory, representational images. Thus, if Truth is ahistorically analogized to the Libyan Sibyl and the Amazon in the prefatory comments, the speech itself seems to assimilate her to the South Carolina slave characterized by a heavy black dialect and the use of the term "nigger," not present in the 1851 version nor, I believe, in any of Truth's other speeches. Thus, the opening lines read: "I tink dat 'twixt de niggers of de Souf and de womin at de Norf, all talkin' 'bout rights, de white men will be in a fix pretty soon" (1:116). The immediate effect of such dialect is to reinforce the image of Truth as a "darkey."

I would argue that Gage's reconstruction of Truth's speech rewrites Truth not only as a "darkey" but also as a masculine body seeking feminization implied in the repeated question "a'n't I a woman?" In contrast, the 1851 account offers an inversion of Gage's paradigm of a quest for feminization as it presents us first with Truth's synecdochic affirmation "I am a woman's rights," which is then followed by a series of statements that emphasize her capacity to do a man's work: "I have as much muscle as any man, and can do as much work as any man." Rather than begging for admission to a sphere of femininity defined by white women, Truth here offers her audience a vision of black womanhood that records the ways in which the specific historical conditions of slave labor have insisted on masculinizing the "brave."

The second noteworthy difference between the two versions of this speech consists in the different placement and wording of the already quoted openings line of the "A'n't I a Woman" speech, which forms the concluding line of the 1851 version but in a different language: "But man is in a tight place, the poor slave is on him, woman is coming on him, and he is surely between a hawk and a buzzard." This sentence is significant in its evocation of slave and woman by means of a folk expression that is simultaneously standard English and African-American. In her juxtaposition of what Blair called "simple expression" and "figure of speech," Truth sought vividly to portray the white man's increasingly tense location vis-à-vis the two groups he has oppressed. The figurative expression "between hawk and buzzard" is a colloquialism of the dominant culture that suggests a positioning between two sufficiently similar but unpleasant entities that can only lead to indecision or paralysis. Yet "hawk" and "buzzard" are also figures from an African-American folktale in which the two vultures are seen as oppositional and come into conflict in a struggle for survival, the buzzard, a descendant of the powerful African "King Buzzard," always gaining the ascendancy.[56] To an African-American audience this colloquialism can be read as the site where the two cultures overlap without converging and makes it possible to see the position of "slave" and "woman" not as symmetrical but as divergent and possibly hostile, thus undermining the kind of coalition that Gage's later 1863 narrative worked so hard to build.

Interesting parallels and divergences exist between Truth's 1851 speech and her 1853 New York convention speech. The latter one is a general plea for women's rights elaborated by means of some of the same figurative analogies employed by white feminist-abolitionists, in particular the figure of the pleading Esther.[57] But the language of Truth's speech also suggests the presence of other cultures—African and African-American—reaching out perhaps beyond her immediate audience of white women to the "brave." Thus, if Truth depreciatingly refers to herself throughout the speech as a "slave," a "colored woman," and an "aged woman" whose right to speak seems questionable, she in fact begins her speech with a powerful Africanism: "Is it not good for me to come and draw forth a spirit." In the Kumina, or "African dance," of the central African Bakongo tribe, the ritual ceremony is performed to the beat of drums and is led by a queen who, initiated into the mysteries of the religion, is both possessed by spirits and able to draw forth spirits.[58] Truth, then, implicitly positions herself here as a kind of African queen come to draw forth the spirit of her audience. Its spirit is, according to her, that of both a goose and a snake ready to hiss her. In this use of animal imagery Truth shifts cultural ground to tap into a colloquialism of the dominant culture whereby the audience mocks the stage performer by hissing at him or her like a goose. Her additional evocation of the snake may be seen, however, as a kind of cultural convergence in which African, African-American, and American values alike interpret the snake as evil and demonic (1:567).

Aware that her audience might not recognize her power as the queen of the Kumina, Truth shifts the ground for establishing her authority as speaker by boldly laying claim to being a citizen of the State of New York. Despite the possibility that her audience might still hiss her "like snakes and geese," Truth's structuring of the rest of her speech suggests that she might in fact be striving to reach an audience of the "brave" that exists beyond her immediate one. For, interestingly enough, although Truth is addressing a "Woman's Rights" meeting, she bases her claim of citizenship on the fact of having been a slave: "I am a citizen of the State of New York; I was born in it, and I was a slave in the State of New York; and now I am a good citizen of this State." It is only after she has asserted the fact of her citizenship that Truth proceeds to speak out on the question of women's rights, allowing slave and woman to conjoin and finally produce the "colored woman." If the end of the 1851 speech had suggested the oppositionality of slave and woman in the figures of hawk and buzzard, here Truth attempts to collapse this opposition into a conflationary "we": "We have all been thrown down so low that nobody thought we'd ever get up again; but we have been long enough trodden now; we will come up again, and now I am here" (1:567). As we shall see in chapter 8, it is this same tension in her thinking between "slave" and "woman," conflict and coalition, that was to shape the politics of race and gender in Truth's postbellum career as a public speaker and social activist.

3

"Humble Instruments in the Hands of God": Maria Stewart, Jarena Lee, and the Economy of Spiritual Narrative

Both Maria Stewart and Jarena Lee were contemporaries of Sojourner Truth, Stewart only five years younger and Lee, born in 1783, older by approximately sixteen years. Although neither woman was born into slavery, both formed part of that steadily growing subaltern class of unschooled and unskilled black laborers who inhabited the northeastern states at the turn of the century. For this class as well as for the black elite, Christianity functioned both as a central belief system and as a source of personal and political empowerment. The Bible offered African Americans narratives that they could readily assimilate to their own experiences. Through the story of Exodus, for example, they could envision themselves typologically as the new children of Israel; through the Christ story they could hope for redemption and salvation. Most importantly, perhaps, the prophetic traditions of the Old Testament offered black Americans a mode of discourse through which they could articulate the despair and aspirations of their people. In antebellum African-American culture then, spirituality provided a gateway to political thought and often functioned as a springboard for discussions of secular history. Furthermore, for women like Stewart and Lee, religious belief, in particular belief in God's divine protection, became a source of self-empowerment, an authorization to act in this world. Yet inevitably a tension was to arise between the beliefs of these women and the very institutions through which they sought to fulfill them. It is from this tension that their narrative impulse originates.

Scattered references to Stewart's and Lee's life and work suggest that at the beginning of their public careers as "doers of the word" both women lacked the requisite skills in literacy that would permit them to engage in sustained acts of literary self-representation. Thus, much as in Truth's case, Stewart's and Lee's social activism was expressed primarily by means of an oratory grounded in biblical rhetoric and infused with traces of Africanisms and African-Americanisms. For Stewart such oratory took the form of political sermonizing, for Lee, that of evangelical preaching; for both, literary composition appeared, at least initially, to be a complex task necessitating the aid of others. In striking contrast to Truth, however, both Stewart and Lee carried out their cultural work primarily within the black communities of the Northeast—Stewart chiefly in Boston, Lee in Philadelphia as well as in those marginal hybrid spaces opened up by the Second Great Awakening. In the process, both women were forced to contend with the prohibitions placed on black women by the power structures of black male institutions and, as a consequence, needed to devise strategies through which to test and overcome these limits. To do so, both Stewart and Lee resorted to geographic displacement either as a necessary means of survival or as an instrument of self-empowerment. Ultimately, they turned to the act of writing to produce a hybrid discourse that reconfigures in interesting ways the genres of spiritual writing that form part of the Western literary tradition.

Shortly before her death in 1879, Maria Stewart reprinted her collected writings from the 1830s under the title *Meditations from the Pen of Mrs. Maria W. Stewart*, which she prefaced with a brief autobiographical narrative. In a series of pithy statements, she informed her readers that she was born Maria Miller "in Hartford, Connecticut, in 1803; was left an orphan at five years of age; was bound out in a clergyman's family," circumstances thus obliging her, much like Nancy Prince and Watkins Harper, to enter into domestic service at an early age.[1] Miller's only education at this time appears to have been attendance at Sunday school, and it instilled in her a profound sense of religiosity that became the foundation of her personality. In 1826 she married James W. Stewart, a fairly prosperous shipping agent who ran an independent business. Her happiness was short-lived, however, as her husband died three years later and she was left destitute when a group of white businessmen defrauded her of her inheritance. Moreover, her husband's death was followed in 1830 by that of her close friend David Walker, leader of Boston's black community and author of the radical pamphlet *Walker's Appeal,* and in 1831 by that of Thomas Paul, another civic leader and pastor of Boston's African Baptist Church, of which Stewart was a member.[2] These deaths propelled Stewart into a period of intense emotional turmoil from which she recovered by means of a religious conversion experience: "[I] was . . . brought to the knowledge of the truth, as it is in Jesus, in 1830; in 1831 made a public profession of my faith in Christ" (4).

It was this same deeply felt grief that appears to have occasioned Stewart's first written publications, *Religion and the Pure Principles of Morality* and the *Meditations,* two short tracts published in 1831 and 1832, respectively. In addition, Stewart gave a series of speeches before promiscuous assemblies in Boston on the subject of community racial uplift and the specific role of black women in it, which were printed in the *Liberator* and published along with her earlier writings by Garrison's press in 1835 under the title *Productions of Mrs. Maria W. Stewart*. The first American woman ever to address a promiscuous assembly, Stewart appears to have raised such controversy within Boston's black community that she abruptly decided to leave the city at the end of 1833. The record of her life thereafter becomes quite sketchy as she traveled south from city to city in search of a local place in which she hoped to continue her community work. The 1830s find Stewart in New York City, where she joined a female literary society, furthered her own education, and taught in the public school system; by the 1850s she was in Baltimore, once again supporting herself by teaching (10). In 1861, at the outbreak of the Civil War, she moved to Washington, D.C., where she remained until her death in 1879.

On the surface many similarities exist between Truth's and Stewart's careers—their emergence from the subaltern class of unskilled workers to prominent roles in antislavery and racial uplift efforts, the intense religious fervor that provided the bedrock of their social activism, their concern with redefining the meaning of black womanhood and the specific role black women were to play within the community. But an attentive reading of the social narrative embedded within Stewart's autobiographical account suggests striking differences between the two. Through marriage Stewart had achieved middle-class status, but the death of her husband left her in precarious economic circumstances and in constant danger of losing her social position. Her desire to maintain her class status is evident in her repeated claims in her autobiography to gentility and ladyhood: "[A]nd being classed as a lady among my race all my life, and never exposed to any hardship, I did not know how to manage. . . . And always had that refined sentiment of delicacy about me that I could not bear to charge for the worth of my labor" (14). It is quite possible that Stewart became convinced at this point of the incompatibility of speaking publicly and being a lady, and that her later decision to leave the Baptist church and join the Episcopal church, most probably in the early 1850s, is indicative of her determination to hold on to her achieved middle-class status. Episcopalianism was the religion of choice among upper-class African Americans, promoting an image of social exclusiveness and prompting "upwardly mobile blacks to transfer their allegiance from Baptist and Methodist denominations."[3] In Washington Stewart joined the white Church of the Epiphany, helped organize Saint Mary's, the city's first black Episcopal church, in 1867, and then affiliated with Alexander Crummell's prestigious Saint Luke's when it opened in 1879 (16–23).

Finally, in joining Boston's racial uplift efforts after her husband's death, Stewart, unlike Truth, chose to work exclusively within the black community, seeking sites of power within its various organizations and aspiring to an institutional legitimacy that Truth never sought. Indeed, in striking contrast to Truth, Stewart adamantly refused to join any liminal community or to transform herself into the marginal figure of the entertainer. Ultimately, of course, Stewart found herself locked out of the black male institutions from which she so eagerly sought a hearing. It was as an outsider that she wrote an article in the July 14, 1832 issue of Garrison's *Liberator*, praising the work of the second annual Convention of People of Color and encouraging young men to become "useful and active members in society." It was again as an outsider that she spoke at Boston's African Masonic Hall No. 28 in February 1833.

The *Meditations* are among Stewart's earliest writings, and it is noteworthy that they were singled out by both Garrison and the distinguished Episcopalian minister Alexander Crummell for special praise in their commendatory letters that prefaced the 1879 edition of her work. In his letter Garrison recollected how Stewart came to him with "a manuscript embodying your devotional thoughts and aspirations, and also various essays . . ." (6) that he then agreed to print on her behalf. Referring specifically to Stewart's "Meditations and Prayers," Crummell recalled his surprise "that *such* a person could compose essays of this kind and give expression to such thoughts and be the author of such a work!" (10). To Crummell the *Meditations* were the literary expression of a young widow's grief, "the outburst of an overwrought soul" (10).

Indeed, Stewart's text consists of a series of fourteen meditations that reflect the anguish of an introspective soul, fully self-absorbed and isolated from society, that has witnessed death at close hand, experienced earthly disappointments, wrongful persecutions, and the temptations of the flesh, and as a consequence longs for a well-regulated life and divine forgiveness; and it charts the struggle of this soul to overcome self-despair and achieve the strength to carry out the Lord's bidding. In this context Stewart's act of writing may be interpreted as a means of rationalizing grief, of relying on the processes of reason to control and order what is otherwise unmanageable sorrow. The composition of the *Meditations* marks, in effect, the transition from affective prayer, characterized by the absence of reasoning, the presence of a multiplicity of affections, and at the extreme the eruption of uncontrolled emotions that submerge the individual in sentimentality and deny the possibility of moral improvement, to discursive prayer, which "proceeds by discursive steps to build up a vision of things . . . aimed at arousing the will to acts of fervor."[4] In addition, Stewart's *Meditations* record a movement from self-absorption to a concern with the social world, from an introspective stance in which "my soul became filled with holy meditations and sublime ideas . . . and my heart is most generally meditating upon its divine truths" (36) to a determination to move out into the community sphere since "my ardent wish and desire have ever been, that I might become a humble instrument in the hands of God, of winning some poor souls to God" (36).

To transform herself into a "humble instrument in the hands of God," Stewart needed to progress from a position of humility to one of greater self-assertion. I would suggest that literary composition and publication came to function for Stewart as just such a sign of self-assertion. Yet the conditions under which Stewart wrote the *Meditations* remain uncertain. In his commendatory letter Crummell explained that his surprise at the excellence of Stewart's essays was due to the fact that their author was "a person who had received but six weeks' schooling, who could not even pen her own thoughts, who had to get a little girl ten years old to write every word of this book" (10). In fact, we have no way of ascertaining the accuracy of Crummell's statement, and it is difficult to believe that Stewart actually dictated the entire *Meditations* to a young girl. What Crummell's comments do suggest, however, is that Stewart lacked well-developed skills in literacy and was largely self-taught.

In her 1879 autobiographical narrative Stewart asserted that her childhood education centered primarily around the study of the Bible: "During the years of my childhood and youth it was the black book that I mostly studied" (36). We do not know whether this study consisted of reading the actual text of the Bible or listening as it was read to her; but it is quite probable that Stewart relied on what another commender called "her retentive memory" (5), characteristic of peoples of oral cultures, and, like Truth, learned large portions of the Bible by heart. I would argue that in either event Stewart lived and studied under conditions of what certain scholars have called secondary orality, in which "oral" and "literate" are not so much a dichotomy as a continuum, mutually interactive and illuminating.[5] The Bible itself is part of this continuum as it is a written text based on the oral traditions of Jewish prophecy as well as Jewish and Christian prayer. It is to this oral/written tradition that Stewart turned to compose her *Meditations,* working either from the written text before her or from memory, either dictating her thoughts to an amanuensis or writing them down herself: "I have borrowed much of my language from the Holy Bible" (36).

It is also difficult to assess whether it was from written or oral sources that Stewart became aware of the tradition of the spiritual exercise and the literary genre of the meditation that emerged from it. The devotional method upon which these forms are based originally consisted of four steps: reading, or "the application of the mind to the Holy Scriptures"; the meditation itself, or "the careful consideration of [religious] truths"; prayer, or "the heart beseeching God"; and, finally, contemplation, or "the soul resting in God"; later methods restricted the steps to three by conflating the last two.[6] Each of Stewart's fourteen individual meditations is loosely patterned on this structure, while the entire volume records, as we have noted, a larger movement from introspection and self-despair to an awareness of the outer world and a desire to engage in spiritual and racial uplift work.

In Stewart's *Meditations* the reading of the Holy Scriptures, which places the supplicant in the presence of God, is carried out by means of the quotation of verse lines excerpted either from hymns by the English minister Isaac Watts, and/ or from selected books of the Old and New Testaments, and inserted at the beginning of several (but not all) of the meditations. As Eileen Southern has noted, Watts's hymns were introduced into the American colonies at the time of the First Great Awakening and quickly became popular among African-American congregants "because of the freshness and vitality of the words."[7] The language of many of Watts's hymns is taken directly from Old Testament psalms whose chief forms are the praise of God, the supplication to him, and the profession of faith, and whose main themes are physical and/or spiritual distress, death and rebirth, and exultation in anticipation of the future.[8] The stanzas quoted at the beginning of Stewart's meditations articulate similar concerns: the contemplation of that which lies beyond earthly life, the desire for death, awe in face of an unknown future, fear of damnation, and devotion to, and trust in, God. In several of Stewart's meditations these hymnal lines are replaced, or supplemented, by biblical quotations taken directly from the Psalms or the books of Jeremiah, Mark, and Matthew, and it is these that provide the actual subject of her meditations: self-despair, the yearning to be healed, the fear of dying without sufficient preparation, God's distinction between the saved and the damned on the Day of Judgment, his protection of the fatherless, his punishment of those who yield to temptation. If the function of the reading is traditionally to reinforce the spiritual thrust of the meditation, in Stewart's text the hymnal lines often serve to contradict it as their message of hope is belied by the feelings of despair voiced in both the biblical quotation and the meditation itself. In Meditation IV, for example, the "Saviour's gracious promise [and] . . . words" from the hymn are juxtaposed to the "cast down" and "disquieted" soul of the speaker of Psalm 43 and, of course, Stewart herself (39). Thus, the dialectical struggle between hope and despair that takes place within the supplicant's soul is already articulated by means of the contiguous placement of the readings.

The reading of the Holy Scripture is followed by the meditation proper as Stewart calls upon her memory, imagination, and intellect to contemplate the subject at hand, arouse the will to devotion, and perhaps even take a specific resolution or action.[9] Stewart's meditations may indeed be seen as "the outburst of an overwrought soul" in which this soul, fully preoccupied with its own earthly predicament, gives vent to anguish and self-despair; they are, in fact, obsessively concerned with the "I" who must one day "appear at the awful bar of God" (36). To prepare for this certain event, Stewart chooses freely to confess her sins and sorrows—the temptations of the flesh (37), her "mad career" and earthly disappointments (39), her horror of an untimely death (46), her fear of divine retribution and of the Day of Judgment (48–49, 53). And, in the process, she variously names herself a sick soul in need of a physician (43), one of the Lord's "fatherless children" (51), or a "poor unworthy worm" (53). Through such confessions Stewart hoped to place herself in the path of Christian submission and forgiveness, making it possible for her to meet death with calm. And her articulation of such confessions is facilitated by her continued reliance on biblical discourse and quotation from books of the Old Testament (Jeremiah, Isaiah, Jonah, and the Psalms) as well as the New (the Epistles of Paul, Revelation).

Despite her intense self-absorption, however, Stewart refused to focus solely on the *I* as several of her meditations transcend preoccupation with the self in order to address themselves directly to the African-American population. This transition from self to people is signaled by a series of "habitation" metaphors, also adapted from biblical discourse. As Mircea Eliade has noted, religious thought often constructs a "homologation house-cosmos–human body" whereby the erected temple alternatively functions as "an *imago mundo*" or assimilates the human body to itself.[10] Thus, in a succession of images, Stewart acknowledged that her ultimate goal was to "make my soul a fit temple for thee to dwell in" (38) before being laid to a final resting place: "Soon I shall be laid in the silent tomb or beneath the sod; and the places that know me now will know me no more forever" (37). Yet for the period that she was destined to remain on earth, Stewart was determined to turn away from the "tents of wickedness" and "whited sepulchres, which indeed appear beautiful without, but inwardly are full of all manner of uncleanliness," preferring instead to inhabit the Lord's "tabernacles" and to be "a door-keeper in the house of my God" (37, 41). Such "habitation" images once again underscore the importance of a constructed local place, here sacralized and spiritualized, in the African-American imagination.

As she addressed herself to the African-American people, Stewart had perhaps a specific constituency in mind, for the title page of the *Meditations* reads "Presented in 1832 to the First African Baptist Church and Society of Boston, Mass." Indeed, in her references to "tents of wickedness" and "white sepulchres" Stewart might well have been thinking of Boston's first African-American church, whose membership had forced the resignation of its founder, Thomas Paul, in 1829 and, without strong leadership, was being wracked by dissension. Historians have suggested that such dissension was caused by internal disagreement over the degree to which the church as an institution should become involved in social activism and interfere, for example, in problems arising from the absorption of newly freed slaves into its congregation.[11] In these more broadly gauged meditations it is perhaps these church members against whom Stewart was inveighing, calling them her "unconverted friends," charging them with a lack of "Christian spirit of fellowship," and exhorting them to repent their irreligiosity before God "execute[s] . . . the fierceness of his anger . . . upon this people" (42, 39, 45).

In these meditations, too, Stewart adopted the prophetic persona of Jeremiah, shaping her text into a kind of jeremiad, a genre that, as we shall see, provided the overt structure of her more politically oriented writings and speeches. Stewart's identification with Jeremiah and his oratory is particularly pronounced at those textual junctures when citation is effaced and Jeremiah's speech is reproduced as her own without quotation marks: "Is there no balm in Gilead, and is there no physician there?" (43); "O, how will they feel in that day to see their skirts filled with the blood of souls?" (37). It is possible, I think, to interpret these moments as instances of "voice merging," a discursive technique that, according to Keith Miller, is characteristic of, and essential to, African-American oral traditions. In contrast to the conventions of literate culture, voice merging rejects the concept

62

of ownership of words; indeed, reliance on the words of other well-known speakers allows the individual to create a more authoritative identity for him- or herself. Moreover, familiarity with such words not only ensures that they will be remembered by the audience but also facilitates the audience's participation in the spoken discourse. Finally, if voice merging signals the adoption of a prophet's persona it also implies the sharing of his "epistemological assumptions" and their articulation by means of typological analogy: "The repetition of equivalent and knowable types of religious experience guarantees the order, predictability, and meaning of history, threading each succeeding generation to those before."[12] Stewart's self-portrait in these meditations is indeed typologically patterned after that of Jeremiah: much like the Old Testament prophet, she represents herself as leaving the security of her home only with the greatest reluctance and with the certain knowledge of forthcoming ridicule in order to guide her people, angrily calling them to account for their wrongdoing and prophesying God's retribution against them.

The prayers that follow several (but not all) of Stewart's meditational reflections represent the final step of the devotional exercise. In them, Stewart as supplicant directly addresses God on her own behalf as well as that of the unconverted. If in the meditational passages Stewart had allowed herself openly to voice emotions of self-despair, fear of death, and anger against her own people, in the prayers we find her beseeching God for relief from this turmoil. Thus, she petitions God for his forgiveness and his blessing, for aid in wrestling against her sins, for help in her attempts to convert the "benighted sons and daughters of Africa" (40), for freedom from the fear of death, for a "well-regulated life" (50), and, finally, for protection. Yet Stewart's prayers do not leave us with a sense of resolution, of "the soul resting in God," but rather with the vision of a restless, tormented individual who has not been able to come to terms with her own people, her earthly existence, or her mortality.

Stewart's *Meditations* constellate, then, largely if not exclusively, around her soul's inner struggles. Her other works, however, all open up onto the outer world, revealing Stewart's intense involvement with the politics of racial uplift within Boston's black community: one essay, *Religion and the Pure Principles of Morality, the Sure Foundation on Which We Must Build* (1831), addressed to "My Respected Friends" (again most probably the congregants of the First African Baptist Church), and four speeches—the Franklin Hall lecture (September 21, 1832), the Afric-American Female Intelligence Society address (spring 1832), the African Masonic Hall address (February 27, 1833), and the Boston farewell address (September 21, 1833)—all of which were published individually in the *Liberator* and then collected as part of the 1835 *Productions*. More overtly political, these speeches and writings were shaped, as Marilyn Richardson has noted, by the influence of David Walker, to whom Stewart was heavily indebted for both her social ideology and her literary form.[13]

Walker was a prominent member of Boston's black community, an agent of and contributor to *Freedom's Journal,* and a lecturer on issues of community racial uplift. Chafing under the restrictions of purely local activism, Walker turned to literary production and in 1829 wrote his *Appeal to the Coloured Citizens of the World,* which went through three editions before he was murdered under mysterious circumstances in 1830. As the title and preface indicate, Walker addressed his *Appeal* to the broadest black audience possible—"all coloured men, women and children, of every nation, language and tongue under heaven" (preface). Much like later black nationalists, Henry Highland Garnet and Martin Delany, for example, Walker was already groping toward a pan-African concept of black nationality, envisioning the construction of local place in global rather than merely U.S. terms. More specifically, Walker's primary objective in writing his *Appeal* was to reach out to his enslaved brethren in the Southern United States; historians have suggested that he was actually able to do so through the intermediary of black seamen who put in at Southern ports.[14]

Walker's *Appeal* constitutes one of the earliest African-American documents that protests American slavery and racism in radical militant terms; and, as Wilson Moses has noted, it forms part of the American literary tradition of the jeremiad.[15] Sacvan Bercovitch has traced the origins of the American jeremiad back to the prophetic discourse of Jeremiah. According to Bercovitch, the Old Testament jeremiad was a political sermon composed of two movements, the first a complaint against both the children of Israel for their faithlessness during the Babylonian captivity *and* their Babylonian captors whose fall he predicts, the second an expression of optimism promising the redemption of the Jewish people. It was later adopted by the New England Puritans as the literary form that could best elucidate their position as a newly arrived people on the American continent. As in the Old Testament sermon, the Puritan jeremiad consisted of a double movement, an invective against the American people for their failure to live up to Christian ideals followed by a more significant prophetic revelation that affirmed God's divine favor and the ultimate success of their errand in the wilderness. Above all, the jeremiad underscored the Puritans' belief that they were God's chosen people whose history would unfold under his divine guidance and for whom the achievement of nationhood was inextricably bound up with Christian ideology. Thus, in the jeremiad secular history is fused with divine history, and secular progress comes to be represented as divine destiny. Yet in this historical narrative the means to the end, the movement from sin to redemption, from failure to success, is never clarified.[16]

Unlike Moses, who argues that the *Appeal* is a rewriting of the Puritan jeremiad, I would contend that Walker made use of the jeremiad in both Old Testament and American forms, adapting it to the specific historical experience of African Americans in the late eighteenth and early nineteenth centuries. Wedded to the Old Testament prophetic language that permeates the *Appeal* is an Enlightenment discourse that borrows both its structure and methods from two important eighteenth-century documents, the Declaration of Independence and the Constitution. Walker's *Appeal* is itself both an African-American declaration of independence and constitution composed of a preamble and four articles that argues by means of characteristic Enlightenment methodologies—observation, rational demonstration, historical evidence, and general book knowledge—that "we, (coloured people of these United States of America) are the *most wretched, degraded* and *abject* set of beings that *ever lived* since the world began, and that the white Americans having reduced us to the wretched state of *slavery,* treat us in that condition *more cruel* . . . than any heathen nation did . . ." (7). In particular, the *Appeal* seeks to answer Thomas Jefferson's contention in his *Notes on the State of Virginia* that blacks occupy the lowest human position on the Great Chain of Being and are thus barely distinguishable from animals by asserting the essential humanity of blacks and blaming their current degradation on the cruelty of white Americans.[17]

Indeed, in his text Walker proposed to analyze the social mechanisms by which African Americans have been reduced to such a degraded state, in the process launching an invective against white America, which has now replaced heathen Babylon as the agent of oppression. Walker's polemic is thus directed against American institutions, specifically the slave system and those organizations that collude with it, most especially the church and the American Colonization Society. It is also directed against such individuals as Thomas Jefferson and Henry Clay, whose self-interest mandates the perpetuation of slavery. Much like Jeremiah's sermons, the *Appeal* is suffused with an anger that even the process of literary composition can barely contain, but that spills over almost uncontrollably onto the written page: "Oh Heaven! I am full!!! I can hardly move my pen!!!!" (22). The rationality of Walker's "demonstration" is in fact repeatedly disrupted by textual markers that underscore the author's wrath and sarcasm: exclamation points, dashes, capitalized or italicized words, indices pointing to passages added in the second edition of the text that single out, in order to denounce, those whom Walker holds responsible for the current degradation of blacks.

If Walker's *Appeal* inveighs loudly against white America, it also constitutes, much like Jeremiah's sermons, a complaint against his own people, whom he accuses of apathy, servility, ignorance, and faithlessness toward one another. Most significantly, in Walker's text it is the black woman who serves as the emblem of black disunity. In response to a newspaper account of a slave revolt thwarted by the actions of a black woman, for example, Walker acidly commented: "But I declare, the actions of this black woman are really insupportable. For my own part, I cannot think it was any thing but servile deceit, combined with the most gross ignorance" (24–25). The *Appeal,* then, functions as a call to mobilization and, in particular, to a form of male empowerment that becomes subsumed under the rubric of "manhood": "Are we MEN!!—I ask you, O my brethren! are we MEN?" (16). For all the militancy of his rhetoric, however, Walker's goal was not radical revolution or the overthrow of the federal government but rather the inclusion of African Americans into a reformed American nationhood, stripped of its hypocritical pretensions of democracy and redirected toward the implementation of true social equality: "Treat us then like men, and we will be your friends. And there is not a doubt in my mind, but that the whole of the past will be sunk into oblivion, and we yet, under God, will become a united and happy people. The whites may see it is impossible, but remember that nothing is impossible with God" (70).

Discerning the operations of divine Providence throughout African-American history, Walker, like the Puritans before him, was able to assert the existence of a covenant between God and his people. And, as with the Puritans, religion—specifically Christianity—became the basis for claiming inclusion into American nationhood such that the entire United States is envisioned in Walker's imagination as a reconstituted African-American local place. True to the tradition of the jeremiad, however, there is no discussion in the *Appeal* of the means by which the goal of national inclusion is to be achieved other than the instrumentality of God, whether divine retribution or forgiveness. Only on rare occasions does Walker's text open up onto possibilities of human action, which is invariably male and violent: "They [whites] do not know, indeed, that there is an unconquerable disposition in the breasts of the blacks, which, when it is fully awakened and put in motion, will be subdued, only with the destruction of the animal existence" (25). In its very excessiveness, however, the agency of the black man is too violent to be specified.

Stewart's 1831 essay *Religion and the Pure Principles of Morality* as well as her 1832 and 1833 public speeches record a shift away from anguished introspection toward a reconfiguration of the black jeremiad as articulated by Walker. Like Walker's *Appeal*, these texts are sermons whose concerns are broadly social and whose political message is grounded in deeply rooted religious convictions. Unlike the *Appeal*, however, but much like Jeremiah's sermons, Stewart's texts constitute invectives directed *primarily* against her own people rather than her people's oppressors; moreover, blame of her oppressors' brutality is balanced by praise of the literary and scientific culture that they have created for themselves.

Such an ideological impulse allowed Stewart to focus more specifically on the question of agency, in particular on the agency of black women. As a result Stewart was able, in a way that Walker was not, to clarify the movement from means to ends, from sin to redemption, from the present condition of black degradation to a future state of social equality, thereby rewriting the genre of the jeremiad. In particular, in Stewart's thinking the gap between promise and fulfillment registers as a primarily female space sustained by women's work and women's culture. Stewart's task became, then, one of specifying the cultural work of black women, of the "brave," positioned between black men, whose institutions of the church, the Masonic lodge, the press, and the convention movement excluded them from positions of authority, and white women, who by the 1830s were already in the process of forging a locus of power for themselves in the public sphere of "female society."[18]

Much like Walker, Stewart addressed herself directly to a black audience, although whites were also in attendance at her lectures; and in both her essay and her public sermons whites are textually present as internal addressees who are excoriated for their racism and held responsible for the current degradation of blacks. In *Religion* and the Franklin Hall lecture, Stewart addressed her audience as "my respected friends," then directed her criticism and recommendations alternatively to black men and women. Yet, although Stewart was the first known American—and African-American—woman to have addressed a promiscuous assembly, there appear to be no contemporary accounts of either her own feelings about, or the public's reaction to, such a display of the black female body; and Stewart's speeches themselves do not directly address the issue of public bodily exposure. Such a void in the written record may perhaps be attributable to the brevity of Stewart's speaking career, her geographic confinement to the Boston area, and/or her limited constituency. Much like Truth, however, Stewart was highly aware of the importance of the press in the dissemination of her ideas. In publishing her texts in the *Liberator,* Stewart was perhaps hoping to reach not only a wider constituency of black Bostonians but also an audience of unconverted whites—whether Southern slaveholders, Northern racists, or abolitionists ignorant of the real condition of free blacks. This decision also reflects the cold reality that, given the financial instability of black newspapers in the early 1830s, no black paper was in operation at that time that could have reprinted Stewart's work.

The introductory portions of Stewart's sermons reflect her awareness of the need clearly to establish her cultural authority as a woman speaker laboring under societal restraints not imposed on black male leaders such as David Walker. The pamphlet *Religion* already gives some hint of Stewart's future narrative self-assertiveness. For if on the one hand the rhetoric of this essay pays lip service to the code of feminine decorum whereby the woman speaker must confess to her inadequacy—"I feel almost unable to address you; almost incompetent to perform the task" (24)—on the other hand it boldly proclaims "that spirit of independence" that has impelled Stewart to devote herself wholeheartedly to racial uplift work. Stewart herself attributed this spirit of independence to her recent religious conversion and her consequent abiding faith in God and his divine protection: "From the moment I experienced the change, I felt a strong desire, with the help and assistance of God, to devote the remainder of my days to piety and virtue, and now possess that spirit of independence. . . ."[19]

In her two 1832 lectures, the first delivered to the Afric-American Female Intelligence Society in the spring, the second in Franklin Hall in the fall, Stewart abandoned this feminine rhetoric of inadequacy as she strove to empower herself as a black female public lecturer. Evidently, Stewart felt no need to appear self-effacing while addressing the members of a black female literary society. Of the approximately forty-six identified black literary organizations in antebellum America, at least eight were composed solely of women and, according to Dorothy Porter, the Afric-American Female Intelligence Society appears to have taken "the lead in the organization of literary societies in Boston." Committed to mutual aid, these black women were supportive of one another's physical needs; committed to intellectual improvement, they read and discussed each other's original compositions, thus undoubtedly enhancing their rhetorical skills and self-confidence.[20] Despite her refusal to admit to inadequacy in her 1832 speeches, Stewart did, however, reiterate her belief in God as both the source of the authority that had enabled her to enter the public sphere of lecturing and community racial uplift work *and* the goal of that work: "Methinks I heard a spiritual interrogation—'Who shall go forward and take off the reproach that is cast upon the people of color? Shall it be a woman?' And my heart made this reply: 'If it is Thy will, be it even so, Lord Jesus!'" (55).

Stewart's 1833 speech delivered in the African Masonic Hall to a promiscuous assembly suggests, however, a fatal rhetorical miscalculation that was perhaps responsible for the abrupt termination of her career as a public lecturer. The task of speaking in this venue must have been a politically delicate one. Although devoted to community racial uplift work as well as to the antislavery cause, black Freemasonry, like its counterpart in the dominant culture, nonetheless constituted a distinctively male space in which black men, particularly of the middle class, sought to work out gender and class roles for themselves in the turbulent years of Jacksonian democracy and the market revolution.[21] In her address, however, Stewart boldly dispensed with any appeal to a spiritual authority other than that of "a holy indignation" that has "fired my soul," choosing instead to locate her authority in an "ambition and force" that she found lacking in black men (66). Given the aggressiveness of her narrative stance in this lecture, it is not surprising to discover that Stewart's final speech in the fall of 1833 was labeled a "farewell address to her friends in the city of Boston" (74) and that it signaled an obedient return to the rhetoric of her early essay whereby God becomes the conduit through which the inadequate woman can come to voice: "And my heart made this reply: 'Lord, if thou wilt be with me, then will I speak for thee so long as I live.' And thus far I have every reason to believe that it is the divine influence of the Holy Spirit operating upon my heart that could possibly induce me to make the feeble and unworthy efforts that I have" (75). Thus, with the notable exception of the African Masonic Hall address, Stewart asserted the workings of God's divine will in order to legitimate her leadership position within the black community and her authority to speak out on issues of racial uplift.

As in the Puritan jeremiad, Stewart's anger found expressive outlet in her appropriation of biblical rhetoric. Indeed, to a greater extent than Walker's *Appeal*, Stewart's sermons are firmly grounded in the language of the Bible and only occasionally make use of Enlightenment discourse. Thus, the introductory paragraph of *Religion* that juxtaposes the passage from Genesis concerning the dominion of all men over animals to the statement proclaiming the freedom and equality of all men under the U.S. Constitution suggests a form of double discourse that is not sustained throughout Stewart's texts. Neither are Stewart's speeches shaped by Enlightenment structures of reason. Less logically constructed than Walker's *Appeal,* they do not pretend to be demonstrations of proposed hypotheses; they offer no statement of a main thesis that is then proved by means of empirical observation, rational argument, or repeated invocations of book knowledge. Such looseness of construction might be attributable, of course, to the fact that the speeches were initially composed for oral presentation. In contrast, biblical discourse pervades Stewart's texts as she self-consciously analogized the present condition of African Americans to that of the people of Israel in the time of Jeremiah: "I really think we are in as wretched and miserable a state as was the house of Israel in the days of Jeremiah" (26). As in the *Meditations,* biblical citations succeed one another with increasing rapidity, often resulting in a merging of Stewart's narrative voice with that of the biblical speaker.

In her political sermons Stewart once again relied heavily on quotations from a wide variety of Old and New Testament books—Jeremiah, Isaiah, Proverbs, Psalms, Matthew, the Epistles of Paul, Revelation. If the line "And Ethiopia shall soon stretch forth her hands unto God" adapted from Psalm 68 functions almost as an incantatory refrain throughout her texts, it is to the book of Matthew that Stewart turned most consistently. As Frank Kermode has suggested, Matthew may be termed the prophet of fulfillment in whose Gospel Jesus' word and deeds explicitly figure as the fulfillment and transcendence of the Laws and prophecies invoked in the old text; and, according to Kermode, such fulfillment finds confirmation of its authority in a rhetoric of excess—whether of righteous love or righteous anger.[22] Yet the righteous anger of humans does not disrupt Stewart's written texts in the same way that it did Walker's (we have no means of assessing the style of Stewart's oratorical delivery). In them, there are no textual breaks occasioned by the emergence of a violence that must be repressed. Instead, Stewart's sermons are structured according to what Marilyn Richardson has called the antiphonal mode of divine providence and historical necessity through which, as we shall see, the way to fulfillment is explicitly charted.[23] Within this framework divine will is represented as God's grace that redeems a sinning people, whereas historical necessity is constituted by human agency and, in particular, the cultural work of the "brave."

In Stewart's sermons God's righteous anger is evoked first of all in her invectives against white America as an agent of oppression. In contrast to Walker, Stewart referred only in the most general terms to the institutions and policies that have oppressed black Americans, North and South, free and slave, and did not presume to examine the social and economic mechanisms that have led to their present degradation. Nonetheless, she repeatedly and emphatically condemned the racism of white America, prophesying divine retribution against the oppressors and eternal salvation for the oppressed. Contained within this invective against white America is an analysis of the effect that slavery and racial prejudice have produced on African Americans. In this analysis Stewart focused not only on how oppression has resulted in the economic and material poverty of blacks but also on their mental and spiritual deprivation, most especially that of black women. Relying on the language of Revelation, she analogized America to "the great City of Babylon," a "seller of slaves and the souls of men . . . [who] has made the Africans drunk with the wine of her fornication . . . and caused the daughters of Africa to commit whordoms and fornications" (72, 33). Criticizing the lack of educational, vocational, and occupational opportunities available to free blacks in the North, she lamented in particular the life of drudge work to which black women are condemned—"continual hard labor deadens the energies of the soul, and benumbs the faculties of the mind" (57)—and the consequent difficulty of all attempts to achieve a literary education: "And what literary acquirements can be made . . . from either maps, books, or charts, by those who continually drudge from Monday morning until Sunday noon?" (57).

Yet, in the true tradition of the jeremiad, Stewart's invectives are directed above all against her own people and the destructive ways in which they have reacted to such oppressive conditions, thus intensifying and perpetuating their own degradation. In her sermons she accused blacks, in much the same way that Walker had, of a lack of seriousness of purpose, of ambition, of energy. Gendering her accusations, black women are condemned for their lack of moral virtue, piety, unwillingness to educate themselves and thereby make themselves useful; black men are charged with a levity of behavior and moral character. As a consequence, the black community is plagued by a disunity that impedes its ability to carry out effective racial uplift work, leading Stewart to complain like Jeremiah: "The general cry among the people is, 'Our own color are the greatest opposers;' and even the whites say that we are greater enemies toward each other than they are toward us. Shall we be a hissing and a reproach among the nations of the earth any longer? Shall they laugh us to scorn forever?" (62–63).

Answering these questions with a resounding no, Stewart proceeded to appoint herself a spokesperson for and within Boston's black community and to articulate a political agenda that would suggest how African Americans might overcome degradation, empower themselves, and re-create a local place in the New World. In so doing she sought to fill in that unnamed space in the jeremiad that lies between sin and redemption, promise and fulfillment, to specify the possibilities of secular history and human agency. As she constructed her social program Stewart emphasized first of all the insufficiency of white benevolent activities, including the antislavery work of "our noble advocate" Garrison (71), the futility of black passivity, and the necessity of energetic self-help efforts: "It is of no use for us to sit with our hands folded, hanging our heads like bulrushes, lamenting our wretched condition; but let us make a mighty effort, and arise; and if no one will promote or respect us, let us promote and respect ourselves" (31). Self-promotion can be achieved, Stewart asserted, by means of concerted racial uplift efforts. Her belief in their ultimate success was fueled by a vision of world history that offered multiple examples of human agency. Yet these historical models centered exclusively on the actions of black men and white women. Much like Truth, Stewart needed to construct an empowering model of cultural work for the "brave."

In her African Masonic Hall address Stewart offered her audience a powerful vision of early African history, adapted perhaps from Walker's *Appeal,* in which cultural achievement and cultural brokers are conceptualized as male. According to this vision, African history is constituted by a cyclic movement: Africa was once an ancient center of learning in the fields of science, philosophy, and law—"the parent of science . . . , the resort of sages and legislators of other nations"— and, though now fallen, is destined to rise once again: "But a promise is left us: 'Ethiopia shall again stretch forth her hands unto God'" (68). Unable to expand upon this male model of African history, however, Stewart fell back on a Christian ideology that maintained that if Africa has fallen in the modern world, it is because of her lack of Christian piety and that consequently religious improvement alone will dispel the "moral gloom" that hangs over African Americans. Thus, Christianity remained the foundation of Stewart's racial uplift program; to follow the tenets of Christianity is to lift oneself from degradation and enter into the world of civilization. Moreover, since Christianity is the very basis of American civilization it thus becomes, as it did for Walker, a means of claiming nationality, of asserting inclusion into American nationhood.

In a final ironic move, highly uncharacteristic of the jeremiad, Stewart's praise of Christianity led her to praise her oppressors' culture—not its social policies, institutions, and leaders but its civilizing ideals. Indeed, according to Stewart Christianity is inextricably linked to other American virtues—the striving for excellence in the arts, sciences, and education, the spirit of enterprise, prudence, and economy—that she believed African Americans should emulate. Thus, as she elaborated the specifics of her racial uplift program, Stewart turned to models of American culture, demanding that black men acquire habits of sobriety and industry, work on the community level to establish educational institutions and temperance societies, and on the national political level to petition Congress to end slavery and grant citizenship to African-American men.

The history of European women offered Stewart yet other examples of human agency and secular progress. Thus, in her farewell address Stewart inserted by means of voice merging a long passage from a book entitled *Sketches of the Fair Sex* that constructs a lineage of exceptional European women who have attained remarkable intellectual and literary achievements and thus become models to be imitated. Stewart's ideology of imitation here would seem to suggest the devastating extent to which the Middle Passage had divorced her from her own history and a past African culture that might well have provided African-American women with models of empowerment. Yet if many of the achievements listed appear to promote a specifically European culture—the study of Latin and Greek, for example—others, especially women's historical role as prophetesses, might also encompass Africanisms and African-Americanisms: "A belief, however, that the Deity more readily communicates himself to women, has at one time or other prevailed in every quarter of the earth" (77). I would thus argue that we need to look beyond Stewart's rhetoric of imitation, which might well have been dictated by the demands of her audience, to speculate on the possibility of hidden Africanisms in her text.

In several of her sermons Stewart invoked American women's antebellum culture—the emergent "female society"—as a model of empowerment that she believed could be adapted to the historical specificity of the "brave" and their racial uplift efforts. Thus, if Stewart, unlike Walker, never attempted to conceptualize black nationality writ large for her audiences, she nonetheless sought to provide a vision of African-American community building. In the Franklin Hall and Afric-American Female Intelligence Society addresses, Stewart's vision of black women's social role appears to be a limited one constrained by the cult of true womanhood, perhaps because the women in her audience were an elite group. Confining black women's agency to a position of moral educators in the domestic sphere, Stewart simply recommended that women seek to exert their moral influence over men in the home. In her farewell address, however, Stewart transcended such a narrow vision of women's agency to promote black women's racial uplift work in both public and private spheres. Her specific suggestions indicate an awareness of the falseness of this public-private dichotomy and the possibilities of forging a community sphere that is neither fully public nor fully private but rather takes the values of the domestic sphere and extends them from the home into the community. In a lengthy passage in *Religion* Stewart had already described how white women of little means had come together under straitened conditions to empower their community and ensure the well-being of their young:

> The American ladies have the honor conferred on them, that by prudence and economy in their domestic concerns, and their unwearied attention in forming the minds and manners of their children, they laid the foundation of their becoming what they are now. The good women of Wethersfield, Conn., toiled in the blazing sun, year after year, weeding onions, then sold the seed and procured money enough to erect them a house of worship; and shall we not imitate their examples, as far as they are worthy of imitation? . . . Let every female heart become united, and let us raise a fund ourselves; and at the end of one year and a half, we might be able to lay the corner-stone for the building of a High School, that the higher branches of knowledge might be enjoyed by us. (31)

What needs to be emphasized here is the degree to which this economic model is also operative in traditional West African societies, where no clear-cut distinction is made between women's "'domestic' economic roles and 'public' economic roles" and women participate in the "society's 'wider economy'" as they engage in "activities such as farming, trading, craft production, or food-processing."[24] Thus, the agency of white American and black African women appears to converge here. And what seemed to be mere imitation suggests, in fact, the possible workings of a kind of cultural unconscious that insists on recalling the example of Stewart's African foremothers and thus imaginatively extends the notion of local place. Such a possibility produces a moment of hybridity in which a "denied knowledge" from the native culture is allowed silently to enter into the text.

Most of our information concerning Jarena Lee's life comes from her two autobiographical narratives, *The Life and Religious Experience of Jarena Lee*, published in 1836, and its expanded version, *Religious Experience and Journal of Mrs. Jarena Lee*, printed in 1849. The focal points of these narratives are, of course, Lee's religious experiences—her conversion to Christ in 1804, followed several years later by her sanctification, defined as a rebirth to a life free of sin and an aspiration to spiritual perfection, and finally her career as an itinerant exhorter preaching the gospel.[25] Yet Lee's autobiographies are also the poignant record of a woman struggling to survive the harsh conditions of black poverty in the northeastern United States at the beginning of the nineteenth century. In the first sentence of her narratives Lee informs us that she was born in Cape May, New Jersey, in 1783 but tells us nothing about her parents, refusing even to divulge their names. It is quite possible that they, like Truth's parents, were firmly rooted in African cultural traditions. Much like Stewart, Prince, and Watkins Harper, Lee was obliged to leave her family while still a young girl to become a "servant maid" to a white family and consequently was never able to obtain "more than three months schooling"; her journal and two narratives constitute, then, remarkable literary accomplishments.[26]

In 1811, several years after her conversion, Lee married and was thus obliged to leave her own religious society and move with her husband to Snow Hill outside of Philadelphia, where he served as pastor of a "Coloured Society." Lee's account of her married life is highly interesting as it suggests that opposition to her preaching was to come not only from the official church hierarchy but also from the domestic sphere. Joseph Lee's refusal to acquiesce to her wish to relocate illustrates the degree to which marriage obliged her to subserve her own spiritual needs to those of her husband, resulting in a loss of community, loneliness, and finally ill health caused by her "discontent" (13).

Joseph Lee's death six years into their marriage enabled Lee to devote herself fully to her religious concerns, but it by no means resolved her feelings of loneliness or her ill health, both of which recur as constant tropes throughout the narratives. Yet if Lee could describe her situation in 1831 as one in which "my money was gone, my health was gone, and I measurably without home. But I rested on the promises of God" (61), she was invariably able to fall back on the support of African-American familial and community structures. To fulfill God's command that she preach the gospel by becoming an itinerant minister, Lee was obliged to separate herself from her family and leave her son in her mother's care for a period of time. Even after lengthy absences, however, she always managed to reunite with her mother and sister, and throughout her life maintained close parental ties with her son, taking joy in his religious conversion and grieving with him in later years over the untimely deaths of his children. Moreover, Lee was also able to rely on nonkin domestic networks within the African-American community, boarding with strangers in her travels and allowing her son to live for several years with Richard Allen, who "with unwearied interest" provided for the young man's education and endeavored to set him up in a trade (61). Finally, Lee also became involved with some of the broader public institutions, in 1840 joining the New York Anti-Slavery Society, a regional affiliate of the American Anti-Slavery Society, and working closely with Richard Allen in the activities of the African Methodist Episcopal Church, both at Mother Bethel and at the annual conferences of the discipline.

Lee's relationship to the AME Church is of particular interest for it illustrates the ambiguous, if not inferior, status accorded women by black male institutions in the ethnic public sphere. From its inception under Richard Allen in 1816, the AME Church had strictly prohibited the licensing and ordination of women preachers; thus, Lee could never become an integral and authoritative member of its organizational structure but was obliged to remain on the periphery. Yet her official relationship to the church was doubled, and at times superseded, by an unofficial personal friendship with Allen. If Allen had initially refused Lee the permission to preach in 1811, maintaining that "as to women preaching . . . our Discipline knew nothing at all about it—that it did not call for women preachers," by 1819 he had reversed his position after witnessing a spontaneous exhortation by Lee at Bethel in which "God made manifest his power in a manner sufficient to show the world that I was called to labor . . . in the vineyard of the good husbandman" (11, 17). Thereafter, Allen appears to have frequently called upon Lee to labor with him "in the vineyard of the good husbandman," inviting her on several occasions in the early 1820s to preach at Bethel, requesting her to accompany him to several discipline conferences, and interceding on her behalf with ministers opposed to female preachers.

Indeed, while Allen exhibited a remarkable liberality insofar as female preaching was concerned, many other clergymen both on the circuit and in Philadelphia mounted a fierce opposition to Lee's attempts to preach. Lee keenly felt the contradiction in the stance of these black ministers, who themselves were subject to racial prejudice but who discriminated against one of their own race on the basis of gender. A passage in Lee's 1849 narrative gives an especially vivid account of the negative attitudes of black men toward her itinerant ministry. Attempting to preach in Reading, Pennsylvania, in 1824, Lee was refused by the local black minister, a Presbyterian, "with his over-ruling prejudice, which he manifested by saying no woman should stand in his pulpit." To overcome his opposition, "the men of color, with no spirit of christianity remained idle in the enterprize"; and it was left to a "sister . . . to open the way" (44). Conditions for women preachers in the AME Church deteriorated further after Allen's death in 1831 and following the ascendancy of Daniel Payne in the church hierarchy; by the late 1830s Lee found her access to the pulpits of Philadelphia's AME Churches severely curtailed.[27] A strong advocate for an educated ministry and opposed to any displays of religious fervor or African and folk survivals in church services, Payne decried those who believed that preaching consists "in loud declamation and vociferous talking; . . . in whooping stamping and beating the bible or desk with their fists, and in cutting as many odd capers as a wild imagination can suggest; . . . that he who hallooes the loudest and speaks the longest is the best preacher." Given such an attitude, Payne could only have opposed those uneducated women preachers like Lee whose only authority to preach was direct inspiration from God. And indeed, in 1850 Payne voiced explicit disapproval of a group of "women members of the A.M.E. Church, who believed themselves divinely commissioned to preach by formal licenses" and consequently organized themselves into an association; he was greatly relieved when "they . . . fell to pieces like a rope of sand."[28]

Excluded from the organizational structure of the AME Church, where, then, could Jarena Lee locate her sources and sites of power? As other scholars have noted, Lee grounded her authority in her firm belief that it was God himself who had singled her out, sanctified her, and appointed her to preach the gospel.[29] Such a source of empowerment led Lee to adopt forms of self-marginalization that were both psychological and geographic.[30] Indeed, Lee's conviction that she was a humble instrument of God allowed her to resist full privatization in the domestic sphere, to set herself apart from others in the community, and to construe God as the enabling force behind both her mystical experiences and her preaching. Safeguarded by his divine protection and favor, Lee was emboldened to place herself before the public, expose herself to its gaze, and risk its perception of her bodily self as disorderly and grotesque; as in Truth's case, Lee's public appearances occasioned the charge that "'I was not a woman, but a man dressed in female clothes'" (23). Finally, Lee sought to legitimate her preaching, which betrayed forms of religious knowledge "illegitimate" for women to possess, by insisting, much like Stewart, that it was God who had endowed her with the ability to speak: "The Lord again cut loose the stammering tongue, and opened the Scriptures to my mind, so that, glory to God's dear name, we had a most melting, sin-killing, and soul-reviving time" (22).

To maintain such a stance of authority Lee, like Truth, also adopted a geographic self-marginalization whose power lay both in constant mobility and in the habitation of those liminal spaces opened up by the Second Great Awakening. Thus, Lee sought to turn her expulsion from the pulpits of Philadelphia's churches to her advantage, deriving strength, as Sue Houchins has noted, from the very fact of travel that itself becomes a form of home.[31] In her 1849 narrative Lee insisted on her obligation constantly to travel: "I felt it my duty to travel up and down in the world, and promulgate the gospel of Christ. . . . I have travelled, in four years, sixteen hundred miles . . . and preached the kingdom of God" (30, 36). In so doing Lee was able to forestall the possibility of any sustained local opposition to her preaching activity and to take advantage of the novelty occasioned by her presence: "They all marvelled at a woman taking such a deep subject, but the Lord assisted the organ of clay, and we had the victory" (95).

Lee's travels, like Truth's, were undertaken within the context of the evangelical movement of the Second Great Awakening. Historians such as Alice Rossi and Carroll Smith-Rosenberg have described how the industrial advances of the early nineteenth century represented improvement in the lives of certain Americans but marked a further loss in social and economic stability for many women and maintained most blacks in an underclass status. They have argued that these marginalized groups consequently turned to evangelicism as an outlet for their frustrations, participating in what Smith-Rosenberg has called the socially and geographically liminal spaces and experiences of the Second Great Awakening in which the carnivalesque flourished. In this space hierarchies of class, race, and gender are deconstructed, the individual self loses its boundaries to merge with the other congregants and with the Godhead.[32] Thus, Lee described an 1824 camp meeting in Delaware in the following terms: "The people came from all parts, without distinction of sex, size, or color, and the display of God's power commenced from singing; I recollect a brother Camell standing under a tree singing, and the people drew nigh to hear him, and a large number were struck to the ground before preaching began, and signs and wonders followed" (45). This space of the clearing is structured not according to a capitalist economy of exchange but rather following what Luce Irigaray has called an alternative economy of mysticism—a transgressive libidinal economy that exists outside the labor market and its symbolic linguistic order and is characterized by the nonrational, the sensual, the oral, the carnivalesque.[33] Lee's awareness of the dominant culture's perceived threat of this transgressive power is evident in her comment that, despite "the good done at Camp meetings," they are "much persecuted" (39).

Discouraged from preaching in Philadelphia's churches and turning to such a space free of commodification, exchange, and profit systems, why would Lee choose to memorialize her religious experiences in writing? Quite clearly, she believed that by writing for publication she could narrate the story of her conversion, sanctification, and call to preach the gospel to a wider audience and thereby gain more converts to the evangelical cause. Furthermore, the act of composition itself allowed Lee both to deflect a curious public's gaze away from her bodily self and to discourage invidious speculations about her gender, as well as to assert her possession of a narrative authority and power of interpretation sanctioned by God. Finally, by selling her life story in "camp-meetings, quarterly meetings, in the public streets, etc." much as Sojourner Truth would also do with her biography and photographs, Lee hoped to find a means of becoming financially self-sufficient (77). Yet Lee was also well aware that in so doing she was reentering the

Jarena Lee. Frontispiece, *Religious Experience and Journal of Mrs. Jarena Lee*, 1849. Courtesy Moorland Spingarn Research Center, Howard University.

dominant system of commodity exchange where value is no longer purely spiritual but is measured in terms of profits and losses, where the economy of mysticism comes into conflict with that of writing. Indeed, having financed the publication of the 1836 narrative at her own expense, Lee remained reluctant to make money from its sale—"to sell them appears too much like merchandize"—yet admitted that the profit, which was used to pay printing expenses, gave her "great tranquility of mind" (77). In striking contrast, a later passage laments the fact that the second printing of the narrative in 1839 "had caused me to be very scarce of money," obliging her to rely on the help of others (86).

Just as importantly, however, I would argue that Lee envisioned literary self-representation—writing and publication—as tools of legitimation that would permit her to forge an entrance into the dominant economy and, in particular, gain acceptance into the all-male hierarchy of the AME Church.[34] In this sense writing became for Lee a necessary supplement. Indeed, the 1849 narrative suggests that, although Lee had kept a private journal for many years, she did not contemplate literary publication until after 1831, when Richard Allen's death signaled the loss of her most powerful protector within the AME Church. The first indication of Lee's interest in publication occurs in her account of her life in 1833, when, impelled by "a great anxiety to publish my religious experience and exercise to a dying world," she paid five dollars to an unknown editor to have a portion of her journal corrected for publication (66). In so doing Lee was perhaps seeking to emulate the example of Richard Allen, whose *Life, Experience and Gospel Labors of the Rt. Rev. Richard Allen* had been published posthumously in 1833. Book writing and publication are not mentioned again until several pages later, however, when Lee records that with the encouragement of friends she was finally able to publish her book in 1836. Although Lee's rhetoric here and elsewhere emphatically insists on the positive reception of the narrative—"my pamphlets went off as by a wind"(85)—it also delineates the much more discouraging institutional context within which her efforts to publish took place, her increasing exclusion from the pulpits of Philadelphia's AME Churches: "I seemed much troubled, as being measurably debarred from my own Church as regards this privilege I had been so much used to; I could scarcely tell where to go or stay in my own house" (77).

I suggest that as a consequence of such a debarment Lee turned to literary composition as a supplement to her evangelical activities in the Second Great Awakening in an effort to erase her "public" bodily self and silence the "private" voice of religious ecstasy in favor of a more "public" language that she hoped would legitimate her preaching in the eyes of institutionalized religion.[35] That she did not accomplish her purpose and that her narratives remained a marginal hybrid discourse are signaled by the refusal of the AME Church's book committee in 1845 to help finance the publication of Lee's second narrative, insisting that it was "written in such a manner that it is impossible to decipher much of the meaning contained in it."[36]

As scholars have noted, Lee's 1836 narrative is written within the tradition of the spiritual autobiography.[37] Such writing represents an instance of Foucauldian counterdiscourse, which has a double function here as it is designed to negotiate the interface between dominant and "minority" discourse, on the one hand, and between the liminality of evangelical experience and the orthodoxy of the AME Church, on the other. While it is impossible to ascertain whether it was Lee or her unknown editor who shaped her journal according to the conventions of the spiritual autobiography, such an appropriation of a genre that has occupied a privileged place in the Western literary canon from Saint Augustine on suggests an implicit desire to place Lee within the master's discourse in order to legitimate her life experiences. It is this very use of the genre that constitutes a form of counterdiscourse as it forcefully asserts Lee's possession of a soul and her conviction that, although "a poor coloured woman," she has been singled out by God and his divine Providence to narrate the story of her "religious experience and exercise," preach the gospel in public, and, in so doing, engage in powerful acts of interpretation.

In her narratives, however, Lee acknowledged her need to defend the authority of women preachers in the aftermath of Richard Allen's initial refusal to allow her to preach. She did so by harkening back to biblical times but shifted the basis of her argument from one of gender to one of class, responding perhaps not only to Allen's specific rejection of women preachers but also to those like Payne who emphatically insisted on the need for an educated ministry. Indeed, I would concur with Jualynne Dodson's suggestion that Lee's assertion of her right to preach was not carried out within a larger theoretical framework of women's rights but was founded on her conviction that all those who felt a special call should be allowed to preach.[38] Following Lee's interpretation, in biblical times the act of preaching was permitted to all individuals who were divinely inspired, including those of the lower classes; indeed, it is perhaps the uneducated who are the most willing to watch "the more closely, the operations of the Spirit" (97). Thus, even "the unlearned fishermen" may tell the "simple story . . . of our Lord," and the issue of gender is thereby rendered secondary (12). It is not surprising, then, that as she overcame her reluctance to preach Lee should have invoked the authority of the poor villager Jonah, who had likewise resisted the Lord's order to prophesy.

In both of her narratives Lee directly addressed the twin issues of the power and problematics of verbal representation, spoken and written. Not only are Lee's acts of preaching portrayed as a coming to voice but so is the moment of conversion itself as it loosens Lee's tongue, enabling her to utter words and tell of God's glory in the presence of a silenced minister (5). Lee's narratives further indicate her awareness that the act of narration itself must carefully negotiate between the extremes of hyberbolic and understated language. In attempting to account for a moment of intense spiritual despair in which she came to fear eternal damnation, Lee acknowledged the potential excessiveness of biblical rhetoric when applied to human rather than eternal time: "This language is too strong and expressive to be applied to any state of suffering in *time*. Were it to be thus applied, the reality could no where be found in human life; the consequence would be, that *this* scripture would be found a false testimony. But when made to apply to an endless state of perdition, in eternity, beyond the bounds of human life, then this language is found not to exceed our views of a state of eternal damnation" (7). Although Lee continued to rely on such hyperbolic language to record her inner mystical visions and dreams, she turned increasingly to "the plain language of the

Friends" (20), particularly in the added sections of her 1849 edition, to record her religious activities in the public sphere. The result is a hybrid discourse, informed by both silences and denied knowledges, that, while seeking to gain the approval of the established church, counters the conventions of spiritual autobiography and constitutes itself as a site of resistance to the discomfort felt over Lee's religious activities in the public sphere.

A close reading of both the 1836 and 1849 autobiographies suggests that at certain narrative junctures Lee deliberately resorted to silence, rejecting any gesture toward narration. Indeed, at times Lee claimed that her religious experience was so intense that no words could articulate it: "So great was the joy, that it is past description. There is no language that can describe it" (10). Moreover, although Lee's stated goal in publishing was to offer an account of her "religious experience and exercise" for the edification of a "dying world," she steadfastly refused to record her sermons in writing. Willing on every occasion to quote the biblical text from which she preached and to describe the effect of her preaching on her congregation, she remained reluctant to represent either the form or the substance of her sermons to a reading public. To do so perhaps would have signaled a fall back into the excessive language of religious ecstasy characteristic of the Second Great Awakening but unacceptable to the ministers of the established church, and would have only served further to delegitimate her. The only sermons available to her readers are, then, the autobiographical narratives themselves in which Lee strove carefully to negotiate between the private language of mysticism and the public language of the institutional church.

Lee likewise refused to specularize herself in the bodily act of preaching but sought instead, much like Nancy Prince was later to do in her travels abroad, to deflect the gaze of her reading public away from her body. The body is presented only once—at the moment of conversion—and this perception is one of self-revelation rather than of vision by others: "That instant, it appeared to me as if a garment, which had entirely enveloped my whole person, even to my fingers' ends, split at the crown of my head, and was stripped away from me, passing like a shadow from my sight—when the glory of God seemed to cover me in its stead" (5). Sue Houchins has argued that such bodily images are evocative of "incarnational theology, which asserts that 'the Word was made flesh,'" and warns against any attempts to "'secularize'" them.[39] Yet other references by Lee to her physical self are illustrative of the "body in pain" that manifested itself during periods of intense spiritual oppression when Lee found herself struggling with demonic temptations such as the impulse to commit suicide, fears of damnation, or unacknowledged feelings of anger. Thus, Lee's apparent acquiescence to the primacy of her husband's pastorate over her own preaching ambitions resulted in her fall into "an ill state of health, so much so, that I could not sit up; but a desire to warn sinners to flee the wrath to come, burned vehemently in my heart . . ." (14). In such instances Lee is indeed a voiceless body in pain who can alleviate suffering, overcome abjection, and transform herself into a bodiless voice of power only by means of the workings of spirituality and its languages: "From this sickness I did not expect to recover. . . . [But the Lord] condescended to hear my prayer, and to give me a token in a dream, that in due time I should recover my health. . . . From that very time I began to gain strength of body and mind, glory to God in the highest, until my health was fully restored" (14).

In adopting these strategies of silence and deflection, Lee's narrative contrasts sharply with an account written by the white abolitionist Lydia Maria Child in letter XI of her *Letters from New York* that openly publicizes the physical and vocal gestures of another contemporary black female evangelist, Julia Pell.[40] Much like Olive Gilbert and Frances Titus, Child functions here as the white literate writer who insists on speaking for the subaltern who cannot record her own story in writing. The dominant culture's perspective is further textually privileged here— and the black female body rendered other—by a framing device in which the comments of a friend who has already witnessed Pell's preaching opens Child's account and those of Father Matthews, Pell's spiritual adviser, closes it. Child readily admits that her initial motivation to hear Pell had been one of "curiosity" rather than religious zeal since "the machinery of theological excitement has ever been as powerless over my soul" (73, 79). In placing Pell through her father in the tradition of the trickster slave, Child seems tacitly to link such curiosity to a fear of being "tricked" by this black woman preacher.

In her portrayal of Pell, Child, unlike Lee, did not hesitate to put the disorderly black female body on display. Terming Pell a "female Whitfield," Child initially observes that "Julia's quiet, dignified, and even lady-like deportment" does not accord with her reputation "in the pulpit, with a voice like a sailor at mast-head, and muscular action like Garrick in Mad Tom" (76). Child's curiosity is fully satisfied, however, when she hears Pell preach the following Sunday: "Such an odd jumbling together of all sorts of things in Scripture, such wild fancies, beautiful, sublime, or grotesque, such vehemence of gesture, such dramatic attitudes, I never before heard and witnessed. I verily thought she would have leaped over the pulpit" (76). Tapping into stereotypes of the black woman public speaker, Child in these and other descriptions analogizes Pell's bodily play to theatrical acting without considering it as a possible expression of the verbomotor lifestyle of oral culture and even more specifically as an adaptation of the ring shout to the limited space of church structures. Further, in her reference to Pell's reputation as another Garrick, she intimates the possible masculinity of Pell's theatricality. Finally, in her later evocation of Pell's former life as a prostitute Child subtly reminds her readers of the dominant culture's alliance of acting, prostitution, and black womanhood. Such descriptions of Pell's physical being are accompanied by a lengthy quotation from one of her sermons, emptied, however, of all rhetorical power. For in attempting to order the disorder of Pell's religious language and legitimate it, Child at the same time undercut its cultural authority by comparing it to the canonical texts of the dominant culture: "It was a beautifully poetic conception not unworthy of Milton" (77).

Lee's desire to adopt a plain language might well have signaled her intent to record her religious experiences chronologically in accordance with the conventions of spiritual autobiography. Indeed, critics have commented upon the linear structure of the genre as it retrospectively charts the progress of the converted individual from an early state of ignorance and sin, through the preparation work for conversion, to the conversion itself, and then to periods of backsliding, concluding finally with the entrance into a state of grace.[41] Such a chronological pattern, for example, structures Richard Allen's 1833 autobiography, with which Lee might well have been familiar. Allen's narrative offers the reader not so much the spiritual history of a repentant sinner as the institutional history of the beginnings of the black church in America. All the stages through which the sinning Christian must pass on his or her way to salvation are articulated in the first paragraph, leaving the rest of the text to narrate in chronological order such external events as Allen's attainment of freedom from slavery, his adherence to the Methodist Church and subsequent separation from it, and his final establishment of the Free African Society and the AME Church. Finally, if Allen's narrative concerns itself most centrally with identifying the proper religious discipline under which African Americans could worship in peace in the late eighteenth and early nineteenth centuries, it also comments perceptively on such practical issues as the economic survival and social welfare of African Americans under conditions of "freedom."[42]

Such a chronological patterning of events serves to produce an intelligible narrative, one whose meaning AME Church members, and readers generally, would find possible to decipher. A careful reading of Lee's 1836 and 1849 narratives, however, suggests the degree to which the temporal architecture of spiritual autobiography dissolves here into a more spatialized organizational form. Lee's— and the unknown editor's—efforts to provide a chronological structure to her 1836 autobiography are evident in the meticulousness with which the opening pages of her narratives record the distinct stages of her spiritual life (ignorance, conversion, backsliding, sanctification) as well as in the later provision of chapter headings that chronicle subsequent important events in her life: "My Call to Preach the Gospel," "My Marriage," "The Subject of My Call to Preach Renewed" (10, 13, 15).

In fact, the linearity of chronological time is disrupted from the beginning as the very first pages of the narrative repeatedly circle back around Lee's moment of conversion, so that although the autobiography progresses by means of a metonymic accumulation of words, sentences, and paragraphs, it also insistently looks back to that single conversionary moment. The first account—"The man who was to speak in the afternoon of that day, was the Rev. Richard Allen, since bishop of the African Episcopal Methodists in America. . . . Three weeks from that day, my soul was gloriously converted to God, under preaching, at the very outset of the sermon"—is supplemented by two subsequent ones: "From this state of terror and dismay [fear of Satan], I was happily delivered under the preaching of the Gospel as before related," and "Through this means [of prayer and supplication] I had learned much, so as to be able in some degree to comprehend the spiritual meaning of the text, which the minister took on the Sabbath morning, as before related. . . . This text, as already related, became the power of God unto salvation to me, because I believed" (5, 6, 8). Following Mircea Eliade, we may view such a representation of time as the configuring of a "sacred time" that reactualizes the past sacred event and "appears under the paradoxical aspect of a circular time," "indefinitely recoverable, indefinitely repeatable . . . that does not 'pass,' that . . . does not constitute an irreversible duration."

Such a reactualization of past sacred events creates, according to Eliade, "a break in profane temporal duration" that, I would argue, appears in Lee's narratives as a spatialization of certain temporal experiences. Thus, Lee's earlier comments on the appropriate application of expressive language to "suffering in time, . . . in human life" as opposed to suffering in "an endless state of perdition, in eternity," transmute the category of time into that of space, invoking in fact both this world and the next. Once again, Lee's reconceptualizations of time and space become comprehensible in the context of Eliade's theological speculations in which the sacred world is defined as a heterogeneous space that "does not only project a fixed point into the formless fluidity of profane space, a center into chaos; it also effects a break in plane, that is, it opens communication between the cosmic planes (between earth and heaven) and makes possible ontological passage from one mode of being to another."[43] Such a capacity to facilitate communication between cosmic planes is, we may note, applicable not only to Christianity but to African and African-American religions as well, in which life and death are perceived as a continuum, death often being envisioned as a door between two worlds or the crossing of a river.[44]

Lee's 1836 autobiography is structured around this concept of a heterogeneous sacred space that enables the ontological passage from one cosmic plane to another. As a result, the narrative is invaded by representations of the "illegitimate" visions of the female mystic, several of which in turn invoke, much as Sojourner Truth's speeches do, denied knowledges of the native—African and African-American—culture. Heterogeneity of sacred space in Lee's narrative is marked first of all by those "fixed points" or "centers," represented by the "secret place" or "closet," and analogous to Truth's "rural sanctuary," to which Lee repeatedly retired to pray for divine guidance (9, 10, 12). More significantly, it is represented by the mystical realm of Lee's visions and dreams that signals her ontological passage from the natural to the supernatural world. As Irigaray has suggested, the function of such a sacred space is to offer the female mystic an alternative local place that would nullify the inequities of a capitalist economy and of male hierarchies.

To articulate her visions, Lee resorted to the traditional Christian iconography of the New Testament: her representation of hell as a bottomless pit derives from Revelation, her dream of the need to keep the sheep away from the devouring wolf echoes a verse from Matthew, and that of the sun obscured by a dense black cloud for a portion of the day is reminiscent of the apostles' description of the day of Crucifixion (6–7, 13, 14).[45] Yet several of Lee's other visions, like Truth's, point to the lingering presence of elements of African and African-American folklore, underscoring both the hybridity of Lee's religious discourse and the complexity of her attempts to recreate local place spiritually in the New World.[46]

Lee's description of her conversion experience, for example, is reminiscent of Truth's in its evocation of spirit possession. Her repeated fantasies of suicide by drowning, although represented from a Christian point of view as satanic temptation, may also express the conviction of newly arrived Africans that death by drowning would ensure a return to one's original local place in Africa.[47] Even more tellingly, Lee's vision of Satan "in the form of a monstrous dog, and in a rage, as if in pursuit, his tongue protruding from his mouth to a great length, and his eyes . . . like two balls of fire" (6) not only reflects the low status of the dog in African folklore but relates more specifically to African-American popular beliefs about animals, many of which, according to Newbell Puckett, were African in origin. Not only is the dog an omen of death—particularly when howling or lying on its back pawing the air—but it was often viewed as the devil himself in disguise. The vision also recalls descriptions of the African-American evil spirit called the Jack-o'-lantern—"a hideous creature, five feet in height, with goggle-eyes and huge mouth, its body covered with long hair, which goes leaping and bounding through the air like a gigantic grasshopper"—whose task it is to lure unsuspecting travelers to their death.[48] Finally, Lee's concept of hell "covered only, as it were, by a spider's web on which I stood" is suggestive of yet another African-American folk belief in which the death process is conceptualized as a spider's web that gradually envelops the dying individual from the feet up to the mouth or, perhaps even more pertinently, in which the claim of conversion is authenticated only for those who have "hung over hell on a spider web."[49]

To some AME Church members and other readers as well, such visions and dreams might indeed be replete with meanings "impossible to decipher." Tacitly acknowledging that these may well be perceived as "fiction[s], the mere ravings of a disordered mind" (9), Lee sought to render her private visions intelligible to her reading public through acts of narration and interpretation. Her aspirations toward intelligibility are evidenced in her decision to have portions of her private journal narrativized for publication and thus contrast sharply with the unpublished spiritual writings of Rebecca Cox Jackson (composed between 1840 and 1864), which remain in a highly fragmentary form.[50] Moreover, in the published narratives themselves Lee took great pains to interpret her two recorded dreams not only for herself but for her readers as well. Here again Lee's writings differ from Jackson's fragments; relatively few of the latter's dreams are subjected to interpretation, but those that are tend to be interpreted several times, suggesting that for Jackson interpretation was a mechanism designed not so much to legitimate her inner visions to a doubting public as to work out her theological beliefs to her own satisfaction. In contrast, Lee's interpretations of her two dreams, both of which occurred during her married life—the one of a flock of sheep threatened by a devouring wolf and the other of the sun temporarily obscured by a black cloud—strike the reader as fundamentally conservative, designed to conciliate the contradictory demands of patriarchal marriage and God's call to preach the gospel. In the first dream Joseph Lee becomes the shepherd chosen by God to protect his flock; in the second, the eventual return of the sun becomes God's promise to Lee of future preaching.

In her 1849 narrative, which adds a significant amount of new material to the 1836 edition, Lee turned increasingly away from a narration of inner mystical experience in order to record in detail her extensive travels as an itinerant exhorter, which took her as far north as the black townships of Canada West, to which Shadd Cary would move in 1850, as far west as Ohio, where Truth was likewise lecturing and testifying to the nation, and south to Baltimore, the city of Watkins Harper's birth. The act of travel itself functioned for Lee as an empowering marginalization as the novelty and skill of her preaching enabled her to attract the faithful while her transience kept her relatively immune to protracted conflicts over the authority of female preachers. Yet travel also came to complicate the process of the recreation of an African-American local place and to raise the question of whether home is ever possible for the African in the New World, a question posed as well by the itinerant careers of Nancy Prince and Mary Ann Shadd Cary.

Lee's longer 1849 narrative also differs from the 1836 version in its expansion beyond purely spiritual concerns to a broader consideration of social issues. Thus, on several occasions Lee's religious goals are conflated with abolitionist ones as, for example, when she attended an antislavery society meeting in Buffalo in 1834 and the annual antislavery convention in New York in 1840: "I felt that the spirit of God was in the work, and also felt it my duty to unite with this Society. Doubtless the cause is good, and I pray God to forward on the work of abolition until it fills the world, and then the gospel will have free course to every nation, and in every clime" (90). On other occasions Lee interrupted the narration of her travels in order to comment on the need to provide African-American children with an education that offers more than mere worldly advancement, "elevat[ing] them to a position that would command respect through the short voyage of life" (80–81). She insisted, much as Stewart had, that education must provide black children with a foundation of piety and industriousness that would enable them to constitute themselves as a "moral people" and create cultural alternatives to the materialistic values of consumer capitalism characteristic of the dominant society: "We, as a people, are generally poor and cannot support so many changes of fashion; th[e children] grow up and crave it, and oftimes substitute evil practices to support themselves, either girls or boys, and often bring a stigma upon their parents and family connexions, though very respectable" (50).

Lee's belief in the importance of the moral education of children is affirmed finally in a curious passage later in the same paragraph in her account of a visit to an Indian village near Buffalo. Her description positions the Indians as cultural Others, different and inferior because of their pagan beliefs. Yet in her initial focus on the village's children—"I could not help admiring the ways as well as gestures of the children"—Lee also envisioned the Indians as children who, despite their appearance as "heathens," are capable of being "civilized and christianized" (51).

The greater length of the 1849 autobiography created, however, certain problems of narration for Lee, revealing, in the absence of a helpful editor, the limitations of her literacy skills as well as her continuing ties to oral culture. The latter are intimated, for example, in Lee's account of her activities for the year 1821 in which she reproduced verbatim a passage from the very same letter by Child that depicted Julia Pell's preaching. In this passage Child had suggested that male objections to female preaching may be answered with the question "'If an ass reproved Balaam, and a barn-door fowl reproved Peter, why should not a woman reprove sin?'" (23). As Lee's insertion of this comment occurs in a portion of the narrative in which she attempts to respond to the church's opposition to female preachers, it may well be that Lee deliberately turned here to a form of voice merging in order to enhance her own narrative authority. Indeed, in Child's text the question itself is patterned after a formula from oral culture—"I have heard that as far back as . . ." (23)—suggesting that the proverbial comment in fact belongs to no one but may be appropriated by any writer and used both to enhance his or her authority and to impress its message on the readers' memory by means of repetition.

In addition, Lee's 1849 autobiography preserves the journal format, characterized by the serialization of dated entries, to a much greater extent than did the 1836 version. Here again, however, time is rendered nonchronologically, as the years, and the experiences contained in them, are often recorded not consecutively but haphazardly; the events of July 1824 are narrated after those of 1825 and the events of 1832 and 1833 after those of 1834, for example. Such random chronicling points to Lee's profound indifference to the workings of profane chronology and suggests instead the extent to which her text is structured around another narrative pattern—that of repetition. On the level of language this pattern consists of the repetition of certain key phrases, many of which are derived from the Bible—"the stammering tongue was loosed," "he caused a shaking of dry bones," "signs and wonders followed the preaching," "backsliders reclaimed, sinners converted, and believers strengthened"—designed to emphasize the narrator's religious authority as well as her primary goal, the conversion of her readership.

A still more significant form of repetition, however, structures Lee's 1849 autobiography—her iteration of each of her returns to Philadelphia at the end of her preaching tours. Here again the temporal organization of spiritual autobiography is transmuted into a spatial one. Resisting the impulse further to narrate her mystical visions or dreams and seeking instead to emphasize the importance of her religious activities in the world, Lee chose in the latter portions of this narrative to depict in great detail her travels as an itinerant exhorter. In this account Philadelphia, home to her cherished son, to the revered Richard Allen, and to Mother Bethel Church, figures as the temporal resting place—and narrative center—to which Lee repeatedly insisted on returning. Here, too, the homogeneous space of the profane world is transformed into a heterogeneous sacred space in which the city of Philadelphia, rather than the secluded secret places of her youth, comes to function as its fixed theological center, as a sacred site around which the formless fluidity of profane space may be organized and an African-American local place finally constructed. Yet even this spatial narrative pattern, which foregrounds this world over the next, proved to be incomprehensible to the AME Church's book committee which, in 1845, found the autobiography "written in such a manner that it is impossible to decipher much of the meaning contained in it." Thus, to the end, Lee's texts remain permeated by that tension between the heterogeneous sacred spaces of mystical vision and of the Second Great Awakening, and the institutional space of the AME hierarchy—a tension that not even the act of writing could reconcile.

4

"Colored Tourists": Nancy Prince, Mary Ann Shadd Cary, Ethnographic Writing, and the Question of Home

In a letter to Mary Ann Shadd Cary's newspaper, the *Provincial Freeman*, published out of Canada West between 1853 and 1859, a correspondent, John N. Still, conceptualized the stance of the "colored tourist" as a means of achieving the "common cause" of racial uplift:

> I find that by a little observation and attention, that volumes of useful information relative to our people, their pursuits, inclinations, circumstances, condition and progress, may be readily obtained. The most that will be required will be to collect it, and arrange it in such a way as to make it useful to the public in general and the travelling portion in particular. . . . I shall endeavor to extend my observations, first to Society, in general; secondly, Churches, Schools, etc., and Business pursuits, in which the colored people are now, or may engage in; and, thirdly, a brief notice of the principle Colored Men and Women in public or private life, etc., etc., under the following heading:—"Incidents, Interviews, and Observations." By a Colored Tourist. (*PF*, June 30, 1855)[1]

If Still appears to have been primarily concerned with the mere ethnographic collection and arrangement of "volumes of useful information," his concept of the "colored tourist" raises a host of theoretical questions surrounding the African-American traveler and his or her strategies of displacement. Although the tourist's chosen objects of observation might well be drawn from "our people," as in Still's project, they may also be located within cultures of the Other. In either event the tourist proceeds by setting forth a plan of travel in which he or she seeks out specific markers perceived as emblematic of the culture under observation. In the nineteenth century, tourist interest both at home and abroad focused not only on natural phenomena but also on those social institutions that were seen to provide moral improvement and a safe retreat to those struggling to survive the chaos of modern life.[2] Still's column suggests that African-American tourism fits this general paradigm. At the same time, the very concept of the "colored tourist" could only problematize the notion of "home" for African Americans in the antebellum period. If African Americans were indeed on tour, where then was home? Can home ever be specified for the African transplanted to American soil? Is the African American not always already a "colored tourist"? Can he or she ever tour at leisure, or is the tour always in some sense an enforced one? What is the particular stance of the participant-observer who, in observing *"our* people," also shifts position to speak of *"their* pursuits"? Finally, what happens when the gaze is returned by the Other and African Americans themselves become the object of tourism? How can they forestall that commodification to which tourism subjects places and peoples?

Such questions were of particular importance to black women in the antebellum period as they toured communities constituted by "our people" as well as more foreign locales—as ethnographic observers, cultural workers in the fields of abolitionism and racial uplift, or lecturers to promiscuous assemblies, exposing themselves to the public gaze. How, then, did such "colored tourists" as Prince and Shadd Cary receive this gaze, how did they return it, and what role did literary representation play in this negotiation? If these women could not specify home, from what sites could they write? If, like Truth and Lee, they were devalued by the surrounding culture, how could they make their perceptions valued, how could they achieve narrative authority?

Answers to such questions could not be provided by the dominant cultural tradition. In early American Puritan travel narratives, such as those of William Bradford, God functions as the source of writing; the narrative is conceived from a transcendent point of view and unfolds according to God's providential design. In later secular travel accounts, composed first by Europeans and later by Americans, the writers' ethnocentric perspective comes increasingly to dominate the narrative. Europe and America respectively become the sites of writing, providing the teleological basis for the narrators' circuitous journey to foreign places and home again. As William Spengemann has noted, however, in the romantic period the locus of narrative authority shifts from the travelers' national point of origin to the travelers themselves in order to emphasize their individual modes of perception and personal reactions to the experience of travel.[3]

Prince and Shadd Cary might well have viewed their lives as unfolding according to providential design, but God was neither the origin nor the goal of their travels or of the narratives that travel produced. Yet neither was the purpose of travel simply an analysis of psychological transformations brought about by geographic displacement. Instead, as Mary G. Mason has astutely noted, the locus of narrative authority resides in the social activism of black women travelers, and home becomes the very attempt to forge an African-American local place by means of such activism.[4] For Shadd Cary the question of home came specifically to focus on the issue of emigration that was revived in the 1850s; and, as she became increasingly involved in this debate, she came to test the institutions of the black press and the annual conventions as no other woman had. As they traveled, finally, Prince and Shadd Cary both had occasion to gaze at the culture of the Other and to be gazed upon in return. Through the literary representation of their travel experiences—Prince's ethnographic and travel narratives, Shadd Cary's newspaper columns—these two "doers of the word" adopted the ethnographic stance of the participant-observer, of the insider-outsider, to record the complex negotiations involved in such gazing.

Nancy Prince represents a black woman traveler whose extensive journeys both empowered and marginalized her, for whom writing constituted the means not only of narrating the Other but also of ordering the disorder, and veiling the public exposure, of the black woman traveler. Little is known about Prince beyond the information contained in her autobiographical account first published in 1850. Born in 1799 in Newburyport, Massachusetts to free parents whose own parents had been kidnapped from Africa, Prince was to some degree aware of her African cultural heritage. Her family was beset by financial difficulties and emotional insecurities, and thus as a young girl Prince, like Stewart, Lee, and Watkins Harper, went "to service in a family" and then later "to learn a trade," thereby hoping to support her family with her meager income.[5] Finding her efforts to be of no avail, she made the decision to start traveling, first to Russia with her husband, Mr. Prince, and then to Jamaica under the auspices of an American missionary, Mr. Ingraham. It was while traveling that Prince came to dedicate herself to a career of social activism that is amply recorded in her two narratives, *The West Indies* (1841) and *A Narrative of the Life and Travels of Mrs. Nancy Prince* (1850). Written most probably for an audience that was primarily black but also included white abolitionists, these accounts are marked by narrative moments in which Prince both yields and withholds information. They also nicely illustrate the stance of the black female social explorer who authorizes herself to gaze at the Other but must in turn, and despite all attempts at self-protection, become a commodity and subject herself to this Other's gaze.

Mary Pratt has outlined two basic models for eighteenth- and nineteenth-century male-authored European ethnographies and travel narratives. The first, Pratt suggests, combines a particularized account of personal experience with a more generalized "objective" description of the habits and customs of the people visited. In this model, great importance is attached to the scene of arrival, which establishes the traveler-ethnographer's twin desire to gaze upon the natives as his ethnographic subjects and to be gazed at as the authoritative European whose right to be there goes unquestioned. If properly presented, neither the validity of his personal point of view nor the generalizations that derive from it are ever at issue, based as they are on assumptions about the European male's cultural superiority and right to gaze. In the second model the gazing *I*/eye of the traveler is self-effaced, hides behind the passive voice, thus depersonalizing the narrative.

Nonetheless, the text exudes European self-consciousness as the *I* invisibly takes over, denuding the landscape of its indigenous people and refusing to record any moments of contact between self and natives.[6]

In *The West Indies*, a narrative of her travels to Jamaica to assess the conditions of the black population after emancipation, Prince combines these dominant ethnographic models in novel ways to produce a hybrid text that inscribes both silences and denied knowledges within it. In the narrative, Prince initially appears to resort to depersonalized ethnographic observation as she steadily fixes her controlling gaze outward, offering "objective" scientific descriptions of Jamaican geography and history while shrouding her personal life and motives in privacy and refusing to allow herself to be gazed at. In fact, however, her text constitutes a moral tract against slavery and its legacy. A hidden critique of colonial history is already embedded within the first pages as Prince gives an account of the natural disasters repeatedly visited upon Jamaica, which function in the text as a sign from God and a trope for the evils of slavery. In the words of a native informant: ". . . then God spoke very loud to *Bucker* (the white people) to let us go."[7]

Prince's narrative is, in fact, an ethnography that is written backward, presenting us first with its ethnographic conclusions and only belatedly introducing us to the field-worker herself. Indeed, it is only well into the pamphlet that Prince repositions herself as a participant-observer, defined by James Clifford as the anthropologist whose authority is based both on the personal experience of being there and on the observation of a society and its institutions from a more distanced and generalizable perspective.[8] In the present instance Prince's stance as a participatory cultural insider is further reinforced by her sense of racial kinship with the Jamaicans as well as her desire actively to participate in the restoration of local place for the newly emancipated slaves. Shedding her cover of objectivity as well as her reliance on God's providential design, Prince finally reveals toward the end of her narrative the real motivation for her journey: "And here I will mention my object in visiting Jamaica. I hoped that I might aid (in some small degree) to raise up and encourage the emancipated inhabitants, and teach the young children to read and work" (13).

In her stance as a participant-observer, Prince launched a severe attack against the island's institutions, emphasizing in the process the regrets of many African Americans who had emigrated there in search of home. If the title page promises us a "description of the islands, progress of Christianity, education, and liberty among the colored population generally," and offers us a medallion commemorating British emancipation with the inscription of a verse from Psalm 118 ("this is the Lord's doing; it is marvellous in our eyes"), Prince's text in fact radically deconstructs all notions of progressive history. The second half of her narrative comes to question contemporary notions of "progress" and "liberty," and to wonder how "marvellous" has been "the Lord's doing." Her sharpest criticisms are reserved for church and school leaders, particularly Baptist missionaries whose venality has earned them the label of "macaroon hunters" (named after the Jamaican coin, the mack) and deprived the slaves of their meager financial resources, leaving them in the same degraded state. Prince's conflict with these Baptist authorities seems to have been occasioned in large part by her presence as a single American woman, since the British allowed missionary women to go to Jamaica only as wives or as sisters and held deep suspicions against American women's social activism: "I do not approve of women's societies; those destroyed the world's convention; the American women have too many of them" (14).[9]

Prince ultimately remained an outsider to Jamaican culture, perceived by many as a mere curious observer: "They wished to know why I was so inquisitive about them" (11). Indeed, Prince's narrative progressively enacts a shift in power relations as she increasingly positions the Jamaicans as subalterns whose consciousness she must retrieve and for whom she must speak, and as her cultural enterprise transforms them into native Others in need of racial uplift. Despite this shift, however, there are ethnographic moments in the text in which narration gives way to dialogue and the voice of the freed slave may be directly heard: "We have nothing left for ourselves, the macaroon hunters take all" (10).

It is only in the concluding paragraph of her text, after she has firmly grounded her authorial power in her political and social activism, that Prince at last narrates a greatly diminished scene of arrival—"dropped anchor at St. Anne harbor Jamaica" (13)—in which neither the right to gaze nor the right to be gazed at is explicitly claimed. Yet here, finally, Prince shows herself willing to risk public self-exposure. Admitting that her narrative strategy has been designed to maintain her privacy and shield her bodily self from the reader's gaze—"my personal narrative I have placed last in this pamphlet, as of least consequence"—she finally relinquishes her stance of ethnographer gazing at the Other and allows the reader to see herself being gazed at, revealing for the first time her racial identity: "He [Mr. Horton, a white missionary] was much surprised to see me, and had much to say about my color, and showed much commiseration for my misfortune at being so black" (15).

Prince's West Indies pamphlet contrasts in interesting ways with a much longer narrative, *Jamaica: Its Past and Present State*, published in 1843 by a British Baptist missionary, James Phillippo. Phillippo's text begins in much the same manner as Prince's with an impersonal survey of the geography and history of the island. Unlike Prince, however, Phillippo goes to great pains to maintain this stance of impersonality to the very end. Historical events are presented as objective facts and, to the extent that they require validation, the authority of other more knowledgeable men is repeatedly invoked: "A portrait shall be given as delineated by men who were too closely connected with the state of things in the colony to be even suspected of exaggeration to the disadvantage of the parties concerned." Yet, if the perspective of the *I* seems to be absent, it is in fact present in Phillippo's many references to himself as "the writer" or "the author." Moreover, as the first chapter makes clear, the text is explicitly centered around an ideological reference point which is that of Christianity conceptualized as an instrument of civilization. Thus, Phillippo's stated desire "to preserve the fidelity of an historical record" becomes instead a highly subjective demonstration of the progressive nature of Christianity that then constitutes the conceptual framework through which the natives are consistently viewed and interpreted. According to this framework, dialect language, superstitutions, and pagan customs, particularly funeral rites that are "unnatural and revolting in a high degree" mark the Jamaicans as fundamentally Other (and, of course, inferior), maintaining them at an insuperable distance from both Phillippo and his British readers.[10]

In a letter published in the May 25, 1843 issue of the *National Anti-Slavery Standard,* Prince wrote of her failure during a second trip to Jamaica in 1842 to establish a Manual Labor School for Girls, given the lack of support from both government and missionary groups. Emphasizing the resilience of the newly emancipated Jamaican blacks, she expressed her intention further "to publish some facts respecting my injured brethren in Jamaica," most probably in an effort to raise funds for the projected school. It appears that Prince never wrote that tract but instead in 1850 published a full narrative of her life, *A Narrative of the Life and Travels of Mrs. Nancy Prince,* reprinted in 1853 and 1856, which gives an account of her childhood and her two trips to Jamaica, as well as her lengthy sojourn in Russia from 1824 to 1833. Although the 1850 edition gives no motivation for this autobiographical impulse, the later editions are prefaced by an explanatory paragraph in which Prince made it clear that she hoped autobiographical writing and publication would constitute a form of self-authorization and would also enable her to "supply my necessities" and "help myself."[11] Perhaps Prince believed that under the cover of female autobiography she could promote interest in moral reform activities both in Jamaica and at home in her readers, most especially those African Americans whom she wished to see more involved in racial uplift work.

As in her West Indies narrative, Prince began her *Life and Travels* by acknowledging the workings of divine Providence and repeatedly invoked it throughout her text. Her autobiography is, then, a narrative of providential design in which she related her life story in a language reminiscent of Bunyan's *Pilgrim's Progress.* In surviving the Saint Petersburg flood of 1824, for example, she writes: "Thus, through the providence of God, I escaped from the flood and the pit" (22). To an even greater extent than in her ethnography, however, Prince was concerned here with how to record in writing both the private facts of her domestic life and her public experiences as a black woman traveler. Public and private coexist in a tense relationship to one another in the autobiography as Prince's narration consistently seeks to foreground public social and moral issues.

Unlike her earlier ethnography, Prince's autobiography begins then with an account of her childhood, thus revising her former contention that personal narrative is "of least consequence." Yet even in this opening section Prince focuses not so much on her own life as on that of the two women closest to her as a child, her mother and her sister Sylvia. Each enacts a specifically female tale of self-dispossession. Her mother's life was one of dependence on male providers resulting in several marriages, the enduring of multiple childbirths and deaths, the burden and scattering of family members, and finally insanity. For Sylvia it was the story of being "deluded away" to ensure her own economic survival (8), thereby reinforcing the dominant culture's linkage of black women to prostitution; and, although Sylvia was saved by Prince's intervention, her life thereafter remained unstable and insecure. Prince's portrait of her family thus underscores the problems faced by African-American women seeking a secure place for themselves within the social and economic systems of the urban North: "My sister . . . wished to procure a place to work out. She tried me much. . . . Care after care oppressed me; my mother wandered about like a Jew; the young children who were in families were dissatisfied; all hope but in God was lost" (11–12).[12]

Prince's additions to this opening section in the 1853 and 1856 editions of her *Life and Travels* are significant in that they further contextualize her early life within both an African cultural heritage and an African-American social community; yet here again the details Prince provides tend to be sociological fact rather than personal feeling. On the one hand, Prince's emendations emphasize her African background as she expands upon the stories of her grandfather's and stepfather's kidnapping from Africa and escape from slavery, relating them in part from a first-person plural point of view: "I have heard my father describe the beautiful moon-light night when they two launched their bodies into the deep, for liberty. . . . In a few minutes, a man with a broad-brimmed hat on, looked over the fence and cried out, 'Halloo boys! you are from that ship at anchor?' Trembling, we answered, yes. He took us kindly by the hand, and told us not to fear, for we were safe" (1853: 6). Africanisms of family structure are also made evident as Prince's efforts to keep the family together emphasize the primacy of consanguineal over conjugal ties.[13]

On the other hand, Prince's additions also detail the real difficulties of African-American familial survival given the harsh socioeconomic system of the urban North. In these passages Prince amplifies her portrayal of child labor, recounting how she and her favorite brother, George, picked and sold berries to supplement the family income, how this same brother "young as he was, caught fish and sold them" (1853:8), and how she suffered under the same kind of brutal labor conditions in domestic service that Harriet Wilson would later "fictionalize" in *Our Nig:* "Hard labor and unkindness was too much for me; in three months, my health and strength were gone. I often looked at my employers, and thought to myself, is this your religion?" (1853:11). Yet none of these endeavors can forestall either poverty or the dispersal of the family. Prince, as we have seen, continued in domestic service and then in trade, while George, like Truth's and Jacobs's sons, went to sea, never to return: "He shipped again to come no more" (12).

Increasingly aware of the futility of such labor within an economic system that has marginalized blacks, Prince asserted her "determination to do something for myself. . . . After seven years of anxiety and toil, I made up my mind to leave this country" (14). Although this determination may strike the modern-day reader as a positive sign of self-assertion, the narrative abruptness of Prince's account here and her silencing of all details surrounding her marriage to Mr. Prince, which was undoubtedly the principal motive for her departure, suggest her ambivalence in placing individual welfare over that of the family. Yet it is approximately at this narrative juncture that the authority of providential design is supplemented by that of the ethnographic participant-observer engaged in the social practice of reconstructing "home" both for herself and for others.[14]

Prince left the United States for Russia to follow her husband, who was a member of the czar's personal bodyguard.[15] Her narrative of her nine-year stay in Russia is remarkable for the great distance that she maintains from her ethnographic subjects, observing them with apparent objectivity and refusing to interpret or generalize about their habits and customs. In so doing Prince's account contrasts sharply with that of the Russian Pavel Petrovich Svin'in, secretary to the Russian consul general, who lived in Philadelphia from 1811 to 1813 and published a travel narrative of the United States. While Svin'in began his account with the assertion that "no two countries bear a more striking resemblance than Russia and the United States," his European gaze underscores the essential difference of African Americans and separates them from the sameness of Euro-American civilization. Thus, his ethnographic descriptions mark African Americans as exotic, even demonized, primitives. Moreover, in his narration of his visit to a black Methodist church in Philadelphia, racial difference is compounded by cultural and class difference. Svin'in's observations of the religious customs and rituals of black common folk are proffered from an ethnographic perspective that is not only European and reminiscent, for example, of Child's framing of Julia Pell, but also elitist in its adherence to classical literary traditions:

> The frightful countenance and the sparkling eyes of the Africans, staring at us in the dim light, filled us in spite of ourselves with a dread which increased even further when they began to howl with wild and piercing voices. I believed myself to be in Pluto's kingdom, amongst all the monsters of hell, and, when the doorman, greatly resembling Cerberus, locked the door, lest anyone depart, I secretly repented my curiosity.
>
> . . . [T]he gallery . . . threatened momentarily to collapse with the convulsions of the possessed, who leapt and swayed in every direction and dashed themselves to the ground, pounding with hands and feet, gnashing their teeth, all to show that the evil spirit was departing from them. . . .
>
> The piercing outcries and howls resembling a chorus of Furies horrify you and make you shudder, whereas the harmony of the singing in a Greek church fills the heart with a sweet emotion.[16]

In contrast, Prince in her narrative openly acknowledges herself to be a commoner who observes and comments upon the customs of the Russian elite, in particular the imperial court. The relative impersonality of her tone is open to interpretation. On the one hand, we may view it as an attitude of respect for the culture under observation, reinforced perhaps by the fact that Russia in the nineteenth century offered African Americans unusual opportunities for social advancement.[17] On the other hand, it may reflect the fact that, unlike Stewart and Lee, Prince never claimed a narrative authority grounded in divine will and thus remained unsure of her power to interpret.

Whatever the underlying reason for her ethnographic stance, instances exist in the narrative in which Prince deliberately positions herself as a commoner gazing at the Russian common folk. Maintaining a relatively detached and neutral perspective, Prince achieves in these textual moments what both Phillippo and Svin'in could not, an ethnographic description that silently underscores some of the "striking similarities" between Russian, African, and African-American folk cultures of which Prince was most probably aware, especially given her own African background. For example, her depiction of the funeral rituals of the Russian common people, in which the mourners shout and eat at the grave site, bears an astonishing similarity to descriptions of African and African-American burial rites. Prince's account reads in part:

> First of August we visited the burying-ground, where the people meet, as they say, to pay respect to their dead. It is a great holiday; they drink and feast on the grave stones, or as near the grave as they can come; some groan and pray, and some have music and dancing. At a funeral no one attends except the invited; after the friends arrive, a dish of rice boiled hard, with raisins, is handed round. . . . [T]hen commence the yells; they drink, eat cake, black bread, and finish their rice. . . . In this manner the common people bury their dead. (18–19)

An eighteenth-century account by Zephaniah Swift describing the funerals of Northern slaves contains many similar elements: "The funeral rites of a slave are performed by his brethren with every mark of joy and gladness—They accompany the corpse with the sound of musical instruments—They sing their songs and perform their dances around the grave and indulge themselves in mirth and pleasantry." And contemporary anthropological scholarship has offered similar accounts of nineteenth-century burial customs among the Mende: "Mende carried to the graveside cooked chicken together with rice and red palm oil. This mixture was placed on a banana leaf and laid by the side of the grave. . . . The family then ate the remainder of the chicken and rice and offered a prayer."[18]

Much as in her West Indies pamphlet, Prince revealed herself in her autobiography to be foremost concerned with investigating those social institutions— the family, the church, schools—where women can work to enhance the welfare of family and community, to construct different versions of home. Given such a feminist perspective, Prince's few explicit evaluations of Russian society are indicative not only of the social respect she wished to accord the country's elite but also of her decisive valorizing of domestic over national politics: the empress is praised as a great maternal figure who nurtures not only her own children but all Russians; the crushing of the Decembrist uprising is analyzed chiefly in terms of how it has torn families apart; serfdom is condemned as a form of slavery but is also recognized as one in which owners "are not suffered to separate families or sell them off the soil" (32). And it is in Russia, finally, that Prince began to work toward her cherished goal of establishing a child-care institution that would help nurture children in need.

Prince's desire to provide a home for young people, particularly girls who might otherwise, like Sylvia, lose their way, is vividly illustrated in her brief account of her life in Boston after her return from Russia and before her departure for Jamaica (1833–40). If Prince attended meetings of Garrison's Anti-Slavery Society "with much pleasure" (36), her narrative makes it clear that her primary concern is the more particularly female one of providing a "home" for "destitute and afflicted" orphans, "where they might be sheltered from the contaminating evils that beset their path" (35). When she then turned to the narration of her Jamaican travels, Prince deliberately reversed the narrative strategy of her earlier pamphlet to announce at the outset her motivation for going—her desire to teach young children and more specifically her wish to help "the poor girls that were destitute" (49) already mentioned in her 1843 letter to the *National Anti-Slavery Standard*. In this portion of her autobiography Prince incorporated all of the material from her West Indies tract but reorganized it, reversing its narrative line so as to make the text conform more closely to the conventions of the travel-ethnography genre. As a result, Prince's stance as a participant-observer becomes fully foregrounded. And, her desire for Jamaican self-determination is perhaps nowhere more evident than in her newly composed historical digression on the Maroons in which she asserted that this people, who had avoided enslavement by hiding in the mountains, are the original population of Jamaica and rightful owners of the island. This digression suggests that maroonage might well provide a model of cultural self-determination and re-creation of local place for blacks in the New World.[19]

As in her West Indies pamphlet, throughout this narrative Prince insists on positioning herself as the subject authorized to scrutinize the Other, refusing to be gazed at, or at least to let the reader see her being gazed at. But as in her earlier narrative, Prince finally allows the reader to see her gaze returned, and all of a sudden her fears become fully understandable. Returning home by way of the coastal Southern states, Prince's boat puts into harbor at New Orleans, and she finds that she cannot escape the gaze of white Southerners who seek to entice her ashore so as to enslave her. Prince now experiences herself as the Other—"a spectacle for observation" (71)—and is obliged to ponder her own social construction, the degree of her difference from the Southern slave. In the process she discovers, as do Harriet Wilson and Harriet Jacobs, that her most effective form of resistance is not physical force but linguistic violence. Resorting to direct discourse placed within quotation marks for the only time in her narrative, she gives us a vivid account of her verbal battle with those who would enslave her: "I found it necessary to be stern with them; they were very rude; if I had not been so, I know not what would have been the consequences. . . . I asked them if they believed there was a God. 'Of course we do,' they replied. 'Then why not obey him?' 'We do.' 'You do not; permit me to say there is a God, and a just one, that will bring you all to account'" (73, 72).

The final section of Prince's 1850 autobiography makes it clear, however, that the free North still cannot offer her salvation, as personal problems—isolation, poverty—continue to plague her upon her return. Prince's text closes with a religious meditation entitled "Divine Contentment," reminiscent of Stewart's meditations although less anguished given its emphasis on humility and faith. The autobiographical structure of Prince's narrative disintegrates at this point as verses from the Bible are linked to one another without narrative commentary and Prince's voice merges with that of Old Testament Prophets and New Testament apostles, suggesting her renewed quest for a convincing narrative authority. Yet Prince's narrative efforts do not end with this collapse into biblical discourse. For, when she reprinted her *Life and Travels* in 1853 and again in 1856 under conditions of severe economic duress, these later editions mark a sharp recovery of narrative voice and authority. In these two editions Prince drastically reduced the concluding religious meditation and, in expanding the introductory account of her early life, relied more emphatically on the authority of cultural experience.

To date, virtually nothing is known of Prince's later life, so we have no way of assessing whether she was in fact able to "supply her necessities" through the sale of her autobiography; nor do we know whether she succeeded in establishing an asylum for young girls or ever traveled again. But scattered comments in the press suggest the degree to which Prince's resistance to "woman's wrongs" continued to be made known throughout the nineteenth century. For example, at the Fifth National Woman's Rights Convention in 1854, Prince recounted her eyewitness observations of American slavery on her journey home from Jamaica along the Southern coast. And in 1894 a brief article in the *Woman's Era* recalled Prince's successful rescue of a fugitive slave in Boston in 1847: "Only for an instance did [her] fiery eyes rest upon the form of the villain, as if to be fully assured that it was he, for the next moment she had grappled with him, and before he could fully realize his position she, with the assistance of the colored women that had accompanied her, had dragged him to the door and thrust him out of the house." In omitting this account from her autobiography Prince, as Anthony Barthelemy has suggested, was undoubtedly once again choosing privacy over public exposure even at the expense of promoting antislavery resistance work.[20]

Born in Wilmington, Delaware, in 1823 into a more well-to-do family than either Stewart, Lee, or Prince, Mary Ann Shadd received formal schooling in the educational system of West Chester, Pennsylvania, where her parents had moved in 1833, and subsequently became a teacher in different townships in Delaware,

Pennsylvania, and New York.[21] By the late 1840s Shadd had also become committed to abolitionist and racial uplift efforts, emulating the example set by her father. Indeed, Abraham Shadd had joined Garrison's abolitionist movement at its inception, participating in the founding of the American Anti-Slavery Society in 1833 and acting as an agent for both the *Liberator* and the *Emancipator;* he had also become actively involved in black reform and protest movements, serving as early as 1830 as a delegate from Delaware to the annual national conventions of black men and working on the Underground Railroad.[22] In 1850 Shadd and her brother Isaac decided to emigrate to Canada. Settling in Windsor, Canada West, in the fall of 1851, Shadd set out from this position of geographic displacement to penetrate the male public sphere of the black press and convention movement. And much like Watkins Harper and Remond were soon to do, Shadd insisted not only on involving herself in issues that focused purely on local communities or woman's sphere but also on conceptualizing a national home place for all African Americans.

In the March 23, 1849 issue of the *North Star* Frederick Douglass had published a letter written to him earlier that year by Shadd from her home in Wilmington, Delaware. In her letter Shadd referred to an article by the New York minister Henry Highland Garnet "relative to the very wretched condition of thirty thousand of our people in your State." Claiming to be "insensible of boundaries," she proceeded to offer suggestions for remedying the wretchedness of blacks not only in the state of New York but throughout the nation. Articulating a set of beliefs to which she would remain faithful throughout the antebellum period, Shadd affirmed "the possibility of final success, when using proper means, . . . the possibility of bringing about the desired end ourselves, and not waiting for the whites of the country to do so." As she ridiculed Garnet's call for yet another national convention as a means "of bringing about the desired end," she insisted that "we should do more, and talk less," specifically proposing that we become "producers" rather than "consumers" by "direct[ing] our attention more to the farming interest."

Throughout her years as a social activist and journalist, Shadd Cary appears to have been impatient with boundaries of all kinds, repeatedly attempting to transcend, if not erase, them. Yet given the attitude of both the dominant culture and the black male elite toward black women, Shadd Cary found herself time and again forced to confront boundaries of race, gender, and even nationality. Both her social ideology and her cultural practice came to function, then, as instruments through which she attempted to deconstruct, manipulate, and reconfigure boundaries in order to bring about "the desired end" of racial uplift.

The first boundary that Shadd Cary sought to deconstruct was that of race. She insisted that racial difference must be viewed not as a fundamental biological difference that separates peoples hierarchically but simply as a superficial difference of complexion. Refusing to name her own people according to either racial or geographic origin—Negro, African, African American, and so forth—she referred to them in terms of "complexional character" only. She further argued that if biological theories of race are to be abandoned, so must those social constructions which derive from them and which condition the lives of African Americans, categorizing them as intellectually inferior, developmentally retarded, morally depraved.

If race was no longer construed as a legal category and racial difference no longer legislated, then maybe African Americans would be given the opportunity to disprove dominant theories of biological and social inferiority. Thus, when the passage of the Fugitive Slave Law in 1850 compelled thousands of ex-slaves and free blacks alike to flee the United States and settle in Canada, Shadd Cary decided to follow suit, hoping that emigration to Canada West—where racial discrimination had no de jure existence—would enable blacks to attain full civil rights, achieve social equality with whites, and find a secure place for themselves in an economy devoted chiefly to "farming interests." Having thus acknowledged the geographic boundary that separated slave nation from free nation in North America, Shadd Cary found herself obliged to confront still other boundaries as she worked for the racial uplift of her people. One of these was the boundary of gender that clearly delineated the separation of spheres within the national convention movement, in which the topics of emigration, Negro nationality, and a homeland for African Americans were being hotly contested.

In October 1855 the National Convention of Colored Men met in Philadelphia to discuss a variety of matters crucial to the welfare of black Americans, among them that of emigration. According to a reporter for the *British Banner*, the convention also rather foolishly took up the issue of the admission of women to its body and, despite the protest of some who argued that "this was not a Women's Rights Convention," proceeded to elect Shadd Cary a member by a vote of thirty-eight to twenty-three. Although this same reporter had no difficulty accepting the equality between black and white, "believing . . . that circumstances alone account for the difference," and although he admitted that Shadd Cary "appears to have made one of the best speeches" on the topic of emigration, he nonetheless remained vehemently opposed to the participation of women in conventions: "Such Conferences are not the place for woman, whose province is ample enough for all her energies of mind and heart—energies alike powerful and precious in their appropriate field; but that field is not the arena of discussion and debate. Had 'Miss Shadd' not had in her bosom more of the male than of the female heart, she would have felt ashamed of her position, and hastened to hide herself amid the soft obscurities of her own sex" (Nov. 20, 1855). Given the number of votes cast against Shadd Cary, these sentiments against female membership in the convention movement were clearly shared by many African-American men as well.

Indeed, from their beginnings in 1831, and in emulation of the dominant culture, black national and state conventions had excluded women from their deliberations as a matter of course. Eventually, however, the status of women was itself to become a subject of debate. Perhaps the most important discussion of this topic took place at the national convention of 1848 held in Cleveland, Ohio. The issue of the social role of black women was brought up early in the convention in connection with a series of resolutions concerning the need for black men to enter "respectable industrial occupations" in order to elevate the race. One delegate took Martin Delany to task for his elitist position concerning female menial labor, in particular for his comment "that he would rather receive a telegraphic despatch that his wife and two children had fallen victims to a loathsome disease, than to hear that they had become the servants of any man." Despite Frederick Douglass's argument that all "necessary" labor should be considered "honorable" rather than "degrading," the resolutions were adopted with near unanimity. These male delegates thus exhibited a singular lack of sensitivity toward black women, most of whom needed to work but few of whom could possibly hope to enter "respectable industrial occupations."

The political aspirations of black women were raised quite unexpectedly toward the end of this same convention as a Mrs. Sanford, echoing the rhetoric of Seneca Falls and speaking on behalf of all "daughters of Eve," pleaded "for the Elective Franchise; for right of property in the marriage covenant," and more generally for the right "to co-operate in making the laws we obey." Reluctant to discuss such controversial issues, several delegates voted to postpone the vote on "the Resolution as to Woman's Rights." Once again, Frederick Douglass intervened to propose an amendment "saying that the word persons used in the resolution designating delegates be understood to include *woman.*" The amendment carried, inviting "females hereafter to take part in our deliberations," but the practical result was in fact an indefinite postponement of any serious discussion of women's rights and of the role that women were to play in future conventions.[23]

This uncertainty over women's roles continued to be reflected in later conventions. At the Ohio State Convention of 1849, a Mrs. Jane P. Merritt rose to complain that the invited women "have been deprived of a voice," and threatened a walkout. A resolution was quickly passed "inviting the ladies to share in the doings of the Convention," but it appears that their participation was limited to the singing of songs. On an even harsher note, the 1855 New York Convention held in Troy simply struck Miss Barbary Anna Stewart's name from the rolls "on the ground that this is not a Woman's Rights Convention." Finally, the National Emigration Convention held in Cleveland in 1854 is generally considered to have been favorably disposed toward the participation of women. A full third of the delegates were women, several women were elected officers, two women were involved in the moving and seconding of resolutions, and the platform issued a statement on female education declaring that "the potency and respectability of a nation or people, depends entirely upon the position of their women." Yet there is no evidence from the deliberations to indicate that the presence of women at this convention influenced the ideological debate over emigration in any way.[24]

Undeterred by such male hostility toward women as public speakers, Shadd Cary refused to withdraw from the public's gaze to bury herself within "the soft obscurities of her sex" but rather insisted on her right to participate in the masculine sphere of public civic debate. Thus, despite the controversy over her presence at the 1855 national convention, she managed to obtain the floor and make a speech. According to *Frederick Douglass' Paper:* "She at first had ten minutes granted her as had the other members. At their expiration, ten more were granted, and by this time came the hour of adjournment; but so interested was the House, that it granted additional time to her to finish, at the commencement of the afternoon session; and the House was crowded and breathless in its attention to her masterly exposition of our present condition, and the advantages Canada opens to colored men of enterprise" (Nov. 9, 1855). A few weeks later Shadd Cary's newspaper, the *Provincial Freeman*, devoted several columns to her debate with a prominent black Philadelphian, Mr. Wears, again on the subject of emigration. In his opening statement, the paper reported, Wears had declared rather superciliously that "he should *treat her in the discussion precisely as he would a gentleman, occupying her position;* assuring the audience that his opponent, though a lady, was too high spirited to crave any *special favor* or *courtesy,* as in fact she was not entitled to any. . . ." But Shadd Cary had quickly obtained the upper hand by "charg[ing] her opponent with having *shunned the issue;* in which she was reminded of the 'Irishman's flea.' 'When he went to put his finger on it, it was not there.' The pertinency of the illustration seemed obvious," the reporter concluded, "and much amused the audience" (Dec. 22, 1855).

Shadd Cary's speeches were, however, often perceived not only as pertinent but as impertinent. In his biographical sketch of Shadd Cary in *The Rising Son*, W. W. Brown remarked that "as a speaker, she ranks deservedly high; as a debater, she is quick to take advantage of the weak points of her opponent, forcible in her illustrations, biting in her sarcasm, and withering in her rebukes."[25] Although we have no record of any of her antebellum speeches other than a few brief quotes reported in newspaper columns, it would seem that in her oratory Shadd Cary made use of what the rhetorician Hugh Blair termed the eloquence of popular assemblies contrasted to the eloquence of the pulpit and that of the bar. According to Blair, this is the most animated form of public speaking, emphasizing argument and debate as the chief techniques of persuasion. Yet while logical reasoning remains the foundation of such a speaking style, great latitude may be given to the expression of passion, warmth, and force: "That ardour of Speech, that vehemence and glow of Sentiment, which arise from a mind animated and inspired by some great and public object, form the peculiar characteristics of Popular Eloquence, in its highest degree of perfection." Furthermore, many aspects of Shadd Cary's rhetoric also reflect that midcentury shift in American oratory recently analyzed by such scholars as Lawrence Buell and Kenneth Cmiel. Joining Cmiel's contention that midcentury America witnessed the emergence of a middling and more democratic form of oratory, Buell has argued that in this period the classical Ciceronian *style périodique* was gradually superseded by the *style coupé*, whose terseness, reliance on interdependent propositions, and sententious brevity mark it as more modern. Taken together, these rhetorical elements endow popular oratory with what Blair asserted to be "an air of manliness and strength."[26]

It would seem that Shadd Cary's lecturing strategies thus differed radically from those of Watkins Harper for example, who, as we shall see, abided by more conventional codes of femininity. Shadd Cary's "unfeminine" speaking style led even those who appreciated the substance of her lectures to admit to her lack of eloquence, to label her delivery as "nervous, hurried." In particular, they felt impelled to reassure the public that, although Shadd Cary had invaded the male public sphere, she nonetheless had remained at all times "in strict keeping with the popular notions of the 'sphere of women'" (*PF*, March 29, 1856): "Although she has mingled much in the society of men, attended many conventions composed almost exclusively of males, and trodden paths where women usually shrink to go, no one ever hinted aught against her reputation, and she stands with a record without blot or blemish."[27]

Shadd Cary herself was very aware of the public's critical estimation of her speaking style, and of Watkins Harper's greater popularity. In a September 1858 letter to her husband from Detroit, Shadd Cary noted that both whites and blacks "are just crazy with excitement" about Watkins Harper. "She is the greatest female speaker ever was here, so wisdom obliges me to keep out of the way as with her prepared lectures there would just be no chance of a favorable comparison."[28] Wisdom thus dictated that Shadd Cary devise other modes of representation more suitable to her talents that would also draw the public's gaze away from any "blot or blemish" that it might imagine recorded on her body. Consequently, she turned to writing and founded a newspaper of her own, the *Provincial Freeman*, the first African-American woman to do so. In the process Shadd Cary probably also hoped that geographic displacement would allow her an independent site of power within the institution of the black press from which she could continue her racial uplift work.

From her earliest days in Canada Shadd Cary had been aware of the importance of the press as a medium through which to articulate and disseminate her views. As early as November 1851, Henry Bibb's *Voice of the Fugitive* had reported that in a speech Shadd Cary had "alluded to the various instrumentalities which should be used as a means of elevation, among which was the Press" (Nov. 19, 1851). By March 24, 1853, Shadd Cary had published the first issue of the *Provincial Freeman*. In its second issue, which did not appear until March 25, 1854, Shadd Cary insisted that hers was to be an independent paper that would transcend ideological differences by insisting on a purely moral approach to political questions: "These remarks will, it is hoped, satisfy all that it is neither

Mary Ann Shadd (Cary). Courtesy of the National Archives of Canada. C29977.

our duty nor inclination to be the advocate of any particular school; but . . . that we endeavor to enforce the broad and comprehensive ground of the moral bearings of the question." Yet the *Freeman* was a newspaper whose very function was to probe the notion of difference. Taking its name from the Philadelphia antislavery newspaper, the *Pennsylvania Freeman*, the *Provincial Freeman* through its very title posed such questions as these: What are the advantages of crossing geographic boundaries and writing from the provinces, specifically the province of Canada West? What are the possibilities of living as a "freeman" in a nation where racial difference has no de jure existence? Furthermore, what is to be gained by crossing the boundaries of gender and publishing from the position of a (black) woman? And, lastly, what can be said to constitute home for African Americans?

Shadd Cary must also have been aware of her newspaper's need to negotiate still other kinds of boundaries as she sought to address multiple audiences of readers and subscribers, men as well as women, the black communities of Canada West as well as the abolitionist communities—both black and white—of the northern and western United States. As the official organ of the Provincial Union, the local benevolent and antislavery association, the *Freeman* encouraged economic self-sufficiency and the achievement of "literary, scientific, and mechanical" skills among the black Canadian population (*PF*, Aug. 19, 1854). Disseminated in addition in the United States among such well-known black abolitionists as Frederick Douglass, Martin Delany, and William Still, as well as white abolitionist groups such as the Philadelphia Female Anti-Slavery Society, whose membership included Lucretia Mott and Sarah Pugh, the *Freeman* also sought both to showcase the progress made by blacks in Canada and to add its voice to the antislavery cause.

In her writings Shadd Cary repeatedly relied on strategies of geographic displacement—crossing the national border from the United States into Canada and community borders within the province of Canada West—in order to question notions of home for the African-American "tourist." Shadd Cary avoided the pitfalls of tourism by deconstructing home as a place of origin and a primary point of reference, by remaining ever aware of her own geographic and social displacement, and by conceptualizing home as a working out of relationships subject to change rather than as a natural and fixed entity. In fact, the tour functioned for Shadd Cary not simply as a site from which to proffer ethnographic observations but as the pretext and context from which to set up a series of sociological arguments about peoples and their institutions.

Shortly after having crossed the northern border to settle in Canada and before starting the *Provincial Freeman,* Shadd Cary published a brief pamphlet entitled *A Plea for Emigration; or, Notes of Canada West,* in which she argued for the certain "political elevation" of black Canadians through sustained racial uplift efforts and promoted Canada as a national home place for African Americans. In her pamphlet Shadd Cary depicted Canada as a northern frontier, a country containing vast tracts of land, made up of rich and fertile soil, waiting to be planted and tilled so as to yield up impressive agricultural products such as cannot be found in the United States. Turning nostalgically back to a Jeffersonian ideal of simple rustic living, Shadd Cary promoted farming as *the* economic system through which African Americans could become self-sufficient producers. In the process she moved away from the push toward the city and industrialization that characterized U.S. society at midcentury, rejecting urban living, capitalism, and trade, insisting that the former would lead blacks to a life of degradation while the latter were quite simply avenues of success still closed to them.

Interestingly enough, Shadd Cary's agrarian philosophy parallels the conservative ideology of neo-Jeffersonians of the 1840s, who feared that the rapid modernization of America would create labor problems similar to those already plaguing the congested cities of Great Britain—capital accumulation in the hands of a few industrialists counterbalanced by a growing dependent wage-earning working class likely to resist capital's growing power through walkouts, trade union activities, and even violence. Rather than permit the creation of such "white slavery," they urged expansion into, and settlement of, western territories, hoping that the United States would remain a predominantly precapitalist agrarian nation where political power would be concentrated in the hands of self-reliant yeomen and planters.[29] If these men envisioned the West as the frontier for the white settler, Shadd Cary promoted Canada for the black. In Canada, she asserted, "there will be no scarcity of land, and a medium, between the extensive operations of capitalists, and the degrading occupations of colored people, generally, in the crowded cities of the United States, thus opens to them a certain road to future eminence, in every way preferable to the sudden changes and chances of trade, exclusively."[30] In her *Notes* as well as throughout the pages of the *Provincial Freeman*, Shadd Cary advocated this agrarian model for black male and female emigrationists alike as she envisioned them working as yeoman farmers to achieve a life of self-sufficiency and dignity.

In the June 30, 1855 issue of the *Freeman*, the same issue in which John Still published his letter on the "Colored Tourist," Shadd Cary announced her resignation as editor. In the early days of the *Freeman*, Shadd Cary had been assisted by Samuel Ringgold Ward, a former slave, author of a slave narrative, minister, and former associate of *Frederick Douglass' Paper*. After her resignation, editorial functions were taken over by several male colleagues, among them William P. Newman, an escaped slave who had studied at Oberlin college and subsequently become a Baptist minister, and her brother Isaac. Her husband Thomas J. Cary, a black businessman from Toronto whom she was to marry in January 1856 and who died prematurely in 1860, was never involved in the workings of the paper. Retaining discreet control over the *Provincial Freeman*, Shadd Cary determined to devote future efforts to obtaining subscribers. To do so she toured settlements in Canada West and the northern United States and wrote a series of letters recording her impressions from this position "abroad" back "home" to the *Freeman*, much as Delany had done on behalf of Frederick Douglass's *North Star* in the late 1840s. The first such columns that I could locate appeared in the July 22 and 23, 1854 issues of the *Freeman* and bore the title "Our Tour"; a letter to "C" modeled on the same format was published in the October 21 issue of the same year. But it was chiefly from September 1855 to April 1856 that Shadd Cary wrote a series of letters to "Mr. Editor" (William P. Newman), which appeared in the correspondence column of the *Freeman* and in which she refined the position and strategies of the "Colored Tourist" as delineated by Still.

In her guise as "colored tourist," Shadd Cary positioned herself from the outset as a participant-observer whose task it was to assess not only the differences between the United States and Canada but also those among black Canadian communities and within the communities themselves. Much like Prince,

Shadd Cary never represents the touring body in her writings. The reader's sense of her physical being is gained only from an outsider's perspective, for example, that of H. J. Williamsom: "In this country, late in the Fall and early in the Spring, the walking is very disagreeable, being very muddy and sloppy, with all this to contend with, to see with what earnestness she went about transacting her business [of collecting subscriptions] first in one place and then in another, and to see the respect paid to her, alike from from whites as well as colored, was particularly gratifying to the observer" (*PF*, Feb. 25, 1856).

The particular hallmark of the participant-observer is, of course, the very fact of "being there." But for Shadd Cary this stance was a complex one, positioning her as both insider and outsider to the black communities, in striking contrast to William Wells Brown, for example, who, in a tour of Canada in 1861, functioned purely as an outside observer whose affiliation with the black communities was determined only by the experience of racial discrimination.[31] Each community Shadd Cary visited thus became a temporary home as she became an insider, a black Canadian vitally engaged in the local politics of racial uplift. Yet Shadd Cary remained an outsider as well, a social ethnographer ever aware of the boundaries that set her apart from these communities.

In publishing her on-site observations of different black communities at regular intervals in the *Provincial Freeman* for her readers back home, Shadd Cary might initially appear to be taking them on tour with her; as she tours, they accompany her. In fact, however, Shadd Cary's columns served to distance her from her readers, reminding them that while she is on tour, they have been left at home. Their knowledge of black Canadian communities comes to them only as it is filtered through Shadd Cary's ethnographic perspective. Refusing in her columns to represent herself as a generalized author or an absolute knowing subject, Shadd Cary explicitly locates her narrative authority in the *I* who creates the perspective from which the observations of the tour are offered. Thus, while her columns emphasize the importance of discourse, and the textualization of experience, they also affirm the impossibility of separating the text from the occasion that has produced it.

The ethnographic occasion that marked Shadd Cary's position as insider/outsider to the community and produced the column was most often a debate entertained with an opponent who did not share a similar program of racial uplift. Shadd Cary's columns were thus designed to win her readers over to her point of view by virtue of her forensic abilities—the eloquence of popular assemblies transferred to the printed page. To accomplish these goals Shadd Cary textualized herself as an agonistic *I* whose weapons are those of the dialogic— the representation, according to Bakhtin, of competing ideological points of view in their own specific social language.[32] Embedded within her own discourse are repeated references to, and quotations from, the discourse of others— C. C. Foote, the director of the Refugee Home Society, whom she accused of promoting "begging schemes" among the fugitive slaves, thus keeping them dependent on white abolitionists and impeding their achievement of autonomy (*Lib,* March 4, 1853); John Scoble, of the Dawn Institute, who has likewise instituted a begging scheme to obtain funds to build a schoolhouse (*PF,* July 22, 1854); Frederick Douglass, whose shifting opinions on emigration render him untrustworthy; and even local women who refuse to contribute to the public work of reform:

> The good people of the places mentioned are resolved on supporting the paper—nothing can exceed the interest shown by the women in its success—a hopeful sign, when one calls to remembrance the apathy of our females generally and especially in the great City of Toronto, until very recently. If there is any one thing that tends to intensify one's contempt for the *muslim* multitude, it is the nothingness the delicate creatures display when invited to aid in a work for the general good. You would be surprised at the pains they take to impress you with their "feebleness." They "would" probably *do something,* but would not for the world "join with others." Why? you ask. "Would have to associate with the circle. Goodness!" Must not think of helping without getting Mr. ——'s comment. Can't get the "sense of it;"—he knows about it—"for he borrows neighbor ——'s paper; knows the enterprise will be well supported though—heard somebody say so." Young ladies who have no Mr. ——'s to think for them, really do not know,—they never read the newspapers; but it would be delightful to go to a tea-meeting: think they might make up some articles;—wonder if there will be play allowed at the donation! What a set! (*PF,* Oct. 21, 1854)

The language of the Other is revived here in order to be turned against its author and reinterpreted from another ideological perspective. In sharp contrast to Watkins Harper's essays and speeches, for example, Shadd Cary's columns thus explode into a polyphonous discourse that underscores the heterogeneity of the black community and its racial uplift agendas.

As a "colored tourist" Shadd Cary remained sensitive to the cultural differences among the black communities of Canada West resulting from specific historical and social circumstances. Thus she analyzed each community in terms of its particular economic advantages and/or disadvantages, its school needs, the presence of different church denominations, the racial attitudes of the local white population, and so forth; yet each analysis is carried out within the context of her agrarian agenda. Writing from Dawn, Shadd Cary praised the industry of the black population, particularly in the areas of carpentry, wagon making, and farming, and encouraged plans to build a school that would be not a caste institution but open to white and black children alike. In a column from the July 25, 1857 issue of the *Freeman,* she painted an idyllic picture of black farm life in the community of Raleigh Plains: "Our farmers are planting, clearing, tending crop. . . . Industry keeps up a musical buzzing throughout the country and in town the working bees are preparing to store away. Men and women are gardening and planting who never dreamed of the necessity before. . . ." Yet, despite her agrarian ideology, Shadd Cary acknowledged the capitalist framework within which farmers were obliged to produce. Thus, in a letter from London, she pointed to the opportunity for some "enterprising capitalist" to buy up lumber and sell it at a higher rate further west (*PF*, Oct. 21, 1854).

Throughout her columns Shadd Cary reiterated her belief that black Canadians could live as independent freemen on an equal basis with whites. She consistently castigated the racism that existed among white Canadians, yet all too often underestimated its power. Writing from Saint Catherines, she decried the presence of Yankeee prejudice among the local white population and denounced the Congregationalist missionary for enriching himself at the expense of local blacks seeking to build up the African Methodist Church (*PF*, Nov. 3, 1855). And from Windsor she condemned reformers like the Reverend C. C. Foote, whose insistence on creating caste institutions played right into the hands of transplanted white Yankees (*PF*, Dec. 6, 1855). To her mind such caste institutions reintroduced erroneous notions of racial difference and boundaries. Yet both the colorophobia exhibited by the white population and the establishment of caste institutions by whites and blacks alike underscored, ultimately, the practical limitations of Shadd Cary's theory of "complexional character."

Reader reaction to Shadd Cary's journalism and editorship was mixed. Many readers were highly impressed by her powerful rhetoric that persuasively detailed the success of racial uplift efforts in Canada West. Thus, a C. S. Depp from Michigan, addressing Shadd Cary as "Dear Sir," paid tribute to her newspaper as a powerful weapon against "pro-slavery party-men": "Whenever I get into an argument with those crazy-headed bull dogs . . . , I throw out a copy of your paper, and tell them that a colored man publishes such a paper in Canada, and that the fugitives are better off in a cold climate, than in a warm one under slavery" (*PF*, Aug. 26, 1854). If readers such as Depp addressed Shadd Cary as "Dear Sir" or "Brother Shadd," we may well wonder how she chose to position and represent herself as a newspaper editor and leader within the black community. As we have seen, Shadd Cary often sought to distance herself from the local women, sarcastically referring to their "apathy" and "feebleness." The intensity of her contempt for such conventionally feminine behavior may perhaps be attributed to the negative criticism she was forced to tolerate as a woman operating in the male sphere of the black press. Indeed, in her "Adieu" column, she attributed her decision to resign as editor to the "difficulties . . . and obstacles such as we feel confident few, if any, females have had to contend against in the same business . . ." (*PF*, June 30, 1855). Her difficulties as a newspaperwoman were further recorded by a correspondent who had observed the continued hardships she was obliged to endure while on a subscription tour in Chatham in "a routine of business" that "for a female looks masculine, in the eyes of some, and is sneered at by the same class, according to the present organization of Society" (*PF*, Feb. 25, 1856).

One of Shadd Cary's most significant conflicts within the sphere of the press occurred, surprisingly enough, with Douglass. As we have seen, Douglass had consistently upheld black women's right to speak at conventions and defended the respectability of female labor. He had also fought for the equality of women within the abolitionist ranks and was an active participant in Stanton and Anthony's women's rights movement. It is difficult, however, exactly to determine Douglass's personal feelings toward Shadd Cary. In the July 4, 1856 issue of *Frederick Douglass' Paper* he gave her a somewhat ambiguous compliment, lamenting that her tone in the *Provincial Freeman* had been "at times harsh and complaining" while simultaneously asserting that "we do not know her equal among the colored ladies of the United States." In turn, Shadd Cary seems to have chafed at what she perceived to be Douglass's dominant role as spokesperson for the black community as well as his underestimation of her newspaper. She felt strongly that the *Provincial Freeman* was unfairly obliged to compete with *Frederick Douglass' Paper* for a hearing within the antislavery movement; in particular she complained that white abolitionists gave exclusive financial support to Douglass's newspaper, thus recognizing him as the single spokesperson for African-American causes. In an article entitled "Plastering etc.," Shadd Cary insisted on the need for blacks to recognize the heterogeneity of their communities and to accept the existence of competing political agendas within them. There is, she maintained, no inherent "bond of union among the colored elements," making it impossible for them to "adopt the same policy." Focusing specifically on the issue of emigration, Shadd Cary expressed outrage at the way in which Douglass in one of his articles had conflated emigration to Canada with the colonization of Liberia, praising both movements simultaneously. In attacking Douglass's views, however, Shadd Cary was simply asserting that hers were the correct ones, substituting her own policy of Canadian emigration, and arguing for the superiority of Canadian blacks over all others as "British subjects without complexional distinction" (*PF*, July 19, 1856).

Beyond her highly personal promotion of Canadian emigration, Shadd Cary also became involved in other political events and controversies surrounding the issues of black nationality and the location of an African-American home place, in particular the John Brown insurrection and the debate over African and Haitian emigration. Shadd Cary's participation in these matters that pertained exclusively to the male sphere of public civic debate and action is attributable in large part to her close friendship with Martin Delany, perhaps the most prominent black nationalist of the period, who had broken rank with Frederick Douglass over the question of black militancy and African emigration.

John Brown's decision to storm the federal arsenal at Harpers Ferry in October 1859 was an expression of this white man's determination to forge a local place for African Americans within the borders of the United States. The exact extent of Shadd Cary's involvement in Brown's enterprise is not known; we do know that a secret convention held in Chatham in May 1858 to debate his policies and plans was chaired by Delany and attended by Shadd Cary's brother Isaac and her husband, Thomas. In addition, Shadd Cary helped to edit a book, *A Voice from Harper's Ferry*, written by Osborne P. Anderson, a black Canadian who had participated in, and survived, the raid. Anderson himself had been in contact with Shadd Cary at least two years earlier when he wrote a letter opposing African emigration that was published in the August 8, 1857 issue of the *Provincial Freeman*. In full agreement with Shadd Cary's own political views, Anderson had endorsed Canadian emigration in opposition to those "pro slavery and colonization parties that claims we can't live on the continent of America, we must be expatriated to the shores of Africa to suffer the fate of a hot embrace beneath an equatorial sun." It is evident, however, that between 1857 and 1859 Anderson had become increasingly radicalized as he moved from advocacy of emigration to one of armed insurrection. His account of the Chatham convention and Brown's project is notable for their reliance—fictionalized in detail in Delany's novel *Blake*—both on violent revolution as the only means to bring about the end of slavery and on secrecy and organization as necessary tools for achieving revolution: "But John Brown reasoned of liberty and equality in broad daylight, in a modernized building, in conventions with closed doors, in meetings governed by the elaborate regulations laid down by Jefferson, and used as their guides by Congresses and Legislatures."[33]

In the aftermath of the failure of John Brown's raid, Shadd Cary was increasingly pressured to give Delany's African emigrationist schemes a hearing. But, given her ideologies of race, gender, and political economy, it was only logical that Shadd Cary would ultimately oppose the emigration movements to Africa and Haiti that proliferated among the black male leadership from the mid-1850s until the eve of the Civil War. In many ways this emigration debate replayed in similar terms one that had been raised in the 1830s in which emigration had been favored by such leaders as Paul Cuffe and opposed by James Forten and, as we saw earlier, Nancy Prince.[34] In the 1850s many black leaders—Delany as well as Henry Highland Garnet, Alexander Crummell, James Theodore Holly, J. M. Whitfield, and others—revived the idea of emigration as the only viable solution to America's race problem. The Fugitive Slave Law of 1850, the Kansas-Nebraska Act of 1854, the Dred Scott verdict of 1857 were all legal decisions designed to undermine the few political and legal rights that African Americans had managed to achieve in the earlier part of the century. Demoralized by these events, many leaders came to the conclusion that blacks had no viable future in the United States, and revived the earlier emigration schemes. This debate over emigration—whether to Canada, to Haiti, or to Africa—was a crucial one, for although it had few practical consequences it addressed on a theoretical level questions that were fundamental to African-American identity in the antebellum period: Can specific mental or cultural attributes be ascribed to peoples of African descent on the basis of race? What constitutes a Negro nationality, and where should its home place be located?

A close analysis of this discourse on emigration suggests, however, that although the issue of gender was never explicitly raised, the project was from the start a male-dominated one. Indeed, if those black male emigrationists who were seeking to found a new "Negro nationality" could be considered politically radical, they tended to be socially conservative. Their values were those of Western bourgeois capitalist society, firmly committed to class and gender hierarchies. For these men Africa (and the nations of the African diaspora) were not sites of empowering cultural traditions as they were for Sojourner Truth, for example, but lands to be colonized and capitalized. Moreover, wherever they located themselves, in whatever country or culture they hoped to establish a new Negro nationality, their agenda for women was a conservative one that emulated the gender ideology of the dominant American culture, in particular its cult of true womanhood. As the topic of emigration was debated primarily in national and state conventions, black women, with the notable exception of Shadd Cary, hardly participated in it. While never directly confronting the socially conservative ideology of a Negro nationality, black women refused by and large to endorse emigration, preferring instead to conceptualize home and community within North America and to reconfigure, as Stewart had, the dominant culture's model of domestic economy to suit their particular purposes.

The emigration movement gained momentum in September 1851 when a North American convention was held in Toronto for the express purpose of promoting emigration. Although this convention backed Canadian emigration exclusively, later conventions, namely, the General Convention of black Canadians held in Amherstburg, Canada West, in June 1853 and two National Emigration Conventions held in Cleveland, Ohio, in August of 1854 and 1856, broadened their concept of emigration to include such locations as the British West Indies, Haiti, and Central America.[35] Committed to western emigration and to a "continental policy" that would keep the migrant population close to their enslaved brethren, and fearful of reviving schemes that would smack of earlier colonization ideas, black leaders resisted all thoughts of African emigration until the topic was introduced by Delany at the National Emigration Convention in Chatham, Canada, in August 1858. The debate over emigration was thus split along several different ideological lines: emigration to a white country, Canada, to which Shadd Cary added her voice, or to a land where blacks already constituted a majority of the population; western emigration, where the transplanted population would remain close to slaves in the South; or eastern emigration back to Africa.

Underpinning all these schemes was the gradual emergence of a masculinist ideology of a Negro nationality that was eventually to receive its fullest expression in Delany's African emigration movement. In a pamphlet published in advance of the 1854 National Emigration Convention, J. M. Whitfield asserted that black Americans had indeed been a "denationalized people" but that the time was now ripe for them to create a new nationality through emigration to a land in which "the negro is to be the predominant race" and "the ruling political element."

Thus, Canada could at best be only a temporary residence for the migrating black. Like most of the black leadership in the mid-1850s, Whitfield held to a "continental policy," asserting that a powerful black nationality in the Western Hemisphere would make it easier to help slaves in the South and would thus constitute a greater threat to the slave system. Like whites, blacks were controlled by a "manifest destiny" that was to result in the creation of a forceful black nation in the Americas that would play its part in "shaping the policy of the American continent."[36]

For many, and in particular for J. T. Holly, Haiti was destined to become that nation. A proponent of Haitian emigration from 1853 on, Holly, along with James Redpath, a white man, and joined briefly in the early 1860s by William J. Watkins, William Wells Brown, and Frederick Douglass, urged African Americans to emigrate to Haiti. Arguing that in the person of Toussaint L'Ouverture Haiti had once proved herself capable of a "heroically achieved nationality," Holly believed it was now the task of African Americans to emigrate there and help elevate that fallen republic through science, Protestant Christianity, and industrial progress; by means of a "reflex influence," Haiti would then regenerate the Negro race throughout the world. In pressing his arguments, however, Holly nowhere defined what he meant by a Negro nationality. Although nationality is clearly identified with raciality in his writings, and is seen to be "inherent in [an individual's] person and in his race," it is never described in terms other than those of raw political power: "We do not simply want a *negro nationality*, but we want a *strong, powerful, enlightened and progressive negro nationality, equal to the demands of the nineteenth centuary [sic], and capable of commanding the respect of all the nations of the earth. . . .*"[37]

Such confusion over the definition of what constitutes a Negro nationality is equally apparent in the writings of Martin Delany, the driving force behind several of the national emigration conventions, in particular that of 1854. At this convention Delany delivered a lengthy speech entitled "The Political Destiny of the Colored Race" in which, with the recent European nationalist movements firmly in mind, he struggled to define the concept of a Negro nationality. Before Holly, Delany identified nationality with raciality and adopted a deeply essentialist position: "We have, then, inherent traits, attributes, so to speak, and native characteristics, peculiar to our race, whether pure or mixed blood; and all that is required of us is to cultivate these, and develop them in their purity, to make them desirable and emulated by the rest of the world." Delany then proceeded to enumerate these native characteristics, asserting that "the colored races have the highest traits of civilization. . . . They are civil, peaceable, and religious to a fault." Although the white race may excel "in mathematics, sculpture and architecture, as arts and sciences, commerce and internal improvements as enterprises," Delany insisted that "in languages, oratory, poetry, music, and painting, as arts and sciences, and in ethics, metaphysics, theology and legal jurisprudence—in plain language, in the true principles of morals, correctness of thought, religion, and law or civil government, there is no doubt but the black race will yet instruct the world."³⁸ Delany's essentialist interpretation of Negro nationality remains highly problematic, however, as it is purely theoretical, relies on Western values and categories, represses cultural and social differences, and creates a myth of raciality unsupported by historical fact.

The National Emigration Convention of 1854 had limited its deliberations to western emigration alone, but by the time of the Chatham convention of 1858 Delany had shifted his goal to African emigration and was actively raising money to finance an exploratory expedition to the Niger Valley. The result of this expedition was the publication of a pamphlet entitled *Official Report of the Niger Valley Exploring Party*. Delany's views on African emigration were complemented during this period by those of Henry Highland Garnet, founder of the African Civilization Society, and Alexander Crummell, resident of Liberia from 1853 to 1873. Together these three men offered a comprehensive vision of Negro nationality through emigration in which, however, they ultimately abandoned essentialist notions of race and instead turned to white cultural models, principally "commerce and internal improvements as enterprises." Following this interpretation, black nationality comes to replicate the values of Western, Christian, capitalist patriarchy.

In their writings Delany, Garnet, and Crummell all agreed that the dual mission of African emigration was to evangelize heathen Africa and, in this process of Christianization, also civilize it by bringing the arts and sciences of the Western world to the degraded African continent. To accomplish this goal, all three men argued that only an elite group of African Americans should be chosen; in Delany's words, "no heterogeneous nor promiscuous 'masses' or companies, but select and intelligent people of high moral as well as religious character were to be induced to go out."³⁹ Ultimately, this notion of civilization became equated with that of capitalism. Both Garnet and Delany believed that the black American in Africa would be able freely to develop his entrepreneurial and commercial talents in a way that had not been possible in the United States. Both men spoke of establishing agricultural and industrial colonies in lands ceded to the emigrants by the local princes and kings. In particular, they encouraged the development of cotton production in Africa. In so doing they hoped to achieve several goals at once: that of enriching native and emigrant cotton growers, thereby "regenerating the race"; that of exporting cotton at competitive prices, thereby reducing the price of cotton in the United States and ultimately destroying the slave system; and finally, that of creating an arena for black men to become traders and businessmen.⁴⁰ The new settlements in Yorubaland would thus replicate Western class divisions and hierarchies.

In stark contrast to their earlier theoretical notions, then, the real motivating force of these African emigrationists appears to have been a pragmatic desire to reorient the commercial balance of power away from America and Europe and toward Africa, and to create a well-to-do middle class of black merchants, traders, and businesmen who would rival, and perhaps even supplant, their white counterparts. If cotton production should prove successful, Delany asserted, "it will be seen and admitted that the African occupies a much more important place in the social and political element of the world than that which has heretofore been assigned him—holding the balance of commercial power, and the source of the wealth of nations in his hands."[41] Here, essentialist notions of Negro nationality are replaced by an ideology that acknowledges the social construction of a heterogeneous international black population.

The rhetoric of African emigration in the 1850s was thus an intensely masculine one that excluded black women from its project; women are nowhere accounted for and one can only infer what kinds of roles they might have been able to play in this emigration process. Given the elitism and class consciousness of such men as Crummell and Delany, their role would probably have been very limited. Both men accepted the patriarchal ideology that recognized the necessity of educating women to be a strong moral influence within the home, but both also sought to restrict women fully to the private sphere. Crummell hoped to establish a female seminary in Liberia that would fulfill the "duty of making woman in this land as superior, intellectual, and dignified, as we all would have her beautiful, and attractive, and moral."[42] Thus excluded from much of the public arena, the one field of activity left to black American women in Africa was missionary work. In his Niger Valley report, Delany refers to many women who were involved in missionary work as wives. But, as women and as wives, their roles could only be ancillary.

Delany's *Report* indicates a certain interest in the social roles of African women, one that might well have been sparked by his close reading of T. J. Bowen's *Central Africa: Adventures and Missionary Labours in Several Countries in the Interior of Africa* before his departure to Yorubaland. Bowen's text provides fascinating reading for his sensitive comments on the need to avoid Western ethnocentricity in the process of civilizing Africa and for his accurate perception of the vital role that the African woman played in the public sphere as a trader and a "free dealer, who labors for herself and supports herself, and has no claim on her husband's property, . . . [who] is sole owner of her property and her earnings." But despite all efforts to avoid ethnocentrism, Bowen ultimately blamed the free dealing status of African women for undermining patriarchy and destroying family unity.[43]

Delany, too, comments on the social role of African women, noting their many varied activities that contribute to the well-being of the household: women are involved not only in domestic work but also in "trading, and gathering in the fields, and aiding in carrying." And he quotes appreciatively a passage from Bowen's text concerning the market activity of African women: "Here the women sit and chat all day, from early morn till nine o'clock at night, to sell their various merchandise. . . ." What is most interesting about Delany's quotation of Bowen, however, is what he elides—Bowen's comments on the aggressiveness of

115

the African woman trader: "The women, especially, always noisy, are then in their glory, bawling out salutations, cheapening and higgling, conversing, laughing, and sometimes quarreling, with a shrillness and compass of voice which indicates both their determination and their ability to make themselves heard."[44] This elision reflects perhaps Delany's discomfort with the critical role played by African women in a tribal market economy at odds with capitalism and further suggests his inability to conceptualize any public function that African-American women might forge for themselves in Africa. Indeed, Delany's appeal for the establishment of "new social relations" in Africa is couched in a rhetoric of class elitism and gender exclusion that is depressingly reminiscent of traditional capitalist, class-conscious, patriarchal social relations.

This emigrationist discourse was countered not only by such black male leaders as William J. Watkins, Watkins Harper's cousin, and Frederick Douglass who, until the 1860s, reiterated with little revision the antiemigrationist arguments of the 1830s, but also by black women like Stewart, Watkins Harper, Remond, and Shadd Cary herself, who refused to endorse either African or Haitian emigration. Although these women were largely silent in the emigration debate, their few comments indicate that they were clearly unimpressed by the entrepreneurial zeal of their male counterparts, dubious of the concept of a Negro nationality, and suspicious of the role that would be accorded them in these male-conceived emigration schemes. They chose instead to develop their own cultural programs for their race and to forge home within the local place of North America.

Ignorant, like black men, of the kinds of lives African women led, and deeply committed to a belief in the civilizing potential of American civilization, black women could only envision Africa as a once-noble, but now degraded, continent. As we have seen, Stewart could only conceptualize Africa as a heathen and "strange land," and insisted that much work of civilization, education, and redemption remained to be done among black Americans. In a similar vein, Remond would later argue: "The coloured people are interested, it is true, philanthropically interested, in the civilisation of Africa, but they are still more interested in the civilisation of America, and they will not leave their country and their homes for any society." Finally, like those black men who were opposed to African emigration, these women asserted that African Americans belonged in America by right, for it was their labor and toil that had enriched this country. Speaking out in opposition to Garnet's African Civilization Society in 1859, Remond asserted this point and suggested that the society could achieve its goal of "effectually putting an end to the American cotton monopoly" without encouraging black Americans to emigrate en masse to Africa (*Anti-Slavery Advocate*, Nov. 1, 1859). As late as 1862, Watkins Harper could be found arguing that African Americans have a "birth right on the soil" of America and sarcastically chastising President Lincoln for his Central American colonization scheme: "The President's dabbling with colonization just now suggests to my mind the

116

idea of a man almost dying with a loathsome cancer, and busying himself about having his hair trimmed according to the latest fashion" (*Christian Recorder*, Sept. 27, 1862).

Throughout the 1850s Shadd Cary remained the only black woman who took an active part in the debate over emigration, favoring Canadian emigration alone. In the aftermath of Harpers Ferry, however, Shadd Cary seems to have gradually shifted from active opposition to African emigration to quiet acquiescence. In this she appears to have been motivated more out of friendship for Delany and antagonism toward Haitian emigration than out of any deep ideological commitment. For while her father and brother both worked actively for Delany and made plans in the early 1860s to emigrate to Africa, Shadd Cary merely lent her name to Delany's projects by agreeing to serve on various boards that he had established. And in editorials in the *Provincial Freeman*, she simply encouraged blacks to reflect upon, and consider, the possibility of emigration anywhere outside of the United States, given the impossibility for blacks to achieve "political elevation" in their homeland.

Shadd Cary's opposition to Haitian and African emigration was both practical and ideological, as she viewed such crossings of geographic and cultural boundaries as highly problematic. She saw these lands as fundamentally alien: in them, the emigrants would be subjected to disease and malnutrition; their religious freedom would be in jeopardy; they would be forced to adapt to foreign social and political systems. And, unlike Prince, Shadd Cary viewed the inhabitants of these lands as strange (and inferior) Others with whom African Americans could have no relationship. Her bitterest comments were reserved for Haitian emigration and its proponents, in particular James Redpath and William J. Watkins, who had briefly been won over to the movement late in 1861. She attacked their schemes in a series of articles published in the *Weekly Anglo-African* between September 1861 and February 1862: "The friends and relatives of your 'contrabands' are deluded to an inconsiderable island in mid ocean with no means of escape to travel the waste of waters between them and Christian lands—to an island where six hundred thousand people now revel in worse than heathen superstition, make 'sacrifices to the God that gives them rain'—practice polygamy, and die both natives and emigrants in frightful numbers with malignant fevers" (Oct. 26, 1861).

Furthermore, Shadd Cary surely must have been opposed to both the theoretical ideologies of Negro nationality on which the African and Haitian emigration schemes were based and the schemes themselves, which, moreover, stood in a tense contradictory relationship to one another. She must have recognized the extent to which such ideologies of Negro nationality ran counter to her notion of race as mere "complexional character." These were, in fact, totalizing projects that remained blind to cultural differences among blacks and held to essentialist notions of "complexional nationality," which, in erasing all other boundaries, could only be a "doubtful advantage" on which to build home and community

(*WAA*, Oct. 19, 1861). And she must have been equally aware of the extent to which Delany and Garnet's vision of African-American capitalist entrepreneurship ran counter to her own agrarian ideology of a self-sufficient neo-Jeffersonian yeomanry.

Indeed, like Stewart, Shadd Cary was particularly appreciative of middle-class white women's domestic economy and was convinced that it could provide a social model that black women could adapt to their own communities. Shadd Cary's feminist agenda, in fact, differed little from that of white American women engaged in moral reform activities in the same period. On one of her subscription tours Shadd Cary had sent a column back home in which she had praised those women who engage in the public work in their communities: "The women—God bless them—see the work of reform to be theirs too, and good sisters in the places I have mentioned, will go to work for an Annual Bazaar" (*PF*, July 22, 1854). Her recognition of shared values with white women is reflected throughout her tenure as editor of the *Freeman* from March 1854 to her resignation in June 1855. During this period she reprinted many articles from the U.S. press by or about women's benevolent activities in the United States. The work and writings of women such as Harriet Beecher Stowe, Lucy Stone, Fanny Fern, and Jane Swisshelm fill the pages of the *Freeman;* articles appear arguing for the need for female influence in the antislavery movement and for the equal opportunity for women in the field of education.

Shadd Cary took as her mission, then, to cross geographic frontiers and move to Canada, where she could test her racial theory of complexional character as well as mount a challenge to Frederick Douglass's leadership. She also sought to cross the frontier of gender and participate in the public debates of black men over issues of emigration and nationality. Finally, convinced of the cultural opportunities for women in homes and communities in North America, she endeavored, like many other black women leaders of the period, to cross the boundary of race and encourage her female readers to join in the public work of moral reform.

5

"Whatever Concerns Them, as a Race, Concerns Me": The Oratorical Careers of Frances Ellen Watkins Harper and Sarah Parker Remond

If religion called many antebellum black women into the liminal spaces of travel and public oratory, so did the more secular social and political causes of abolitionism and racial uplift work. Through these movements black women involved themselves in a variety of benevolent reform activities within their local communities—education, temperance, and mutual aid, for example—as well as in antislavery lecturing to promiscuous assemblies. Rather than simply labor for these causes within the community sphere, however, women like Frances Ellen Watkins Harper and Sarah Parker Remond chose to carry out their work as "doers of the word" within a wider context of travel. Such travel enabled them to circumvent to a certain extent the exclusionary policies of black male institutions in the ethnic public sphere. Yet, if such geographic displacement functioned as a site of freedom and empowerment, it nonetheless could never entirely relieve these women of the necessity of mediating the boundaries between masculine and feminine codes of behavior and in particular of negotiating the public exposure of the black female body. As public speakers, and in particular as antislavery lecturers, both Watkins Harper and Remond sought to reject the dominant culture's vision of the black woman as grotesque and to ground their authority in middle-class respectability. They did so by appropriating the discourse of sentimentality that characterized so much of the writing of middle-class white women at mid-century and by reconfiguring it in their oratory—and in Watkins Harper's case in her recited poetry—in order to articulate the particular needs of the "brave." By the 1860s, however, Remond was already discarding sentimental rhetoric in favor of the discourses of the social sciences that would become increasingly available to black women in the postbellum period. For these two women, finally, literary representation functioned as it had for Lee, Shadd Cary, and others as a means of negotiating the boundaries between public and private, of testing the limits imposed on their activities in the ethnic public sphere, and of reaching out to a broader audience.

Born in Baltimore in 1825, Frances Ellen Watkins was orphaned at an early age and brought up by her uncle, the Reverend William Watkins, attending his Academy for Negro Youth until about the age of thirteen. Thereafter, like Stewart, Lee, and Prince, she went into service with a family who, however, allowed her to pursue a program of self-education while taking care of the children and sewing for the household. According to her chief biographer, William Still, Watkins left Baltimore for the free states of Ohio and Pennsylvania around 1851, supporting herself by teaching. But the consequences of the Fugitive Slave Law for African Americans in the free North made her forcefully aware of the horrors of slavery and resulted in her decision to "pledge myself to the Anti-Slavery cause."[1] During this period Watkins participated in such ancillary antislavery activities as the Free Produce movement that advocated the boycotting of products of slave labor and of which her uncle was an active member.[2] In addition, Watkins at this time began her lifelong involvement with other reform causes to which she would become institutionally affiliated after the Civil War, notably temperance and women's rights; according to Daniel Payne, she even contributed an essay entitled "Women's Rights" to the *Christian Recorder* sometime in the early 1850s.[3]

Located initially in Philadelphia, Watkins soon discovered that "but little known, being a young and homeless maiden (an exile by law), no especial encouragement was tendered her by Anti-Slavery friends in Philadelphia"; and even as late as 1857 a newspaper column described her as "almost entirely a stranger in Philadelphia."[4] As a consequence, Watkins chose—like Truth, Lee, and Shadd Cary—to embark on a highly public traveling career, lecturing chiefly on the margins of antislavery centers. In August 1854 she gave her "maiden lecture" in New Bedford, Massachusetts on "the Elevation and Education of our People," and thereafter traveled into Maine, New York, New Jersey, Pennsylvania, Ohio, and Indiana. After her marriage to Fenton Harper in 1860, Watkins Harper "invested in a small farm near Columbus, and in a short time . . . entered upon house-keeping," confining her lecturing activities to the Columbus area until her husband's death in 1864.[5]

Watkins Harper became engaged in antislavery and racial uplift work after her uncle had left these movements but at a time when his son William J. Watkins had become a prominent leader; the former wrote for Garrison's *Liberator* and was a member of the American Moral Reform Society, while the latter remained closely allied to Frederick Douglass throughout the 1840s and 1850s and was an associate editor of *Frederick Douglass' Paper* for several years.[6] To date no historical evidence has been uncovered that might specify the kind of collaborative work that might have occurred among Watkins Harper and her male relatives. Such a lack of evidence is difficult to interpret. Given the fact that both men explicitly condemned the black community's apathy toward reform work, maintaining in the words of William Watkins that "we are, as a body, too blind to our interests, . . . too many of us are grasping at unsubstantial forms," it would be reasonable to suppose that they heartily welcomed, and commented upon, Watkins Harper's social activism. Yet it is also possible that, given the attitudes of the black elite toward women's activities in the public sphere, they might have been uncomfortable with her presence. And indeed, the masculinist rhetoric that pervades William J. Watkins's editorial "The Reformer" published in the April 7, 1854 issue of *Frederick Douglass' Paper,* suggests the degree to which he might well have perceived "woman" and "social reformer" as incompatible categories: "The bold and dashing Reformer, who walks to and fro, with the besom of destruction in his right hand—whose business seems to be to scatter, tear, and slay, meets with opposition from almost every quarter. . . . He comes with his flaming sword, and must penetrate, if he would be successful in the end, the incrustations of ignorance, in which he finds imbedded, man's mental and moral organism."[7]

As she traveled Watkins Harper constructed a kind of moral geographic map of the northern and midwestern United States much as the younger Charlotte Forten was simultaneously doing, thereby revealing her acute awareness of the significance of local place for African Americans. According to this map, Pennsylvania figures prominently as the primary place of racial harassment to which black women were particularly vulnerable: "Now let me tell you about Pennsylvania. . . . Of all . . . places, this is about the meanest of all, as far as the treatment of colored people is concerned. . . . On the Carlisle road, I was interrupted and insulted several times. Two men came after me in one day." In contrast, "dear old New England" is, just as for Forten, a place of brightness, sunshine, and kindness (*Lib,* April 23, 1858).[8] But it is, of course, Canada that figures most brilliantly as "the land of Freedom" to which neither the rock at Harpers Ferry, the ocean off the New England shore, nor the falls at Niagara can compare (*NASS,* Sept. 12, 1856).

In her lecture tours Watkins Harper spoke to varied audiences, often integrated, but sometimes all black: "I am going to spend part of this fall visiting and lecturing among the colored people" (*Anti-Slavery Bugle,* Sept. 29, 1860). Her reports of audience reaction ranged from accounts of "rowdyism," which "passed off without much serious injury" (*ASB,* Nov. 13, 1858), to the more frequent comments of quiet and orderly assemblies and lectures that are "well-received." Watkins Harper herself spoke depreciatingly of her own talents as a public speaker, at one time mockingly referring to herself as "an old maid . . . going about the country meddling with the slaveholders' business, and interfering with their rights" (*ASB*, April 23, 1859), and at another comparing herself unfavorably to Frederick Douglass, "who may come to you with lips freighted with eloquence and utterance clothed with power" while "my words might seem like feeble and purposeless utterances" (*ASB*, Sept. 29, 1860). Most often, however, the public had nothing but high praise for her lectures: "Seldom have we heard a more cogent, forcible, and eloquent lecture upon any subject, especially from a woman" (*Christian Recorder*, May 21, 1864).

How did Watkins Harper, in contrast to Shadd Cary, for example, so consistently elicit this kind of praise for her public speaking? A review of one of her lectures in the *Liberator* may provide a clue: "Mrs. Frances Watkins Harper, who, by speech and poetry has enlisted many hearts in the cause of oppressed colored Americans, delivered an eloquent and interesting address . . ." (March 24, 1865). Indeed, much as Sojourner Truth had alternated song and speech in her public performances, so Watkins Harper occasionally and particularly in the postbellum period accompanied her lectures with recitations of her poetry, which she also collected in volumes for publication and sold at the close of her lectures. Reviews of such public performances in both the antebellum and postbellum periods—by William Wells Brown, Lydia Maria Child, Grace Greenwood, Monroe Majors, and Phoebe Hanaford, among others—often go well beyond the mere description of her speeches as eloquent. In striking contrast to Truth, Watkins Harper is portrayed in bodily appearance as "quiet," exhibiting "feminine modesty"; her gestures are "few and fitting. Her manner is marked by dignity and composure. She is never assuming, never theatrical." Rhetorically, her language is "pure" and "chaste." In affective impact, her performance is stirring because of the highly expressive quality of her voice, which is "melodious" and "musical."[9]

What is at stake when a black woman's physical comportment and verbal expression are described in such terms in the nineteenth century? I suggest that these comments, in contrast to those about Truth, constitute attempts to decorporealize Watkins Harper by emphasizing the quietness of her body, the chastity of her language, and the purity of her voice. A close reading of reviews of the most famous black female singer of the antebellum period, Elizabeth Taylor Greenfield, clarifies this point. Called "the Black Swan" and often compared to the internationally acclaimed Jenny Lind, Greenfield was a singer of classical opera whose musical talent was generally acknowledged. But reviewers in the white press often had difficulty reconciling the blackness of the diva with the beauty of her voice and were unable to devise appropriate criteria for evaluating her singing. Greenfield is invariably positioned—positively and negatively—within a frame of radical Otherness; she is never perceived on her own terms. Thus, the appellation "Black Swan" led to further comparisons to an "African crow" or a "biped hippopotamus." Greenfield's tremendous vocal range brought forth the complaint that her baritone register "is as bad as a bride with a beard on her chin and an oath in her mouth." Her race, rather than her musical ability, evoked inevitable

Frances Ellen Watkins Harper. Frontispiece, *Iola Leroy*, 1895. Courtesy Moorland-Spingarn Research Center, Howard University.

comparisons with minstrelsy that patronizingly asserted that she was "a good deal above the 'Dandy Jim' and 'Lucy Long' school." Still other attempts to cast her in a more favorable light condescendingly claimed that she sang "like a child," or that "although coloured as dark as Ethiopia, she utters notes as pure as if uttered in the words of the Adriatic." Greenfield's, and her audience's, solution to this perceived incongruity of body and voice was to deemphasize the body. Indeed, like Watkins Harper, Greenfield sought to make her body "quiet," bringing forth, however, the criticism that she exhibited at all times "the same rigidity of face and body." For its part, her audience sought to obliterate the body altogether: "Upon the suggestion of another, we listened to her without looking toward her during the entire performance . . . and were at once and satisfactorily convinced that her voice is capable of producing sounds right sweet."[10]

The reviews of Watkins Harper's lecture performances suggest a similar attempt to eliminate the public presence of the black female body perceived as sexualized or grotesque, and to promote the voice as pure melody, insubstantial sound, a negation of presence. What results is a complex compromise between presence and absence: the body is rendered as "quiet" and "modest," the language represented as "pure" and "chaste," and the voice promoted as intangible music. In a short story published in 1873 Watkins Harper herself was to analogize poetry to music as the protagonist remarks: "'I would scatter the flowers of poetry around our paths; and would if I could amid life's sad discords introduce the most entrancing strains of melody. I would teach men and women to love noble deeds by setting them to the music, of fitly spoken words'" (*CR*, April 24, 1873). Yet this appeal to music remains ambiguous. For if one philosophical approach claims music to be insubstantial sound, another holds it to be the most immediate expression of human emotions, a manifestation of the passions themselves, thus connecting music directly to personality and body, and reading it as a sign of plenitude.[11] Watkins Harper's poetry and speeches are an effort to negotiate these extremes, to situate themselves somewhere between the plenitude of passion and the hollowness of pure sound; between the public exposure of the body and the intangibility of feeling; between, finally, the audience's image of the black woman as body and the poet's construction of self. To accomplish these negotiations Watkins Harper turned, I suggest, to her faith, evangelical Unitarianism, to fashion herself as a poet and a preacher composing poetry that obeys what Lawrence Buell in another context has called an "aesthetics of restraint."[12]

Critics such as Joan Sherman and Maryemma Graham have noted that although Watkins Harper assiduously participated in activities of the AME Church throughout her life, she was a lifelong member of the Unitarian Church; but they have stopped short of interpreting this biographical fact.[13] Evangelical Unitarianism enabled Watkins Harper to envision herself as a poet-preacher whose faith in the particular figure of Christ empowered her to promote social engagement in order to achieve the goal of universal harmony. Indeed, Unitarianism of the antebellum period was grounded in Christian specificity—the belief that the supernatural revelation of Jesus Christ as recorded in the Bible is the ultimate source of salvation. Further, although adherents to Unitarianism were sufficiently affected by the Second Great Awakening to believe that religion should touch the heart, they were also convinced that faith must be rationalized, assented to on the basis of intellectual reasoning. Rather than encourage the free flow of emotions, Unitarians argued that individual "character" must be attended to in order to create moral beings whose duty it would be to work for social cohesion in a disordered world. Religion thus became a form of social work in which "experimental activity, the use of books, magazines, lectures and voluntary associations," was of paramount importance. In particular, Unitarians looked to the spoken word in its many forms—preaching, prayer, hymn singing—as an important instrument for evoking those emotions that would elevate moral conscience and bring about social transformation.[14]

Poetry—in both its recited and printed forms—was just such an experimental activity for Watkins Harper, serving as a structural frame through which she could fashion herself in the public role of poet-preacher in order to articulate her vision of nineteenth-century America. In accordance with Unitarian literary theory, in which the British novelist Maria Edgeworth and poet Felicia Hemans were put forth as models of good taste, Watkins Harper conceived of poetry as moral and didactic preaching in which originality was less important than the ability to create character in the reader. In particular, sentimentality became a mode whose purpose was not to unleash an excess of emotion in the reader but rather to channel feelings toward benevolent and moral ends, develop Christian character, and forge social bonds that would commit the individual reader to work for the betterment of society.[15] Thus, Watkins Harper's poetry was designed to rationalize the emotions in order to encourage her audience's social activism.

In appropriating sentimentality to fashion her poetic discourse, Watkins Harper was of course working with a mode that had come to dominate antebellum literary discourse. Relying on contemporary modernist norms, early twentieth-century critics have tended to devalue her work because of this very sentimentalism and didacticism. In *To Make a Poet Black*, for example, Saunders Redding condemns Watkins Harper both for being "a full-fledged member of the propagandist group," indulging in "particular" rather than "general" feelings, and for allowing herself to be "overwhelmed" by "the demands of her audience for the sentimental treatment of the old subjects" and thus "gush with pathetic sentimentality." His comments further suggest that Watkins Harper's popularity—her acquiescence to the taste of her nineteenth-century public—was a sign of artistic weakness which "led her into errors of metrical construction."[16] Such evaluations dehistoricize Watkins Harper's poetry, ignoring the cultural work it performed. It is only recently that revisionist scholarship on sentimental culture has been able to place Watkins Harper's poetry in its proper cultural context that would help us understand her enormous popularity in the nineteenth century.

While a more developed discussion of sentimental culture will be presented in chapter 6, it may be noted here that sentimentality in America was an outgrowth of the ideology of separate spheres that sought to establish a strict dichotomy between the public male sphere and the domestic female one. Written largely by and for women, sentimentality took as its main subject such domestic themes as the family, the home, motherhood, and childhood. More specifically, according to Philip Fisher, sentimentality occupied itself with the socially weak and helpless whose plight was most often inscribed upon the body, rendering it a highly bodied form. Such a pitiable portrayal of the weak was designed to evoke feelings of pathos in the reader, to create, in Fisher's words, "an inward and empathetic emotional bond." Yet, if sentimentality initially seemed to locate itself within the private worlds of domesticity and feeling, in the hands of many writers—both white and black—it quickly extended itself to more public and political themes. Much sentimental literature, in fact, illustrates the extent to which the public comes to infiltrate and inhabit the domestic, thereby politicizing it, and conversely the degree to which metaphors of domesticity are appropriated to express the political, thereby domesticating it. Ultimately, sentimentality's demand that its readers respond with compassion and sympathy to the plight of the oppressed dictated, as Fisher has noted, a "public" extension of the reader's private self out toward the other.[17] It is important to note, however, that in the case of many black writers, Watkins Harper included, their reading public was conceptualized not merely as female but also as male; and at all times their goal remained the public one of stirring moral conscience in order to effect social change.

An analysis of one of Watkins Harper's earliest poems, "The Syrophenician Woman," may serve to illustrate some of the ways in which sentimental discourse is deployed in her poetry. The poem inaugurates her earliest volume of poetry available to us, *Poems on Miscellaneous Subjects*, first published by a Boston house, J. B. Yerrinton and Sons, in 1854 and then in a slightly enlarged edition by a Philadelphia printer, Merrihew and Thompson, in 1857 (there are no extant copies of *Forest Leaves* [1845], which Still has named as Watkins Harper's first published collection). The selection of "The Syrophenician Woman" as a first poem is revealing, since several other poems in the collection ("Eliza Harris," "The Dying Christian," and "Ethiopia") appear to have been written earlier. But "The Syrophenician Woman" is a highly appropriate inaugural choice as it encapsulates themes and techniques that recur throughout Watkins Harper's poetry and illustrates her early awareness of poetry as experimental activity.[18]

Cast as a narrative, Watkins Harper's poem focuses on the Syrophenician woman as the weak and oppressed subject whose plight is designed to evoke the reader's compassion. It is a revision of the New Testament story told in Mark 7 of the mother who begs Jesus to cast out unclean spirits from her daughter. The theme of the fallen woman is common in Watkins Harper's poetry, yet it is present here only indirectly—as the biblical source of poetic inspiration. Although the biblical verses might well resonate in the reader's ear, Watkins

Harper's poem actually depicts the mother's attempt to save her (ungendered) child from death by hunger. The poem universalizes the themes of hunger and poverty, but it also allows those readers who so choose to apply these circumstances to the specific historical experience of African Americans; and it remains possible that such experiences were evocative of Watkins Harper's own childhood as well. As in Mark's account, Watkins Harper's woman remonstrates with the Lord who at first fears "wast[ing] the children's bread" but then acknowledges her moral superiority. She thus takes on a preacherly function, becoming the voice of moral conscience itself. Finally, the poem also illustrates the basic thrust of Watkins Harper's narrational strategies. For if the poet initially positions the Syrophenician woman as a first-person narrator, in the third stanza she becomes a character in a third-person narrative, distanced from the reader and mediated by the interposition of an authoritative narrator who, in telling her story, seeks to stir the moral conscience of her readers just as the woman had Jesus': "With a purpose nought could move, / And the zeal of woman's love, / Down she knelt in anguish wild—" (5).

Like "The Syrophenician Woman," many of Watkins Harper's other antebellum poems also insist on a reconfiguration of the categories of public and private. Her poetry functions, then, on one level as "public" poetry that narrates multiple social histories through the characterization of representative types: slavery in "The Slave Mother" and "The Slave Auction," temperance in "The Drunkard's Child," poverty in "Died of Starvation," appropriate marriage choices in "Report" and "Advice to the Girls," female sexuality and the double standard in "The Contrast," and finally, Reconstruction racial uplift work in her poems of the 1870s. On occasion it may also represent, very indirectly, the "private" history of Watkins Harper's own life in which feelings stemming from the autobiographical facts of orphanhood or death find covert emotional expression as, for example, in "The Dying Christian": "She faded from our vision, / Like a thing of love and light; / But we feel she lives for ever, / A spirit pure and bright" (18).

Yet in Watkins Harper's poems the public-private dichotomy finds itself repeatedly deconstructed. Thus, if the public history of African Americans is seen most often to unfold within the "private" familial sphere, the poems' depiction of the slave mother's or the fugitive's wife's fate, for example, historicizes African-American family life and demonstrates the degree to which it is never "private." These characters are representative because history has inscribed itself on their bodies; yet Watkins Harper's narrational strategy is one that, unlike the sentimental discourse of the dominant cultural, seeks carefully to deemphasize the African-American body and focus instead on emotional response. In addition, as the poems' narrating persona, Watkins Harper empowered herself to comment upon their events, thus giving public voice to her own private opinions. And, in availing herself of contemporary public poetic conventions to portray her own private emotions, concerning orphanhood and death, for example, she was able to make public her deepest feelings while simultanenously veiling them behind the anonymity of conventional poetic discourse. Finally, just as other African-American writers sold their slave narratives or spiritual autobiographies after delivering antislavery speeches or sermons, so Watkins Harper sold her books of poems to the audiences that had come to hear her lecture. In this sense her poetry can be interpreted as autobiography, as an indirect account of an individual life.

If such poetry relied on sentimental discourse in order to call attention to the plight of the weak and the oppressed while refusing to scrutinize their bodily form, it was also designed in public performance to rationalize the speaker's body. To achieve these goals, Watkins Harper made use of an "aesthetics of restraint" whose chief "coping strategies," in Buell's words, were "narrative and meter"; in this aesthetics, emotion is contained "within formal limits conceded themselves to be limited."[19] Indeed, as critics like Frances Smith Foster, Maryemma Graham, and Patricia Liggins Hill have noted, Watkins Harper most often chose the narrative mode over the lyric, implicitly suggesting her desire to avoid the lyric, traditionally associated with the spontaneous expression of emotion.[20] In Watkins Harper's poetry, passion is subdued and rationalized by means of narrativization. In order to narrate different nineteenth-century "public" and "private" histories, Watkins Harper relied on highly conventional poetic forms just as she utilized highly traditional rhetorical modes in her public speaking; it was perhaps the very traditionalism of her verse that made publication with a mainstream press possible and ensured her popularity throughout the nineteenth century. Specifically, the poetic forms she appropriated were the ballad and the hymn, and in the Reconstruction period, the epic as well, all three of which are ancient poetic modes grounded in incontrovertible forms of narrative authority and designed to bring together in community the disparate elements of the audience.

In appropriating the ballad form, Watkins Harper turned to the work of such contemporary poets as Longfellow who had adapted the European ballad to American subjects. In its origins the ballad grew out of oral folk culture as the product of an anonymous author who voices the concerns of the community; in addition, in the British tradition the broadside ballad came into being as a vehicle for political expression. As she made use of the ballad form, Watkins Harper invoked its oral, communal, and political functions in order to recount diverse social histories embedded in nineteenth-century American culture at large. In these ballads, plots unfold around social themes as characters interact with one another, often by means of dialogue, while Watkins Harper as narrator intervenes on occasion to provide authorial judgments and reinforce the moral point of the poem, as, for example, in "The Slave Auction": "Ye who have laid your love to rest, / And wept above their lifeless clay, / Know not the anguish of that breast, / Whose lov'd are rudely torn away" (15). Rather than view such authorial commentary as a sign of excessive sermonizing and didacticism, we should recognize its important function as a vehicle that enabled Watkins Harper to authorize, and make public, her own personal opinions on social issues. It also encouraged her in other poems to become the poetic protagonist and speak out directly in her own voice as, for example, in "Free Labor": "I wear an easy garment, / O'er it no toiling slave / Wept tears of hopeless anguish, / In his passage to the grave" (35).

Watkins Harper's awareness of the need to temper personal political passion through narrative control is articulated in her poem "A Mother's Heroism," which depicts Elijah Lovejoy's mother's reaction to the news of her son's death: "It seemed as if a fearful storm / Swept wildly round her soul; / A moment, and her fragile form / Bent 'neath its fierce control." Watkins Harper's personal convictions about mob violence are here projected onto the poetic protagonist. But speech enables Lovejoy's mother to regain control of her emotions and consequently to articulate a narrative of liberty: "'Tis well! 'tis well!' the mother said, / 'That thus my child should die. / 'Tis well that, to his latest breath, / He plead for liberty; / Truth nerved him for the hour of death, / And taught him how to die'" (26). If narrative here is a means of emotional and physical containment, allowing Lovejoy's mother's "fragile form" ultimately to resist the "fearful storm's" "fierce control" in order to impose its own control, so is Watkins Harper's conventional use of the ballad's formal elements—the four-line stanza composed of alternating iambic tetrameter and trimeter lines, whose brevity makes metrical substitutions difficult, and an ABAB (or ABCB) rhyme scheme that need not be technically perfect. In its origin, the simplicity and regularity of this stanzaic form served the purposes of memorability and popular appeal in oral folk culture. In Watkins Harper's poems the conventionality and formal limitations of the ballad stanza further served the poet's imperative of emotional restraint.

Familiarity with the ballad enabled Watkins Harper to experiment with another verse form not usually encompassed under the rubric of poetry—the hymn, whose stanzaic form is identical to that of the ballad. For, like other contemporary Unitarians and abolitionists such as Lowell, Longfellow, and Whittier, Watkins Harper wrote poems that are hymnal in nature and intent. As public poetry designed for oral performance and to move the entire congregation, the hymn is grounded in a literary philosophy of simplicity and clarity. As Isaac Watts, the great English hymn writer, whose compositions were freely adapted by American Unitarians, admitted: "In many of these composures, I have just permitted my verse to rise above a flat and indolent style . . . because I would neither indulge any bold metaphors, nor admit of hard words, nor tempt the ignorant worshipper to sing without his understanding."[21]

It was Watkins Harper's genius to take the hymn form beyond religious exaltation to social appeal and, in the Reconstruction period, to political argument. Thus, "That Blessed Hope" speaks in traditional language of the poet's desire to join Christ in Heaven: "Help me, amidst this world of strife, / To long for Christ to reign, / That when He brings the crown of life, / I may that crown obtain!" (17). But other poems directly address current social and political conditions in a discourse that, unlike that of the ballad, does not center on representative types but rather is given to reflective commentary that will stir the readers' moral conscience and commit them to social action. "Ethiopia," for example, predicts God's deliverance of this nation's sons from slavery—"Redeemed from dust and freed from chains, / Her sons shall lift their eyes" (12)—while "Bible Defence of Slavery" specifically attacks the American churches' support of slavery and the hypocrisy of their missionary efforts abroad: "Oh! when ye pray for heathen lands, / And plead for their dark shores, / Remember Slavery's cruel hands / Make heathens at your doors!" (9). If the hymn verse in its simplicity and regularity was designed, like the ballad, to appeal to popular understanding, it also enabled Watkins Harper once again to contain her own political passion within formal limits and thereby legitimate the radicalness of her political stance.

Watkins Harper's poems also appeared, of course, in printed form, thus allowing her to abstract herself from the public's gaze and invert that strategy of looking away adopted by Greenfield's audience in order to appreciate her music as "sounds right sweet." Published singly in newspapers, the poems were also brought together in book form, making it possible to read the poetic volume as a continuous narrative and seek out links between the poems. Although we have no way of knowing to what extent Watkins Harper was able to control her own publication process, we may nonetheless speculate as to how the sequence of poems in each volume might add to our understanding of both her social ideology and her methods of appealing to contemporary audiences. Like the collected volumes of Lydia Sigourney and other contemporary white women poets, none of Watkins Harper's volumes may be said to form a progressive linear narrative; instead, they appear to resist strict organization. But the poems within each volume, as well as from volume to volume, are unified by a common ethos— evangelical Unitarianism—and by the recurrent emergence of related themes; moreover, the positioning of the first and last poems of each volume as well as the additions made from edition to edition function as a kind of cultural statement.

If there is a particular structural principle operative in Watkins Harper's two surviving antebellum collections of poems, I suggest that it is a framing device in which the first and last sets of poems tend to constellate around a particular topic, or in which the last poems function as a kind of counterweight to the first. Thus, the initial and final poems of the 1854 *Poems on Miscellaneous Subjects* focus for the most part on the topic of slavery, while those of the central section are concerned with multiple themes—death, temperance, marriage, female sexuality, and so forth. Such a framing device tends to foreground the material of the frame itself rather than that which is placed inside it. In this instance it embeds within the frame some of Watkins Harper's most personal concerns—death, orphanhood, the social construction of women's sexual and marital roles—allowing these to recede somewhat from the reader's line of vision. But it also points to the presence of a common thread that unites all these social issues—the perversion of power relations between strong and weak, whether between master and slave, man and woman, or rich and poor—of which slavery remained for Watkins

Harper the most egregious. The dominance of slavery in Watkins Harper's thinking is further reinforced by the addition of a new group of poems at the end of her 1857 edition of *Poems on Miscellaneous Subjects*, almost all of which focus on this one topic—"The Tennessee Hero," "Free Labor," "Lines," "The Dismissal of Tyng," and "The Slave Mother (A Tale of the Ohio)."

The very last poems of both the 1854 and 1857 editions of *Poems on Miscellaneous Subjects*, however, explicitly seek to link the social oppression of women within the "private" sphere to larger political issues. They portray women whose lives are constrained, even destroyed, by male political action, be it American slavery or other forms of bondage. Thus, "Eva's Farewell," a retelling of the death of Stowe's Eva, who refuses to live any longer within the context of Southern slavery, concludes the 1854 edition, while "The Slave Mother (A Tale of the Ohio)," a poetic account of Margaret Garner's murder of her child in Ohio in 1856, is appended to the 1857 edition. Finally, two biblical poems, "Rizpah, the Daughter of Ai" and "Ruth and Naomi," complete the 1857 volume. If "Ruth and Naomi" recounts the well-known story of female friendship in which the widowed Naomi exiles herself from the land of Moab and returns to Bethlehem accompanied by her faithful daughter-in-law Ruth, "Rizpah, the Daughter of Ai" narrates a much less familiar story. Turning to the biblical account of Joshua's conquest of Canaan, it retells from the woman's point of view Rizpah's sorrow over David's sacrifice of her sons to the Gibeonites as a penance for Saul's betrayal. All four poems thus illustrate how from biblical times to the present women within the supposedly protected domestic sphere have been made to suffer as a consequence of male political actions.

Watkins Harper's poems, as we have noted, occasionally served as accompaniments to her speeches. Indeed, in Watkins Harper's canon verse and lectures cannot be considered isolated aesthetic objects that exist separately from one another but must be viewed as coextensive not only with each other but with her essays and fiction as well. Poems and prose interact continuously as social concerns find their way equally, and often in exact detail, into both forms. As Frances Foster has shown, for example, Watkins Harper's description of "the stain of blood and tears upon the warp and woof" of cloth made by slave labor is woven into both her poem "Free Labor" and her 1855 "Free Labor Movement" speech; and her antebellum praise of Moses in the essay "Our Greatest Want"—"I like the character of Moses"—is later developed in her postbellum epic.[22] Aunt Chloe's Reconstruction political efforts in "Sketches of Southern Life" are echoed by the fictional character of Aunt Linda in *Iola Leroy* (1892), just as the poetic hero's martyrdom in "A Story of the Rebellion" is embodied in the slave Tom in the same novel. Watkins Harper's appeal to the "women of America" to demand justice for the Negro in her 1892 speech "Woman's Political Future" is reiterated in the 1895 poem "An Appeal to My Countrywomen," and the 1895 poem "Only a Word" is actually embedded in a later essay, "True and False

Politeness" (1898). Throughout the volumes, poems on slavery and temperance make concrete the abstract propositions set forth in the speeches and essays. And finally, Watkins Harper's belief in the redemptive power of Jesus Christ reverberates as a constant theme in all her writings, poetry and prose.

Indeed, Watkins Harper's speeches, much like her poetry, are suffused with a Unitarian conviction in the power of the spoken word to bring about social change by elevating the moral conscience of whites and building character among her own people. To effect such transformations, Watkins Harper relied on what Hugh Blair termed the eloquence of the pulpit rather than that of popular assemblies favored by Shadd Cary. Indeed, a review of an 1866 speech analogized Watkins Harper's lecturing platform to the pulpit, commenting that "she *felt* that she had been ordained to this ministry—for the service of the pulpit is not the only ministry that God had appointed" (*CR*, Sept. 15, 1866). A truly popular form of oratory because it must appeal to the masses, the eloquence of the pulpit is directed at the heart. But if it allows for "warm and glowing expressions" and the display of "the most passionate figures of Speech," it must nonetheless preserve the gravity, simplicity, and dignity of expression required by its subject.[23] Ignoring the shift in American oratory toward democratic eloquence and the more modern *style coupé*, Watkins Harper fashioned her rhetorical style by turning to models of classical rhetoric, in particular the Ciceronian *style périodique* characterized by flowing periodic structures, convoluted syntactic constructions, the accumulation of modifiers, parallelisms, and antitheses, and the use of anaphora, hyperbole, extended metaphors, and images.[24]

For Watkins Harper it was perhaps the very traditionalism of this rhetorical style that, like the conventionality of her poetic form, made it so useful to her. Highly familiar to many in her audience, having been employed to great advantage in Sumner's 1856 "The Crime against Kansas" speech, for example, this style functioned as a marker of social status, suggesting the presence of a well-educated and cultured mind. As such, it contrasts sharply with Truth's more "modern" ethnic discourse. But in its very traditionalism it fulfilled an authenticating role similar to Douglass's use of classical rhetoric in his 1845 *Narrative*, which led Garrison to declare that "compressed into it is a whole Alexandrian library of thought, feeling and sentiment."[25] Even more to Watkins Harper's purposes, this form of oratory offered her audiences the necessary ethical proof that, in Blair's words, "the Preacher himself [is] a good man."[26] The ability to advance such proof to her audience was of critical importance to Watkins Harper, who, in an early essay/speech published in *Poems on Miscellaneous Subjects*, "The Colored People in America," spoke of the need to accomplish the goals of racial uplift so "that ere long we may present [ourselves] to the admiring gaze of those who wish us well . . ." (55).

The goal of Watkins Harper's public speaking was quite simply the recreation of the American nation as a local place for all African Americans, necessitating the abolition of slavery, the achievement of racial uplift, the building of character in her people, and in the 1860s the successful conclusion of the Civil War. Given the lack of historical evidence to date, it is difficult to assess to what extent this social agenda might have been influenced by that of her uncle and cousin. But it is evident that all three shared the same broad principles of racial uplift that stressed the incompatibility between slavery and Christianity, condemned the indifference of individual blacks to social activism, and insisted on the importance of education. In her antebellum speeches, the issue of the social role of black women is raised infrequently and only then within these broader contexts. Somewhat paradoxically, Watkins Harper's program seems to have been more at odds with that of William J. Watkins, who, as a close associate of Frederick Douglass, frequently criticized white abolitionism, actively supported the Free Soil and Republican parties, and in the early 1860s backed Haitian emigration, than with the agenda of the older William Watkins, whose social activism remained firmly grounded in a fundamentally Christian vision.[27]

Indeed, as in her poetry Watkins Harper sought in her speeches to place her ideas within a framework of rational Christian belief and to articulate them by means of logical exposition. In an early lecture entitled "Christianity," delivered in Boston in September 1854 and published at the end of *Poems on Miscellaneous Subjects*, Watkins Harper declared Christianity to be a "system claiming God for its author, and the welfare of man for its object" and so "uniform" that the "speculative researches" of philosophy and science must acknowledge her preeminence (48). Christianity disseminates her claims by means of the Word of God, which "is in harmony with that adaptation of means to ends which pervades creation" (51). Emulating her creator, Watkins Harper insisted that her speeches likewise functioned as an adaptation of means to ends. Her means were, as we saw, classical oratory whose potential excessive energy is channeled by means of rational exposition. Thus, rather than resort to the narration of personal experience to build her argument as did Truth and even Shadd Cary, Watkins Harper effaced herself from her speeches, appealing instead to impersonal proofs. In particular, she relied on argument by definition, most especially in her openers, presenting from the outset as unarguable fact what was in reality personal interpretation; to the definition of Christianity cited earlier we may note as well the opening statement in her address to the Fourth Anniversary of the New York City Anti-Slavery Society: "The law of liberty is the law of God, and is antecedent to all human legislation" (*NASS* May 23, 1857).

To buttress such generalizations, Watkins Harper resorted to accumulated illustration, detailing, for example, the personal degradation caused by slavery as it tears families apart and reduces slave mothers to utter helplessness. Yet, further to reinforce her narrative authority, she determinedly moved beyond the exposition of mere individual circumstance to adopt a broader historical and sociological perspective, to argue her case not by individual or personal example, but by historical analogy, both biblical and secular. Thus, her address at the Fourth Anniversary of the New York Anti-Slavery Society as well as the one at the

Twenty-Fifth Annual Meeting of the American Anti-Slavery Society both begin with a geographic survey of the United States that indicts state after state for its protection of slavery and perversion of freedom, respectively; they then proceed to a historical investigation that in the first instance demonstrates the extent to which other nations—Austria, Great Britain, France—protect the slave, and in the second argues for the importance of social reform movements throughout history, adducing in particular the beginnings of Christianity and the Protestant Reformation as examples (*NASS*, May 23, 1857; *NASS*, May 22, 1858). Finally, in a letter to the *Christian Recorder* written in the thick of the Civil War Watkins Harper worried about America's lack of "contrition for the wrongs of the Indian or the outrages of the negro" and pointed to the fates of Egypt and Babylon as warnings to the nation: "This lesson she should have learned amid the wrecks of ancient empires, buried beneath the weight of their crimes" (Sept. 27, 1862).

Yet undergirding Watkins Harper's sweeping moral vision of universal freedom lay her awareness of the raw economic issues surrounding slavery, giving rise, for example, to a speech in defense of the free labor movement in which she maintained that "our moral influence against slavery must be weakened, our testimony diluted if . . . we are constantly demanding rice from the swamps, cotton from the plantations and sugar from the deadly mills . . ." (*Frederick Douglass' Paper*, June 29, 1855). Such an awareness of economic issues also provided the framework for Watkins Harper's racial uplift program. In a letter to the *Anti-Slavery Bugle*, dated July 9, 1859, that describes a lecture tour of the Midwest, she noted the number of blacks engaged in productive farming in these states and proceeded to argue that "better political economy" dictated that they be educated and uplifted rather than oppressed and treated like criminals. Indeed, Watkins Harper's hope for blacks lay in their establishment of a network of social institutions dedicated to racial uplift—schools, newspapers, churches ("The Colored People in America," 54–55). Not the least important was the building of strong homes and the female influence that would emanate from them. To accomplish these goals, what is needed is not "gold, or intellect, but more soul, more unselfishness, earnestness, and sterling integrity" (*ASB*, April 23, 1859)—the development of character that will ultimately result in social change: "To teach our people how to build up a character for themselves—a character that will challenge respect in spite of opposition and prejudice; to develop their own souls, intellect and genius, and thus verify their credentials, is some of the very best anti-slavery work that can be done in this country" (*ASB*, Sept. 29, 1860).

The early 1860s found Watkins Harper delivering lectures chiefly on the topic of the Civil War in which her economic arguments became increasingly foregrounded. If she saw the war in biblical terms as a necessary punishment inflicted by God on a proud nation, she was also aware of how that nation had made war inevitable by founding itself on a document that had given a "fatal permission," economically motivated, to slavery (*Lib*, March 3, 1865). In turn, Watkins Harper marshaled economic arguments of her own in support of black Reconstruction. The American soil is the birthright of all African Americans since they have enriched it with their toil. As a consequence, Lincoln's colonization scheme is mere political expediency; in fact, a more persuasive economic argument is that no nation, the United States included, can afford "to part with four millions of its laboring population" (*CR*, Sept. 27, 1862). The achievement of postwar Reconstruction can be brought about only by giving the black man the elective franchise to ensure his independence from the old slaveholding class (*Lib*, March 3, 1865) and, most radically, by forging a labor alliance "between the poor white men and the poor black men of the South" (*Lib*, Aug. 11, 1865).

Although a number of Watkins Harper's lectures were printed at the end of her volumes of poetry, most were published primarily in white antislavery newspapers, most notably the *Liberator*, the *National Anti-Slavery Standard*, and the *Anti-Slavery Bugle*, whose readers were both black and white, or in black organs, the *Christian Recorder* and the *Anglo-African Magazine*, which addressed themselves specifically to an African-American readership. The effects of such print dissemination were twofold. On the one hand it ensured that the social content of Watkins Harper's speeches would reach a much larger audience than that of a mere lecture hall. On the other hand it also led Watkins Harper to participate in that general trend toward the institutionalization of oratory that occurred toward the end of the antebellum period and enabled the expansion of a new professional arena for women—both black and white—in the postbellum era.[28]

If the influence of William Watkins and William J. Watkins on Watkins Harper's antislavery activity remains unclear, written testimony has amply documented the role of the famous black abolitionist lecturer Charles Lenox Remond in shaping the antislavery career of his sister, Sarah Parker Remond. Sarah Parker Remond was born in 1826 into one of the most prosperous black families of Salem, Massachusetts. Her father, John Remond, had emigrated from Curaçao late in the eighteenth century and, after a stay in Boston where he met and married his wife Nancy, settled in Salem, where he went into business as a barber, hairdresser, caterer, and trader. Both John and Nancy Remond were active in the antislavery movement as members of the Massachusetts Anti-Slavery Society and other local organizations, as supporters of Garrison, and as part of that larger circle of black abolitionists that drew together members of the African-American elite residing in the major cities of the northeastern and Atlantic seaboard states. In 1838 their eldest son, Charles, became an agent for the Massachusetts Anti-Slavery Society and one of the earliest black abolitionist lecturers, touring the northeastern United States between 1838 and 1840, and England in 1840–41.[29] In addition to advocating the cause of the slave, Charles Remond became a passionate defender of women's activities in the public sphere of abolitionism. Financed by several of the local New England female antislavery societies that made his trip to England possible, he collected contributions from British women abolitionists for the annual Christmas bazaar of the Boston Female Anti-Slavery Society. Even more importantly, when the World's Anti-Slavery Convention held in London in 1840 refused to accept women delegates, Charles Remond protested in the strongest of terms: "In the name of heaven, and in the name of the bleeding, dying slave, I ask if I shall scruple the propriety of female action, of whatever kind or description. I trust not—I hope not—I pray not."[30]

It is not surprising that Sarah Parker Remond, reared in such an antislavery household, should herself have become an active abolitionist. She was a member of the Salem Female, Essex County, and Massachusetts Anti-Slavery Societies and, in 1856, was appointed an agent of the American Anti-Slavery Society. In an autobiographical essay, published in London in 1861, she indirectly attributed her antislavery interest to her brother Charles: "My eldest brother, early in the conflict, publicly advocated the cause of his enslaved countrymen, and from my earliest days, until I left the States, fifteen months since, I have attended the public meetings of the abolitionists." In 1857, "urged by a few friends to speak in public" but worried "that I was in need of a good English education," Remond was finally convinced to join a group of Garrisonian antislavery lecturers that included her brother, and spent 1857 and 1858 lecturing throughout New England and in New York State.[31] In 1858 she also attended the annual women's rights convention in New York City.[32] Finally, in September of the same year Remond decided to follow in her brother's earlier footsteps and carry the antislavery cause to England. The reasons for her decision were multiple. If, on the one hand, Remond was motivated by U.S. attempts to legalize the slave trade, she was also impelled by more personal reasons—"an intense desire to visit England, that I might for a time enjoy freedom" (286) coupled with a firm determination "to depend upon myself."[33]

Remond's autobiographical sketch enables us to gain greater insights into her emotional and psychological makeup than was possible in Watkins Harper's case. Commissioned by Matthew Davenport Hill for a collection of essays, entitled *Our Exemplars, Poor and Rich,* and designed to portray "the rise and progress to wealth and eminence of men who, by the exercise of their own powers of mind and body, have risen from the humbler classes" (vii), Remond's sketch makes public—in brief glimpses at least—the racial anxiety suffered by upper-class black women that also pervades the more private writings of Charlotte Forten. In her essay Remond carefully positions herself as a member of the upper-class black population of Salem and Newport that has thoroughly assimilated fundamental American virtues: "The coloured population was of an elevated character, and for industry, morality, and native intellect, would compare favourably with any class in the community" (282). In particular, her description of her home upbringing, grounded in the dominant ideology of domestic economy, suggests, much as Stewart's writings did, the forging of a cultural alliance between black and white women of the middle class: "We were all trained to habits of industry, with a thorough knowledge of those domestic duties which particularly mark the genuine New England woman" (276).

Given such an elite concept of self, Remond by her own admission was fully unprepared for the racial discrimination to which she was repeatedly subjected in the schools of Salem and Newport as well as in a variety of public places—hotels, vehicles of transportation, places of amusement: "In joy or sorrow, whether pursuing the pleasures or business of life, it [prejudice against colour] has thrust itself, like a huge sphinx, darkening my pathway, and, at times, almost overwhelming the soul constantly called to meet such a conflict" (277). Indeed, Remond's narrative suggests her initial expectation that membership in an elite class should have provided her protection from the sphinx of racial hostility and bitter disappointment that it did not. From this particular perspective the narrative further articulates Remond's deeply held conviction that the prejudice experienced by upper-class blacks is all the more cruel because it is expressed by members of one elite toward those of another: "The more intelligence and refinement they [proslavery men and women] possess, the more liable they are to insult. The chivalry of America seems to take immense satisfaction in insulting those who will feel it the most keenly" (281). In the aftermath of such public racial humiliation, the private pleasures of reading and music functioned, at least temporarily, as a welcome antidote. But, influenced by her mother's enthusiasm for, and her brother's activity in, Garrisonian abolitionism, Remond soon found herself drawn to antislavery work. Her emergence into the public sphere of abolitionism was motivated all the more by her acute awareness, similar to that of Shadd Cary and Watkins Harper, of the impact of the slave laws on the free black population and by a recognition that, ultimately, class status could not shield her from the fact of racial difference: "The laws which emanate from the compromises of the constitution, as the Fugitive Slave Law, and the Dred Scott decision, are most keenly felt by all the coloured race" (283).

History has left us an extensive record of Remond's antislavery lectures in Great Britain, which were reported in such widely distributed abolitionist newspapers as the *Liberator* and *Frederick Douglass' Paper* in the United States and the *Anti-Slavery Advocate* in Great Britain as well as in local British newspapers like the *Warrington Times* and *Standard*, the *Manchester Weekly Times* and *Examiner*, the *Leeds Intelligencer* and *Mercury*, the *Scotsman*, and the *Derbyshire Courier*. These reports make evident that, if American audiences were unused to female lecturers, British ones were even more so. Indeed, as observed by Prince, the constraints on female activities in the public sphere, even when these were specifically dedicated to moral and benevolent reform, were much greater for British women than for their American counterparts. Thus, when Remond lectured to women's groups such as the Dublin Ladies' Anti-Slavery Society or the Edinburgh Ladies' Emancipation Society, the meetings were chaired by men

Sarah Parker Remond. Circa 1865. Courtesy Peabody Essex Museum, Salem Massachusetts.

while the women sat silently on the platform. Furthermore, before Remond actually delivered her speech, the chairman often felt impelled, as had Robert Gaskell, the mayor of Warrington, to explain the presence of a female lecturer: "However common this might be on the other side of the water, it was an uncommon thing in this country. And perhaps it was as it ought to be. We in England all looked to the past—we all looked to antiquity, and prided ourselves on the habits of the past; and it had not been a habit to admit ladies prominently into public." Consequently, these men often deemed it necessary to defend Remond against the charge of female impropriety: "He did not think himself, however, there was anything, the slightest, approaching to indecorousness in a lady addressing her remarks to the public" (*Lib*, March 11, 1859).

In the mind of the well-known British abolitionist George Thompson, charges of female impropriety could readily be overcome and permission for women to lecture granted by means of a reconceptualization of antislavery work that *de*-publicized it, incorporating it into the "private" sphere of sentimental culture whereby woman's essential moral nature dictated her wholehearted concern for the slave. Thus, according to Thompson, if "some present might think it a strange thing that a woman should stand up in public to speak on the subject of slavery," it must be remembered that "men were too much engaged in secular occupations to give more than an occasional attention to the wrongs of the slave; but when a woman became interested, her whole soul was absorbed in the subject, and she was constant, in season and out of season, in her efforts for the redemption of the oppressed" (*ASA*, July 1, 1859).

Despite Thompson's sentimentalization of women's antislavery activity, Remond's lecturing style appears to have been forged largely, although not fully, outside of this cultural framework. A review of one of her early speeches in Warrington characterized Remond's oratory as a "calm and deliberate appeal to the understanding of her auditors without any attempt to captivate the imagination" (*WStandard*, Jan. 29, 1859); another report of a later speech praised her "calmness of manner" and "womanly dignity," asserting that the very absence of "excitement in her tone [and] exaggeration in her language" made it possible for her to reach "the understandings and the hearts of those before her the more effectually on this account" (*ASA*, Oct. 1, 1859). Such an interpretation of Remond's oratorical strategy as calm and rational might well have corresponded to her actual mode of presentation. Indeed, the few newspaper accounts that gave full reports of Remond's lectures in the first person—one in the September 17, 1859 issue of the *Manchester Weekly Times*, another in the November 1, 1859 issue of the *Anti-Slavery Advocate*—indicate no greater degree of rhetorical hyberbole or pathos. Consequently, it is tempting to theorize that, in contrast to Watkins Harper, and more like Shadd Cary, Remond might well have been part of that midcentury oratorical shift from the more elaborate *style périodique* to the terser *style coupé*. At the same time we may also want to speculate that, if Watkins Harper's oratory was grounded in what Hugh Blair termed the eloquence of the pulpit and Shadd Cary's in that of popular assembly, Remond's was based on the eloquence of the bar. According to Blair, the object of such oratory is conviction rather than persuasion: "It is not the Speaker's business to persuade the Judges to what is good or useful, but to show them what is just and true; and, of course, it is chiefly, or solely, to the understanding that his Eloquence is addressed." To accomplish this goal the orator must avoid adopting a "high vehement tone" and must refrain from giving his imagination too great a scope; rather, his language must be "sober and chastened," "calm and temperate," and the structure of his speech should be built upon a clear debating method and close argumentative reasoning.[34]

It is true, however, that on occasion, particularly in the early part of her tour, Remond moved beyond attempts to "show . . . what is just and true" in order to "persuade . . . to what is good or useful." Such an oratorical impulse had the effect of undercutting the rhetoric of rationality that characterized the majority of her lectures and of opening up a discursive space from which Remond could deploy a language of pathos and sentimentality in order to achieve different but complementary goals. At such moments Remond shifted from an exposition of the socioeconomic facts of slavery to a pathetic narration of the story of an individualized, though most often anonymous, slave woman in a highly sentimental language. Following the conventions of sentimentality, these stories are grounded in domestic and familial plots that center on a victimized heroine and invite the audience to empathize with her plight; thus, pathetic accounts of the tragic destiny of female slaves find their way into several of Remond's early speeches. Given the British public's familiarity with such sentimental discourse through the novels of Dickens or even Henry Mayhew's sociological writings about the London poor, it would appear that Remond's sentimental narratives did elicit a tremendous emotional response from a sizable segment of her audience.

The most detailed of such sentimental accounts was perhaps one offered by Robert Gaskell by way of concluding Remond's second Warrington speech. Ostensibly a true story taken from an American newspaper, it rehearses the typical "tragic mulatta" plot in which a beautiful young girl is brought up as the mistress of her slaveholding father's house only to discover that her mother was in fact a slave, that she is consequently tainted by black blood and is to be sold into slavery to pay off her father's debts; she and her white lover despair, but, while most tragic mulatta plots end with the death of the heroine, Gaskell's account assured the audience of a "happy termination" in which the lovers manage to escape to Canada (*WStandard*, Feb. 5, 1859). Such a sentimental story was calculated in particular to move the female members of Remond's audience who could readily identify with the heroine and whose "whole soul," to repeat Thompson's words, would as a consequence become "absorbed in the subject, and [who would be] constant, in season and out of season, in [their] efforts for the redemption of the oppressed."

On occasion Remond herself narrated similar sentimental accounts of the tragic destinies of slave women. Even when she opened her lectures by asserting that she would abide by "unquestionable facts instead of personal statements" (*WTimes*, Feb. 2, 1859), these facts often become enmeshed in both the personal and the pathetic. For example, in an early speech Remond recounted the story of the escaped slave Margaret Garner, who chose to kill her three-year-old daughter rather than allow her to be remanded into slavery (*WTimes*, Jan. 29, 1859). In later lectures she focused, as Gaskell had done, on the figure of the mulatta whose white inheritance commands a high price on the auction block: "The lecturer read an affecting account of the sale by auction of a woman who was recommended on account of her being undistinguishable by complexion from the white race, for her unsullied virtue, her personal beauty, and her elevated piety, and who, for these reasons, brought a high price that she might become the mistress of some depraved monster" (*ASA*, July 1, 1859). Such an account, delivered by Remond and reported by a British newspaperman, possesses all the quality of a fictional story narrated in the common currency of sentimental language. And, in fact, one of the most interesting aspects of Remond's reliance on sentimental culture in her speeches is her appeal to fictional characters—particuarly those of

Uncle Tom's Cabin—to authenticate the historical lives of slave women. If she does mention Topsy and Eliza, it is to Cassy that Remond turns most especially as the emblem of those slave women whose "higher natures . . . feel and writhe under their intolerable injuries" (*ASA*, Sept. 1, 1859). Like other black women in the antislavery movement—Harriet Jacobs in particular—Remond was well aware of the ways in which the language of sentimental fiction could help shape feminist-abolitionist discourse.

It is important to note, however, that the published versions of Remond's speeches were dictated, and to a certain extent constrained, by the conventions of British journalism at midcentury. Following these conventions, the speeches of the nation's most prominent political leaders were faithfully transcribed and reprinted verbatim in newspapers with a minimum of commentary or interpretation. In contrast, those of lesser spokespersons or of foreign dignitaries tended to be summarized by the reporter in third-person accounts that permitted a modicum of editorializing and commentary.[35] The newspaper reports of Remond's lectures fall, with few exceptions, into the latter category; as a result, we have no way of ascertaining their absolute accuracy and cannot treat them as Remond's own text. In fact, the shift from verbatim reporting in first-person direct discourse to summary reporting in third-person indirect or free indirect discourse marks a shift from imitation to representation; and, to the extent that the reporter in this process comes to impose his own imprimatur on the account, what is increasingly at stake is not only the accuracy of the reporting but also the expressive qualities characteristic of the speaker. What results, then, is the opening up of a representational gap between the lecture as given and as reported; and it is in this gap that we may locate the shift from Remond's authorial control to that of the reporter in his efforts to represent and contextualize Remond and her antislavery work to his readers.

A close reading of British newspaper coverage of Remond's speeches suggests a concerted attempt by reporters to shape these accounts to conform to their own stated perception of the speaker. Thus, interestingly enough, what might have "captivated the imagination" or evoked pathos in Remond's lectures is frequently condensed or even omitted. For example, in the same newspaper account in which women's right to public speaking is defended as decorous, the reporter deliberately brackets Remond's detailing of the horrors of slavery: "She . . . would read the audience a letter she had received, telling of the horrors of slavery. (The letter was then read by the lady, the writer describing various heart-rending scenes, with great force)" (*WStandard*, Feb. 5, 1859). In still other reports the contents of Remond's speeches are so condensed by means of indirect discourse or the passive voice that little affective value is retained: "Miss Remond proceeded to detail a number of interesting cases of the escape of slaves" (*ASA*, Sept. 1, 1859); "Deep regret was expressed that England had ever given up the right of search, as the African slave trade was fast reviving in consequence" (*Manchester Examiner*, Sept. 21, 1859). It is difficult to ascertain exactly why British journalists chose to abbreviate the sentimental and pathetic elements in Remond's speeches so severely. It is quite possible that they might have felt highly uncomfortable with the presence of a woman speaker. More particularly, even though sentimentality was associated with femininity, they might have felt some anxiety over its bodied nature and thus chosen to underplay, bracket, or even elide it altogther.

In fact, sentimental discourse was by no means the major rhetorical mode of Remond's lectures. We may wonder whether Remond herself did not come to believe that it was too bodied a form and that too great a reliance on it might encourage her audience to confuse her with the slave victim of the pathetic domestic plot. Thus, as her tour progressed Remond seems to have turned increasingly to rhetorical strategies that relied on the exposition of socioeconomic facts and the development of analytical argument. Such strategies were not unlike those of the British sociologist Henry Mayhew, whose contemporary writings about the London poor were initiated within a "sentimental moral frame" but then evolved into a form of sociological analysis "close to the analysis of capitalism Marx was developing."[36]

In the process, however, Remond needed to negotiate with her audience not only issues of race and gender but also those of class. Indeed, if Remond increasingly adopted a rhetorical strategy of "calmness of manner" at the expense of "excitement of tone," this decision might well have been dictated by her need to work out a highly complex set of social relations between herself and her audience. Not only was Remond a black woman speaking to promiscuous assemblies of whites; she was also a member of a social elite whose remarks were frequently addressed to working-class groups. Although one of the abolitionists' transatlantic strategies was to promote an ideological alliance between black American slaves and white British workers based on an analogy of wage labor to slavery, racial and class differences between Remond and her audience could not so easily be erased. The cultural contradictions that emerged as an upper-class African-American woman lectured from a position of greater intellectual knowledge to a white working-class audience were not readily reconcilable. It is quite possible that Remond's working-class audience resented her class status given that, in the words of one of her sponsors, she "was now as they saw—an educated woman— well read in English literature and the English poets" (*Lib*, March 11, 1859), and consequently asserted its racial superiority by construing her as a victimized tragic mulatta or a grotesque black body. To avoid the surfacing of such social tensions that might well have resulted in the loss of her audience's sympathy, it is understandable that Remond should have turned increasingly to the discourses of the social sciences and their accompanying rhetoric of rational exposition and argument.

In her first speech in Great Britain, Remond rationalized her lecture tour by couching it in terms of a necessary project of black self-representation. Much like the editors of *Freedom's Journal* and the *North Star*, who claimed, respectively, that "we wish to plead our own cause. . . . Too long has the publick been deceived by misrepresentations" (March 16, 1827) and "it is evident we must be our own representatives and advocates, not exclusively but peculiarly" (Dec. 3, 1847), Remond asserted that "[since blacks] were misrepresented by the American press . . . that was one reason why they were bound to represent themselves" (*WTimes*, Jan. 29, 1859). In particular, Remond sought to legitimate her own speaking role in Britain by conceptualizing herself not only as the "representative also of that body of abolitionists in the United States, reproachfully called Garrisonians" but more importantly as the "representative in the first place of four millions of human beings held in slavery in a land boasting of its freedom—of 400,000 persons of colour nominally free, but treated worse than criminals" (*ASA*, July 1, 1859). To speak on behalf of her race and plead the truth of its "cause," Remond, as we have speculated, adopted a rhetoric of rationality, constituting herself as "advocate" and her audience as a "jury" that would "judge coolly, justly and impartially on a subject so artfully slurred over and misrepresented by interested parties . . . and give a verdict according to their conscience" (*ASA*, April 2, 1859). Remond's firm belief in the power of legal discourse to shift allegiances and sway convictions is evidenced in her brief but telling portrayal of Daniel Webster as a highly respected New England statesman who managed to persuade a reluctant people to obey the Fugitive Slave Law by convincing them that "the Alleghanies were higher than the other mountains, so this law was ranged higher than the feelings of common men" (*WStandard*, Feb. 5, 1859).

The newspaper reports of Remond's lectures suggest that, in constituting herself as an advocate pleading the cause of her own people and the reconstitution of the American nation as an African-American local place Remond relied above all on a careful narration of the facts of American slavery and prejudice in order to make her case to the British people. Unlike Sojourner Truth but much like Watkins Harper, Remond in her speeches resisted appealing to the authority of personal experience, turning instead to the impersonal proofs offered by history. As we have speculated, however, Remond rejected the use of that grandiloquent Ciceronian rhetoric characteristic of Watkins Harper's oratory in favor of the terser and more deliberate style so admired by British journalists. Her rhetorical strategy was, then, to convince her public of the evil of racism and slavery by means of a sheer accumulation of facts. Indeed, in one of her earliest lectures Remond self-reflectively asserted her preference for "unquestionable facts instead of personal statements" (*WTimes*, Feb. 5, 1859). Other speeches equally appear to construct themselves around a logical exposition of the causes, facts, and consequences of American racism. An early Warrington lecture, for example, makes its case first by analyzing the institutions that oppress African Americans (the courts of law, the federal government, the churches), then by demonstrating their pernicious effect on the black population (free blacks, slaves in general, slave mothers in particular), and lastly by suggesting possible means of redress to be taken by the British people (*WTimes*, Jan. 29, 1859). A later speech begins by rehearsing the history of slavery in America, then proceeds to address the present conditions of slaves in the South and of free blacks in the North before turning to analyze once again those institutions that collude with the slave system—the churches, the press, the armed forces—and finally to call on the British to take action (*ASA*, Nov. 1, 1859).

Remond was well aware, of course, that it would be difficult to persuade many Britishers, whose textile manufactures depended on U.S. raw materials produced by slave labor, that their best economic self-interest dictated the abolition of American slavery. Indeed, several of her lectures indicate that she understood the increasing globalization of industrial manufacturing and commodity capitalism as well as Martin Delany and that she consequently needed to forge a set of arguments that would convince the British laborer to work for the abolition of slavery. Acknowledging that in the cities of Manchester and Liverpool "she had found something that approximated more to the pro-slavery spirit of America" (*ASA*, Nov. 1, 1859), Remond sought to counter the propaganda disseminated by visiting slaveholders who "made cotton growing and the question of the supply of cotton the ground of their appeal to selfish and commercial interests" (*ASA*, April 2, 1859). In a speech given in Manchester in September 1859, Remond reminded her audience that the slave cotton picker is never rewarded for his labor. This fact is further developed in an 1862 address delivered before the International Congress of Charities, Correction and Philanthropy, in which Remond pointed to a double connection between American slave labor and British free labor. Indeed, despite the three thousand miles of ocean that lie between the two groups, "almost personal relations" exist between them, as British workers have accepted to "manufacture the material which the slaves have produced."[37] Yet if these same British workers may be accused of profiting from slave labor, they are equally entrapped in the slave system since the wages they receive are approximately one-seventh of the profit the manufacturer makes from the cotton trade. The conclusion of Remond's argument, never explicitly stated, is to suggest the analogous position of American slave and British wage worker in the newly globalized system of commodity capitalism.

Remond could not elaborate upon these issues in any greater detail without engaging in a sustained critique of the economic system upon which the wealth of her host country was based. In her speeches, her economic arguments thus remained underdeveloped and were amplified by moral arguments more in keeping with the agenda of other Garrisonian abolitionists lecturing abroad.[38] From this perspective Remond's narration of the facts of slavery was designed, in Blair's words, not so much "to persuade the Judges to what is good or useful, but to show them what is just and true." Through factual enumeration, Remond hoped to convince her British audiences of the absolute truth of the injustice of American slavery and thus lead them to exert all the force of their moral power to combat it. In the process Remond acknowledged that she was not merely addressing human "understanding" but was in fact "appealing to that high moral feeling which every man's heart could appreciate—viz., the idea of love to God and man which was implanted in the heart of every man" (*WTimes*, Jan. 29, 1859). In turn, she expected the British, whose antislavery crusade had already been so effective within their own commonwealth, to "raise the moral public opinion until its voice reaches the American shore" (*Manchester Weekly Times*, Sept. 17, 1859).

To reinforce such an appeal to British moral sensibilities, Remond suggested to her audiences that a compassionate response to abolitionist efforts would be exactly analogous to those generous sentiments with which they had reacted to other national liberation movements, in particular those that had swept through Europe a decade earlier, reminding them, for example, of how they had offered refuge to Neapolitan exiles in 1848. And yet at other times this same humanitarian appeal led Remond to voice a fulsome praise of British mercantilism and imperialism that never acknowledged the fact that such "progress" could be achieved only at the expense of other subordinated groups who were neither European nor African-American: "Great Britain had now reached a degree of influence and civilization, such as had never before been attained by any country. . . . Her navies covered the ocean; ships freighted with her merchandize crowded the harbours of the old and new world. Her colonies were flourishing in every region of the globe, and the sounds of the morning and evening drums of her garrisoned troops encircled the whole earth" (*ASA*, April 2, 1859). It is only in the aftermath of the Civil War, at the time of the black rebellion in Morant Bay, Jamaica, that Remond felt herself able openly to attack the British "West Indian interest," accusing it of colluding with its "natural allies," the Southern Confederates, in order "to neutralize the interest felt for the oppressed negroes, and to hold them up to the scorn and contempt of the civilized world" (*Daily News*, Nov. 22, 1868).

In the postbellum period, Remond's and Watkins Harper's oratorical careers would take increasingly divergent paths. Having "enjoyed freedom" abroad and rapidly disillusioned with the politics of Reconstruction, Remond returned to Europe, settled in Italy, married, and entered the medical profession. In contrast, widowed by 1864, Watkins Harper became increasingly engaged in social reform movements, boldly forging a broader field of activity for herself both in public lecturing and in literary production.

6

"Forced to Some Experiment": Novelization in the Writings of Harriet A. Jacobs, Harriet E. Wilson, and Frances Ellen Watkins Harper

The 1850s constitute a significant moment in the history of African-American literary production as they were the first decade to bear witness to the publication of full-length fictional narratives written by blacks, both male and female. Indeed, between 1853 and 1862, black writers published at least seven texts—two novelized autobiographies, Harriet E. Wilson's *Our Nig; Or, Sketches from the Life of a Free Black* (1859) and Harriet A. Jacobs's *Incidents in the Life of a Slave Girl* (1861), two short stories, Frederick Douglass's "The Heroic Slave" (1853) and Watkins Harper's "The Two Offers" (1859), and three novels, William Wells Brown's *Clotel; Or, The President's Daughter* (1853), Frank J. Webb's *The Garies and Their Friends* (1857), and Martin R. Delany's *Blake; Or, The Huts of America* (1859–62). Such multiple publishing within a nine-year period immediately invites a series of questions: What are the advantages of fiction writing and, more specifically, of novelization, to a given culture or individual writer? How does this writer perform as a "doer of the word"? What circumstances dictate the appearance of fiction at a particular historical moment? Or, as phrased by the turn-of-the-century novelist Pauline Hopkins in 1900, "Of what use is fiction to the colored race at the present crisis in its history?"[1]

Although the narrative writings analyzed in the three previous chapters— spiritual autobiography, travel narrative, the essay, the newspaper column—are all obviously constructed narratives, they do not rely so consistently on fictionalizing techniques nor announce themselves so self-consciously as fiction as do the texts to be examined in this chapter. As critics of the novel have suggested, fictional narrative tends to make its appearance at those moments of crisis when, in

Bakhtin's words, a national culture is decentralized and loses "its sealed-off and self-sufficient character." The 1850s were just such a critical moment for African Americans as they witnessed the dramatic deterioration of race relations, marked by the passage of the Fugitive Slave Law, the Kansas-Nebraska Act, and the Dred Scott decision, as well as the growing exclusion of blacks from industrialization in the North and increased demand for slave labor in the South. African-American fictional narrative came to give particular expression to such social transformations, becoming, to quote Bakhtin again, "inseparable from social and ideological struggle, from processes of evolution and of the renewal of society and the folk."[2] It stands as a striking example of how novelization may become a profoundly political act designed to disrupt hegemonic notions of history, to preserve tradition and community, and to reconstruct a local place that in this instance was abrogated by the Middle Passage and the forces of internal colonization.

Following William Andrews, I would suggest that fictionalization functioned as a means through which early African-American writers could counter or supplement "official" historical accounts by narrating their own version of history, whether that of the social group, of individuals within it, or of the self.[3] Thus, at the beginning of "The Heroic Slave" Douglass's narrator complains that, given the absence of an official written record, his hero Madison Washington "holds now no higher place in the records of that grand old Commonwealth than is held by a horse or an ox" and poignantly relates his futile search for that "great character" that ultimately leaves him no other alternative but fiction writing: "But alas! he is still enveloped in darkness, and we return from the pursuit like a wearied and disheartened mother, (after a tedious and unsuccessful search for a lost child,) who returns weighed down with disappointment and sorrow. Speaking of marks, traces, possibles and probabilities, we come before our readers."[4] Seeking to answer her own question about the uses of fiction, Hopkins herself offered one "possible" by emphasizing the ways in which fiction may work to preserve a written record of "the growth and development of a people":

> [I]t is the simple, homely tale told in an unassuming manner which cements the bond of brotherhood among all classes and all complexions. If the writer is true to life, he will give us pictures of manners and customs, present the religious, political, and social condition of a people, preserving in this way a valuable record of the growth and development of a people from generation to generation. No one will do this for the race. They must themselves develop the men and women who can and will do this work faithfully.[5]

In "fiction," "history" is most often related by means of biography in which the narrator focuses on a central character's life and allows his or her story gradually to unfold. We have seen, for example, how in her efforts to give a compelling account of the evils of slavery Sarah Parker Remond shifted on occasion from an exposition of the socioeconomic facts of slavery to a sentimental narration of the plight of an individual slave, even invoking fictional characters such as Cassy and Topsy as authorities of experience. Remond's gradual abandonment of this form of narration, we noted, might well have resulted from her fear that her audience might confuse narrator and character, believe biography to be autobiography.

That African-American fiction also originated in autobiography is made fully evident by the tendency of midcentury slave narrators to turn increasingly to novelization.[6] In writing slave autobiographies under the aegis of white abolitionism, black writers all too often found themselves producing conventionalized narratives that offered increasingly stereotyped images of the slave both as narrated and as narrating *I*. Traditional studies of autobiography have theorized the presence of two such *I*s in autobiographical narrative and have insisted on the need to view them as distinct and separate entities for whom the use of the same graphic sign is an act of confusion, creating a false unity. In the slave narrative these two *I*s correspond, respectively, to the slave still enmeshed in the slave system and the escaped slave whose acquisition of literacy and ability to tell his or her story mark the narrator as unique. Paul Smith has further argued that a third *I* tends to emerge in autobiography as the moral "guaranteeing subject" whose function is to vouch for the ideological doxology of the text. This *I* is conceptualized as a fixed and coherent subject, whose effect is to close down the enunciatory gap.[7] The slave narratives sponsored by white abolitionists—*Narrative of the Life of Frederick Douglass, Narrative of the Life of William Wells Brown, Narrative of the Life of Moses Grandy, The Life of Josiah Henson*, for example— underwrite just such a project. Teleological in structure, they conform to an antislavery doxology that mandates the progression of the autobiographical *I* from slavery to a "freedom" whose implications are never fully analyzed. This singular *I* is represented as a coherent guaranteeing subject whose essentialized identity is suggested by the signature "written by himself/herself."

Slave narrators such as Frederick Douglass and William Wells Brown, for example, soon discovered that the autobiographical act, far from freeing them from commodification, tended to reinforce their status as commodities. In writing their lives they often found that they had created alienated images of themselves. And, in agreeing to sell their life experiences on the marketplace, they further exposed themselves to the gaze of an alien audience, whether well-intentioned abolitionists, prurient readers seeking titillation in the accounts of slave nudity or whippings, or simply those eager to consume private lives. Novelization thus helped these writers to avoid the self-commodification of the slave narrative by disguising those traces of the self they desired to keep hidden.[8]

Furthermore, as William Andrews has noted, early African-American novels intermingled fact and fiction so that they came to occupy a special, and potentially empowering, "marginal position between authenticatable history on the one hand and unverifiable fiction on the other."[9] If novelization could function as a blind, making consideration of serious political issues more palatable to a readership seeking entertainment rather than edification, its strength also lay in the fact that fiction often is, in Gerald Graff's terms, "hyper-assertive rather than non-assertive," capable of "making stronger, more universalizable" statements than the "factual" discourse of history or autobiography.[10] Indeed, these novelized texts offered alternative worlds that, unlike history or autobiography, permitted an exploration of the future and the representation of endings of African-American life stories. Unlike the slave narrative in particular, these fictional narratives resisted teleology, offering a discursive space for a larger meditation on the "economics of freedom."

Third-person fictional narration in particular—exemplified here by Wilson's *Our Nig* and Watkins Harper's "The Two Offers"—provided greater narrational possibilities than traditional autobiography. By explicitly inscribing the third person within the text, such narration effectively opened up the enunciatory gap closed down by slave autobiography, acknowledging the split between narrating and narrated personae. African-American writers took advantage of this split, embodying themselves in the text as narrator and character(s). As narrators they could adopt authoritative omniscient perspectives denied them by history. As characters they could turn the uncomfortable alienation of slave autobiography to their advantage by distancing themselves from painful past events, and encourage personal expansion by reinventing themselves as singular or multiple selves. Fiction also enabled them to provide different perspectives on a given subject, especially the self. Finally, through fictional characterization these writers worked to dismantle essentialized notions of black subjectivity, conceptualize identity as socially constructed, and explore the multiple facets of African-American experience.

Just as importantly, however, in appropriating novelizing techniques African-American writers were simply adapting themselves to the economy of the dominant culture in which the novel was fast becoming one of the most popular and lucrative forms of writing in the first half of the nineteenth century. Indeed, such was the popularity of the novel that the 1850s witnessed the appearance of more fictional best-sellers than any previous decade. To explain the explosion and influence of the novel as a genre, Nina Baym has suggested that it was its very flexibility and absorbency that made possible its incorporation of almost any topic and thus its appeal to a broad and heterogeneous audience. To support her argument, Baym quotes from a review in *Graham's:* "'We have political novels, representing every variety of political opinion—religious novels, to push the doctrines of every religious sect—philanthropic novels, devoted to the championship of every reform—socialist novels, philosophic novels, metaphysical novels, even railway novels.'"[11]

Given its popularity and influence as well as the all-inclusiveness of its subject matter, the novel would appear to be an ideal vehicle through which African Americans could speak to one another in the mid-nineteenth century and thereby imagine community. This community impulse is fully articulated, for example, early in Webb's novel *The Garies and Their Friends* as Mrs. Garie seeks to redirect the conversation of her cousin who has just returned to the South from Philadelphia: "'Oh, George, never mind the white people,' here interposed Mrs. Garie. 'Never mind them; tell us about the coloured folks; they are the ones I take the most interest in.'"[12] Yet at the same time African-American writers often found themselves dependent on a white readership and thus found their freedom of expression constrained by larger socioeconomic issues of commodification, readership, and publication, especially since they ultimately sought to profit from the sale of their books. In her preface, for example, Wilson asserted that she was "forced to some experiment" in order to make enough money to care for her sick son, while Brown hoped his novel would finance his stay in Britain so that he would not be obliged to "beg" his living from white abolitionists. Both Jacobs, who had escaped from slavery in 1842, and Delany were eager to use the proceeds from their book sales to further their espoused social causes—Jacobs, the antislavery movement, Delany, African-American emigration to the Niger Valley. To achieve such goals these writers often found themselves obliged to compromise with both publishers and readers.

As we have seen, there were no black institutions in the antebellum period that could readily accommodate African-American book publication. The publishing possibilities open to black writers were few—printing at one's own expense, publication by a white abolitionist press, publication in Britain, or the remote possibility of publishing with a commercial press. The publishing history of African-American novels and novelized autobiographies at midcentury is instructive. If Wilson was able to bring out *Our Nig* with the Boston firm of Rand and Avery, both Brown and Webb initially had their books printed in England. Watkins Harper and Delany were able to publish their works in the United States by resorting to serialization in the *Anglo-African Magazine*, the first African-American monthly magazine, started by Thomas Hamilton in 1859 as an act of imagining community: "This Magazine will have the aim to uphold and encourage the now depressed hopes of thinking black men, in the United States—the men who, for twenty years and more have been active in conventions, in public meetings, in societies, in the pulpit, and through the press."[13]

The correspondence of both Jacobs and Delany tellingly reveals the extent of the publication difficulties experienced by these writers. With Jacobs's acquiescence, the white abolitionist Amy Post had written to Stowe sometime in 1852, requesting her aid in helping Jacobs write her life story.[14] But Jacobs refused any collaboration with Stowe when the latter wrote back not to her but to her employer, Mrs. Willis, asking for verification of certain events in Jacobs's life and violating confidential facts concerning the birth of her children. Proceeding on her own with the composition of her narrative, Jacobs completed a draft in 1857 and subsequently wrote to Post on June 21 that "I would so like to go away and sell my Book—I could then secure a copywright—to sell it both here and in England" (243). Unsuccessful in this attempt, Jacobs was eventually forced to allow Lydia

Maria Child to take out the copyright in her name. Writing to Jacobs on September 27, 1860, Child informed her that "I have signed and sealed the contract with Thayer & Eldridge, in my name, and told them to take out the copyright in my name. Under the circumstances *your* name could not be used, you know. . . . I want you to sign the following paper, and send it back to me. It will make Thayer & Eldridge safe about the contract in *my* name, and in case of my death, will prove that the book is *your* property, not *mine*" (245–46). In a letter to Amy Post dated October 8 of the same year, Jacobs further noted that Thayer and Eldridge were insistent that the book contain a preface "by some one known to the public—to effect the sale of the Book" (246–47). Thayer and Eldridge went bankrupt, however, and *Incidents in the Life of a Slave Girl* was finally published by a Boston printer "for the author."

Delany likewise sought to orchestrate the publication of *Blake* with great care, securing the copyright to the novel and initially allowing the *Anglo-African Magazine* to publish only a select number of chapters in its first issue: "We publish in this issue Chapters 28, 29, and 30, of a new work of thrilling interest, with the above title, on the manuscript of which the author (Dr. M. R. Delany), now holds a copyright. . . . We do not give these Chapters because of their particular interest above the others, but that they were the only ones the author would permit us to copy." But, much like Jacobs, Delany was eventually obliged to appeal to a white abolitionist, Garrison, to intercede on his behalf with "a good publishing house" so that he could "make a penny by it [*Blake*]."[15] Apparently receiving no answer from Garrison, Delany finally allowed the successor to the *Anglo-African Magazine*, the *Weekly Anglo-African*, to publish the novel in weekly installments from November 1861 to May 1862.

In order to interest a good publishing house while remaining faithful to their ideological agendas, African-American writers had to produce commodities that would please both a white audience, unfamiliar with African-American culture, and a black readership seeking to imagine community. As they charted new terrain within the tradition of American fiction, these writers inherited novelistic conventions from the dominant discourse that ultimately revealed themselves inadequate to express their concerns. Subverting, revising, and adapting these conventions while simultaneously introducing "denied knowledges" from their native traditions, African-American writers created hybrid forms of novelized discourse.

The history of African-American writers' tentative shift from autobiography to novel, from first- to third-person narration, is fully inscribed in the texts of *Our Nig* and *Incidents in the Life of a Slave Girl*. It suggests the degree to which autobiography in general—and the slave narrative in particular—already contains within it subversive fictional techniques,[16] and it underscores the extent to which the grammatical choice of person, like that of genre, is not a purely formal act but a profoundly political one. It points, finally, to the presence of yet another liminal space created and occupied by antebellum black women in which they could give voice to the tense and contradictory impulses of legitimation and subversion that lay within them.

In the first instance, both Jacobs's and Wilson's narratives effectively displace the primary position of the white abolitionist preface whose purpose was to authenticate the truthfulness of black experience and authorship. Wilson placed authenticating documents at the end of her narrative, beginning instead with her own preface that delivered a stinging attack on "our good anti-slavery friends" and specifically appealed to her "colored brethren" to become her readers.[17] And while Child's introduction demanded by Thayer and Eldridge is still present, it is preceded by Jacobs's own authenticating preface. Yet, as female-authored novelized autobiographies, *Our Nig* and *Incidents* bear burdens of narration not as evident in male-authored autobiographical narratives. Both Wilson and Jacobs seem to have required a permission to narrate necessitated by their vulnerability as black women to the violence of race prejudice and slavery and signaled by their use of fictitious names and signatures. Thus, the common "written by herself" that signs Jacobs's slave narrative is preceded in the title by the pseudonym "Linda," suggested initially by Child as a means of protecting Jacobs's Northern employer and agreed to by Jacobs, who then used the name "Linda Brent" throughout her text.[18] Wilson signed her narrative with the self-consciously objectified signature "Our Nig" and then referred to herself as Frado in her text. The presence of the pseudonym in these autobiographical narratives problematizes notions of essentialist identity, opens up onto questions of selfhood, and works to resist commodification. It may also acknowledge the underlying "violence of the letter" that often accompanies the revelation of proper names within an oppressed group in quest of "freedom."

Still other novelizing techniques function as permissions to narrate, as through them Jacobs and Wilson strove to resist bodily exposure, veil not only their physical selves but also their interior lives, and in particular deflect feelings of anger and vulnerability whose expression is often so problematic for women writers. Using characters with fictional names to recast their life stories, both Jacobs and Wilson endeavored to distance themselves from such powerful emotions by containing them within a "fictional" world. They demanded that their fictional rather than their factual selves bear the physical and emotional brunt of both racial violence and the sexualized male gaze; they sought to make these fictional selves carry the burden of their own anger as well as to redirect this anger against fictional characters rather than historical persons and actual readers.

On the level of narration, Wilson established a third-person narrator whose function was to maintain full control over the plot, achieve a perspective of omniscience unattainable in traditional autobiographical narrative, and permit multiple outside viewpoints on the fictional self. At the same time Wilson sought to conceal her "actual" self and thereby escape commodification by obscuring the distinction between fact and fiction. For while she affirms that her entire narrative is autobiographical, the appended letters confirm as "factual" only the earliest and latest events in her life; the bulk of the narrative, Frado's years in service with the Bellmonts, receives no other textual confirmation. Wilson's difficulties in maintaining narrative distance become evident in the remaining traces of the first person at the beginning and end of the text, the confirmed autobiographical sections.[19] The fact that the first person coheres only around the terms "mother," "father," "home," and "narrative" suggests the degree to which Wilson's auto-biography strives, despite the dominance of third-person narration and her attempts to split apart the autobiographical *I*, to unify narrating and narrated *I* into a coherent self.

While maintaining a first-person narration throughout *Incidents*, Jacobs none-theless adapted novelizing techniques to the autobiographical mode. She developed forms of double discourse that enabled her to negotiate feelings of anger: chapter titles whose vagueness or banality belies the harshness of the incidents depicted (chapter 16, "Scenes at the Plantation," narrates Brent's plan to escape slavery); direct appeals to the reader whose conventionality masks real aggression ("O, you happy free women, contrast *your* New Year's day with that of the poor bond-woman!", 16); maxims whose broad generalizations veil forceful *personal* judgments ("It [cunning] is the only weapon of the weak and oppressed against the strength of their tyrants," 100–101). Finally, much like Wilson, Jacobs sought self-empowerment by shifting the terms of the narrating *I*'s relationship to the narrated *I*, endowing the narrator with much of the authority associated with third-person narrators. Thus, Jacobs relates events and conversations that she herself did not directly witness as if she were an omniscient narrator. And, by relying extensively on dialogue, she seems to turn Brent, the narrated *I*, into a third-person character, while remaining careful not to allow other characters to develop a sustained perspective on her. In fact, in striking contrast to Wilson's narrational strategies, dialogue and letter writing appear to be the only narrative modes in *Incidents* that allow for a perspective outside that of Brent. If *Our Nig* is a third-person narration that strains toward the first, *Incidents* is a first-person narration that strains toward the third.

In fact, *Our Nig* and *Incidents* differ radically in their negotiation of necessary compromises with white sponsorship. Having established close relationships with Amy Post and Child, and having been able openly to express her distress over Stowe's attempts to appropriate her story, Jacobs could accept collaboration as historically inevitable and seek to turn it to her advantage. The exact extent of Child's editorial role in shaping Jacobs's manuscript has been extensively debated by critics and is in fact impossible to ascertain. Yet it is clear that Child allowed Jacobs a much greater authorial role than she had the evangelist Julia Pell, perhaps because of her greater degree of comfort with Jacobs's more "feminine" story. Child herself insisted in the introduction that "such changes as I have made have been mainly for purposes of condensation and orderly arrangement. I have not added any thing to the incidents, or changed the import of her very pertinent remarks. With trifling exceptions, both the ideas and the language are her own. I pruned excrescences a little, but otherwise I had no reason for changing her lively and dramatic way of telling her own story" (3). Thus, the presence of the conventional discourse of sentimental/seduction fiction in Jacobs's narrative need not be seen as a sign of Child's editorial encroachment but rather as the shaping of a "floating writing" that suggests the disappearance of the "author" and emergence of an authorial anonymity through which Jacobs could attempt to escape commodification.[20] In contrast, Wilson's text is marked by an angry acknowledgment of Northern race prejudice and a refusal to compromise with white abolitionism that, given the realities of the 1850s, was highly unrealistic. As a consequence, the third person of the narrative collapses into the ideological *I* of doxological autobiography in Frado's letter reprinted in an appended document, whose humility of attitude and tone belies both the preface's appeal to an exclusively black readership and the narrative's self-assertiveness.

To tell their life stories, Jacobs and Wilson both turned—in different ways and with different degrees of explicitness—to the sentimental figure of the tragic mulatta whom Remond was simultaneously invoking in her speeches across the Atlantic. Briefly summarized, the tragic mulatta plot centers on a beautiful fair-skinned young girl whose father is most often her master but who remains ignorant of her slave identity. Socialized as a young lady, she is courted by a white gentleman who endows their relationship with all the trappings of romance. At the moment of narrative crisis, her slave condition is discovered, or remembered, and she is remanded into slavery. Unable to escape the laws of slavery, she is separated from her lover and most often dies a tragic death. Karen Sánchez-Eppler has perceptively analyzed the importance of this literary convention to the sentimental culture of white feminist-abolitionists and to antislavery literature.[21] But I would argue that the tragic mulatta figure has even earlier antecedents. Indeed, America's first novelistic genre was the seduction novel, whose plot uncovered the economic contract of middle-class marriage in which white women figured as objects of exchange subordinated within the home as regulators of a domestic economy owing its existence to the labor and capital of their husbands; the endings invariably punished the heroine who resorted to the free expression of her sexuality in an attempt to disrupt this capitalist system of exchange. Nina Baym has shown how this plot was abandoned by women writers after the 1820s;[22] yet seduction novels such as Hannah Webster Foster's *The Coquette* continued to be read. Thus, cultural anxieties about women's sexuality did not disappear but were invested in the tragic mulatta plot, in whose heroine sexuality and blackness became conflated.

Traditional interpretations of the tragic mulatta have suggested that the convention ostensibly functioned as a socially acceptable literary device that would allow white abolitionist women to speak openly about the plight of the female slave and perhaps even identify with her. Yet it also had its more insidious side. If the tragic mulatta figure erases the physical blackness of the slave woman, as Spillers and Sánchez-Eppler have noted, it nonetheless reveals the culture's apprehension over what constitutes blackness. The proliferation of such terms as *mulatto, quadroon,* and *octoroon* suggests the impossibility of defining that space in between pure whiteness and pure blackness, and even of defining whiteness and blackness themselves. This anxiety over issues of race and sexuality could be allayed only by the sacrifice of the black woman. Thus, beneath its idealized surface, the tragic mulatta plot suggests just how insidiously "romance" privatizes and manipulates the heroine: the object of the white male gaze and desire, the mulatta renders female sexuality available; she legitimates the act of seduction, perhaps even of rape.[23]

As in the seduction novel, however, the sexual plot of the tragic mulatta story is undergirded by an economic one. In the economy of slavery the mulatta was a commodity sold at high profit as a "fancy girl" or exploited to produce more slaves. Yet she also constituted a surplus value produced for the personal consumption of the slaveholder, for whom the economic system of slavery was underwritten by an aristocratic social code emphasizing luxury consumption rather than thrift, accumulation, and profit.[24] In this context the mulatta functions as a fetish, a material object onto which the social properties of aristocratic consumption have been transposed. In the literary representation of this figure, the libidinal surplus of the tragic mulatta is thus doubled by an economic surplus, and her story results from the convergence of two plots that produces the narrative crisis and the subsequent unfolding of the story. In the first the mulatta is a luxury commodity to be enjoyed (consumed) by the slaveholder. In the second she is converted into capital and reinvested (through sale and/or reproduction) in order to accumulate additional capital for the slaveholding class. One important function of African-American novelization in the 1850s, then, was to critique the tragic mulatta plot and, more generally, sentimental culture.

As we saw in chapter 5, Watkins Harper had readily appropriated certain features of sentimental culture into her poetic compositions. Sentimental culture, we may remember, was premised on the ideology of separate spheres whereby men inhabit the public sphere of the marketplace and women the domestic sphere of the home, posited as the site of moral goodness. In the antebellum period it produced a literature that was written largely by and for women, creating what Lauren Berlant has termed a "feminine counterpublic sphere." In the literary representation of this domestic sphere particular attention is attached to the socially weak—slaves, women, children, and, quite specifically, the tragic mulatta—whose plight demands a compassionate response from the reader, a sympathetic extension of the self that ideally leads to corrective social action. Additionally, as Gillian Brown and Richard Brodhead have noted, as the sentimental novel developed its characterization of the heroine, it came increasingly to invest domestic ideology with values of individualism, interiority, and private feeling; in particular, it is love, or what Brodhead has called "disciplinary intimacy," that will correct social evil and solve the social problems besetting the nation.[25]

In their texts Jacobs, Wilson, and Watkins Harper all engage sentimentality in order, then, to reject it. Watkins Harper, as we saw, reconfigured sentimental values in her poetry by insisting on the extent to which public interests at all times infiltrate the private sphere of African-American familial life. In their narratives these three women writers further dismantled this private-public sphere ideology by focusing on the portrayal of an "anomalous" single woman—Linda Brent, Frado, Janette Alston—whose very existence and actions reveal not only its inapplicability to the lives of black women but also its confusion of values. For all three writers were acutely aware of the extent to which this ideology was constructed and held in place by market forces—slavery in the South and capitalism in the North—with which white women often collaborated. More specifically, in appropriating the tragic mulatta figure, Jacobs and Wilson explicitly separated the economic plot from the libidinal in order to foreground the former. In their narratives the tragic mulatta becomes emblematic of African-American economic dispossession and homelessness, of the difficulties of forging home on American soil, of the need to continue working toward the construction of an African-American local place that is defined by neither public nor private spheres. In the process of developing their plots, these narratives further undermine sentimental culture by illustrating the inadequacy of love and sympathy as mechanisms to correct social evil in a world of racial hostility.

As in the case of Jarena Lee and Nancy Prince, the facts of Jacobs's life are available to us through the written record of autobiography. Born in 1813 in Edenton, North Carolina, Harriet Jacobs was a slave in the Horniblow/Norcom family until her escape in 1842. Her narrative of her childhood in slavery focuses in particular on the repeated sexual advances of her master, Dr. Norcom (Dr. Flint in the text), the various strategies she adopted in order to elude him, and the help and comfort given to her by her grandmother (Aunt Marthy) and others in the community. But Jacobs's narrative also provides details of her escape to the North, her situation as a domestic in the New York home of Nathaniel Willis, a popular purveyor of sentimental culture, and the uncertainty of her life after the passage of the Fugitive Slave Law until the purchase of her freedom by Mrs. Willis in 1852 (Mr. and Mrs. Bruce). Finally, additional information concerning Jacobs's life in the North may be gleaned from her correspondence with Lydia Maria Child and Amy Post, indicating the extent to which she agreed to work, much like Truth, within the structures of the white antislavery movement up to the outbreak of the Civil War.

In writing *Incidents in the Life of a Slave Girl,* Jacobs explicitly constructed her textual self, Linda Brent, as a mulatta. In the opening paragraph of her narrative Brent informs us that "in complexion my parents were a light shade of brownish yellow, and were termed mulattoes" (5). And later, in one of the few instances of the insertion of "factual" discourse into the narrative, she reproduces the text of Flint's advertisement of her as a runaway: "$300 Reward! Ran away from the subscriber, an intelligent, bright, mulatto girl" (97). Yet Brent's narrative proceeds severely to rewrite the sentimental plot of the tragic mulatta by revising the private-public sphere ideology and its attendant values, revealing the limits of sympathy as a response to the evils of slavery, redirecting its narrative energies toward the construction of African-American home places, and, finally, addressing a specifically black readership in order to imagine community.[26]

Brent's interaction with Dr. Flint (and his wife) immediately exposes the fallacy of the separate sphere ideology in relation to the female slave. First, the Flint household provides full corroboration of Elizabeth Fox-Genovese's contention that the very constitution of the Southern slave household undermines the private-public sphere dichotomy as it contains within it essential aspects of both productive and reproductive relations, regulating both the labor and sexual relations of master and slave classes. Furthermore, Brent's narrative insistently reiterates the extent to which it is the private rather than the public sphere that constitutes the site of danger for the female slave. This point is first made in chapter 2 in Brent's account of Flint's attempt to avoid selling her grandmother at a "'public sale of negroes, horses, etc.'": "Dr. Flint called to tell my grandmother that he was unwilling to wound her feelings by putting her up at auction, and that he would prefer to dispose of her at private sale. My grandmother saw through his hypocrisy; she understood very well that he was ashamed of the job. . . . [I]f he was base enough to sell her, when her mistress intended she should be free, she was determined the public should know it" (11).

Similarly, Brent's narrative of Dr. Flint's conduct toward her suggests her early awareness of the dangers of privacy in the life of a slave girl. Flint's sexual advances do not of course become the basis for a romantic plot but constitute an attempt at rape. To escape him Brent realizes that the best strategy of resistance lies in publicity and that privatization, so common in tragic mulatta stories, can only work to the advantage of the slaveholder. She repeatedly expresses her relief that she lives in a crowded town rather than on an isolated plantation: "I had escaped my dreaded fate, by being in the midst of people" (53). Well aware of the advantages of privacy for himself, Dr. Flint, in a kind of parody of the heroes of tragic mulatta stories, seeks to privatize Brent: "In the blandest tones, he told me that he was going to build a small house for me, in a secluded place, four miles from the town. I shuddered; but I was constrained to listen, while he talked of his intention to give me a home of my own, and to make a lady of me" (53). It is this attempt to transform Brent into a tragic mulatta that goads her to the public action of taking another white man, Mr. Sands, as a lover and bearing two children by him. While critics have noted the rhetorical ambiguity of Brent's sentimental narration of this episode in which she both apologizes for, and defends, her decision, the action itself represents, I think, Brent's early recognition of the limitations imposed on the "socially weak" and the need for self-assertion.[27]

The second half of *Incidents* consists of an account of Brent's resistance to what Kristeva has termed "abjection." Always aware of the advantages of privacy, Flint concocts a plan to remove Brent and her children to his son's distant plantation, thinking "it was a good place to break us all in to abject submission to our lot as slaves." It is her discovery of this plan that "nerved me to immediate action," that of escape (93–94). Brent's escape from slavery, however, leads her first to a seven-year confinement in her grandmother's attic. Such confinement can be read as a grotesque parody of the dominant culture's efforts to privatize the female, to shut her up within the family, and to hystericize her body. As one of her slave friend's exclaims: "'Lor, chile,' she said, putting her arms around me, 'you's got de highsterics'" (108). And indeed, Brent's bodily history ironically prefigures that of later nineteenth-century hysterical women who were to play such an important part in the psychoanalytic discourse of the dominant culture: attempted seduction by an older father figure; the display of such symptoms as numbness, paralysis, loss of speech (*aphonia*), persistent coughing (*tussa nervosa*), unsociability; seclusion within the family; the obsessive concern of the medical profession (Dr. Flint tells Brent that "he, as a physician, could have saved me from exposure," 58); and finally, the questioning of the social structure of the patriarchal family (implied in Brent's exclamation "What tangled skeins are the genealogies of slavery," 78).[28] But Brent refuses to succumb to that madness so often inflicted on slave women compelled to bear the children of white men (51). And, unlike Freud's later hysterics, she insists on entering the symbolic order to write an autobiography that is grounded not in hysterical discourse but in a careful manipulation of the plots and conventions of the dominant literary culture.

Thus, *Incidents* narrates Brent's decisive rejection of the traditional fate of the tragic mulatta—commodification, privatization, hystericization, consumption, reinvestment, and ultimately death. Instead, her actions insistently unmask the economic basis of the incidents in her life and her use of "femininity" as a site of resistance to the patriarchal system of slavery. As Houston Baker has noted, Brent deliberately commodifies herself as a sexual object and gives herself to Mr. Sands in order to disrupt the slaveholders' control of the slave exchange market. She insists on negotiating her own labor power and later that of her children, first by turning her womb into a site of (re)production, then by her acts of mothering and nurturing, and finally by commodifying her children in order to free them.[29]

If the slave owner's household represents one geographic locus in *Incidents*, Brent's grandmother's house represents yet another. While Brent's narrative fully acknowledges the fundamental homelessness of the slave as the first chapter, for example, describes how the deaths of her mother and her first mistress lead her from one home to another, it also offers Aunt Marthy's house as a constructed African-American home place. Critics have commented on the conservatism of this older woman's social ideology—her firm belief in a ruling Providence that would seem to deny the possibility of individual agency, her insistence that Brent uphold the values of true womanhood despite her slave condition, her discouraging reaction to Brent's desire to escape North to freedom, her unquestioning loyalty to the Flint family, her (most often futile) choice to work to buy her own children's freedom rather than attempt escape.[30] And indeed, Brent's description of Aunt Marthy's home in the chapter on the Nat Turner rebellion entitled "Fear of Insurrection" seems fully to conform to the dominant cult of domesticity by representing this home as a site of privacy and interiority. In fact, however, this description serves the important political function of inverting racial and social hierarchies, portraying the white invading rabble as the true insurrectionists and Aunt Marthy's home as emblematic of African-American community stability.

Even more importantly, homes like that of Aunt Marthy and Brent's father are suggestive of the ways in which, despite their enslaved condition, slaves worked to achieve autonomy, and offer the reader a vision of slave culture that lies beyond its supposed "degradation" that was so frequently invoked by free blacks in the North. Thus, if the first chapter poignantly portrays Brent's own homelessness, it also foregrounds in its very first paragraph the figures of her father and grandmother, who, as carpenter and baker, respectively, are important economic providers for family and community and work to maintain homes on the margins of the slaveholders' economy. In particular, Brent's grandmother's house illustrates how the African-American domestic sphere is neither private nor public but generates an in-house economy in which children are sheltered, goods produced, and the community taken care of. Even Brent's garret, the most private of spaces, is transformed from a prison into a productive domestic space through the activities of reading, letter writing, and sewing. Such a reconstruction of this place of confinement forces a reassessment of the dominant culture's assumed notions of domesticity.

Brent's depiction of the larger slave community in which these homes are located demands, finally, that we reconfigure notions of private and public, as suggested in chapter 1. Indeed, this community functions as a kind of intermediate sphere located somewhere between the public and the private. It is public in that it is not confined to a single home, but it is also domestic in that it carries the values of home into the community; most importantly, perhaps, it is private insofar as it manages to keep many of its activities hidden from the eyes of the slaveholding class. Thus, Brent's account of her own life and of those of individual slaves is interspersed with descriptions of "denied knowledges"—institutions and folkways—from slave culture that point to the importance of collective action in the slaves' effort to forge local place: the African-American church, the burying ground, Johnkannaus celebrations, funeral rituals, and so on. Given this tremendous valuation of community networks and relationships, we may more readily understand Aunt Marthy's reluctance to escape slavery for the uncertainties of life in the urban North.

The extent of Jacobs's subversion of the tragic mulatta plot may be perceived more readily by a comparison with William Wells Brown's novel *Clotel,* published eight years earlier than *Incidents*. Taking as its starting point the sexual relations between Thomas Jefferson and one of his female slaves, called Currer here, *Clotel* opens with an attack on Southern slave laws, which refuse to acknowledge the marriage relation for slaves, and closes with the happily-ever-after marriage of Currer's granddaughter Mary. In between, Brown traces the sad fate of Currer's other progeny, in particular, her daughter Clotel. Writing his tragic mulatta plot by incorporating entire passages from Child's short story "The Quadroons," in what constitutes perhaps yet another instance of voice merging, Brown on the surface yields to its romantic conventions and ideology. What is particularly interesting about Brown's adaptation is the degree to which the mulatta characters are not unique but appear in a kind of inflationary proliferation (Currer, her two daughters, and their daughters). The plot's development consists, then, of the circulation of these tragic mulattas, as undifferentiated characters, through the libidinal economy of Southern slaveholding society, ostensibly as objects of romantic desire but in fact as luxury commodities designed for the private consumption of the slaveholders. And it concludes with their reconversion into capital for further reinvestment; resistance to reconversion results, of course, in death. Given his sister's and mother's own sexual histories as slaves, Brown could never have unquestioningly accepted the conventional tragic mulatta plot but, as a faithful Garrisonian, could only register a highly indirect subversion. For example, both Clotel and Mary acquire forms of agency uncharacteristic of the traditional tragic mulatta as they attempt escape or resistance by disguising themselves as men. And Currer becomes part of a slave community whose comic surface masks its collective resistance to the slave system.

The only character to escape the fate of the tragic mulatta is Mary, who escapes to France and marries the heroic mulatto George. While it is impossible to underestimate the importance that Brown attached to marriage as an institution that legitimates the sexual relations of African Americans, it is important to note that Mary and George's marriage isolates them from the slave community to which they once belonged and also privatizes her. In striking contrast to the activist careers of the women we have been studying, Brown's narrative can only conclude by claiming that "a woman's whole life is a history of the affections," and by conceptualizing as an appropriate ending for his surviving heroine her relegation to the private sphere.[31]

If Jacobs's autobiography exposes the flawed premises and confusion of values inherent in the separate sphere ideology on which sentimental culture was grounded, it also lays bare the limits of sentimental sympathy as an adequate corrective to the social ills besetting the nation. Franny Nudelman has perceptively noted how in her narrative "Jacobs tries to work within a sentimental tradition . . . , using self-revelation to effect an alliance between white and black women that will transform the radical inequality that her suffering denotes." Nudelman goes on to argue that "because the social consequences of this project—Jacobs's publication of her sexual impurity and her consequent violation of the purity of her female audience—are intolerable, sentimental conventions are, for her, dysfunctional." And she concludes by suggesting that while "Jacobs never abandons a preoccupation with suffering as the basis for communication with her white audience," she resorts "at points in the narrative" to a "rhetoric of contrast" that relies on difference rather than identification as a mode of appeal.[32]

I would extend Nudelman's analysis to argue that Jacobs's disenchantment with sentimental sympathy in fact runs much deeper. Valerie Smith has already noted how Miss Fanny's sympathy for Aunt Marthy and her family does not extend to action but to a wish for their deaths as the only way to achieve peace (89).[33] I would suggest that we can read a more generalized critique of the superficiality, hypocrisy, even danger, of sentimental sympathy in Jacobs's description of Mrs. Flint's reaction to Aunt Nancy's death. Having "slowly murdered" her foster sister through constant hard work, Mrs. Flint "now . . . became very sentimental" (145, 146). The pure externality of her sentimentality is made evident in her plan to provide a "beautiful illustration of the attachment existing between slaveholder and slave" by having Nancy buried in the Flint family burial place (146). Such an illustration is not only hypocritical but disempowering to the slave community, for whom, as Albert Raboteau has shown, funeral rituals are acts of resistance and the burial ground a sacred place; in fact, it is a visit to her parents' graves that finally results in Brent's decision to escape.[34]

In further positing that "Northern travellers" are readily taken in by such sham sentimental performances, Jacobs effectively extends her critique to question Northerners' proper understanding of sentimental values: "Northern travellers, passing through the place, might have described this tribute of respect to the humble dead as a beautiful feature in the 'patriarchal institution;' a touching proof of the attachment between slaveholders and their servants; and tenderhearted Mrs. Flint would have confirmed this impression, with handkerchief at her eyes. *We* could have told them a different story" (146). If Jacobs comes to tell a different story, it is a story that not only details the horrors of the Southern slave system but also exposes the collaboration of the North, in particular its acquiescence to the Fugitive Slave Law; as this story unfolds, sentimental appeal is increasingly replaced by political denunciation: "The Fugitive Slave Law had not then passed. The judges of Massachusetts had not then stooped under chains to enter her courts of justice, so called. . . . I relied on her love of freedom, and felt safe on her soil. I am now aware that I honored the old Commonwealth beyond her deserts" (187). It is at narrative moments such as these when Jacobs turns to contemplate Northern collusion with the South (from which white women are not excused) that the depth of her anger is most intensely felt.

I would argue, however, that Jacobs's most important "different story" lies in a subtle narrative shift in addressee from the "women of the North" invoked in her preface to members of the black community. *Incidents* must then be read not only as a text that engages sentimental culture in its appeal to the sympathies of women of the North but also as a narrative that seeks to imagine community

Harriet A. Jacobs. 1894.

among African Americans. Although Jacobs did not serialize her text in the *Anglo-African Magazine* or the *Weekly Anglo-African* as Watkins Harper and Delany did, the book was reviewed in the April 13, 1861 issue of the *Weekly Anglo-African*, thus confirming its reception by a black readership. The unsigned review is remarkable for the degree to which its tone differs in its assertion of anger from that of the *Liberator* and *National Anti-Slavery Standard* reviews, transforming Jacobs's text into a call to arms:

> No one can read these pages without a feeling of horror, and a stronger determination arising in them to tear down the cursed system which makes such records possible. Wrath, the fiery messenger which goes flaming from the roused soul and overthrows in its divine fury the accursed tyrannies of earth; will find in these pages new fuel for the fire, and new force for the storm which shall overthrow and sweep from existence American slavery.

In Jacobs's text the fire and storm that will overthrow American slavery are not explicitly named. But I would suggest that one mechanism for social change may be found in "beautiful illustration" that is not the attachment between slave mistress and slave but one similar to the portraits shown to Brent by Mrs. Durham in Philadelphia: "One day she took me to an artist's room, and showed me the portraits of some of her children. I had never seen any paintings of colored people before, and they seemed to me beautiful" (162). Although Jacobs never denies the value of white women's sympathy (190, 194), her real commitment is to defining the "beauty" of "colored people" and appealing to them to exhibit it in their behavior. Within her text, African-American beauty is located in the South in the promotion and maintenance of community values, best illustrated through the character of Aunt Marthy, and in the North in the twin acts of self-assertion and self-control. Condemning black servants' submission to the degradation of Northern racism, for example, Brent chastises them in a rhetoric not unlike that of Walker and Stewart and then launches an appeal to her people as a whole: "My answer was that the colored servants ought to be dissatisfied with *themselves*, for not having too much self-respect to submit to such treatment; that there was . . . no justification for difference of treatment. . . . [F]inding I was resolved to stand up for my rights, they concluded to treat me well. Let every colored man and woman do this, and eventually we shall cease to be trampled under foot by our oppressors" (177). Beauty is be to found finally in the value of self-control that in the African-American community replaces the sentimental ethic of disciplinary intimacy as the regulation of blacks' emotions and behaviors comes to originate within the self so that outside restraint is unnecessary. Jacobs's narrative of her life in slavery insistently reiterates how such self-control is lacking in the conduct of the slave master and mistress but is a necessary mechanism of survival for the slave. Indeed, Jacobs achieves her rights in the incident related earlier precisely because she is able to preserve her self-control.

If this discourse of racial self-assertion was acceptable to a white abolitionist audience, such was not the case with Jacobs's chapter on John Brown that Child told her in a letter dated August 13, 1860 "had better be omitted. It does not naturally come into your story, and the M.S. is already too long. Nothing can be so appropriate to end with, as the death of your grandmother" (244). While I have argued that Child's editorial role ought to be seen largely as a form of collaboration rather than encroachment, I think we cannot foreclose the possibility of a real divergence of interests here between Child and Jacobs. Child fully supported Brown from a moral point of view but could not bring herself to condone the use force to bring about the end of slavery. Thus, her request in this same letter that Jacobs develop the Nat Turner chapter is motivated by her desire for a fuller account not of Turner's violent actions but of the subsequent victimization of slaves by the white mob: "My object in writing at this time is to ask you to write what you can recollect of the outrages committed on the colored people, in Nat Turner's time" (244). Jacobs's inclusion of the Brown chapter would, in fact, have been quite "natural." Indeed, in their accounts of John Brown's raid, African-American writers frequently invoked Turner's rebellion in order further to debate the means of black liberation. Thus, the December 1859 issue of the *Anglo-African Magazine,* which Jacobs might well have read, juxtaposes accounts of both episodes in order to pose the following question to its black readership: "The one is the mode in which the slave seeks freedom for his fellows, and the other, the mode in which the white man seeks to set the slave free. . . . So, people of the South, people of the North! men and brethren, choose ye which method of emancipation you prefer—Nat Turner's or John Brown's?"[35] Jacobs's desire to conclude with such a chapter represented yet a final effort on her part to imagine community.

Despite the omission of this chapter, the ending of *Incidents* does problematize notions of black liberation and freedom as it narrates in some detail the difficulties of forging an African-American local place in the urban North. Jacobs's unusually lengthy account of her life after her escape from slavery suggests an aloneness in New York's black community similar to that experienced by Sojourner Truth a decade earlier and illustrates the complexities of black economic survival in the North. The juxtaposition of the last two chapter titles, "The Fugitive Slave Law" and "Free at Last," severely questions the meaning of freedom when slave laws can so easily penetrate to the North. And the content of these chapters fully acknowledges Jacobs's continued dependent status as a domestic worker to a white woman, the dispersal of her children, and her lack of a "hearthstone of my own" (201). Given these facts, we can more readily appreciate Aunt Marthy's conservatism and reluctance to abandon the slave community of the South. Consequently, we can also recognize the degree to which Jacobs's nostalgic reference to her grandmother in the very last lines is not a sentimental but a political act of remembrance that suggests her valuation of past bonds forged in slavery and her recognition of "retrospection"—and the narration of retrospection—as a vital means of creating community. In making the decision to move to Alexandria, Virginia, in 1863 to bring relief to the contrabands of war,

Jacobs would once again find herself living within a black community and working for its welfare.

The difficulties of African-American economic survival and community preservation in the North are fully exemplified in Harriet E. Adams Wilson's novelized autobiography, *Our Nig.* Recent research by Barbara White has uncovered further information to add to Henry Louis Gates's reconstruction of Wilson's life. Adams was born sometime between 1824 and 1828. The 1840 census shows her working in Milford, New Hampshire, for the Nehemiah Hayword family, the lives of whose members correspond closely to the Bellmonts'. Other Milford records list Adams's marriage to Thomas Wilson of Virginia in 1851, the birth of their son, George Mason Wilson, in 1852, as well as his death in 1860, approximately six months after the publication of *Our Nig.* Finally, the Boston directories list Wilson as living widowed in that city between 1856 and 1863. Beyond that date, nothing more is known of her life.[36]

In her novelized autobiography Wilson's Frado is a mulatta who participates in a double seduction plot—her mother's and her own—that strips bare all romance surrounding the tragic mulatta story and exposes both the economic and sexual politics through which capitalism has systematically kept underdeveloped certain classes of people. Frado's mother, Mag, is a poor white woman who is seduced and abandoned but who, unlike her middle-class fictional counterparts, cannot die and must struggle to survive in undignified poverty. When she does marry it is out of economic necessity and to a black man, Jim: "'I can do but two things,' she said, 'beg my living, or get it from you'" (13). This marriage is a union of white and black in which the white partner represents pure economic motivation, interested only "to subserve her own comfort," while the black is portrayed as "kind-hearted," "industrious," bespeaking "a finer principle," reflecting the union of the nation at large (15, 9, 14, 10). Jim proudly hopes to take possession of Mag as his "treasure" (14) but soon dies of consumption, victim of both disease and a life of hard work; the union between black and white is dissolved and its product, Frado, discarded as waste.

In the narrative Frado is thus made to carry the burden of black self-representation alone. From the first she is described as a mulatta, but the distance between her and the conventional tragic mulatta is immense; her function is to expose the romanticization of this figure and point to its economic basis. Inverting the convention, Frado follows the condition not of her mother but of her "free" father and becomes "Our Nig," an appellation that calls attention to her blackness and erases her mother's whiteness. This inversion underscores the hypocrisy of those laws that define civil status according to the mother and affirms the inescapability of race as the primary social category in the free North.

When Frado is discarded as waste by her mother and stepfather, Seth Shipley, she becomes an indentured servant in the house of a white family, the Bellmonts. Indentured servitude had been a fairly common form of labor in colonial America, based on the importation of servants from both Africa and Europe, but had then waned in the latter part of the eighteenth century given the shortage of imported European labor. According to Sharon Salinger, it had a brief revival in the North after the 1780 Gradual Abolition Law, when manumitted slaves were made to pass through a period of indenture. In this system the servant voluntarily gave away his or her labor power to an employer who then owned it for a specified period. Sometimes children were placed into indentured servitude by their parents not for profit but to ensure that they would have a means of gaining a livelihood as adults. Written contracts were commonly drawn up that were designed to protect the servant by specifying the locale of servitude, its length (generally seven years for farm workers, three to four years for apprentices to professionals), the provisions for freedom, as well as the care, shelter, and sometimes remuneration to be provided by the employer. Employer abuse (including sexual assault) was not unknown, however, and the incidence of runaways, particularly in rural areas, was often high.[37] In *Our Nig* Frado's labor power is given away by Mag and Seth without a written contract, perhaps as a preferable alternative to total abandonment, which undoubtedly would have resulted in remittance to the poor farm. Frado never attempts to reclaim her labor power nor to run away, and tacitly agrees to a term of servitude of approximately twelve years; it is only toward the end of this period that she seeks—successfully—to control her labor power. Frado stays, I would argue, because she is motivated by a desire to "be in some relation," in particular to be in a relation—emotional, economic?—"to white people she was never favored with before" (28).

During her twelve-year stay with the Bellmonts Frado, then, does not seek to own her labor power; in fact, she owns nothing. The issue of proprietorship is central to *Our Nig*, a text that at least indirectly raises the questions: Who owns? Who is an heir? Who can inherit? To inherit property one must be in possession of a patronymic. Of the black male characters in the text, neither Jim (Frado's father) nor Samuel (her husband) have a patronymic; they inherit no property and have no inheritance to leave her. Frado can only inherit that potential legacy of "parental disgrace and calumny" invoked by the narrator in her description of Mag's sexual downfall: "How many pure, innocent children not only inherit a wicked heart of their own, claiming life-long scrutiny and restraint, but are heirs also of parental disgrace and calumny, from which only long years of patient endurance in paths of rectitude can disencumber them" (6). If the narrative does in fact intimate that Frado is heir to Mag's disgrace, it also suggests that the sign of her disgrace might well be her black skin, the only inheritance left her by her father.

In striking contrast to Jacobs, who maintained firm control over the process of self-representation, Wilson eschewed the conventions of autobiography whereby the perspective of the *I* largely governs the narrative. Instead she told her life story by means of multiple outside perspectives on her fictionalized self, Frado, in an effort perhaps to accommodate her double audience of both black and white readers.[38] According to these outside perceptions, Frado is not socialized into the feminine graces of traditional tragic mulattas. Instead, like Stowe's Topsy, she is depicted as "a wild, frolicky thing" (18) whom white readers might well have viewed with condescending mockery rather than identification but in whom black readers might well have recognized a figure of resistance. Indeed, Frado is repeatedly represented as a figure of minstrelsy through which the dominant culture constructed and economically exploited black stereotypes. She performs, for example, for her schoolmates by puffing on a cigar and hiding it in the teacher's desk so that he might believe its smoke to be a sign of fire. And she performs again for Jack Bellmont when, in order to eat from Mrs. Bellmont's plate, she has her dog wipe it clean. Clearly an act of resistance to Mrs. Bellmont's tyranny, it is also a source of amusement to Jack, who throws her a silver half-dollar, "saying, 'There, take that; 't was worth paying for'" (72).

Beneath this comic surface, however, Frado is doubly constructed by the Bellmonts as sexual and economic object—represented by the appellation Our Nig—thus bringing to the surface the latent contradictions in the conventional tragic mulatta figure. It is significant that minstrelsy itself both sexualized the black woman in the role of "Negro wench" and undercut her sexuality by masculinizing her, unmasking the male impersonator beneath the female costume at the show's end.[39] Frado is first sexualized by her stepfather in his deliberations about giving her away: "'There's Frado's six years old, and pretty. . . . She'd be a prize somewhere'" (17). Later, as Our Nig, Frado again functions as a sexual object. The term is invented by Jack, the younger Bellmont son, and is used consistently up to the point where both he and his older brother, James, disappear from the plot. It is clearly sexualized: "'She's real handsome and bright, and not very black, either'" (25); and Frado participates in this sexualization by becoming attached to both men: "How different this appellative sounded from him [Jack]" (70). Although the narrative specifically refrains from portraying an explicit sexual relationship between Frado and either of these men, such language remains highly suggestive, particularly given the social realities of the indentured female servant.

If Frado as Our Nig represents black female sexuality to these two men, she is seen by others, particularly Mrs. Bellmont, as a desexualized worker whose labor power, or "worth," is to be exploited much as Nancy Prince's had earlier been (90). Initially construed as a male worker when Mag remembers that "Mr. Bellmont wants to hire a boy to work for him" (18), by the end of her indenture Frado has come to incorporate within her both, or neither, sexes: "Mrs. B. felt that she could not well spare one who could so well adapt herself to all departments—man, boy, housekeeper, domestic, etc." (116); and it is this interpretation of Frado, rather than the sexualized one, that survives to the end of the narrative and even beyond in the appended documents. Mrs. Bellmont's shrewd assessment of Frado's "worth" should not surprise us, for of all the characters in the narrative it is she who is the most preoccupied with the issues of acquisition, ownership, and accumulation of property. The Bellmont "two-story white house," we are told, had been acquired by Mr. Bellmont's father and then "passed into the hands of a son" (21). But it is Mrs. Bellmont who arrogates unto herself the duty of maintaining her husband's estate through Frado's labor and of enlarging it by seeking Aunt Abby's right in the homestead and plotting to marry Jane to a wealthy landowning neighbor (45, 56).

As she appealed to a readership of "colored brethren" for "patronage," Wilson offered them the portrait of a white woman that subverts the private sphere ideology, in particular the sentimental responses of sympathy and disciplinary intimacy as social correctives; and her subversion here is even greater than that of Jacobs. Mrs. Bellmont perverts the feminine values of the private sphere first of all by reconstructing it as a place organized according to a capitalist ethic of ownership and accumulation. In this sphere, moreover, Mrs. Bellmont insists on regulating Frado's behavior not only by confining her to the "L chamber" (26) but also by implementing an ethic of "severe restraint" rather than that disciplinary intimacy through which Stowe's Eva and Ophelia had controlled Topsy. We may note that this discipline of restraint had already been initiated by Mag; and indeed, Mrs. Bellmont's lack of emotional self-control and willingness to use physical force suggest her replication of Mag as an authority figure. Finally, Mrs. Bellmont openly opposes sentimental values by denigrating the sentimentality exhibited by other members of the household, both male and female: "She would not have Jane too sentimental" (56). Given such a realignment of values, it is not surprising that Mr. Bellmont repeatedly leaves the domestic home "to await the quieting of the storm" (45).

The plots of sentimental fiction required the presence of an authority figure who abuses her power over the socially weak.[40] But her authority is generally balanced, and corrected, by the sympathy of those characters who embody sentimental culture. In *Our Nig,* however, these characters—Jane, Aunt Abby, and particularly James—are impotent. Indeed, if Frado appears to be Stowe's Topsy transplanted to the North, James embodies the traits of a conventional nineteenth-century heroine. He is a revised Eva, gentle, religious, and forgiving, whose death is described in a rhetoric strangely reminiscent of Stowe's: "'Hark! do you hear it?' . . . Look, look, at the shining ones! Oh, let me go and be at rest!' At midnight the messenger came" (97). Hazel Carby has suggested that James represents the well-intentioned but ineffectual Northern abolitionist whose economic interests, we may note, are ultimately allied with capitalism.[41] More generally, however, James represents the inefficacy of masculine sentimental sympathy as a means of correcting social ills. James sees Frado in fully sentimental terms: "A frail child, driven from shelter by the cruelty of his [*sic*] mother, was an object of interest to James" (50). But neither James's sympathetic responses nor his attempts at disciplinary intimacy have any power over the economic forces arrayed against Frado. Indeed, James participates in Frado's oppression; for underneath its sentimental surface their relationship is one of labor exploitation as Frado ruins her health nursing James on his deathbed.

The conclusion of *Our Nig* suggests some effort by Frado to control her own labor power; she successfully threatens to withhold her labor in a verbal altercation with Mrs. Bellmont: "'Stop!' shouted Frado, 'strike me, and I'll never work a mite more for you'" (105). The performative power of her words here makes it abundantly clear why Mrs. Bellmont's severe restraint invariably takes the form of driving a wedge in Frado's mouth, thereby rendering speech impossible. Yet even after the termination of her indenture Frado can find neither a safe haven in the domestic sphere nor escape from economic exploitation. In her marriage to Samuel, who seduces and then abandons her, Frado is forced to become the primary bread earner. And as a laborer in the New England cottage industries of sewing and straw weaving, she must allow work to invade the private sphere. Finally, while the Bellmont sons and daughters can rely on geographic mobility to improve their economic condition—traveling north to Vermont, south to Baltimore, and out west—Frado finds herself confined to her village, deprived of a community of "people of color," without a home of her own, and thrown back on public assistance for a period of time. It is perhaps the ultimate irony that at the narrative's end Frado chooses to commodify the one object that she now owns—herself—to sell on the literary marketplace, but that not even this act of commodification can ensure her son's survival.

Although Gates has contended that by signing her text as "Our Nig," Frado has moved from being the object of the dominant discourse to being the subject of her own and has reversed the power relation involved in the issue of who names,[42] I would suggest that Frado ironically becomes imprisoned by those outside perspectives, allowed by fiction, that impose their definitions of black womanhood on her. Frado develops no self-identity independent of the Bellmonts, and the last line of the narrative leaves us with a sense of her continuing obsession: ". . . she will never cease to track them till beyond mortal vision" (131). Frado's inability to escape these definitions underscores the difficulty of constructing black subjectivity in isolation from community, and suggests the degree to which identity is never individual but part of a larger collective consciousness. As such, the emergence of the ideological *I* around the terms "mother," "father," "home," and "narrative" become fully comprehensible—a desperate gesture to claim self-possession, ownership, relationship.

Delany's novel *Blake* stands in striking contrast to *Our Nig* as a text that extols the black male hero who self-consciously positions himself above his community and insists on absolute freedom of movement in order to forge black nationality and economic power beyond continental boundaries, thereby rewriting history. To a somewhat lesser extent than Wilson's heroine, Delany's protagonist is a fictional projection of the author, recast as a picaresque hero who contemplates the possibilities of black revolution. A genre employed early in American literary history, the picaresque is a novelistic form that celebrates difference, acknowledging the aspirations of the economically underdeveloped; it is linked to the rise of commodity and merchant capitalism, and reflects its economic and social instability. Standing as an emblem of this society in flux, the picaro is an isolated individual, an insider and an outsider, contemptuous of the dominant culture's devotion to capitalism yet eager to share its spoils. His story unfolds in an untotalized narrative, filled with ambiguities and irreconcilable contradictions, often ending on a note of irresolution.[43]

From the first chapter the narrative action of *Blake* unfolds around two plots, one private, the other public. The first plot is initiated by the sale of a mulatta slave, Maggie, by her master Colonel Franks; the second, by the refitting of an old ship, the *Merchantman*, by a group of American and Cuban men, among whom figures Colonel Franks, who hope to revive the slave trade, open up Cuban sugar plantations to U.S. interests, develop external colonization, and expand global capitalism. The novel thus fictionalizes political events that were taking place in the Caribbean during the 1840s and 1850s and Delany's reactions to them before he turned his full attention to African emigration in the mid-1850s.

Blake is moved to heroic action not because of these political developments but because of the sale of his wife, Maggie. Running away from Colonel Franks and seemingly motivated by a sense of common interest with other slaves, he travels throughout the Southern states organizing a slave revolt. As a composite of past African-American leaders who resisted the exploitation of their labor power through revolutionary acts—Toussaint L'Ouverture, Denmark Vesey, Nat Turner, Madison Washington—Blake embodies collective African-American history. Yet he remains a single hero—a picaro—who sets himself above the rest of his community. While he seeks to create community by linking the "huts of America" to one another in a revolutionary organization, he always remains apart from their inhabitants. Indeed, as the narrative progresses, Blake increasingly positions himself as an elite figure detached from the mass of slaves for whom he speaks. Rejecting both the conjure and Christian beliefs of slave culture as avenues of black empowerment, Blake relies instead on an organizational strategy that unites the huts of America by means of secret rituals, disguises, symbols, and the cult of silence reminiscent of Delany's own organization of the 1858 Chatham convention in which John Brown participated.

Delany may well have borrowed such forms from the Freemason movement of which he was a member and about which he had written a pamphlet claiming Freemasonry to be Egyptian—and thus black—in origin. Mark Carnes has recently suggested that Freemasonry flourished in the antebellum period as an essentially middle-class urban institution that arose in response to male anxieties created by the market revolution. This new capitalist order forced the restructuring of male gender roles, guiding men into competitive capitalism and allowing them sanctuary not in a feminized church but in masculine Freemasonry. This movement simultaneously adopted the values of the emerging middle class by preaching hard work, sobriety, and self-restraint, and subverted these values by creating mysterious rituals that undermined capitalist discipline.[44] In the novel, Blake's use of such rituals to create an organization of slaves under his control within an African-American male space reflects Delany's own aspirations as an educated and secularized black man to create a strong black male network that might eventually intervene in the new capitalist order.

The second half of *Blake* begins with the reappearance of both the *Merchant-man* and Maggie. The sexual and economic plots conjoin here in a twin colonization—that of Cuba by American slaveholding interests, and that of Maggie by the black male. Much like Brown's heroine Mary, the freed Maggie is privatized not by a white slaveholder but by the conditions of black patriarchy and capitalism, and disappears from the novel. The rest of part 2 focuses on the recolonization of Cuba as Americans, Spanish, Creoles, and blacks compete for the wealth provided by her plantation economy. Although Delany's narrative attempts to forge an alliance between American and Caribbean blacks as well as Creoles through the organization of a Grand Council, such an alliance appears unsustainable. The loss of the last chapters of the novel prevents us from knowing the ultimate fate of Cuba, the Grand Council, and Blake himself. But the increasingly episodic quality of the plot suggests Delany's difficulty in sustaining a vision of a revolutionary organization composed of a heterogeneous black population, of imperialism as a model of social change in the African diaspora, and, not unlike Jacobs and Wilson, of an African-American local place in the New World.

In 1859 Watkins Harper published a short story, "The Two Offers," in the *Anglo-African Magazine*, thus inaugurating a long career of fiction writing for a broad audience of black readers that would complement her public lecturing and continue until the end of the century. Like Jacobs and Wilson but to somewhat different ends, Watkins Harper in her story appropriated sentimental ideology and its construction of the private-public dichotomy to critique it and celebrate instead the single woman who, like herself, insists on seizing the public sphere as her field of action. Given that public speaking was, to return to Hugh Blair's words, the province of "good men" and thus exposed female lecturers to charges of unfeminine behavior, it is possible that in turning to fiction writing Watkins Harper was seeking to deflect the public's gaze from her bodily self. To establish an unquestioned narrative authority in her story, Watkins Harper created a disembodied third-person omniscient narrator who is neither gendered nor racialized.

The form of sentimental fiction enabled Watkins Harper to explore those seemingly private issues of romance and marriage that in fact have wider social implications. Indeed, what initially appears to be a conventional courtship plot in "The Two Offers" quickly becomes a cautionary temperance tale, as drink infiltrates the domestic sphere, destroys both the drunkard and his family, and thus rends the social fabric. In accordance with sentimental ideology, temperance stories posit a beneficent feminine domestic sphere ruled by pure moral values that stands in opposition to the male public sphere whose corrupt values are symbolized by the spaces of the saloon, the gambling house, and the brothel. In emphasizing the isolation, dependence, physical vulnerability, and social immobility of married women, such stories underscore the extent to which they are victims of intemperance.[45] "The Two Offers" constructs itself around such values, privileging the home as an almost sacred moral space and largely blaming the drunkard's frivolous mother for his viciousness. Interestingly, in this story it is upon the male rather than the female body that sentimental evil is inscribed. The narrator refuses to give the reader a detailed physical description of her heroine; instead, it is the body of the drunkard husband alone, upon which are written the ravages of intemperance, that is exposed to the reader.

In "The Two Offers," however, another plot emerges alongside the temperance tale that insists on reconfiguring the place of woman. Although the story initially focuses on the heroine, Laura Lagrange, and her poor marriage choice to a future drunkard, it is in fact a hybrid text that gradually reveals a second plot, that of Laura's cousin, Janette Alston. Janette's story frames Laura's and seems at first to serve a purely functional purpose. It is Janette who initiates the opening expository conversation that enables the reader to learn about Laura's two offers; it is Janette's earlier unhappy romance that foreshadows Laura's later doomed marriage; finally, it is Janette's independence and self-reliance that underscore Laura's weakness. Yet "The Two Offers" is also centrally about Janette, the "old maid" in whom "nature . . . put . . . a double portion of intellect."[46] For Janette is a writer who can authorize her own life in a way that Laura cannot. This point is tellingly made at the beginning of the story as Laura finds herself unable to make a choice between her two marriage offers and thus cannot finish writing her letters to her suitors. Laura's choice of husband occurs, in fact, outside the narrative frame, and, once it is made, she is unable to make any further narrative choices; after her marriage she simply becomes a "weary watcher at the gates of death" (313). In contrast, Janette is able to make choices. If at the beginning of the story the narrator informs us that the heartbroken Janette has chosen the vocation of poet, by the tale's end she has transcended the status of fictional character to enter into history and merge with both Watkins Harper and the disembodied narrator.

In "The Two Offers" the reader is never explicitly informed of the narrator's identity; yet it is clear that her authority derives not only from her capacities as a fiction maker but from her firm grounding in, and understanding of, history. Indeed, in an important passage midway through the story, the narrator interrupts the flow of her narration to shift from fictional to sociohistorical discourse and contrast the woman of fiction, described as "a frail vine, clinging to her brother man for support, and dying when deprived of it" to the "true woman" of social history in whom "conscience should be enlightened, her faith in the true and right established, and scope given to her Heaven-endowed and God-given faculties" (291). Laura obviously conforms to the definition of the woman of fiction, who has accepted confinement in the domestic sphere, lives entirely within the private world of emotions, and "trie[s] to hide her agony from the public gaze" (312). To the narrator she is not interesting, and thus must die not only as a character but as a model for black women. Over her the narrator chooses Janette, the true woman, whose life bears a close resemblance to Watkins Harper's own. By the end of the story Janette has decisively rejected the values of sentimentality—"Neither was she always sentimentally sighing for something to love"—and embraced the anomalous status of the single woman: "She was an old maid; no husband brightened her life with his love or shaded it with his neglect. No children nestling lovingly in her arms called her mother. No one appended Mrs. to her name" (313). Instead, Janette, like Watkins Harper, chooses to devote the rest of her life to service in the community and public spheres, in particular to the "unpopular cause" of abolitionism and the development of "right culture" in women (313).

Yet the story does not only offer the reader a parallel between Janette's life and Watkins Harper's own; it suggests as well a conflation between the narrator and Watkins Harper herself. Indeed, in the passages on womanhood as well as in the final discussion of Janette's choices, the narrator turns to Watkins Harper's speeches to find models for her own narrative discourse; the eloquence of the pulpit is transferred to the printed page and made respectable for use by a woman writer. In an account of one of her lecturing tours placed in the same *Anti-Slavery Bugle* article in which she had described herself as a meddling old maid, Watkins Harper exhorted her black audiences in much the same terms as the story's narrator: "We need women whose hearts are the homes of a high and lofty enthusiasm, a noble devotion to the cause of emancipation, who are willing to lay time, talent, and money, on the altar of universal freedom."[47] Janette, then, merges not only with Watkins Harper but with the narrator whose fictional self depends on Watkins Harper's historical existence, yet whose body remains shielded from the public's gaze. "The Two Offers" suggests, then, the degree to which history and fiction are interdependent and fiction functions as an important strategy for the representation of both self and African-American social history.

In remaining faithful to the autobiographical "facts" of their lives, neither Jacobs nor Wilson could realistically represent the community sphere as a fully successful site of resistance to racial oppression or as a place of African-American economic empowerment. At the close of "The Two Offers" Watkins Harper offers only a brief description of her heroine's engagement in community and public spheres. Frank J. Webb's novel, *The Garies and Their Friends,* is all the more remarkable, then, in its use of fiction to conceptualize an African-American local place in the urban North and thereby imagine community. A review published in the December 4, 1857 issue of *Frederick Douglass' Paper* offers an acute appraisal of Webb's motivations as it applauds the ability of "one of the persecuted people . . . to take up the pen and paint their manners in vivid and pleasing colors and struggle against their wrongs and oppression, with a weapon which never yet failed the just cause. . . . If he has turned author in order to give us some idea of the inner life of his race, he has done good service to the cause of humanity and progress."

The very title of Webb's novel announces community in its reference to a group of people rather than a single heroic figure; yet it also suggests the separation of the Garies from their friends. The opening chapters of the novel boldly initiate a revision of the tragic mulatta plot as the slave master, Mr. Garie, has installed his slave, Emily, in his house as his wife. Ostracized by the slaveholding class in the South and hoping to escape the fate of the tragic mulatta, Emily soon convinces Mr. Garie to resettle in the free North. But even as a married couple in Philadelphia they remain isolated; Webb refuses to offer legal wedlock as a solution to the dilemma of the mulatta heroine. Midway through the novel, a race riot occurs and the Garies are murdered. In *The Garies*, then, the tragic mulatta figures more as a pretext for narrative action than as its center.

Indeed, Webb's chief interest in his novel is to probe the social and economic conditions of African Americans in the urban North and to theorize strategies of survival. Philadelphia's black community is represented as a hybrid space characterized by a heterogeneity of neighborhoods, social classes, and inhabitants, whom city life brings together in unpredictable ways. Through its main characters—the Ellis family, the De Younges, and Mr. Walters—it practices an "economics of marginality" designed to counter black underdevelopment and translate marginality into social and economic autonomy based on community interdependence.

On the one hand the novel acknowledges black dependence on white social and economic structures, as Mrs. Ellis and her daughters sew for white families, and Charlie Ellis must seek employment with white businesses. On the other it illustrates the potential of black entrepreneurship in the figure of Mr. Walters, a wealthy investor in real estate, black craftsmanship in the carpenter, Mr. Ellis, and black small business ownership in the secondhand clothes store of the De Younges. Though the novel openly endorses capitalism as an economic model for black empowerment, it celebrates not so much individual achievement as the way the characters attend to the collectivity, returning surplus value to the community rather than serving their own particular interests. Community values emerge most strongly during the race riot and its aftermath, which form the central episodes of the novel. The defense of Mr. Walter's house—the bastion of black capitalism—during the riot becomes emblematic of black community interdependence as men and women of all social classes come together to protect it. After Mr. Ellis is injured by the mob in a futile attempt to warn the Garies, the ordinarily self-reliant Ellis family suddenly finds itself deprived of economic resources and is sheltered by Mr. Walters. The family's resilience and ultimate triumph demonstrate the effectiveness of an economics of marginality that resists racial oppression and relies on collective action in order to forge an empowering African-American local place in the urban North.

In the 1850s, then, African-American writers—both male and female—seized upon the new possibilities offered them by novelization. In their writings they turned to fiction, or made use of fictionalizing techniques, to counter the dominant culture's versions of their history and reconceptualize the social construction of African-American identity on their own terms. In particular, they took advantage of the nonteleological nature of fiction to explore the different possible shapes and outcomes of the experiences of blacks in America. In so doing they hoped that fiction would serve as a yet another instrument not only of social protest but also of empowerment, enabling both the entrance to a broader literary marketplace and, most especially, the creation of community.

7

Seeking the *"Writable"*: Charlotte Forten and the Problem of Narration

Unlike the black women lecturers, travelers, and writers discussed in the previous chapters, Charlotte Forten never emerged as a fully public "doer of the word," either in speech or in print. Indeed, in her early years Forten appears to have lived in dread of public self-exposure and to have assiduously avoided entering any of those liminal spaces that had enabled earlier black women to carry out their cultural work. Forten's verbal reticence is puzzling since she was almost a full generation younger than these older women and benefited greatly from the cultural expansion that was taking place among the northeastern African-American elite in the decades before the Civil War. In stark contrast to the illiterate Sojourner Truth, for example, Forten was not only fully in command of the requisite skills for literary composition but also came to intellectual maturity during the burgeoning of African-American literary and oratorical traditions. She knew Charles Lenox Remond and Sarah Parker Remond well and, indeed, as an adolescent lived with the Remond family in Salem for several years. She was familiar with Phillis Wheatley's poetry from childhood and met the novelists William Wells Brown and Frank J. Webb during the 1850s after the publication of their respective novels, *Clotel* (1853) and *The Garies and Their Friends* (1857).

Forten's elite status alone singles her out as remarkable. She was born in 1837 into an upper-class Philadelphia family whose members were well educated, cultured, genteel, and dedicated to racial uplift. Her grandfather, James Forten, was a wealthy sailmaker and an active leader in both black and white social reform movements; he held a prominent place not only in the black American Moral Reform Society but in Garrison's American Anti-Slavery Society as well, and was an early supporter of the *Liberator*. In contrast to James, the next generation of Fortens appears to have been affected by declining economic fortunes, reflecting perhaps a general trend of downward occupational mobility that beset antebellum Philadelphia from the 1830s on as large merchant-manufacturers came to erode the power of smaller craftsmen and traders.[1] Thus, Charlotte's father, Robert Bridges Forten, achieved neither the economic nor the civic prominence of his father. Although termed "the most gifted . . . of the four sons" by Daniel Payne and clearly dedicated to racial uplift and abolitionism, Robert Forten seems to have been much less self-assured than his father in both his occupation and his social activism.[2] After the death of his first wife, Mary Virginia Wood, he sent Charlotte to live with the Remonds in Salem, remarried, and moved with his second family to Canada and then to England in 1858. Returning to the United States to participate in the Civil War, he enlisted in the Union army in March 1864 only to die the following month.

Charlotte Forten's early life was marked, then, by a profound sense of desertion and homelessness that, as I shall later argue, provided the emotional impulse behind her diary writing. Sent by her father to Salem to avoid the segregated educational system of Philadelphia, Forten lived with the Remonds and went to the local schools. Upon her graduation, she taught school until ill health forced her to move back to Philadelphia, where she lived intermittently from the spring of 1857 to 1859 and then for a sustained period from October 1860 to the summer of 1862; it was at this time that Forten made the bold and surprising decision to go south to teach the newly freed people of the South Carolina Sea Islands. While still living in Philadelphia, Forten came intensely to dread the city's racially charged atmosphere. And yet it was there that she found herself surrounded by loving and socially active family members, her aunts Margaretta, Sarah, and Harriet, who were affiliated with the Philadelphia Female Anti-Slavery Society, the Free Produce Society, and the Philadelphia Vigilant Committee, as well as Harriet's husband, Robert Purvis, who had succeeded his father-in-law as the city's most prominent black spokesperson. It was also there that Forten became reacquainted with many of the black and white abolitionist leaders whom she had met earlier in Salem. Yet despite her constant contact with these public figures, Forten herself never fully emerged as a public speaker or writer.

In her diary, which she began in 1854 at the age of sixteen, Forten repeatedly stated her ambition to acquire a public voice through either speaking or writing. Thus she wrote alternately of her desire to emulate Sarah Parker Remond and "become what I often say I should like to be—an Anti-slavery lecturer" or to compose poetry in the tradition of English romanticism: "Oh! that I could become suddenly inspired and write as only great poets can write, or that I might write a beautiful poem of two hundred lines in my sleep as Coleridge did."[3] Yet Forten never followed Remond's example, and her published writings consist chiefly of some poems, travel descriptions and art appreciations, as well as a series of letters to the editor, most of which were printed in the *Liberator,* the *National Anti-Slavery Standard,* the *Atlantic Monthly,* and, in the postbellum period, Boston's *Commonwealth* and *Christian Register.* In lieu of published writings, Forten kept a private journal, which offers us only tentative clues that would fully elucidate her relative silence.

One possible explanation for Forten's reluctance to engage in public lecturing might be found in the social ideology of her class, which, to a much greater extent than that of Jarena Lee or Maria Stewart, for example, discouraged female public self-expression and sought to contain women within the domestic circle of true womanhood. Indeed, in 1836 one of Forten's uncles, James Forten Jr., addressed the Philadelphia Female Anti-Slavery Society, of which his mother and three sisters were members, suggesting that women's best means of achieving the goals of abolitionism was to make it "the topic of conversation amidst acquaintances, in every family circle and in the shades of private life."[4] Yet, as we have seen, such prohibitions against the public activism of elite women were not strictly adhered to; indeed, twenty years later Forten would be able to observe within her intimate circle of friends and relatives the highly effective, if somewhat unique, example of Sarah Parker Remond in her role as a Garrisonian antislavery lecturer.

A more plausible explanation for Forten's public silence might perhaps be the psychological and intellectual insecurities to which she gave poignant expression in entry after entry in her diary.[5] In them Forten repeatedly confessed to a paralyzing shyness that left her, unlike "Miss R.[emond] who can *always talk*" (247), strangely silent: "I do not know how to talk. Words always fail me when I want them most. The more I feel the more impossible it is for me to speak. It is very provoking" (433). So strong was this inhibition that after having been urged to join a literary society in Philadelphia, Forten expressed the hope that "I shall not be called upon to do anything more than write. Indeed it would be utterly impossible for me to read or recite" (339). Yet even the more private act of writing itself occasioned intense self-doubt in Forten. Literary composition became "a most formidable undertaking for me, and one which, I greatly fear, is quite beyond my powers" (153); its results were invariably "poor," "miserable," "not worthy," "doggerel." This sense of intellectual inadequacy was further reinforced by acute feelings of racial oppression: "None but those who experience it can know what it is—this constant, galling sense of cruel injustice and wrong. I cannot help feeling it very often, it intrudes upon my happiest moments, and spreads a dark, deep gloom over everything" (111). Accompanying such feelings of intellectual inadequacy and personal worthlessness was, finally, a sense that literary composition, and in particular the genres of poetry and fiction, necessitated forms of self-revelation that could in fact be very painful. Thus, even Forten's diary, that most private of literary forms, is marked throughout by signs of emotional self-repression that, by her own admission, constituted a fundamental aspect of her "nature": "I know not why it is that when I think and feel the most, I say the least. I suppose it is my nature, not to express by word or action how much I really feel" (94).

Faced with such a resistance to self-revelation that not even Forten's diary can dispel, we are left with a series of questions: What kinds of literary texts might Forten have wanted to write and publish? Given her commitment to her race, would she have insisted on producing a racial literature? Or might she have chosen to write about nonracial subjects in the hopes of escaping the pain of race prejudice and self-revelation? What kind of audience might she have wanted to appeal to? What publishing house would have been willing to print her work? What compromises might she have been forced to make in order to accommodate white publishers and readers?

Answers to these questions can only be speculative. Forten's few published antebellum pieces appeared mainly in white newspapers and magazines such as the *National Anti-Slavery Standard,* the *Liberator,* and the *Atlantic Monthly,* and, to a much lesser extent, and only when pressed by Daniel Payne, in the AME Church's *Christian Recorder.* Although it is quite possible that Forten was thereby seeking to address as broad an audience as possible, we may also wonder to what extent her close ties to white abolitionism detached her from African-American literary traditions and, as in Sojourner Truth's case, drew her away from an African-American readership. In her diary Forten never makes reference to such black newspapers as the *North Star, Frederick Douglass' Paper,* the *Anglo-African Magazine,* or the *Weekly Anglo-African;* nor does she mention Brown's or Webb's novelistic production, nor any of Watkins Harper's works. And although Wheatley is praised as a gifted poetess, she seems to represent in Forten's imagination the intellectual possibilities of an Other radically different from herself, the "African slave": "Her character and genius afford a striking proof of the falseness of the assertion made by some that *hers* is an inferior race" (92, emphasis mine).

It would seem, then, that in her antebellum years Forten was unable to make use of the African-American literary and oratorical traditions that were developing around her in order to fashion an empowering mode of public self-expression. Forten's alienation from these burgeoning traditions was quite possibly due to what I would call her lack of a "usable past." Indeed, separated from Southern slaves by virtue of both geography and civil status, and from a large segment of Northern blacks by virtue of her class, Forten in her early years could not find within the African-American culture that surrounded her a past from which she could construct a sustained narrative of self, community, and history.

A reading of her diary indicates that, in the antebellum period, Forten did make serious efforts to write and publish in two of the genres readily available to women of this time, the short story and poetry. Forten's diary entries suggest that she wrote at least two, if not three, short fictional narratives in her early life. The first was started in April 1857 and was on the "subject 'prejudice against color'" (212); it was either that same story, or a second one, entitled "The Lost Bride," that Forten sent to the *Home Journal* in December 1857 but apparently never heard about further (271); the last story mentioned was one on an unknown topic begun in April 1858 but not referred to thereafter (302). Given our lack of knowledge about these stories, any comments about them must remain highly speculative. Forten's decision to send "The Lost Bride" to the *Home Journal,* for example, seems significant in that it raises interesting questions of both genre and audience. The New York periodical, which bore the marked imprint of its editor, Nathaniel Willis, the same man in whose house Jacobs had lived after her escape from slavery, was devoted primarily to news about society and fashion as well as to the dissemination of sentimental literary culture.[6] In sending her story to the *Journal*, it seems clear that Forten envisioned her readership as white and upper-class; we may also speculate that, given its title, the story was probably written in the genre of American sentimental fiction that was so popular in the 1850s.

It is significant, I think, that in Forten's many discussions of novel reading in her diary, it is Scott and Dickens who figure most prominently, suggesting that Forten may well have hoped that these writers would ultimately serve as her fictional models. Yet it would seem that both Scott's historical romances and Dickens's more sentimental social novels may have finally proved unsuitable representational forms for Forten. For unlike Scott, who was able to mine a usable historical past in which the violent conflict of class, national, and ethnic forces could be reconciled through the romance form, Forten seems to have been unable to recover a past through which she could begin to unravel and make sense of the complexities of race relations in the United States on the basis of her knowledge and experience of American and African-American history. And, unlike Dickens, who did not shrink from imaginatively projecting his autobiographical self into his fiction, Forten, given her exquisite racial sensitivities, might well have found even the form of the sentimental social novel insufficiently distanced.

Forten was more successful in her efforts at both poetry writing and publication. At least eight of her poems were published in newspapers and magazines in the antebellum period: "To W. L. G. on Reading His 'Chosen Queen'" (*Lib*, March 16, 1855); two hymns written for school ceremonies in 1856, "A Parting Hymn" (printed in William Wells Brown's *The Black Man* in 1863) and an untitled poem (*Lib*, Aug. 24, 1856); "The Angel's Visit" (written for the *Christian Recorder* in 1858 and printed in Brown); "The Two Voices" (*NASS*, Jan. 15, 1859); "The Wind among the Poplars" (*Lib*, May 27, 1859); "The Slave Girl's Prayer" (*Lib*, Feb. 3, 1860); and "In the Country" (*NASS*, Sept. 1, 1860).[7] The first three poems, written during Forten's school years in Salem, are, like Watkins Harper's later verse, hymnal in tone, substituting for the congregant's praise of Father and Son the adolescent's admiration of teachers and other moral leaders along with admonitions to her peers to emulate them. These poems are highly impersonal; the poetic persona effaces herself in the presence of those she admires or exhorts, and relies on conventional imagery to articulate her feelings. Thus, Forten's first poem, addressed to William Lloyd Garrison, is devoted to praise of the reformer's commitment to abolitionism formulated in the allegorical and metaphoric language of chivalry. Abolitionism is imaged as a "Queen," a "champion of Truth," who "should be th' acknowledged sovereign of all." To Garrison, however, she is not simply "that bright Queen," but most significantly a "chosen Queen." Represented as having consciously and deliberately chosen abolitionism to be his sovereign, Garrison is then figured as her "loyal subject," who not only pays her "homage" but engages on her behalf in the "battles" of "moral warfare" "with truer weapons than the blood-stained sword." The poem convincingly concludes with the triumphant declaration that "thy chosen Queen shall never find / A truer subject nor a firmer friend."

Forten's other two early poems are meditations upon the moral duties of the graduating students of Salem Higginson Grammar School and State Normal School, both of which Forten attended. In each poem Forten remains self-effaced, hiding personal concerns behind her educational goals. In "A Parting Hymn" she addresses those "parting" friends whom she "within these walls shall meet no more": "Forth to a noble work they go: / O, may their hearts keep pure." In the second poem she includes herself within the group of aspiring students: "But, with hope of aiding others, / Gladly we perform our part." Both poems are permeated by an impersonal vocabulary of moral obligation to educate the young. Thus, in "A Parting Hymn" she exhorts: "May those, whose holy task it is / To guide impulsive youth, / Fail not to cherish in their souls / A reverence for truth." This obligation consists, more specifically, both in helping "the poor and the oppressed" and in teaching "hatred of oppression" to those who were born more fortunate.

Forten's later antebellum poems were written mostly during that particularly difficult period of her life in Philadelphia when she found herself "unable to work, and having but little congenial society, and suffering the many deprivations which all of our unhappy race must suffer in the so-called 'City of Brotherly Love.'" So intense was Forten's unhappiness that she found herself unable to confide it even to her diary: "But over these weary months it is better to draw the veil and forget" (363). Instead, her feelings of despair are articulated in a series of narrative poems that, in contrast to the earlier ones, are revelatory of deeply felt personal emotions. Although the subject matter of some of these poems is racial and others nonracial, the poems nonetheless express a similar emotional content by means of similar poetic techniques, suggesting that ultimately the separation of racial from nonracial material was impossible for Forten to make.

For example, at least three of these poems, "The Angel's Visit," "The Two Voices," and "The Wind among the Poplars," are structured around a dialogue—either between self and other or between two warring aspects of the self; yet only the second is explicitly racial in theme. In all three poems, poetic dialogue appears to serve both as an outer manifestation of those deep divisions (both racial and nonracial) afflicting Forten and as a mechanism for breaching these divisions and achieving oneness. It is also possible that poetry functioned at this time as a means through which Forten felt she could enter into a kind of spiritual dialogue with her absent father. Indeed, according to Daniel Payne, Robert Forten was himself "gifted with a poetical vein"; not only had he pub-lished poems in the *Pennsylvania Freeman* in the 1840s and 1850s, but an album belonging to Charlotte's mother, Mary Virginia Wood, which eventually came into Charlotte's possession, reveals that he had wooed his first wife through verse: "And by these lines perchance you think on me / I am your friend and always wish to be."[8]

The central theme of "The Angel's Visit" consists of a dialogue between the poet and her dead mother. This dialogue is contextualized by the poet's evocation of those beneficent natural forces that surround her and focuses primarily on the "gentle moon" who "lovingly . . . smiled on me" as well as the "night wind" whose song "sang to me of peace." The dialogue itself records Forten's deep sense of loss over her mother's early death, her anguished cry for guidance, and her desire, born of despair, to go "home" to God. Falling into a "dreamy spell," she is visited by her "angel mother," who promises her a "brighter day"; upon awaking, the poet finds that her prayers have been answered and that "from my heart the weary pain / Forevermore had flown." In contrast, "The Two Voices," which Forten herself described as "stanzas which express what I've *felt*" (350), portrays conflicting voices that explore issues of race internal to the poet herself. The first is a voice of despair that images Forten as a "homeless outcast," invites her to yield to racial hatred and vengeful thoughts, and tempts her to contemplate the grave as her only "haven"; the second is a voice of struggle that asserts that "the life that's passed in struggling / Is the true, the only life," and bids Forten to live, to "strive and suffer," and to "work for others." As she listens to these voices the poet finds that her resolve has grown and she decides "Bravely will I bear earth's burdens, / Ere I pray to rest in Heaven."

On the surface, two other poems, "The Wind among the Poplars" and "The Slave Girl's Prayer," appear to contain little revelation of personal feeling but, on the contrary, to narrate totally fictive plots. "The Wind among the Poplars" consists of a dialogue between two characters, Clare, who invites her companion to enjoy the "strange, wild music" of the wind that induces her soul to exultation, and Bertha, who can interpret this music only as a requiem for her drowned lover. It is possible that this poem is in fact a fictionalization of the death at sea of Jacob Gilliard, the husband of Forten's close friend Helen Putnam, whose ship had foundered in the Atlantic returning from San Francisco to New York; thus, Bertha would represent Helen, and Clare, Forten herself.[9] It is also possible that Bertha and Clare may serve as externalizations of those two contradictory dialoguing impulses in Forten, the one leading her to exultation, the other to anguish. Similarly, "The Slave Girl's Prayer" is a fictional narrative that rehearses the conventional plot of a slave girl—perhaps a tragic mulatta—who begs to die rather than be sold into slavery. Told in the first person, this poem again invites us to read beneath its fictive surface to uncover Forten's own personal anguish over "the doom of shame and sorrow" that American slavery and racism have brought to black womanhood. As such, it stands in striking contrast to an earlier poem, "The Appeal," written by her father and published in the February 19, 1852 issue of the *Pennsylvania Freeman*. In this poem "the poor, the outcast slave" figures as a subaltern who cannot speak: "Oppression's heel hath crushed / His native genius, which, if early train'd / Had grown to honor'd usefulness, and rush'd / Onward among the fam'd"; it is the literate narrator who, asserting his distance from the mute slave, delivers an appeal on the latter's behalf.

Finally, the poem "In the Country," written in the summer of 1860, when Forten's health compelled her to try a water cure at a hydropathic clinic in Worcester, Massachusetts, differs significantly from the others in the serenity of its tone. It was at this clinic that Forten met Dr. Seth Rogers, who would figure so prominently—and romantically—in her later Saint Helena diary entries. Unable to give direct and full expression to her intense personal emotions, Forten composed a nature poem that functions as an imagistic projection of her feelings. Unlike many of her earlier poems, "In the Country" is not structured around dialogue but from the outset strives to achieve unity both with nature and with self. Enjoying the harmony offered by such natural elements as the birds, the sun, the sky, the shadows, and the air, the poet finds "a strange, sweet rapture" in the "loving breast" of "Mother Earth" and is gradually transported from emotional turmoil to peace: "Passion hath passed away, / And weariness and woe; / Wrapt in the glory of this perfect day, / Sweet peace at last I know."

As with Watkins Harper's poetry, these latter poems must be seen as a product of midcentury American sentimental culture. And, as in the case of the older poet, Forten's preferred poetic form was the ballad through which she narrativized the plight of the socially weak—the orphan child, the bereft lover, the slave girl, the racially oppressed—repeatedly invoked sentimental culture's obsession with death and mourning, and interpreted nature as a redemptive force, all the while seeking to evoke a sympathetic response from her readers. In addition, Forten's poems appear to have been influenced by her readings in British romanticism as they suggest an assimilation of some of its most characteristic images. For example, in "An Angel's Visit" Forten's "angel mother" is symbolically represented in imagistic language reminiscent of Brontë's *Jane Eyre* (which Forten had read as early as 1854) as the moon who descends in a "flood of rosy light" to bring solace to her daughter. Both "The Wind among the Poplars" and "The Two Voices" make central use of what M. H. Abrams has called the romantic metaphor of the correspondent breeze in which the sound made by the storm's wind functions as an outer analogue of the poetic personae's inner emotion, whether it be joy ("Lov'st thou not the strange, wild music / Of this March wind bold and free?") or sadness—"Ah, the wind among the poplars / Hath a mournful sound to me, / For it moaneth to me ever / Of a loved one, lost at sea" ("The Wind among the Poplars").[10] Unlike Watkins Harper, however, Forten was not able to master the poetical techniques of the ballad form, and her poems show none of the metrical regularity or "aesthetics of restraint" that characterized Watkins Harper's verse. Indeed, in striking contrast to Watkins Harper, Forten in her poetry exhibited little control over her own emotions and revealed herself much more willing to make public her private world of inner feelings. In the process, she came to violate her own dictum of emotional self-repression—a betrayal which perhaps became the reason for her abandonment of poetic composition until the mid-1870s.

At the same time that she was experimenting with fictional and poetic form, Forten kept a several-hundred-page journal in which she addressed, directly and indirectly, those issues of representation and self-representation that were besetting her. Margo Culley has suggested that diary writing is most often motivated by the experience of some form of "death."[11] For Forten this "death" could only have been her separation from her father, Robert Forten, occasioned by her move to Salem in order to take advantage of its nonsegregated school system. Compounded by the early death of her mother, this separation left Forten an orphan, in need of reconstituting a "home" for herself. Through diary writing she sought to construct a social space for herself in which she could work out definitions of self and the relationship of self to the larger community.

In the nineteenth century diary writing was a highly respectable occupation for young American women. It was, in fact, not only culturally acceptable but expected, functioning as a form of mental discipline as parents mandated that their daughters record not girlish fantasies but moral progress.[12] Intensely self-conscious about her writing project, Forten began her diary by reflecting on its significance. She conceptualized it as a private document in which she would function simultaneously as author, text, and reader, thus creating a closed circuit that would preclude any possible intrusion of the public's gaze. Furthermore, diary writing encouraged Forten to emphasize her inner self and thereby render herself bodiless. Her body is, in fact, represented only as sick and devitalized; indeed, Forten was plagued throughout her life by a respiratory illness that manifested itself in headaches, colds, lack of strength, and exhaustion. If, for many women of the dominant leisure class, invalidism was a crucial sign of social status, wealth, and ladyhood, for African-American women it was a brute physical reality intensified by the difficulties of living in a racially oppressive environment. It is perhaps not accidental that Forten's first mention of illness in her diary—a "distressing headache"—is occasioned by the noise of firearms set off during a Fourth of July celebration (81). It is equally possible, of course, that her illness might have been exacerbated by the tense convergence of physical sickness, racial oppression, and the cult of invalidism condoned by upper-class ideologies. Whatever its causes, Forten's invalidism during this period of her life operated as a constraining force that severely limited her bodily movements and thrust her back into her inner self whose life she meant to record in her diary.

Forten began her diary in the hopes that it would appeal to her retrospective mind by helping her to recall "in other years" friends much loved, books read, and places seen, and by "enabl[ing] me to judge correctly of the growth and improvement of my mind from year to year" (58). This last comment suggests the depths of Forten's desire to focus on her inner being and chart the formation and progression of a coherent self made intelligible through the act of writing. Such a project would prove to be dangerous, however, ultimately leading to self-censorship. Forten's upper-class social position as James Forten's granddaughter, her economic status as a member of a family whose fortunes were in decline, her racial identity as a black, her position as a woman privatized by her own community but perceived as grotesque by the dominant culture, her fetishization by white abolitionists, all converged to create a heterogeneous self, a compound of different, and finally irreducible, elements. Given such heterogeneity of self, Forten's project of coherent self-writing ultimately became impossible. So fraught was it with psychical danger that Forten, as we have already observed, often recoiled from self-expression. To say, to feel even, may lead to insanity. Reacting, for example, to the bitterness and agony of racism she wrote: "To me it is *dreadful, dreadful.* Were I to indulge in the thought I fear I should become insane" (183).

How, then, could Forten indulge in thoughts in her diary without going insane? To accomplish this end she developed a set of rhetorical strategies that, as critics have noted, give her private writings a peculiarly public voice.[13] Thus, within the narrative contract established in the diary, the narrating *I* is invoked only when the self is experienced as relatively stable. As a consequence, Forten records no entries during the difficult months spent in Philadelphia or the emotional summer spent at Dr. Rogers's clinic in Worcester (1860–62), nor does she write during the period surrounding her father's death (winter of 1863 through spring of 1864). Events narrated are also selectively chosen. An entry made April 11, 1863 from Saint Helena's, for example, underscores Forten's exquisite narrative discrimination. Having moved to the South Carolina Sea Islands during the Civil War to teach the freed people, she renewed with great intensity her acquaintance with Dr. Rogers, who was surgeon in Thomas Wentworth Higginson's regiment of First South Carolina Volunteers. Watching the Volunteers prepare for combat from the window of her house, Forten insisted, however, on abiding by self-defined notions of literary propriety: "Meanwhile I sit composedly down taking notes; and shall now occupy myself with darning a pair of stockings for the doctor until something further occurs which is *writable*" (475).

What constitutes the writable for Forten? The main "plot" of her diary during the Salem and Philadelphia years consists of a narration of the "social body," the black and white abolitionist society in which her grandfather had figured so prominently earlier in the century. Such a narration allowed Forten to express her admiration for leading abolitionists—Garrison, Phillips, Whittier, and others—and to voice her aspiration to become a worker one day for the antislavery cause. Equally importantly, however, it allowed her to portray relatives and friends within the black elite—the Remonds and Putnams of Salem, the Fortens and Purvises of Philadelphia—who substitute for her dead and absent parents. Indeed, given the early death of her mother, the remarriage of her father, his departure to Canada, and his emotional remoteness, Forten's sense of homelessness was acute and pervades diary entry after entry: "But as I cannot go to either of my homes—to Canada (where father has recently moved) or to Phila.[delphia], I must try not to think of them" (144). Her detailed account of the pattern of her daily life within the black community—from the "sweet converse" held with friends and acquaintances to the more dreadful insanity-provoking discussions of racial prejudice to the combined pleasures and tensions within the different Remond households to the deaths of beloved ones—suggests the degree to which Forten sought to reconstitute home within this extended family of kin and non-kin.

Forten's diary entries concerning Sarah Parker Remond are of particular interest for they open onto the possibility—never fully realized—of the formation of a lasting female friendship and mentorship between these two antebellum black women. Eleven years her senior, Remond was the object of Forten's intense admiration as one in whom "I particularly admire the uncompromising sincerity which is a prominent trait of her character" (115). The catalyst for her interest in antislavery work, the person most responsible for introducing her to such white abolitionist leaders as Garrison and Whittier, Remond was Forten's earliest role model. Yet the relationship never developed into one of equality, and Forten ultimately chafed at Remond's mentorship role. To Forten, Remond's "perfect sincerity and candor" (115) eventually came to alternate with a "careless indifference" (139) toward her which she keenly resented. At the same time, Forten's admiration of Remond's antislavery work, in particular the success of her 1856–57 lecture tour of New York and Canada, gradually gave way to feelings of envy: "Am afraid much of envy stole into the pleasure with which I listened to Miss R.[emond]'s animated account, for the friendship of a great, a truly noble *genius* has, since childhood been one of the most fondly cherished of my many dreams" (200). It appears that such competitive feelings were ultimately returned by the older woman, as Forten's last diary entry concerning Remond reports a hostile comment made about Forten's first major publication since her schoolgirl poems, the article "Glimpses of New England," published in the *National Anti-Slavery Standard* in 1858: "Miss S.[arah] P. R.[emond] I hear has burst out most venomously upon my poor 'Glimpses.' . . . I *pity* her" (338).

Yet Forten was able to establish intimate and lasting relationships with other women, both peers and elders, forged in large part around the sharing and discussion of books that are amply recorded in her diary. Forten appears to have been especially interested in travel literature, in particular in books that depict the relationship of literary figures to geographic place, and specifically to home. The reading of such books became a form of travel itself: "I went determined *not* to take a book of travels, for already the foreign fever burns high enough. But on opening the book, the magical names of places and people fascinated me, and I could not resist the temptation" (237). Thus, in her diary Forten repeatedly mentions her pleasure in reading William Howitt's *Homes and Haunts of the Most Eminent British Poets*, the different essays of *Homes of American Authors*, and the chapters entitled "Authors Associated with Places" in Mary Russell Mitford's *Recollections of a Literary Life*. Constituting a distinct and highly popular genre during the antebellum period, books such as these were part of a broader cultural movement that focused its attention on "cultivated country life" and sought to imbue the country house—both its architecture and its surrounding grounds— with significant moral attributes and influential powers. According to this ide- ology, the country house serves as a respite from an aggressively utilitarian and competitive society and is meant to foster, in Nathaniel Willis's words, "a most careful culture of *home associations*" that would strengthen the individual's sensi- bilities and affections.14 In Forten's imaginative vision, people are invariably associated with a place that is not simply part of the natural world but possesses a spirit of its own, a *genius loci*. In particular, literary people are not merely associated with place but also influenced by it; and in the process of composition the spirit of the place comes to imbue the work of art.

Interestingly enough, Forten's narration of the social body in her diary is repeatedly interrupted by her own descriptions of landscapes and places. Although many of these descriptions are based on her observation of places in and around Salem that she had actually visited, others derive from paintings and illustrations contemplated in museums and books, and thus anticipate Forten's art criticism of her postbellum years in Washington, D.C. In the diary these descriptions are juxtaposed to the main plot without necessarily converging or overlapping with it. They are presented as set pieces that appear to be static and impersonal in their focus on such literarily conventional elements as the ocean and the elm tree. In fact, however, these landscapes are both lyricized and mor- alized. They function as projections and transformations of Forten's bodily self into a natural place already inhabited by guardian spirits and suffused with moral meanings. Thus, the elm, which in American literature symbolizes the spiritual core of a community, acquires particular resonance in Forten's writings as it comes to bespeak at once durability and survival for an oppressed people and serenity for Forten herself: ". . . the grand old elm trees. Peaceful, happy thoughts came lovingly to me as I paced slowly along under the arching branches. To me there is always a strange, sweet influence pervading these noble elms. I love them" (254).15 The ocean waves, accompanied by the "wild sounds" evoked by the wind, function, as in her poetry, as an outer analogue of inner movement. If the "correspondent breeze" typically connoted a vital release of imaginative fac- ulties in romantic ideology, for Forten the "wild sounds of the waves" also came to signify "liberty, glorious, boundless liberty" (88) as well as personal release from psychic bondage and consequent self-fulfillment: "As they [the waves] receded, my whole soul seemed drawn away with them, then when they rushed back again upon the steadfast rocks my being thrilled, glowed, with joyous, exultant life" (365–66).

Landscape description thus functioned for Forten as an indirect strategy of self-expression that would allow her to write the self without going insane. Yet these descriptions are also constrained by a politics of the picturesque that remains fundamentally conservative, suggesting just how complex self-definition was for her. The impulse of the picturesque is to improve nature, to tame its wildness, by means of representational techniques that render it decorous, proper, congruous.[16] In the process, as Alan Liu has noted in another context, the picturesque landscape becomes a moment of arrested desire in which narrative is transformed into atmosphere, people are marginalized, and passion has no outlet. According to Liu, such a pictorial arrest of desire is occasioned in late-eighteenth-century England by the workings of specific political, economic, and administrative institutions that were then reorganizing the English countryside and consequently were able to "project a new, carefully reposed discipline of freedom" into landscape painting while refusing "to assimilate certain anomalous forms into the formal integrity of the whole."[17] In Forten's landscape descriptions desire is arrested, I would argue, because it has been impeded and stifled by the social and economic barriers erected by the institutions of American slavery in the South and racial prejudice in the North. If the self is still present in Forten's descriptions, it is a disembodied solipsistic self cut off from both the thread of African-American history and the web of the national social body. Moreover, because of its isolated state this self cannot enact that crucial movement—characteristic of both the eighteenth-century local-meditative poem and the greater romantic lyric—from description to meditation that enabled the poet to organize his poem "around an emotional issue pressing for resolution."[18] The resistance to meditation thus points here to the impossibility of resolution. Landscape description in Forten's diary is indicative, then, of an absence of history, of the lack of a usable past.

Forten's alienation from African-American history and her inability to narrativize any aspects of it are intimated in her few diary comments on Northern black folk as well as in her article "Glimpses of New England," published in the June 19, 1858 issue of the *National Anti-Slavery Standard.* Although Forten makes no mention in her diary of blacks outside her social circle in Salem, she does so in two of her Philadelphia/Byberry entries. If whites were able to construct a racial ideology that would enable them to reject Forten from ice cream parlors (230), Forten in turn relied on her upper-class status to distance herself from, and objectify, the African-American folk of Philadelphia from a perspective of high culture. A "woman seated by the road-side, her bonnet thrown off, and evidently bent on enjoying the cool of the day" is condescendingly perceived by Forten as "a picture of ease and comfort" and "wicked[ly]" called "Jane Eyre" by her aunt (318); the driver of their carriage serves to "amuse . . . —such an odd, wide awake, droll little black boy" (326). Not part of the elite African-American social body of which she is a member, these Northern blacks are simply picturesque elements easily assimilable into the Pennsylvania landscape.

"Glimpses of New England" initially appears to be a travelogue of little historical significance. It is a text that once again points to the primacy of local place in Forten's imagination. Geography here is explicitly moralized following a structure of polarity as Philadelphia, whose genius loci is racial hatred, comes to represent the darkest aspects of American race relations while New England is populated by "warm, true, loving *hearts.*" Yet in this article place ultimately functions as a kind of palimpsest as the tourist's glimpses of New England give way to a deeper historical perspective. History here is largely that of the dominant culture, specifically the early Puritans—the "old-time heroes"—who settled Salem at the beginning of "American" history. Forten's attitude toward this history is in itself ambiguous, as the Puritan past is alternately seen as the site of religious delusions *and* as the repository of a cultural authenticity only recently superseded by an inauthentic modernity in which Forten herself is currently imprisoned. At certain textual junctures, however, the essay opens up onto considerations of the place of African Americans within American history. Forten's depiction of the natural beauties of New England, for example, leads to an evocation of its moral beauties and to a praise of New England abolitionism—specifically the Female Anti-Slavery Society of Salem, Wendell Phillips, and Boston abolitionist activities. This discussion, however, remains highly abbreviated and embedded within conventionally picturesque landscape descriptions that focus on the elm, the cemetery, and the sea. One may well wonder whether it was not such an ellipsis of African-American history that led Sarah Parker Remond to "burst out most venomously upon my poor 'Glimpses'—accusing them of being pro-slavery and heaven knows what all" (338).

Yet Forten was eventually to discover a usable past that would enable her to confront, however tentatively, her problematic relationship to African-American history. This discovery was initiated by her journey to the South Carolina Sea Islands during the Civil War to participate in what was known as the Port Royal experiment. After the Union forces had captured Port Royal harbor in late 1861 and the slaveholders had abandoned their plantations to flee inland, the federal government needed to resolve the fate of the thousands of slaves left behind. At the urging of General Sherman, it devised a social experiment whereby "'suitable instructors [would] be sent to the Negroes, to teach them all the necessary rudiments of civilization, and . . . agents properly qualified . . . [would] superintend the work of the blacks until they be sufficiently enlightened to think and provide for themselves.'"[19] Shortly after this plan was implemented by Edward Pierce of the Treasury Department in early 1862, its control was transferred to the military under the command of General Saxton. While the government selected agents to supervise the work of the freed slaves on the abandoned plantations and the army requested Thomas Wentworth Higginson to recruit black soldiers for the regiment of First South Carolina Volunteers, Northern abolitionist societies such as the Port Royal Commission set about raising funds to send teachers south, among them Charlotte Forten.[20]

Forten's journey to Port Royal is recounted as if motivated purely from the outside, as her diary entry of August 9, 1862 simply notes: "W.[hittier]

Charlotte L. Forten. Photographs and Prints Division. Schamburg Center for Research in Black Culture. The New York Public Library. Astor, Lenox and Tilden Foundations.

advised me to apply to the Port Royal Com.[mission] in Boston. He is very desirous that I sh'ld go. I shall certainly take his advice" (374). In her decision to leave Philadelphia and its black elite, which had sheltered her during her growth to maturity, we may perhaps read a tacit acknowledgment of a fundamental homelessness similar to Shadd Cary's and a wish somehow to take advantage of such a dispossessed condition. Like Shadd Cary's move north, Forten's journey south was a physical displacement that, while forcing a public exposure of the body, also enabled the discovery of a site of self-authorization. For like Shadd Cary, Forten here revealed her determination to construct a positive role for herself out of her geographic dislocation. To her stated desire "to find my highest happiness in doing my duty" to the "poor freed people" of the Sea Islands (376) came the unexpected discovery of a usable past through the culture of these same people.

Forten's Sea Islands diary entries (October 1862 to May 1864) are here too shot through with picturesque descriptions of landscapes. In this Southern location it is the swamp that comes to supplant the ocean, and the moss-draped oak the elm.[21] Once again the landscape is conventionally moralized; the swamp bespeaks a kind of religious austerity: "The whole swamp looks wonderfully like some old cathedral, with monks cloaked and hooded, kneeling around it" (457), and the moss of the oak tree becomes suggestive of funereal solemnity ("This moss is singularly beautiful, and gives a solemn almost funeral aspect to the trees," 391). Yet, unlike Forten's Northern landscape, this Southern landscape is peopled by bodies; desire is no longer arrested, but history is made alive and present. It is peopled most romantically by Seth Rogers and Forten herself, whose friendship is renewed with increased intensity in the natural world of the Sea Islands: "Dear A. I can give you no idea of the ride homeward. I know only that it was the most delightful ride I ever had in my life. . . . I shall never forget how that rosy light, and the moon and stars looked to us as we caught them in glimpses, riding through the dark pines. How wild and unreal it all seemed and what happiness it was . . ." (454–55). If actual consummation with the married Dr. Rogers is not possible, erotic desire is nonetheless unleashed and enjoyed.

Yet just as importantly, Forten's Southern landscapes are inhabited by the "poor freed people" whose desire has not been sapped by slavery but whose vital folk culture attests to a determination to construct a local place for themselves in the New World. The question that confronted Forten was whether she could make of this culture a usable past and thereby claim a place for herself in African-American history, some aspect of which she might one day be able publicly to narrate. In entry after entry in her diary Forten represents slave culture in vivid and careful detail. Many of her descriptions are devoted to an analysis of the moral nature of the newly freed people in which she emphasizes the degree to which they exhibit traits highly valued by the dominant culture: the industriousness of their labor force, the courage of black conscripts in the Union army, the willingness of many to accept the Christian rituals of baptism and marriage. Yet Forten was also highly appreciative of a variety of folkways derived from African culture that had given the freed people the strength to endure and survive slavery. Thus, she praised what she believed to be an innate sense of courtesy in the ex-slaves and also expressed delight in their colorful mode of dress. Above all, Forten paid homage to the aesthetic forms of the spiritual and the shout through which the freed people expressed their religious beliefs. If the spirituals are based primarily on Christian hymns, Forten seems to have been aware of their African influences, as both the incomprehensibility of some of the lines and their accompaniment by the counterclockwise circular dance movement of the shout suggested a foreign presence: "They sang beautifully in their rich, sweet clear tones, and with that peculiar swaying motion which I had noticed before in the older people, and which seems to make their singing all the more effective" (391).[22]

In her confrontation with slave culture Forten, like Shadd Cary in Canada West, found herself positioned as a kind of ethnographer; yet her stance as insider/outsider to the observed culture was even more complex. Much of Forten's knowledge of the freed people was derived initially from events observed and anecdotes heard at the local store opened by the Northern Quaker Mr. Hunn, who, along with his daughter Lizzie, had accompanied Forten to Saint Helena. If Hunn's store functioned as a marketplace where the ex-slaves could buy provisions in an (unequal) economic exchange, it was also the site of an (unequal) ethnographic exchange whereby Forten, and others, could gaze upon the freed people as interesting exotics: "I foresee that his store, to which people from all the neighboring plantations come,—will be a source of considerable interest and amusement" (395). Thus, Forten's initial perspective on the ex-slaves was as an outsider who perceived their customs as strange. Despite such cultural estrangement, however, Forten never resorted to the racist rhetoric employed, for example, by Laura Towne, the white head teacher of the school and physician to the black community, who in her diary repeatedly referred to the freed people as "darkies" with "woolly heads" who live in "nigger houses," and to teachers from the North as "nigger teachers."[23] Moreover, as Forten's stay lengthened, the strange became increasingly familiar to her as she found both her affective and bodily self drawn to the ex-slaves' ceremonies. Witnessing a shout she noted: "L.[izzie] and I, in a dark corner of the Praise House, amused ourselves with practicing a little" (482). In this description Forten's Southern landscape is once again peopled and she herself inscribed within it.

Most importantly, Forten's diary entries betray a sensitive awareness of the complex process of transculturation that was unfolding on the Sea Islands. They bear witness to the back-and-forth traffic between dominant and subordinate cultures as, for example, the freed people learned Whittier's songs and the white abolitionists Negro spirituals. Yet Forten herself was well aware that transculturation tended to move in a single direction: the imposition of dominant cultural forms on people of the subordinate culture. Thus, if she records one exciting moment of cultural hybridity in which a Fourth of July celebration is marked by the singing of both "The Star-Spangled Banner" and "Roll, Jordan, Roll" (491), she also remains aware of how hybridity may dissolve once again into unicity: "We c'ld . . . hear them singing hymns;—not their own beautiful hymns, I am sorry to say. I do so fear these will be superseded by ours, which are poor in comparison" (477).

What is most startling about this observation is Forten's use of pronouns in which the third person refers to the black freed people and the first to Northern white Christians. In this comment Forten aligns herself with the dominant culture; yet within the context of the Port Royal experiment, if Forten was not a freed slave, neither was she a white abolitionist. She functioned, in effect, as a lonely middle term between these two extremes, suggesting the degree to which American culture cannot embrace any element that destabilizes its hierarchically fixed binary oppositions. In fact, for the entire period that Forten spent on Saint Helena, she remained ambiguously poised between the two social groups, gazed at by each as radically Other, and unassimilable into neither. Her alienation from each of these communities is marked, on the one hand, by the ex-slaves' initial resistance to her difference. According to Laura Towne: "The people on our place are inclined to question a good deal about 'dat brown gal,' as they call Miss Forten. Aunt Becky required some coaxing to wait upon her and do her room. Aunt Phyllis is especially severe in the tone of her questions. I hope they will respect her."[24] It is suggested, on the other hand, by Towne's relative disregard of Forten in her diary, in striking contrast to Forten, whose own diary is filled with references to the "delightful," "remarkable" Miss Towne and her friend Ellen Murray, "one of the most whole-souled warm-hearted women I ever met" (392).

Forten's diary entry of November 23, 1862 poignantly elucidates her own profound sense of cultural alterity. Although represented as "wild and strange," the spirituals of the freed people affect Forten in such a way as to bespeak a deep, hidden familiarity: "The effect of the singing has been to make me feel a little sad and lonely to-night. A yearning for congenial companionship *will* sometimes come over me. . . ." Yet if such companionship cannot be found with the freed people in the slave huts, neither can it be found with the whites (Mr. Hunn and Lizzie) with whom she is living: "Kindness, most invariable,—for which I am most grateful—I meet with constantly, but congeniality I find not at all in this house" (402–3).

Ultimately, such cultural alterity came to shape Forten's published writings about her Port Royal experiences and to inhibit her further invention of a master plot that would allow her to narrativize her experiences. Early in her stay Forten wrote two letters to Garrison that were published in the December 12 and 19, 1862 issues of the *Liberator;* in its May and June 1864 issues the *Atlantic Monthly* published at Whittier's request a two-part article by Forten entitled "Life on the Sea Islands," based largely on personal letters to Whittier. It is significant that these published writings are composed substantially of material that Forten culled from her diary—analyses of slave culture, landscape descriptions, accounts of teaching experiences, political events, and interactions with important public figures—suggesting the degree to which this private document was, from its inception, largely a form of public self-expression.

Forten's two letters to the *Liberator* as well as "Life on the Sea Islands" represent her efforts to create a sustained narrative out of her Saint Helena diary entries. Given her awareness of her own problematic cultural in betweenness, and given the fact that she was addressing an overwhelmingly white readership, it was perhaps inevitable that Forten, in these published writings, should have ultimately fallen back on traditional ethnographic models.[25] Indeed, these accounts are marked by a repression of intimate personal experience and a retreat into the disembodied stance of the ethnographer who observes the culture of the (primitive) Other. In the first *Liberator* letter, written less than a month after her arrival, Forten began by rehearsing her decision to go to Saint Helena, then proceeded to a description of its inhabitants. The reader is initially confronted with the strangeness of their culture in Forten's brief reference to the "peculiar wildness and solemnity" of the songs of the "negro boatmen," which is soon followed by a longer commentary suggesting, much like some of her diary entries, the degree to which the fundamental ways of knowing and being of the freed people may be readily assimilated to the familiar values of the dominant culture: thus, the "negro pickets . . . do their duty well"; the workers are "honest, industrious, and sensible"; the people possess a "natural courtesy of manner"; the children are "well behaved, and eager to learn." Such a cultivation of the ethnocentrically familiar gives way in the second letter to a more open acknowledgment of the strangeness of slave culture represented from a distanced perspective. Indeed, the letter is safely framed by references to white political culture, beginning with praise of the *Liberator*, "familiar as the face of an old friend," and those national leaders dedicated to emancipation, and concluding with a nostalgic evocation of New England. In the central section, however, Forten invites the reader to enter an unfamiliar world which she likens to "a strange wild dream," as she offers a vivid portrayal of the slave quarters, former slave masters, and individual slaves.

Forten concluded her second letter to the *Liberator* with a contrast between the winter cold of New England and the warm sunlight of South Carolina, which is also that of freedom: "The sunlight is warm and bright, and over all shines gloriously the blessed light of freedom, freedom, forevermore." Yet even more than her *Liberator* letters, Forten's "Life on the Sea Islands" records this narrative of freedom from a highly detached ethnographic perspective. Unlike Prince, Forten began her account by narrating the scene of arrival in which she permitted herself freely to gaze upon her ethnographic subjects but, much like Nancy Prince, disallows any return of the gaze: "A motley assemblage had collected on the wharf,—officers, soldiers, and 'contrabands' of every size and hue: black was, however, the prevailing color."[26] Most of the rest of part 1 of the article is organized according to a temporal chronology that is based on the activities of the ethnographer—"it was on the afternoon of a warm, murky day," "the next morning," "the Sunday after our arrival," "during the week," "the first day at school" (67, 68, 69, 70, 71)—but gives way repeatedly to description, while part 2 eschews temporal structure almost entirely. As we have indicated, both parts consist largely of segments taken from the diary, in particular descriptions of public events: the reading of the Emancipation Proclamation on Thanksgiving Day, attended not only by General Saxton but also by Frances Gage, who was soon to write her "Reminiscences" of Sojourner Truth; emancipation day itself; encounters with the rebels; the death of Colonel Shaw. To the extent that new material is included, much of it focuses on the ex-slave population and its central meeting place at Mr. Hunn's store, that site of unequal exchange. In much of this material Forten attempts to iᵢ dividuate the black community by positioning herself as a participant-observer authorized to relate to the reader anecdotes about specific persons—Harry, Cupid, Amaretta, Celia, and others; yet even in these descriptions, these individuals remain predictable stock figures representing black folk naïveté, religiosity, wit, and so on.

Suppressed in this article, then, is the narration of intimate experiences with slave culture whereby the *I* may come familiarly to inhabit the strange. In its stead the reader is presented with an indeterminate and pluralized "we" who observe "the people." To the extent that the *I* is employed, it is most often not an experiencing *I* but a narrational *I*, the writing subject engaged in the difficult task of ethnographic reporting: "While he [Cupid] is thus engaged, I will try to describe him" (70). On the few occasions when Forten does represent herself in the text, she does so as a detached ahistorical *I*. She portrays herself, for example, as seeking from a safe pedagogical distance to construct a history for the freed people by offering them a biographical narrative of Toussaint: "I told them about Toussaint, thinking it well they should know what one of their own color had done for his race" (71). Or she insists on interpreting the shout from an ethnocentric Christian perspective as the "barbarous expression of religion, handed down to them from their African ancestors, and destined to pass away under the influence of Christian teachings" (74). Within such a narrative framework, Forten's ethnographic *I* can claim cultural identification with the freed people only by speaking in the concluding paragraph through the voice of another, that of the Bible: "While writing these pages I am once more nearing Port Royal. . . . I shall dwell again among 'mine own people'" (86). As we shall see in the next chapter, Forten's affinity with the freed people would only diminish in the aftermath of the Civil War and her search for voice in the postbellum period take increasingly complex and problematic forms.

8

Home/Nation/Institutions: African-American Women and the Work of Reconstruction (1863–1880)

To the majority of the antebellum black leadership—male and female—the Civil War brought the hope of an end to racial hostilities, North and South, and the promise of a new era in which all African Americans would finally achieve full civil rights and forge that local place denied them by the historical experiences of the Middle Passage, slavery, and institutionalized racism. In this concluding chapter I bring together those "doers of the word" whose antebellum careers were treated in greater detail in earlier chapters in order to analyze their political, cultural, and literary activities in the Reconstruction era. I treat these women collectively here because my analyses are meant to be suggestive rather than exhaustive. I merely want to trace in a very general way the extent to which emancipation fulfilled—or denied—the implementation of these women's antebellum social ideologies, and to assess their reactions to the complexities of Reconstruction politics on both national and community levels. Given our uneven knowledge of the postbellum careers of these women, a collective treatment seemed advisable: to date, virtually nothing is known about the Reconstruction activities of Jarena Lee, Nancy Prince, and Harriet Wilson; large gaps remain in our knowledge of the postbellum work of Harriet Jacobs and Sarah Parker Remond; our recovery of the writings of Frances Watkins Harper has been much more extensive than that of Mary Ann Shadd Cary or Charlotte Forten. Ongoing and future archival research will undoubtedly supply much of the missing information.

As historians like Eric Foner have noted, Reconstruction posed certain crucial questions to its contemporaries: What was to be the meaning of freedom for both freeborn and newly freed African Americans in the wake of emancipation? What form and shape would this freedom take? What would be the institutional mechanisms by which freedom would be achieved and in which it would be embodied?[1]

From a national perspective, the federal government needed to determine the basis upon which the defeated Confederate states would be governed and restored to the Union. With respect to its black population, it needed to assess the new terms on which this people would be incorporated into American society. As it groped toward a formulation of these terms, it created a number of organizations—notably the Freedmen's Bureau—designed to oversee the welfare of the newly emancipated slaves by redistributing abandoned or confiscated land among them, establishing a public school system, supervising labor relations between employers and freed people, and finally by offering what modicum of protection it could against white violence. It also passed three constitutional amendments abolishing slavery, guaranteeing citizenship to all African Americans, and granting the franchise to black males, and a series of civil rights bills mandating the free access of African Americans to federal courts, the end of racial discrimination in public places, and the enforcement of these laws by federal troops.

For African Americans, emancipation meant the opportunity to create a local place that might truly become home. To do so they continued to rely on many of the same social institutions that had ensured their survival in the antebellum period in both the slave South and the free North: familial and domestic networks, the church, schools, community benevolent societies. But they also stepped onto new terrain opened up by Reconstruction legislation, hoping that the nation itself might become home. On the political front they sought to influence national and local politics by running for, and winning, state and local offices and by voting for those candidates they believed would best represent their interests. In the economic arena they strove to address the means by which they could achieve economic autonomy by controlling their own labor power, whether as agricultural or industrial workers. More broadly and theoretically, they needed to scrutinize capitalism itself as a viable economic system for African Americans and contemplate the possible alternatives to it.

By the mid-1870s national Reconstruction efforts were already starting to unravel as state rights doctrines became increasingly prominent, a spirit of sectional compromise between North and South became more and more evident, and as Republican opinion moved closer toward Democratic conservatism; by the late 1870s the South could announce itself fully redeemed. If accusations of rampant corruption against politicians of the Grant era was one reason for the failure of black Reconstruction, its underlying causes must also be attributed to the economic instability of the period. The return of land to former plantation owners, the depression of the 1870s, the failure of the Freedmen's Savings Bank, the erosion of free labor ideology leading to increased tensions between capitalists and workers all had the effect of severely curtailing African Americans' search for economic autonomy; and these factors further exacerbated the still tense race relations between whites and blacks, resulting finally in the restoration of white supremacy in the South.

One important consequence of Reconstruction for the black community was a deepening of class and gender divisions that had already made themselves felt before the Civil War. Indeed, the postbellum period witnessed the slow emergence of a new class structure and sensibility that separated the mass of common laborers from a growing black professional and business class. This class was not always able to comprehend the labor issues facing black workers and felt at times that the political and social interests of the two groups no longer necessarily coincided. Moreover, within this nascent bourgeoisie black women found themselves increasingly pressured toward privatization in the domestic sphere, and their presence in the ongoing public work of racial uplift often unwelcome. They discovered that the achievement of citizenship placed them, in fact, in a highly complex position. Denied the right to vote, black women were now distinguished by law from black men as second-class citizens. Thus positioned, they needed to decide whether to cast their lot with the white women's suffrage movement in the hopes of forging a new interracial female political culture that would take the place of the antebellum cultural model of "female society." Or, given the vocal opposition of many of the suffragist leaders to the passage of the Fifteenth Amendment, should they agree with Harper's contention that "when it was a question of race, [they should] let the lesser question of sex go."[2] Cutting through differences of race, class, and gender, finally, were issues of economic power and control that were ultimately to spill over the boundaries of the black community and play themselves out on the national level.

In the face of such turmoil, Sarah Parker Remond early voiced her frustrations with Reconstruction politics and in October 1866 fled America as a self-imposed exile in search of a home in Europe. In a letter published in the November 3, 1866 issue of the *National Anti-Slavery Standard,* Remond described her southward journey across the Alps into Italy, inviting her imagination to envision this country as an untroubled promised land—"all that one ever dreamed or imagined of the sunny, cloudless skies of Italy burst upon my vision"—while constructing her own birthplace as a tyrannous nation in which racial prejudice has threatened the liberty of blacks and whites alike: "Is this to be the result of your war—that neither black or white men have rights which tyrants are bound to respect?" Most significant in this letter, however, is Remond's admission of literary defeat, of the insufficiency of words to narrate the historical experiences of African Americans: "What a record could the victims of this terrible hatred present against the dominant race. It will never be written. It never can be written."

If Remond was to concede defeat, other black women struggled on, determined to continue their tradition of social activism by organizing, speaking, and writing, while establishing greater formal networks among one another. Faced with the complexities of Reconstruction politics and their problematic place within it, they turned increasingly to national institutions as mechanisms through which to work for freedom, participating in growing numbers in the organizations and discursive practices of black men and white women. In addition to Truth's and Harper's continued lecturing on behalf of the postbellum antislavery movement, for example, Jacobs, Forten, and Truth worked with the contrabands, escaped slaves who took refuge from their masters in camps established by the Union army, under the auspices of the Freedmen's Bureau and its related agencies. While Harper affiliated with the American Woman Suffrage Association, Truth and Cary joined the rival National Woman Suffrage Association; Cary, moreover, came to play a vocal role in the nascent black labor movement. By century's end the "brave" would thus find themselves ready to create national institutions of their own. Finally, in order to promote their cause to a broader audience these black women turned increasingly to the medium of the press— antislavery and women's rights vehicles as well as more mainstream newspapers. Harper and Forten in particular sought, with varying degrees of success, to take advantage of the postbellum expansion and institutionalization of literary culture.

COLLABORATING WITH THE FREEDMEN'S BUREAU: FORTEN, TRUTH, AND JACOBS

Writing at the turn of the century, Du Bois praised the impulse that gave rise to the Freedmen's Bureau while noting that this social experiment was doomed to failure. Established as a temporary agency, the bureau could not hope to solve the problem of freedom in the short time allotted to it; treating the freed slaves as "helpless wards" of the nation, it could not provide the mechanism through which they could become self-reliant; unable fully to address the vast labor problems facing the South, it could not prevent the rise of "economic slavery" resulting from peonage.[3] Despite these shortcomings, Forten, Truth, and Jacobs all eagerly participated in the efforts of the bureau and undoubtedly came into frequent contact with one another. Their scattered references to this relief work suggest a commonality of point of view that emphasizes their strong sense of racial solidarity with the freed people. In conjunction with Harper, they could affirm: "Still I am standing with my race on the threshold of a new era. . . ."[4] Fundamental to their activities with the Freedmen's Bureau was a conviction that the newly emancipated population must become self-sufficient and achieve community autonomy by means of "home building," education, and employment. Their emphasis on domesticity cannot be interpreted as an attempt to privatize black women according to the dominant culture's middle-class ideology of proper femininity but must be seen instead as a continuation of those antebellum practices that viewed domestic economy as an instrument of family and community empowerment.

After teaching on Saint Helena Island, Forten returned to the North and worked from 1865 to 1871 as a clerk for the Teachers Committee of the New England Freedmen's Union Commission in Boston. During her tenure she helped the committee keep a journal of its activities and wrote letters to educators in the field, particularly in South Carolina, to whom it offered financial assistance. These documents reflect Forten's desire for community self-sufficiency, as she expressed her interest in the work of the "native teachers" of that state and her hope that, for example, "after this year the colored people [of Edisto] will support the school themselves."[5] Similarly, both Truth and Jacobs worked during and after the war in Virginia with the contrabands. In her narrative Titus relates how Truth was appointed a counselor in Freedmen's Village in Arlington Heights in 1864, where she sought to assist the freedwomen, most of whom had known only field labor, by instructing them in housekeeping and domestic duties. Transferred to Freedmen's Hospital in 1865, she worked toward the goal of "promoting order, cleanliness, industry, and virtue among the patients" (183).

In a letter to J. Sella Martin written in 1863 from the Alexandria contraband camp in which she had settled, Jacobs fully acknowledged the extent to which the memory of her slave past "has served to bind me more closely to those around me" (*Freeman's Aid Society*, April 1863). As in Truth's case, one of Jacobs's chief concerns was to encourage the freed people in home building—a concept encompassing not only the construction of a physical edifice but also the implementation of domestic economy and the consolidation of domestic relations—as a prerequisite to community building. Writing to Child, Jacobs noted that the freed people had managed to build approximately seven hundred cabins over an eight-month period, and although in some "chaos reigned supreme. There was nothing about them to indicate the presence of a wifely wife, or a motherly mother," others "showed marks of industry, neatness, and natural refinement" (*NASS*, April 16, 1864).

Jacobs herself participated in this process of home building by teaching sewing classes to both children and adults; and less than a year later, her daughter Louisa was able to write of the substantial improvement in the domestic organization of the freed people: "I contrasted their homes of today with those of a year ago. The comparison was favorable. The inmates were more tidy in person, while the rooms of many of them were clean an [*sic*] orderly" (*NASS*, Feb. 25, 1865). Discovering in addition that in many instances the "marriage law has been disregarded, from old habits formed in slavery," Jacobs herself engaged in "a long battle about the marriage rites for the poor people" and in another letter to Child reported happily on eight weddings performed in one day (*Freeman's Aid Society*, April 1863; *Lib*, April 10, 1863). If Jacobs felt obliged to emphasize the importance of conjugal relations as a means of ensuring community stability, she did not have to stress the necessity of maintaining strong nonkin domestic networks. Seeking to provide shelter for orphaned children, she found the refugee women fully committed to preserving such supportive social arrangements familiar to them from slavery days: "I have never known them, in any one instance, refuse to shelter an orphan. In many cases, mothers who have five or six children of their own, without enough to feed and cover them, will readily receive these helpless little ones into their own poor hovels" (*Lib*, April 10, 1863).

Of equal importance to Jacobs was the education of both contraband children and adults. Her efforts resulted in the construction of a new school that, according to the *Freedmen's Record*, was "named in her honor, and presided over by black and white teachers, working harmoniously together" (Feb. 1865, 19). Besides offering instruction in basic literacy to the newly freed slaves, the freedmen's schools also raised crucial issues of black self-reliance. Much like Forten, Harriet and Louisa Jacobs made clear that while they welcomed all those willing to teach the contrabands, they placed most pride in schools staffed exclusively by "native" teachers and maintained entirely by support from the black community; such was the case of several of the institutions with which they came into contact during their stay in Savannah, Georgia, in 1866 (*FR*, March 1866, 55). Moreover, Jacobs was well aware that in schools where black and white teachers worked together relations were not always harmonious. In her 1864 letter to Child she related a dispute that took place in her Alexandria school over whether black or white teachers should be the superintendents. As trustees of the school, the freedmen were asked to resolve the matter and did so in favor of the black teachers. To Jacobs this decision was a positive indication of increasing black self-reliance and of the gradual emergence of black community leadership: "The fact of their giving preference to colored teachers, as managers of the establishment, seemed to us to indicate that even their brief possession of freedom had begun to inspire them with respect for their race" (*NASS*, April 16, 1864).

Yet both Harriet and Louisa Jacobs were well aware that the crux of black community building was free and independent labor, that in order to become self-reliant the freed people needed not only to find employment but, more importantly, to achieve economic autonomy from whites. Jacobs attributed much of the degradation evident in the Alexandria Freedmen's Village to the fact that its women were unemployed and the men dependent on government work. In a letter to Garrison dated August 1862 she wrote: "The old schoolhouse is the Government headquarters for the women. This I thought the most wretched of all. In this house are scores of women and children with nothing to do, and nothing to do with. Their husbands are at work for the Government. Here they have food and shelter, but they cannot get work." She further contrasted the Alexandria contraband camp to the Arlington Heights Freedmen's Village, referring to the latter in glowing terms. The inhabitants of the Alexandria camp are debilitated by illness, confinement, and idleness, many also appearing "so degraded by slavery that they do not know the usages of civilized life," but those of the Arlington camp have found fulfillment through work: "The men are employed and most of the women. Here they have plenty of exercise in the open air and seem very happy. . . . It is a delightful place for both the soldiers and the contraband" (*Lib*, Sept. 3, 1862).

FORGING LOCAL PLACE: SOUTHERN HOMESTEADS, WESTERN LANDS, AND THE EPISCOPAL CHURCH

Beyond the temporary activities of the Freedmen's Bureau lay a broader and more fundamental set of questions: To what extent could African Americans forge a permanent local place for themselves within the borders of the United States? Or were they destined to remain "colored tourists" in the New World? If home is a concrete geographic place constructed around intimate interpersonal relationships and delimited by "familiar, safe, protected boundaries," it is also, as Martin and Mohanty have noted, a politically constructed community whose stability and identity are repeatedly subject to reformulation.[6] In the Reconstruction period the black women under study sought to forge a local place for the newly freed people—and African Americans generally—by calling for the uplift of rural communities in the South, encouraging the exodus to western lands, and promoting Northern churches as a space of spiritual power. In the process their cultural work foregrounds the very material and historical nature of home.

Both Jacobs and Forten addressed this issue of an African-American home place in their journeys south shortly after the Civil War. Recording her reactions to her first return visit to Edenton in a letter to Ednah Cheney, Jacobs conceptualized home not so much as an imprisoning physical structure whose memory can only cause pain but as a community of people whose love and devotion in turn fill her with love: "I had long thought I had no attachment to my old home. As I sit here and think of those I loved, of their hard struggle in life, their unfaltering love and devotion toward myself and children, I love to think of them. They have made the few sunny spots in that dark life sacred to me."[7] Returning to South Carolina in 1871 to teach at the Shaw Memorial School in Charleston, Forten wrote an article about a brief visit to Port Royal in which she also addressed the issue of home. While the essay commented extensively on the Reconstruction work of Northern businessmen and teachers on the Sea Islands, its main thrust was to emphasize the continuing efforts of the freed people to reconstruct home as a space of meaningful work and freedom: "Most of them own little lots of land, upon which they work industriously, and some are building themselves nice houses" (*Commonwealth*, Sept. 21, 1872).

For Harper a journey south in 1867 and then again in 1871–72 offered her for the first time an unmediated vision of black Southern home life. These visits enabled her to rethink her earlier totalizing vision of the degradation of slave culture and persuaded her that "the South is to be a great theatre for the colored man's development and progress. There is brain-power here. If any doubt it, let him come into our schools, or even converse with some of our Freedmen either in their homes or by the way-side." Fully appreciative of the rich and potent legacy of slave culture, Harper was convinced of the ability of the newly freed slaves, particularly the women, to forge domestic spaces in which they would "plant the roots of progress under the hearthstone."[8]

For Jacobs, Forten, and Harper the foundation of an African-American home place in the South lay in land ownership. In one of her public lectures Harper exhorted her audience: "Get land, every one that can, and as fast as you can. A landless people must be dependent upon the landed people. A few acres to till for food and a roof, however humble, over your head, are the castle of your independence."[9] Similarly, in her *Commonwealth* article Forten emphasized the importance of land ownership among the Sea Island people as a prerequisite to the construction of home. In these homes, "however humble," the freedwomen were to devote themselves to the same forms of home building that Truth and Jacobs had encouraged in the contraband camps—a domestic economy centered on respect for women, the marriage relation, and domestic order, which would then serve as a basis for community strength. Complementing the work of the home would be that of the social institutions of school, church, and temperance societies, as well as the political instrument of black men's newly acquired right to vote.

Yet Forten, Harper, and Harriet and Louisa Jacobs all remained aware of the extent to which these newly created African-American home places were threatened from without. In their writings from the South, these women repeatedly commented on the difficulties faced by the freed people in their efforts to achieve economic independence given the meagerness of the proceeds from their land, the disadvantageous labor contracts forced upon them by former plantation owners, and the high taxes assessed on their land by county officials. In her *Commonwealth* article Forten reported how the increase in taxes effectively undercut the supposed autonomy of land ownership, forcing farmers to supplement their own provisions by working for, and thus becoming dependent on, "the larger planters around them." Writing from Savannah in 1866, Louisa Jacobs complained of the unfair contracts that some white landowners had forced upon black farmers, thereby restricting their ownership of animals, their ability to raise produce, and their freedom of movement, leading her to inquire sarcastically: "Is this freedom, or encouragement to labor?" (*FR*, March 1866, 56).

As they articulated their vision of an African-American home place in the South, Harper, Jacobs, and Forten often contrasted North and South while remaining sensible of the permeability of the boundaries that divided the two regions and increasingly allowed for the penetration of Northern influences in the South. Given her new appreciation of the vitality of the ex-slaves' communities, Harper reversed her antebellum evaluation of the relative merits of Northern and Southern black culture to argue that the freedman's simultaneous acquisition of freedom and suffrage meant that "he is not forced to go through the same condition of things here, that has inclined him so much to apathy, isolation, and indifference, in the North."[10] In contrast, on her return home to Edenton the Southern-born Jacobs brought with her what she considered to be superior Northern agricultural technologies, which she attempted to impart to the freedwomen: "I have spent much of my time [on] the plantations distributing seed and trying to teach the women to make Yankee gardens. They plant everything to mature in the summer, like their corn and cotton."[11]

It is Forten, however, who in her *Commonwealth* article exhibited the greatest sensitivity toward the complex nature of Northern influences in the South. If on the one hand she anticipated the progressive transformation of the "picturesque" landscape of Port Royal into a "thriving and prosperous" town provided "some industrious, energetic Northern settlers could be imported," on the other she condemned the blatant racism of these same Northern traders "who, coming down solely to make money, seem to expect perfection from a people so recently delivered from slavery, and are disgusted with the whole race because they do not find it." Furthermore, Forten readily acknowledged the high cost exacted from slave culture by Northern notions of progress as she witnessed its increasing contamination by the forces of modernization. As in her earlier journal entries, she lamented the disappearance of spirituals from the freed peoples' church services in favor of Northern hymns: "We regretted that they did not sing any of their old hymns, 'spirituals,' as they call them. The teachers told us that they still sing these during the shouts in their 'praise-houses,' but never at church. They now sing from ordinary hymn-books, and often make sad havoc of words and tune."

Expanding her antebellum interest in communitarian forms of living, Sojourner Truth also worked throughout the Reconstruction period to establish a home place for the newly freed slaves. In contrast to Forten, Jacobs, and Harper, however, Truth envisioned this place outside the South. As early as 1866 and well before the mass exodus of blacks to Kansas in the late 1870s, Truth began encouraging the freed people to migrate west and petitioned Congress to set aside land for this purpose; many of her speeches of this period were designed to convince her audience to sign such petitions. The impetus for Truth's project lay in her horrified reaction to the terrible conditions under which the newly emancipated population of Washington, D.C., labored. According to a report written by the District of Columbia superintendent of police and reprinted by Titus in her narrative, contrabands from Virginia had settled in the nation's capital, where, unable to find gainful employment, they congregated idly in crowded and unsanitary shanties; "these places," the report asserted, "can be considered as nothing better than propagating grounds of crime, disease, and death" (191). Much like Cary, who in the 1850s had conceived of Canada West as a northern agricultural frontier receptive to African-American emigration, Truth envisioned Kansas as a western frontier where American blacks would be able to achieve economic self-sufficiency.

In promoting western migration Truth thus hoped that the newly freed people would escape not only the poverty and degradation of city life but also their growing dependence on federal government charity. Yet she adamantly refused to join any of the contemporary movements that favored emigration to Liberia, insisting, according to Titus, that "our nerves and sinews, our tears and blood, have been sacrificed on the altar of this nation's avarice. Our unpaid labor has been a stepping-stone to its financial success. Some of its dividends must surely be ours" (197). Truth's project anticipates by several years that of the Southerners Henry Adams and Benjamin Singleton, who, propelled by white mob violence and fears of reenslavement, spearheaded a migratory movement from the Southern states of Louisiana, Texas, and Tennessee to Kansas from about 1874 to 1879. If their movement initially sought to carry out its mission by means of petitions to Congress much as Truth's had, it soon acquired millenarian overtones likening the migration to the Exodus, each emigrant to Moses, and Kansas to the promised land of Canaan.[12]

Typical of Truth's emigration speeches is one delivered on January 1, 1871 at the Commemoration of the Eighth Anniversary of Negro Freedom in the United States.[13] Although the purpose of this speech was to persuade her audience to sign a petition authorizing Congress to set aside land in the West, Truth in fact did not reveal her goal until the concluding lines. Conscious of the need to gain her audience's attention, Truth relied on many of the same rhetorical patterns that had structured her antebellum speeches. From the outset she sought to establish her authority as a speaker by means of an appeal to personal experience, invoking and reconfiguring in particular notions of birth and generation. Reconceptualizing herself as reborn at the time of emancipation, Truth insisted that she was now standing at the very beginning of life rather than near its termination. Further rewriting herself as a child, she then proceeded to recall and reiterate her mother's admonitions to her long ago in Ulster County. Yet in this very reenactment of Mau-mau Bett's role, Truth discursively replaces her mother, and it is with this maternal authority that she can then address her audience as "chilern" (213).

Having established her authority as a speaker, Truth needed, then, to develop a set of rhetorical strategies that would help her attain her pragmatic goal of acquiring signatures. The strategies she adopted eschew millenarian rhetoric in favor of a double discourse—Christian and African—that might appeal to a double audience of whites and blacks. Indeed, millenarian rhetoric based on the necessity of divine intervention rather than human agency appears to be largely absent from Truth's speeches and dictated letters of this period. It seems to appear only in the late 1870s, most probably brought to the fore by the later emigration movements; for example, in the memorial appendix to the 1884 edition of the *Narrative* Truth is said to have stated to a reporter some years before her death: "I have prayed so long that my people would go to Kansas, and that God would make straight the way before them. Yes, indeed! I think it is a good move for them. I believe as much in that move as I do in the moving of the children of Egypt going out to Canaan, just as much."[14]

Instead, Truth's 1871 speech relies covertly on Africanisms that might have served both as a source of personal empowerment and as a means of imagining community among African Americans, and overtly on a discourse of Christian humility directed at whites in her audience. In appropriating her mother's discourse, Truth incorporated Africanisms in her speech thereby preserving "native" beliefs by means of oral transmission, itself a "native" tradition. Truth recounts how she used to sit under "a canoby ob ebben" in the company of her mother, who would tell her to "look up to de moon an' stars dat shine upon you father an' upon you mother when you sole far away, an' upon you brudders an' sisters, dat is sole away," for God, who "sits in de sky," will hear and answer her prayers (213–14). God is presented not only as materially everywhere but also as spiritually immediate to the child who becomes convinced that she can converse and negotiate with him as if he were right before her. As we saw in chapter 2, such beliefs in the presence of God in the moon and the stars, in the lack of distinction between spiritual and material world, and in the primacy of the oral such that speech alone can transform vision and desire into a reality, are Africanisms handed down by Mau-mau Bett to Truth as sources of cultural power.

If Truth chose to ground her representation of her mother and her younger self in an African belief system, she explicitly constructed her present self in Christian terms as a convert who has found humility and serenity through acceptance of Jesus as her only "marster." In particular, she asserted—whether out of sincerity or manipulation it is difficult to tell—her love and forgiveness of whites: "I used to hate de wi'te pepul so, an' I tell ye w'en de lobe came in me I had so much lobe I didn't know what to lobe. Den de w'ite pepul come, an' I thought dat lobe was too good fur dem. Den I said, 'Yea, God, come, an' I'll lobe ev'ybuddy an' de w'ite pepul too'" (215). Using the rhetorical question "Ain't it wonderful dat God gives lobe enough to de Ethiopins to lobe you?" as a segue to her concluding statement, Truth then directly argued her case for western emigration to the "you," the white people in her audience: rather than allow the "culud pepul" to continue living in a state of degraded dependency in Washington, the government should set aside land for them in the West where they could construct a home place for themselves, work, and gain an education. In finally requesting her audience to sign her petition, Truth subtly dropped her mask of humility; by exchanging the positionality of whites and blacks, her construction of the freed people as all-forgiving suddenly reads as an implicit challenge. If blacks can "lobe de wi'te pepul" who had once enslaved them, then certainly the white people can love them in return and demonstrate this love by signing the petition: "I speech dese tings so dat when you have a paper come for you to sign, you ken sign it" (216).

Shortly before her death in 1879, having recovered her husband's pension funds and become reacquainted with many of her old abolitionist friends, Maria Stewart republished her 1835 *Productions*. In the one-page preface and short autobiographical narrative that served as introductions to this edition, Stewart addressed her "friends" within the black community and, like the other women discussed earlier, articulated her aspiration to forge a home place for African Americans in the aftermath of the Civil War; in this instance, as Stewart's narrative makes evident, home is envisioned as the Episcopal Church. To fulfill her goal, Stewart conceptualized herself, just as she had in the 1830s, as an instrument of God chosen by him to carry out his bidding: "For God . . . uses such instruments as He sees proper to bring about His most wise and glorious purposes" (iii). In the process she insisted, much as Truth had, on the fact of her own rebirth. It is the "God-send" of the republished *Productions*, "suppressed for forty-six years," that attests to the material and psychological rebirth of the author—her recovery of her husband's government pension and the redissemination of those early writings that bear witness to her antebellum racial uplift efforts.

In addition to her claim of being an instrument of God's "most wise and glorious purposes," Stewart also appealed to secular authorities for legitimation. Her preface is followed by several letters and commendations signed by Garrison as well as by various leaders of Washington's black community, among them the Episcopalian minister Alexander Crummell. Much like the white abolitionist documents that had introduced the antebellum slave narratives, these letters have an authenticating function. Specifically, they serve to legitimate Stewart's claims to her husband's pension, to assert her central role in antebellum and Reconstruction racial uplift efforts, and, most especially, to buttress her aspirations to an elite social class position. Thus, in the opening lines of the preface Stewart represents herself in the third person as a sorrowful widow "struggling . . . to maintain her dignity and standing as a woman and a Christian in poverty's dark shade" (iii) and later self-consciously positions herself as "your heroine" (16); the commendations that follow fully corroborate this self-image, calling the reader's attention to Stewart's ladylike "modest and very retiring" demeanor (7).

Such an emphasis on Stewart's ladyhood was designed to differentiate her from the African-American population that surrounded her, to foreground her as a unique individual, a worthy subject of autobiography. As the preceding quotations suggest, Stewart sought both to attract the readers' gaze to her unique person and to elicit their sympathetic interest in her fate while maintaining them at a safe distance from herself as the autobiographical subject. To do so she resorted to narrational strategies reminiscent of those employed earlier by Wilson and Jacobs, in particular self-references in the third person and the appropriation of fictional-dramatic discourse: "Yet your heroine was a sufferer, with scarce the necessaries of life. The say was: 'She belongs to white folks' church, let them take care of her.' The curtain falls thus, and ends the scene" (16).

What in fact distanced Stewart from, and rendered her a "stranger" to, Washington's black community was her affiliation with the Episcopal Church, the "white folks' church," whose openly racist and elitist attitudes had alienated many African Americans and discouraged them from joining. Yet if Stewart had converted to Episcopalianism to achieve social distinction, she nonetheless insisted that this church become the institutional base from which she could establish a

Sunday school and thereby not only sustain herself economically but also create a spiritual home for the children of the community. Stewart's narration of her efforts to find a site in which to worship and locate her school emphasizes the importance of the specificity and materiality of local place in community building: "[A]nd one of the motives that induced me to come to this city was to seek a habitation for my God to dwell in, not dreaming that I should ever own a house adapted to that purpose" (15).

Indeed, denied financial aid by the Episcopal Church because of her blackness and by the black churches because of her commitment to Episcopalianism, Stewart could find no local place within which to situate her Sunday school and was eventually forced to hold prayer meetings in her own "dwelling-house" (18). Without institutional support such a mode of worship could only remain precarious, resulting in repeated dislocations: "A lady said to me: 'When we were getting up our church, we met in the same room for one year, and then we moved in a body; but when you go from house to house, half of the persons do not know where the different places of meeting is'" (20). It is only through the determined efforts of a "handfull of us poor lone colored women followers of the cross" (22) that Stewart was finally able to find a "habitation for my God to dwell in" in the organization in 1867 of Saint Mary's, Washington's first black Episcopal church, pastored by Alexander Crummell; a decade later, when Crummell decided to leave Saint Mary's and found a new church, Saint Luke's, Stewart moved with him. It is these two churches that provided many black Washingtonians, among them Frederick Douglass, a local place in which to worship. Beyond that, Episcopalianism was to provide Stewart with a home that she envisioned as neither merely physical nor local but spiritual and global: "[A]nd rejoice that I now feel that I have a home not only in the Protestant Episcopal Church, but in the Holy Church Catholic throughout the world" (22).

IMAGINING LOCAL PLACE: HARPER AND FORTEN

As noted in chapter 6, the imagination provides yet another mechanism through which oppressed peoples may aspire to restore the local place expropriated by colonization. The literary careers of Frances Harper and Charlotte Forten suggest two very different modes through which African-American women writers appropriated the imagination as an agent of decolonization and sought to benefit from the expansion and institutionalization of literary culture during the Reconstruction period. As in the 1850s, all African-American literary expression in this era was constrained by crucial issues of production—patronage, publication venues, marketing strategies, readership, and so on. Such limitations placed on African-American writers are fully exemplified by a curt rejection letter sent to Cary in September 1873: "Thanking you for the favor of being allowed to consider your ms. I am, for Messrs Harper and Bros., R. R. Sinclair."[15]

Of all the writers of this period, it is perhaps Harper who fared the best: her antebellum Philadelphia publishers continued to publish her poetry throughout the 1860s and 1870s, and the *Christian Recorder* opened up its pages for the printing of both her short stories and her longer fiction. In turning to this publication venue, Harper obviously made the decision to write from within, and for, the black community. In contrast, Forten accepted the patronage of Whittier and Higginson, who sought to provide her access to such magazines and newspapers as *Scribner's Monthly,* the *Christian Register,* and Boston's *Commonwealth,* the management and readership of which were largely white. In so doing Forten hoped to take advantage of the expansion of literary culture and its marketplaces during the 1860s and 1870s, which was marked by the development of such quality magazines as the *Atlantic, Scribner's,* and *Harper's.* Richard Brodhead has argued that one important aspect of this expansion was a differentiation within the American literary system and its reading public between highbrow and lowbrow. Adopting the literary tastes of her patrons, Forten came to identify with highbrow culture, perhaps best symbolized by the *Atlantic Monthly,* where Whittier had placed her "Sea Island" articles in 1864. As Brodhead further notes, this highbrow literature was no longer based on the antebellum "domestic-tutelary model of writing" but instead reflected the leisure values of the new middle class.[16] As in the composition of her "Sea Island" articles, the "writable" now became for Forten not merely what she desired to narrate but also what the literary system would allow her to, resulting in thematic tensions not apparent in Harper's work.

HOME AND NATION: SOCIAL VISION IN THE POETRY AND FICTION OF FRANCES HARPER

The 1860s and 1870s saw the publication by Harper of three volumes of poetry, *Moses: A Story of the Nile* (1869), *Poems* (1871), and *Sketches of Southern Life* (1872), an allegorical story "The Mission of the Flowers," published at the end of the *Moses* volume, a series of short sketches entitled "Fancy Etchings" or "Fancy Sketches" that appeared in the *Christian Recorder* between 1871 and 1874, and two short novels, *Minnie's Sacrifice* (1869) and *Sowing and Reaping* (1876–77), both of which were serialized over a period of several months in the *Christian Recorder.* Taken in its entirety, Harper's Reconstruction literary production suggests a reorientation of both form and content. Its subject matter reflects Harper's insistence that her imaginative vision serve her social agenda by opening up onto a meditation of how home and community might become the basis of nation building and conversely how nation might be made into home. In the process it points to Harper's gradual abandonment of sentimentality as a mode of political expression. Finally, it illustrates how new experiments in poetic technique and narrative strategy subserve this social vision.

Harper's publication of three collections of poetry within a three-year period suggests a focusing of thematic concerns. I would argue that it is possible to read the three volumes as a single narrative that considers one of the fundamental problems of Reconstruction—the assimilation of African Americans into the national body politic—from multiple perspectives. In both *Moses* and *Sketches,* characters, plots, and action are located, explicitly or by means of allegory, within the black community. As Maryemma Graham has pointed out, *Moses* retells the Old Testament story in order to meditate upon the problematics of leadership under conditions of slavery, while *Sketches* narrates the struggle of Southern common folk to resist oppression and empower themselves.[17] In contrast, though the subject matter of the thirty-one poems of the 1871 *Poems* is highly eclectic, a good number insist, by direct reference, historical analogy, or allegory, on the post–Civil War responsibility of whites to reconstruct the nation as a home for African Americans.

In the late 1860s Harper undertook to experiment with the epic, perhaps the most "public" and certainly one of the least sentimental of poetic genres, and wrote *Moses: A Story of the Nile,* portions of which she recited in public as early as 1868 as part of her lecturing engagements. Written in free verse without measurable meter or rhyme, *Moses* consists of a sustained narration of events and records a further movement away from the realm of lyric poetry toward prose. In adapting the epic form to the African-American experience, Harper could find no suitable models of emulation in the American literary tradition. American poets of the late eighteenth and early nineteenth centuries, like Timothy Dwight and Joel Barlow, had appropriated the epic as a literary form through which to express American nationalist sentiments. In so doing they strove to conciliate traditional feudal military action with contemporary republican civic virtue, often choosing George Washington as the embodiment of their epic ideal. Above all they sought to articulate a vision of a future world order that would promote notions of freedom, independence, and economic and cultural progress based on ideologies of American republicanism. Yet these epics remain histories of conquest rather than liberation. Timothy Dwight's *The Conquest of Canaan* (1771–85), for example, typologically rewrites the biblical story of Joshua's bloody conquest of Canaan in order to narrate both the history of European settlement in the New World and the achievement of American independence over British domination. Almost a century later, Harper's contemporary Walt Whitman returned to the epic form in his *Leaves of Grass.* Abandoning the tradition of his revolutionary forefathers, he constructed what critics have called a "lyric-epic" that upheld the ideals of American democracy by means of a celebration of individual selfhood in its spiritual and physical manifestations, and posited the rebirth of these ideals through the Union's victory in the Civil War.[18]

As both a woman poet and an outsider to the dominant culture, Harper could not make either of these literary models serve her ideological purposes. Rather than construct an epic of conquest that would extol recent events in American history or engage in revelatory acts of lyrical self-representation, she chose simply to retell without explicit allegorizing the story of Moses and the Exodus of Israel from Egypt; to endow her narrative with authoritative power, she simply merged her narrator's voice with those of the composite narrators of the Old Testament. Yet any attempt to interpret the poem as an allegory of national liberation gives rise to a central indeterminacy. Moses is represented as a type prefiguring Jesus who brings with him the promise of salvation: "'Tis an old story now, but then 'twas new / Unto the brethren,—how God's anointed ones / Must walk with bleeding feet the paths that turn / To lines of living light; how hands that bring / Salvation in their palms are pierced with cruel / Nails. . . ." In Harper's epic, however, this national savior is as yet unknown and unnameable. In an 1859 essay, "Our Greatest Want," Harper had portrayed Moses as "the first disunion-ist . . . [who] would have no union with the slave power of Egypt."[19] Under the leadership of Abraham Lincoln, the Civil War had achieved "union" rather than "disunion," and by 1869 Harper must have wondered exactly what the nature of this union was. Rather than anticipate national union and consider its multiple meanings, Harper's epic simply looks back to rehearse the major events of Moses' life.

Unlike the earlier American epics, then, the central theme of *Moses* is not the actual achievement of freedom but a consideration of the necessary choices that confront leaders of an oppressed group.[20] The particular form that Moses' choice takes concerns the "private" sphere of family and home. It is a dilemma that the mulatta heroines of Harper's postbellum fiction must also face and suggests once again the degree to which these "private" institutions must in fact be recognized as historically constructed and subject to change. In the opening lines of the epic Moses makes known his decision to leave his home in Pharaoh's palace and his adoptive mother to inhabit the lowly hut of Jewish slavery where his biological mother lives. If this initial choice is presented as a *fait accompli,* the notion of home nonetheless remains highly problematic throughout the poem. Indeed, as Moses and Zipporah later leave Midian to return to Egypt, Zipporah is portrayed as "looking back / With tender love upon the home she had left," while Moses is seen "with eager eyes tracking / His path across the desert, longing once more / To see the long-lost faces of his distant home" (153). And at the poem's conclu-sion the children of Israel have not yet come to "possess the land and pass / Through Jordan to the other side" (163).

The forging of a national home place for the oppressed remains unresolved at the epic's conclusion, yet the poem does clarify the means to achieve this goal. As the epic progresses, the complexities of Moses' "private" family life recede to the background and the narrative action moves into the more "public" national arena to consider the mechanisms through which an oppressed people may attain its freedom. In this process Moses must consider the uses and abuses to which violence may be put. After killing the Egyptian, he comes to question the value of violence as he witnesses two brothers engaged in a private quarrel that echoes the public strife of the Civil War: "[He] saw two brethren striving / For mastery; and then his heart grew full / Of tender pity. They were brethren, sharers / Of a common wrong: should not their wrongs more / Closely bind their hearts, and union, not division, / Be their strength?" (151). As a consequence of these events, Moses rejects violent action in favor of thought: "Men grow strong in action, but in solitude / Their thoughts are ripened" (151); when he returns to action, it is not to physical violence but the action of words. Moses' words enable the children of Israel to escape bondage in Egypt, but "broader freedom"—the achievement of nationhood—remains, as it did in the antebellum jeremiads of David Walker and Maria Stewart, unfulfilled: "But though they slumbered in the wild, they died / With broader freedom on their lips, and for their / Little ones did God reserve the heritage / So rudely thrust aside" (163). Yet the very evocation of Moses, who figured so prominently as the slaves' redeemer in antebellum spirituals, may be said to constitute a promise of African-American freedom.[21]

It is in the 1872 cycle of Aunt Chloe poems in *Sketches of Southern Life* that Harper attempted to work out the meaning of this "broader freedom" by locating the poems' action within the homes of Southern black folk. Like her poems of the 1850s, these are ballads; unlike the earlier poems, however, these ballads are no longer grounded in sentimental culture. Home is no longer the sentimental site of the socially weak, of those individuals and families victimized by the slave system whose destinies demand the readers' empathetic response. Instead, it is a political locus in which the socially active and empowered work collectively to implement black political Reconstruction. The poems narrate the history of a group of Southern black folk, Uncle Jacob, Jakey, and especially Aunt Chloe and "we women radicals"—the mothers, sisters, and wives who had gradually withdrawn into the background of *Moses* but now dominate the foreground as political activists. The history of this folk is conceptualized as a progressive one that proceeds from the dark days of slavery when families were torn asunder, to the Civil War when blacks prayed and fought for freedom, and finally to the contemporary Reconstruction period as the struggle to achieve full political and social equality is taking place. In the process home becomes the place of nation building as its inhabitants debate, and work toward, the incorporation of blacks into the national body politic by means of literacy, education, and the ballot.

"Broader freedom," finally, is linguistically marked in these ballads by Harper's abandonment of her antebellum third-person narrator who is located outside the circle of slavery and her consequent authorization of the freed people to narrate their own history—the private, the familial, the communal, the political—in the speech of the community. To this end Harper invented a linguistic form that is not black dialect but in which, as Sterling Brown has suggested, "truth to idiom is more important . . . than truth to pronunciation" and pronunciation must be aurally imagined by the reader. I believe Harper was attempting here to erase the dichotomy between white literary frame and black dialect that John Wideman has argued hierarchizes speech usage as it interprets the white frame as "matured" and the black dialect as "infantile," "chaotic," and in need of containment. According to Wideman, the task facing twentieth-century black writers has been "to escape [this] literary frame which *a priori* devalues black speech."[22] I would argue that such a freeing is exactly what Harper accomplishes in her Aunt Chloe cycle as she deconstructs the binary opposition of white literary frame and black dialect and invents a black idiom that exists on its own terms, unframed by the language of the dominant culture. Through such a manipulation of idiom Harper rejected the notion that black language, thought, and action must inevitably be framed by a white perspective and instead locates the point of view of freedom squarely within the black community: "After years of pain and parting, / Our chains was broke in two, / And we was so mighty happy, / We did'nt know what to do. / But we soon got used to freedom, / Though the way at first was rough; / But we weathered through the tempest, / For slavery made us tough."[23]

In contrast to the Aunt Chloe poems, Harper's 1871 volume of poems reveals very little in the way of technical innovation, as the ballad, the hymn, and a conventional narrative voice dominate; it does, however, offer new thematic material that interrogates the national politics of Reconstruction. In her poetic collections of the 1850s Harper chose, as we saw earlier, to narrate the histories of "private" individuals victimized by different public institutions. These sentimentalized individuals—the Syrophenician woman, the slave mother, the drunkard's child, the fugitive's wife—function as metonyms of the disorders that are rending the social fabric of the nation. In contrast, many of the poems of the 1871 collection specifically address the nation itself ("the American people," "men of the North," "the oppressing nation") or its most committed leaders (Thaddeus Stevens, Charles Sumner, President Lincoln) and thus explicitly enact a shift from the "private" sphere of the family to the "public" arena of political action.

Building upon the familiar poetic forms of her antebellum verse, Harper extended here her use of the hymn in order forcefully to uphold her own support of Reconstruction policies—emancipation, the Fifteenth Amendment, protection of the civil rights of all African Americans—and to challenge the nation's leaders and citizens to implement these policies. Thus, poems such as "Lines to Hon. Thaddeus Stevens," "President Lincoln's Proclamation of Freedom," or "Fifteenth Amendment" directly address or comment upon current political issues, pay homage to the actions of Republican politicians now dead, and, in typical Unitarian fashion, work to stir the moral conscience of readers and commit them to social action: "There is light beyond the darkness, / Joy beyond the present pain; / There is hope in God's great justice, / And the negro's rising brain. / Though before the timid counsels / Truth and Right may seem to fail, / God hath bathed his sword in judgment, / And his arm shall yet prevail."[24]

As in her antebellum poetic volumes, the structural principle operative in Harper's 1871 collection seems to be a framing device in which the first and last sets of poems tend to constellate around a particular topic and provide a frame for a more eclectic group of middle poems. Once again, such a framing device tends to foreground the material of the frame itself rather than that which is placed inside it. The material within the frame consists here of poems on slavery written in the late 1850s ("The Dying Fugitive," "Bury Me in a Free Land") as well as some of Harper's most personal poems dealing with death, mother-daughter relationships, and orphanhood; their embedded placement allows them to recede somewhat from the reader's line of vision. In contrast, the frame consists of those poems that address issues of Reconstruction politics, either directly ("Lines to Hon. Thaddeus Stevens," "An Appeal to the American People," "Words for the Hour," "President Lincoln's Proclamation of Freedom," "Fifteenth Amendment"), through biblical analogy ("Retribution," "The Sin of Achar"), or by means of allegory and symbol ("Truth," "The Little Builders," "Light in Darkness"). "The Little Builders" in particular illustrates the way in which Harper sought to make home function as a metonym for nation. Although "the little builders" are indeed "building man a home," this home cannot simply be made "with mortar, brick and stone." For the home they are building is in fact "freedom's temple," which resides within the hearts of the nation's citizens, "the hearts that love her best" (44–45).

If Harper was able to publish her poetry quite consistently as printed volumes from the 1850s on, her first book-form novel, *Iola Leroy,* was not to appear until 1892. As yet we have uncovered no evidence to suggest that Harper had attempted to publish her earlier novels with a mainstream publishing house but had been rebuffed as Cary had been by Harper and Bros., or that these publishers might have felt that African-American poetry in its apparent conventionalism was safer and thus more marketable than potentially subversive fictional narratives. What the recent archival research of Frances Foster has ascertained, however, is that from the late 1860s on the AME Church—in contrast to its earlier treatment of Jarena Lee—opened up the pages of its official organ, the *Christian Recorder,* to Harper, which thus became the chief vehicle through which her fiction was able to find a public. Harper's fiction is addressed, then, to a black readership and its content focuses on issues concerning the construction of African-American domestic and community space.

Harper's seven known short stories ("Opening the Gates" [October 28, 1871], "Fancy Etchings" [February 20, April 23, May 1, May 22, and July 23, 1873], and "Fancy Sketches" [January 15, 1874]) consist of conversations conducted between two characters, Jenny and her Aunt Jane, and on occasion a minor third character. If Jenny insists "'that conversation ought to be made one of the finest and most excellent of all arts'" (Feb. 20, 1873), Harper herself asserts the dialogic to be her principal narrative strategy; each sketch raises a social issue of vital importance to the black community—the worth of women's work, the value of literature, the advantages of industrial associations—which is then debated from different perspectives. Aunt Jane's perspective exhibits greater experience and moral sensitivity, and Jenny's greater educational achievement. The two characters represent, of course, two different facets of Harper herself—the older woman who has survived the difficult material conditions of antebellum black life and the younger woman who would like to write "a book that will make people better and happier because they read it" (Feb. 20, 1873) and become "a poet, to earn and take my place among the poets of the nineteenth century" (April 24, 1873).

If Harper's poems often came to voice at the public podium, her short fiction would seem to emerge from the private place of home where Jenny and Aunt Jane practice the "excellent art" of conversation. Yet Jenny makes it clear that she conceives of "poetry" as a means of "teach[ing] others to strive to make the highest ideal, the most truly real of our lives"; poetry is in fact "one of the great agents of culture, civilization and refinement" (April 24, 1873). Thus, even though women's writing in these stories is initiated in the privacy of home, it is also directly connected to concerns of the public sphere.

These stories stand in contrast to Harper's two Reconstruction novels, *Minnie's Sacrifice* and *Sowing and Reaping,* that revolve around the sentimental figures of the tragic mulatta and victims of intemperance, respectively; in fact, the latter novel is a mere elaboration of "The Two Offers." These narratives construct plots in which the characters' private and domestic choices are shown to have social consequences that reverberate throughout the fictional black communities, yet they remain rooted in an antebellum sentimental sensibility. In contrast, the conversations of the plotless short stories explicitly raise social issues that the African-American leadership itself was debating at that time. They suggest Harper's awareness of the limitations of sentimental discourse in expressing the complexities of black Reconstruction. Of particular interest are those debates between Aunt Jane and Jenny that raise the crucial question of labor relations and black entrepreneurship during this period. In "Opening the Gates" Aunt Jane argues: "As we are shut out from workshops and other places of industrial departments, then there is greater reason why we should combine together to bring different trades and businesses within our reach" (Oct. 28, 1871). This proposal is further developed by Jenny in "Fancy Sketches" as she recommends the development of black "civil associations": "[I]t would be an excellent plan if some of our colored men who possessed money could only unite upon some plan by which we could build up some thriving industries of our own. . . . [C]ould not this thing be effected among us by the power of combination?" (Jan. 15, 1874). It is just such an acknowledgment of the insufficiency of the antebellum model of domestic economy in forging a national home place for African Americans in the postbellum period that led black women like Harper to insist more and more forcefully on gaining access to national institutions.

HOME AND EXILE: BIFURCATED NARRATION IN THE WRITINGS OF CHARLOTTE FORTEN

Forten's Reconstruction literary production stands in striking contrast to that of Harper in its relative paucity, its thematic diversity, and its publication venues. In a biographical sketch published in 1892, Lawson Scruggs suggested that both ill health and domestic obligations incurred by her marriage to Francis Grimké in 1878 were perhaps responsible for the fact that Forten never achieved her goal of "becoming an authoress": "Her life in the District has not been an eventful one, much of her time being spent in church work, and therefore she has not done as much literary work as she had hoped to do. She sometimes tries to find some consolation in the thought that possibly this is why her long-cherished dreams of becoming an authoress have never been fully realized."[25]

Yet Forten's literary endeavors in the 1860s and 1870s raise important issues that move beyond the personal realm to questions of production and reception, patronage and readership. To become an authoress, Forten, unlike Harper, did not position herself within the black community and avail herself of its institutions, literary organs, and readership. Instead, she relied on the patronage of such men of letters as Higginson, whose literary disciple she had been during her stay on the Sea Islands, and Whittier, who had made possible the publication of her essay in the *Atlantic Monthly*. It was perhaps through the intermediary of these two men that she was able to publish in the *Christian Register*, the *Commonwealth*, and *Scribner's*, enjoying, according to Monroe Majors, "the reputation of being a costly correspondent."[26] In this condition of racial "exile," Forten needed perforce to negotiate with her patrons, publishers, and readers. It is somewhat ironic that one of Higginson's early acts of literary patronage was to arrange for Forten to translate one of Erckmann-Chatrian's "national novels," *Madame Thérèse*, for Scribner's. Forten's relationship to revolutionary history here is not to the U.S. Civil War but to the French overthrow of the ancien régime, and it is expressed not through original composition but through translation. Left unanswered are such questions as the following: What kinds of texts would Forten have wanted to write in the postbellum period? Would they have promoted a vision of the past (American, African-American, both) that was "usable" to Forten? Would they have reaffirmed an ideological commitment to the picturesque? What publishing house would have agreed to publish these writings?

What in fact characterizes Forten's Reconstruction oeuvre is a bifurcation of sensibility that underscores the complexity of literary expression for an African-American woman with links to both the black and white communities. Indeed, in the 1870s Forten wrote a series of angry letters to the editors of the *Christian Register* and the *Commonwealth* that evince her readiness to respond to racist statements made by opponents of Reconstruction and to defend the progress of Southern blacks. Yet during the same period Forten also published several pieces of art criticism that directly address the highbrow cultural sensibilities of the postbellum leisure class. These art appreciations may be seen as an extension of Forten's childhood pastime of contemplating pictures in books. Thus, they might well have functioned as a strategy of containment that would have allowed Forten to inhabit a realm of pure art emptied of political content and at the same time accommodate the ideological constraints demanded by patrons and publishers, much as her antebellum cultivation of the picturesque had abetted her censorship of self.

A poem published in the July 18, 1874 issue of the *Christian Register* commemorating the death of Charles Sumner indirectly illuminates Forten's difficulties in coming to voice.[27] In the first stanza of the poem the poet starts off by recalling Sumner's house in Washington, D.C., and the art objects in it; much as in her antebellum writings, Forten's vision here is grounded in a sense of local place presided over by a genius loci whose power and voice have, however, faded in death: "Only the casket left, the jewel gone / Whose noble presence filled these stately rooms, / And made this spot a shrine where pilgrims came— / . . . To listen to the wise and gracious words / That fell from lips whose rare, exquisite smile / Gave tender beauty to the grand, grave face." In this silent and empty casket of a house, Forten is left alone to contemplate the paintings on the wall "whereupon thy artist eye delighted dwelt." As she imagines Sumner's artistic delight, Forten conflates her stance as an art appreciator with that of Sumner. Rather than maintain this perceptual stance throughout the poem, however, Forten shifts position to identify herself with the art objects on display, in particular a painted figure of Psyche. This identification is occasioned by the anxiety generated by the silencing of Sumner's voice in death and the desire to hear it once again: "Thy favorite Psyche droops her matchless face, / Listening, methinks, for the beloved voice / Which nevermore on earth shall sound her praise" (2:24).

Forten's evocation of Psyche is particularly significant since in the classical tradition she is an allegorical personification of the erring human soul in search of perfection and fulfillment—emblematized by a union with Eros, the god of love— who may attain her goal only through separation and suffering. Through identification with this allegorical figure, Forten appears to acknowledge the inevitability of suffering as a means toward the fulfillment of desire and to accept the necessity of entering the "dark . . . way" of historical experience—however racialized that history may be. But the poem ends with the recognition that the living are still silent and the (vain) plea that Sumner grace them with a sign that will allow them to come to voice: "All these remain—the beautiful, the brave, / The gifted, silent ones; but thou art gone! / . . . Oh friend beloved, with longing, tear-filled eyes / We look up, up to the unclouded blue, / And seek in vain some answering sign from thee."

Two letters to the editors of the *Christian Register* and the *Commonwealth* published in the mid-1870s testify to Forten's refusal to remain silent and her willingness to speak out on racial issues. Written as responses to published articles expressing racist attitudes, Forten's counterattacks derive their rhetorical force from their immediacy and personal tone. Furthermore, both letters are constructed as debates between two opposing parties, as Forten relied on a strategy of inserting quoted material taken directly from her opponent's document into her own, to which she then offered a point-by-point rebuttal. Forten's argument in each letter—the first, an argument against school segregation, the second, against the justification of slavery—turns on the necessity of analyzing African-American experience as historically constructed rather than racially essentialized and determined.

Forten began her first letter, published in two parts in the June 20 and June 27, 1874 issues of the *Christian Register,* with a lengthy nature description of Columbia, South Carolina that, as in her earlier diary entries, abounds in picturesque details of trees, flowers, and fountains. But landscape description is quickly displaced here by an analysis of historical experience, specifically the experiment in classroom integration at the state university. Referring her readers to a recently published article in *Scribner's Monthly* criticizing integration, Forten responded with forceful counterarguments based on the need to contextualize human behavior historically, and in particular to see moral degradation—both black and white—as a result of slavery. As she developed her arguments, Forten sought to reinforce their effectiveness by underscoring her authority as an eyewitness to the historical events of slavery and Reconstruction; what she has directly observed in her travels in the North and South become irrefutable facts that invite generalization.

The second letter, "Mr. Savage's Sermon, 'The Problem of the Hour,'" published in the December 23, 1876 issue of the *Commonwealth,* is not framed but is articulated from the outset in a tone of intense anger and bitterness that reflects Forten's sense of betrayal over Savage's racial attitudes expressed in a sermon printed in the *Commonwealth's* December 9 issue: "In most respects—I say it with sadness—this sermon is worthy of a veritable Southern slaveholder, born and bred. It is hardly possible to believe that it could have been delivered by a Republican" (2:121). In the first part of the letter Forten angrily denounced Savage's justification of slavery, employing the same rhetorical strategy of direct quotation from her opponent's argument in order to rebut it. Midway through the letter, however, Forten shifted from an analysis of the nation's slave past to a critique of the present failure of Reconstruction. To Savage's accusations of black corruption in the South and his sympathetic construction of white Southerners as victims of a harsh Northern Reconstruction policy, Forten perceptively responded with an incontrovertible truth—that white Southerners "had not, and have not, any desire to grant their rights to the colored people, but, on the contrary, a determination to reduce them to a condition as nearly like that of slavery as possible" (2:126). The heart of her evidence lies in her quotation of Savage's assessment of blacks in freedom as *"disagreeable and barbarous and ape-like colored people"* (2:124). Italicized by Forten herself and reiterated three times in the course of the letter, this quotation obviously burned with an intense viciousness in Forten's mind, reminding the reader that if such was indeed the representation of the African American in the white imagination, Reconstruction was doomed to failure.

At the same time that she was embroiled in such personal polemics over racial issues, Forten also wrote and published several pieces of cultural and art criticism—for example, a brief article entitled "A Visit to the Birthplace of Whittier" that appeared in the September 1872 issue of *Scribner's*, two essays that review the Corcoran Art Gallery's permanent collection in Washington, D.C., as well as a three-part account of the opening of the 1876 Centennial Exposition in Philadelphia published in the July 22, July 29, and August 5, 1876 issues of the *Christian Register*. The Whittier piece looks back to Forten's antebellum readings, as it is patterned after the literary genre that centers on the description of a home place that is then associated with its author-inhabitant. The later art appreciations are, however, more expressive of a postbellum bourgeois sensibility. They reflect the bourgeois status of the viewer who has both the cultural background and the leisure time to appreciate such high-culture artifacts. In its emphasis on the formal qualities of the work of art, the art appreciation is often conceptualized as an apolitical form that represses ideology. Forten herself in one of her Centennial Exposition articles explicitly affirmed the realm of the aesthetic as one in which the "too painful" must be forbidden entrance and quoted in seeming support a line from an Elizabeth Barrett Browning sonnet: "They say that ideal beauty should not enter the house of anguish" (2:73). But Browning's sonnet, which Forten cites in its entirety in one of her Corcoran Art Gallery pieces, is in fact a meditation on Hiram Powers's Greek Slave statue that emphatically resists the dichotomy between "ideal beauty" and "anguish"; it demands that the "passionless perfect" of the statue serve to "break up ere long / The serfdom of this world!" (2:39). These quoted lines indicate Forten's own recognition of the possible cohabitation of "ideal beauty" and "anguish."

In her two articles on the Corcoran, "Midsummer Days in the Capital" and "The Corcoran Art Gallery in Winter," Forten's imagination transforms the gallery into a "refuge," removed from the "heat and turmoil of the town," within whose "walls much of the glory and beauty in nature and in art, to which we cannot go is brought to us" (2:34–35). Critics such as Susan Stewart have recently analyzed the cultural politics that undergird the constitution of the museum. In bringing together disparate art objects to form a collection, the museum obfuscates the material history of the objects' origins; the relation of labor to the production of these objects is erased, and they enter into the dominant exchange economy as commodities. Historical content is thus lost and replaced by a new framework based on formal classification that emphasizes the uniqueness of the individual object whose use value is thereby fully aestheticized. In viewing the art object, the spectators participate in its aestheticization; identifying with the bourgeois class that has produced the museum, they are educated into its cultural values and adopt its politics of containment.[28]

As she constructed a narrative of her visits to the Corcoran Art Gallery, Forten appears to have entered into just such a dehistoricized world of formal beauty in which the art object is commodified and to have identified with the cultural values of the bourgeois class. Moreover, if Forten was indeed remunerated for the writing of her articles, these also come to operate as commodities within an exchange economy. As she toured the gallery, Forten deliberately turned away from those "exquisitely-finished French pictures" whose worldly subjects were altogether too reminiscent of the social world of Washington, D.C. (2:43). She exhibited instead a decided preference for classical statuary and landscape paintings. Forten's admiration for such statues as the Venus de Milo, the Apollo Belvedere, and the Mercury in Repose betrays a nostalgic longing for what Nietzsche has called the Apollinian principle in which art pertains to the sphere of dreams and appears as "the beautiful illusion of the inner world of fantasy" whose "higher truth" and "perfection" contrast sharply with "the incompletely intelligible everyday world."[29] Forten appears, then, to seek aesthetic delight in those art objects whose Apollinian characteristics beckon her into a world of dream and illusion. But embedded in, and countering, this aestheticizing tendency is her description of Powers's Greek Slave statue and her gloss of it by means of Browning's poem.

Forten's complex relationship to aesthetic experience is even more apparent in her three articles on the 1876 Centennial Exposition, in which the cultural politics that shaped the exhibition are never explicitly invoked. Historians such as Robert Rydell have demonstrated how this federally initiated and funded exposition was conceived by politicians eager to celebrate U.S. national unity and to reinforce the nation's status as God's chosen people. More particularly, the exposition was meant to foreground U.S. economic growth in the Gilded Age and to illustrate the critical relationship between patriotism, economic growth, and sociopolitical stability. To underscore the nation's astounding economic development, its accomplishments were charted in comparison to those of other countries. American nationhood was thus defined within an international perspective through which the exposition organizers boldly constructed a world in which the U.S. exhibits served as the geographic center and gave it coherent representation by means of racial mapping. Immediately adjacent to the U.S. displays, and thus of almost equal importance, were the European exhibits, of France, England, Germany, the Austro-Hungarian Empire, and their colonies. Located across the way were those of Mexico and Brazil, while the Chinese and Japanese were relegated to another wing.

As Rydell has emphasized, the exposition's ideology explicitly linked economic progress and industrial growth to notions of race and nationality in which nonwhite peoples were perceived either as benighted or as threatening. In the United States exhibit in particular, native Americans were portrayed as savage antiprogressive forces, while African Americans went totally unrepresented with the exception of several statues by Edmonia Lewis and Edward Bannister's painting *Under the Oaks*. Despite their attempts to participate, black women were refused exhibition space in the Woman's Pavilion. Finally, if the Centennial Exposition was organized according to a chauvinist principle of American nationalism, it was also dominated by a broader ideology of mercantilism in its presentation of highly prized art objects to which a monetary value was explicitly affixed. As in the case of the museum, we can view the 1876 exhibition as a collection of discrete artifacts placed within a representational framework that transforms them into commodities defined purely by their exchange value.[30]

Forten's account of her visit to the exposition is interesting both for what it explicitly states and for what it silences, underscoring once again the complex cultural negotiations in which she found herself embroiled. Interestingly, in her articles Forten refused to dwell at any length on the accomplishments of U.S. manufacturing and also withheld judgment on the relative lack of an African-American presence at the exposition. Her only references are a quite evenhanded critique of Edmonia Lewis's contributions to the Art Building and a more vigorous complaint over the organizers' neglect during the opening ceremonies to emphasize the "emancipation of a race" and to invite Wendell Phillips to speak (2:64). Given the demands of her publishers and readership, such commentary might well have been Forten's only possible form of political protest.

What Forten does record at great length is her contemplation of luxury items of all kinds and from all provenances—jewels, china, and crystal from England; Indian carving in silver and gold as well as cashmere carpets; feathers from New Zealand; French lace, tapestries, fans, and engravings; Florentine mosaics; Russian malachite, lapis lazuli, furs, and velvets; and paintings from diverse European countries. Forten's gaze here suggests what Remy Saisselin has called the bourgeois fascination with the bibelot, as the collecting of works of "high art" is replaced in the second half of the nineteenth century by the accumulation of bibelots in the bourgeois household, which function as markers of social status and exemplify this class's emphasis on acquisition, possession, and market exchange.[31] Gathered together in an international exhibition, these objects become for the spectator a substitute for the actual journey to, and experience of, foreign nations. Serving as a metonym for the foreign culture, the exhibited artifact points to its loss of original context, its displacement from its own history, in particular that of its material production, and its increasing function as a fetish.

Forten's position as a spectator of these exhibits underscores the intensely contradictory nature of her relationship to American society; if on the one hand she appears to participate in the dehistoricization and commodification of the foreign cultures displayed, to delight in the contemplation of pure beauty, and to identify with the social values of the dominant bourgeoisie, on the other hand she knew that she could never fully gain acceptance into this class. Her presence at the exposition was also an acknowledgment of the degree to which travel abroad must for now take the form of spectatorship. As she herself recognized: "If we can't see Europe, Asia and Africa, in short, make a tour of the world, (not in eight days) this is certainly the next best thing" (2:66). Forten, in fact, intimates that such substitutions may be the only forms through which she can apprehend these foreign cultures. And, finally, given the probable constraints of publication imposed on her, we may wonder to what extent narration here could adequately translate such substitute experiences into a literary form that Forten could claim as her own.

A short fictional piece, "The Flower-Fairies' Reception," published in the August 8, 1874 issue of the *Christian Register,* offers a vivid illustration of how Forten was able to make use of the aestheticization of human experience— specifically here its allegorization—to mask the social. Of particular interest is the way in which Forten's allegorical concerns converge here with those of Harper's short vignette "The Mission of the Flowers," appended to the 1869 edition of *Moses.* Both stories appropriate, in order to rewrite, the American myth of the nation as garden. In the nationalistic versions of the myth, first New England as another Eden, then the South with its vast plantations, and finally the West with its open frontiers are represented as gardens that offer their spiritual and earthly wealth to the enterprising (white male) settler. In contrast, Forten and Harper present the reader with an already landscaped Victorian garden in need of re-cultivation.

In her story Forten's imagination seemingly invites the nameless protagonist to leave the realm of history to inhabit a dreamworld that is explicitly allegorized. With her younger sister she leaves her own garden to go to the woods and pick wild flowers, passing Mount Auburn Cemetery on the way. Ann Douglass has shown how Mount Auburn was typical of those nineteenth-century picturesque rural cemeteries that were carefully landscaped and planned according to the same system of sentimentality that regulated the domiciles of the living; as such, they were designed to cultivate "home associations" and to freeze such memories of the past into a timeless present.[32] Yet the protagonist's foray beyond the cemetery does not bespeak an abandonment of the cultivated in favor of the wilderness, for the woods with their "wealth of flowers" merely constitute another form of the garden (2:78), and the picking of flowers is to result in a floral arrangement.

Upon her return the protagonist falls asleep and enters into the dreamworld of the flower fairies' garden, an allegorical realm in which the garden seems to stand for a secure pastoral world, autonomous and permanent, redeemed from the ravages of history. In this context the flowers themselves appear to function as emblems of universal and eternal truths imbued with transparent meanings. Yet the flowers are also allegorized in terms that move beyond the universal to confront the culturally particular. As a literary form, allegory is structured according to a double level of meaning and relies on rhetorical strategies through which ideological signification is kept "secret in the act of making public," is simultaneously veiled and unveiled. Here the flowers are ideologically coded as they form part of a specific cultural construction, the Victorian language of flowers, in which the speaker's very knowledge of this language designates her social status and group identity, and the flowers' very meanings are reflective of Victorian culture's moral values.[33] The allegorical process that structures the protagonist's dream suggests Forten's own awareness of the Victorian language of flowers, made available to her perhaps through such compilations as Sarah Josepha Hale's *Flora's Interpreter,* thus placing her firmly within middle-class sentimental culture.

Yet in her allegorizing, Forten's protagonist endows the flowers with specific moral meanings of her own. In individual interpretations "the noble Queen Calla Lily" becomes "a fitting type of the Divine Purity and Love," "little Lady Heliotrope" symbolizes modesty, and "Princess White Camellia Japonica" is emblematic of arrogant pride. Even more significantly, the protagonist also creates broader social and geographic categories, whereby the humility of the country flowers is prized over the haughtiness of the city flowers, and the sweetness of the New England flowers is preferred to the showiness of those from the South: "I thought most of them more showy, but less delicate and refined, than our Northern Flower Fairies" (84). In Forten's vignette, then, the flower fairies' garden does not simply represent universal moral values or reflect culturally coded conventions but instead becomes an allegory of the nation in which country is preferred to city, New England to the South, and community-building values to individualistic ones. As such, it exhibits striking similarities to Harper's allegorical "Mission of the Flowers," in which the dictatorial rose refuses to accept the heterogeneity of the garden-nation; insisting on the need for homogeneity, she turns all the other flowers into roses. The moral lesson that she ultimately learns is respect for difference: "She had learned to respect the individuality of her sister flowers, and began to see that they, as well as herself, had their own missions."[34]

INSTITUTIONS AND SOCIAL DISCOURSES

As Forten's and Harper's allegories of the nation make clear, black women in the Reconstruction period aspired to a comprehensive political vision that would encompass the place of African Americans within the nation as a whole. To construct a place for blacks within the nation, they needed to assess not only the strengths and weaknesses that lay within domestic and community spheres but also such questions as the commonality of interests between black and white women, the ballot as a tool of national Reconstruction, and the function of black labor within the nation. Harper had already broached certain of these issues in her lecturing, writing, and work among the black communities of the South, but in the 1860s and 1870s she, along with many other black women, sought to expand their influence by affiliating in increasing numbers with national organizations headed by black men or white women—the women's rights movement, temperance associations, labor unions, the press, legal institutions. Participation in such organizations during Reconstruction ultimately facilitated the creation of national institutions of their own that by the century's end could provide black women with their own home place.[35]

From the mid-1860s on, black women participated with increasing frequency and interest in the women's rights movement, attending and addressing its various annual conventions. Sojourner Truth, who, as we saw in chapter 2, had been a frequent and vocal presence at many of these meetings, was now joined by Harper and Cary. Harper attended a New York state convention in 1866 as well as the contentious 1869 Equal Rights Association Convention when the organization split in two over the issue of black male suffrage and allegiance to the Republican Party. Harper chose to affiliate with the more "moderate" American Woman Suffrage Association (AWSA) whose membership was composed largely of antebellum abolitionists supporting radical Reconstruction and the Fifteenth Amendment. It was at this convention that Harper, acknowledging her complex position as one of the "brave," affirmed both her allegiance to "race" over "sex" and her distance from white women whose racism continued to oppress the black woman worker.

In striking contrast, Truth and Cary chose to participate in the activities of Stanton and Anthony's more "radical" National Woman Suffrage Association (NWSA), whose platform was based on a denunciation of the Democratic and Republican parties, opposition to the Fifteenth Amendment, and a determination to lobby Congress for the passage of a federal woman's suffrage amendment. Truth's affiliation with the NWSA thus provided her with a forum from which to speak out on behalf of woman's suffrage. To an even greater extent than Truth, Cary joined the NWSA in order to lobby the federal government. Although the *History of Woman Suffrage* contains no reference to any speeches delivered by Cary, it does note that she participated in the NWSA conventions of 1874, 1877, 1878, and 1880, and it is possible that she also attended others. Cary's loyalty to the NWSA leadership seems assured by her February 5, 1874 *New National Era* article in which she praised these white women for their "talent of a higher order," "indefatigable zeal and splendid accomplishments," and "unselfish efforts in every noble cause."

If such complimentary language suggests full allegiance to the NWSA and the choice of "sex" over "race," other of Cary's writings belie such an interpretation. Drafts of articles and speeches in the Moorland-Spingarn collection, for example, show evidence of Cary's commitment to political action as a means of advancing the specific cause of black women. In a document entitled "A first vote almost," Cary gave a lively account of the attempt to vote by "sixty-three women citizens who voluntarily proposed to divide with them the onerous responsibility but were summarily refused."[36] To the argument that moral logic dictates that black women should be given the same rights as black men under conditions of freedom, Cary added the more political contention that the vote of black women is needed to ensure respect of the Fourteenth and Fifteenth Amendments, which neither Democrats nor Republicans seemed inclined to protect vigorously: "It is not merely a question whether the women shall vote by reason of their own established amendments, it is a virtual admission of the rebel claim that there is nothing in those amendments by which the people should be bound." Finally, in direct contrast to the NWSA's refusal to support either political party, Cary openly proclaimed at the 1878 annual convention that "colored women would support whatever party would allow them their rights, be it Republican or Democratic."[37]

Black women thus exhibited a growing interest in the question of women's rights during the Reconstruction period as entry into citizenship made them aware of the extent to which neither political, legal, nor social institutions necessarily ensured the equal treatment of men and women and the extent to which their own historical specificity distinguished them from both black men and white women. Thus, while Harper, Truth, and Cary expressed their concern in concert with white women over such issues as the ballot and equal protection of all women before the law, they also refused to focus solely on the single category of Woman and her rights. For these black women the broader claims of what Harper called "all humanity," and the specific needs of the heterogeneous groups within it, were of the utmost importance. Truth's and Harper's women's rights speeches delivered during the 1860s and 1870s are thus fully informed not only by the category of gender but by those of race, class, and political allegiance to the Republican Party, as well as the racism of the very white women whom they were addressing. For them, the position of the "brave" was indeed complex.

In the 1860s and 1870s Sojourner Truth continued to attend and address many women's rights conventions, delivering, for example, three speeches to the American Equal Rights Association Convention held in New York in May 1867 on its first anniversary.[38] These speeches should not be read in isolation from one another but must be seen as symptomatic of Truth's continuing struggle to define her position as one of the "brave." Indeed, Truth refused any systematic alliance with her "sex" over her "race" but instead undertook a series of complex ideological negotiations between the categories of race, sex, and class. In contrast to some of her antebellum lectures, however, Truth's goal here—the achievement of woman's suffrage—was identical to that of the white women in her audience. To achieve this goal, Truth seems to have shifted rhetorical strategies, relying less on Africanisms and resorting instead to biblical analogy and, increasingly, humor.

In her first speech to the 1867 convention Truth following her antebellum rhetorical pattern, began by addressing the members of her audience with an appeal to personal experience. Yet while she referred to them as "my friends," thereby suggesting a degree of shared values and experiences, Truth simultaneously intimated the potential for disagreement given her own radical alterity: "I come from another field—the country of the slave." And, in fact, the remainder of the speech focuses on Truth's apprehension of her otherness, of her difference from both black men and white women, in tones that could as yet allow for no humor but only bitterness. Black men are distinguished by the fact that "they have got their liberty," since they are about to "get their rights." The inevitable consequence of such a difference can only be, according to Truth, a deepening of gender divisions within the black community, as "colored men will be masters over the women, and it will be just as bad as before" (20).

In constructing her argument against the mastery of black men, Truth sought to forge a rhetorical alliance with white women. Yet if she was able to generalize the category of woman—"I wish woman to have her voice"—she simultaneously articulated differences that existed among white women as well as between white and black women. By virtue of their race and class, "white women are a great deal smarter, and know more than colored women, while colored women do not know scarcely anything. They go out washing, which is about as high as a colored woman gets" (20). These white women are smarter, then, because they do not need to engage in the brutalizing menial jobs that black women must accept. At the same time, however, Truth allied herself experientially with "the German women" who, like her, work in the field but are paid much less than the men. Truth asserts here the commonality of interest among working women whose labor ought to be compensated equally to men's. Yet Truth also set herself apart from all of these classes of women by insisting, on the one hand, on her greater generational experiences that position her as "mother" to all those "chil'n," and, on the other hand, on her specificity as a "colored woman" fighting for the rights of other colored women: "I suppose I am about the only colored woman that goes about to speak for the rights of the colored women" (20).

If the first part of this speech is structured around issues of difference, the second half seeks to erase such distinctions in favor of commonalities of gender and race. Thus, the only thing that should matter is not distinctions among women or between black men and women but the longstanding oppression by white men: "You have been having our rights so long, that you think, like a slaveholder, that you own us." What matters most of all, perhaps, is Truth's commitment, beyond the gender divisions in the black community, to racial solidarity in order to achieve the uplift of her people: "I have been in Washington about three years, seeing about these colored people" (21).

Truth's second speech to the convention, delivered on the following day, is linked to the first by means of images of stirring through which Truth voiced her continued determination to agitate for women's rights. Thus, the colloquialism "I want to keep the thing stirring, now that the ice is cracked" is reconfigured in the

226

second speech as "while the water is stirring I will step into the pool." But this speech differs significantly from the first in its refusal to articulate its argument by means of a rhetoric of racial divisiveness, its consistent inclusion of all women, as well as its double appeal to biblical authority and to subversive forms of humor. Thus Truth began her speech by expressing her "gladness" that black men have got the vote and by construing the enfranchisement of all women as complementary to theirs. To build her case Truth retold the biblical parable from Luke in which Jesus cast seven devils out of a woman, and she did so from an African-American perspective of humor in which hierarchies are ridiculed and inverted. If the woman did indeed have seven devils in her, man had legions; if the devils are cast out of man, they promptly seek out "as good a place as they came out from," the swine known to be "the selfishest beast." After having ridiculed "man," Truth's rhetoric turns serious as she asserts Jesus' greater love of "woman" because of woman's, particularly Mary's, greater sense of fidelity. Truth's own reconstruction of the parable thus allowed her to conclude with a unifying vision not of "colored people" but of "woman": "Just so let women be true to this object, and the truth will reign triumphant" (63).

In Truth's third speech, delivered the same day as the second, the attempt to transcend difference and build coalitions across race and gender lines is made explicit at the outset, and humor—this time gentle rather than biting—becomes the mechanism for achieving these goals. Basing her remarks once again on the authority of personal experience, Truth described the antebellum abolitionist movement, in particular the "anti-slavery meetin's," as a time in which there was always "great grumblin' and mutterin' goin' on" (67). In contrast, she proclaimed to much "applause and laughter" the harmony of the present women's rights convention that has brought "so many people together—both male and female" who "seem to feel more for one another. Certainly I never saw so many people together and nobody tryin' to hurt anybody's feelin's" (67).

Yet as she argued her case in favor of the enfranchisement of women, Truth appealed through elaborate punning to a very specific authority of female experience: the experience of working women—homeowners like herself in Battle Creek—who were not only "taxed" but also "taxed" to build roads: "They went on the road and worked. It took 'em a good while to get a stump up. (Laughter). Now, that shows that women can work. If they can dig up stumps they can vote. (Laughter). It is easier to vote than dig stumps. (Laughter)" (67). Through this example Truth reasserted, albeit humorously, her own difference from the middle-class white women in her audience who have never been taxed to build roads. Such difference is reinscribed in an 1870 speech to a woman's suffrage convention in Providence, Rhode Island, in which Truth apparently chastised the women in the audience for the artificiality of their dress: "What kind of reformers be you, with goose-wings on your heads, as if you were going to fly, and dressed in such ridiculous fashion, talking about reform and women's rights?" (*Narrative*, 243). As she concluded her 1867 speech Truth hinted at the origins of her alterity as deriving from African cultural tradition in her announcement that she would close with a song whose words are unwritable and untranslatable: "They can't put things down on paper as we speak, though I speak in an unknown tongue" (68).

By the end of the Civil War Harper was lecturing with increasing frequency on such diverse topics as women's rights, Reconstruction, home building, and Northern racial uplift efforts. In contrast to her antebellum career, Harper now found herself able freely to promote her services as a public lecturer. One advertisement, printed in the December 21, 1872 issue of the *Christian Recorder,* and reprinted for almost a full year thereafter, ran as follows: "Mrs. F. E. W. Harper would respectfully give notice to Lyceums, Societies, and Churches of her readiness to fill any engagement." Reviewers still claimed Harper to be one of the most effective female lecturers of the period, justifying her preeminence by viewing her oratory as a form of preaching: "If Mrs. Harper be not a preacher of righteousness, then we have none" (*CR,* Jan. 28, 1871). A closer examination of two of Harper's Reconstruction speeches—one on women's rights, the other on Reconstruction—suggests, however, a greater degree of oratorical flexibility than that intimated by the reviewers, as Harper on at least one occasion abandoned the Ciceronian *style périodique* in favor of a more "middling rhetoric."

A speech delivered at the Eleventh National Woman's Rights Convention in May 1866, three years before the movement's split, points to Harper's willingness to experiment with different rhetorical modes.[39] In this speech, perhaps her maiden lecture on the topic of women's rights, Harper admitted at the outset to be new to the movement—"I feel I am something of a novice upon this platform" (45)—and then proceeded to deliver a lecture that was new not only in content but also in style. Indeed, this address differs markedly from almost all of Harper's other speeches in the degree to which she sought, in a manner reminiscent of Sojourner Truth, to ground her authority in personal experience and her subject matter in the revelation of intimate emotions. The personal nature of the speech was prompted by Harper's memory of the recent death of her husband, Fenton Harper, and her sudden awareness of how little protection the laws offers widowed women:

> But my husband died in debt; and before he had been in his grave three months, the administrator had swept the very milk-crocks and wash tubs from my hands. I was a farmer's wife and made butter for the Columbus market; but what could I do, when they had swept all away? They left me one thing—and that was a looking-glass! Had I died instead of my husband, how different would have been the result! By this time he would have had another wife, it is likely; and no administrator would have gone into his house, broken up his home, and sold his bed, and taken away his means of support. . . . I say, then, that justice is not fulfilled so long as woman is unequal before the law. (45–46)

In this personal anecdote Harper positioned herself squarely as "woman" in opposition to "man," specifically as a woman whose economic labor is carried out within the domestic sphere of the home and who, when denied the necessary means of production after the death of her husband, must assert the absolute need for woman's equality before the law. Yet the remainder of Harper's speech contains an implicit rejection of the unitary category of "woman" in favor of the more complex category of "humanity"—"we are all bound up together in one great bundle of humanity" (46)—which is but a secularized version of the framework of Christianity that had structured many of Harper's antebellum speeches. If humanity, like Christianity, is one great unifying force, it is nonetheless composed of multiple, heterogeneous elements, each of which cannot be ignored but must be attended to. Thus, Harper's speech at this point shifts from a single focus on "woman" to a more encompassing perspective that includes the "negro," oppressed by centuries of slavery, and the "poor white man," marginalized by the antebellum plantation economy (46). As a consequence of this broader human perspective, Harper comes to reinterpret herself as one of the "brave"—at once, "negro," "woman," and "unprivileged"—and she does so by aligning herself primarily against "you white women" whose skin color operates as a badge of privilege that Harper believed should be used to help the less privileged: "I do not believe that white women are dewdrops just exhaled from the skies. . . . While there exists this brutal element in society which tramples upon the feeble and treads down the weak, I tell you that if there is any class of people who need to be lifted out of their airy nothings and selfishness, it is the white women of America" (46, 48).

In this same speech Harper lamented that the "brutal element in society," combined with the indifference of white women, has rendered living conditions for African Americans almost intolerable in Northern urban communities. Relying once again on personal experience as a metonym for a more comprehensive racial experience, Harper proceeded to detail the difficulties she herself had encountered in her attempts to establish an African-American home place in the North: "To-day I am puzzled where to make my home. I would like to make it in Philadelphia, near my own friends and relations. But if I want to ride in the streets of Philadelphia, they send me to ride on the platform with the driver" (47).

This broader goal of locating a home place for all African Americans within the nation became the topic of a later address at the Centennial Anniversary of the Pennsylvania Society for Promoting the Abolition of Slavery held in Philadelphia on April 14, 1875.[40] Perhaps because Harper was speaking to an antislavery audience, the rhetoric of this speech belongs more to the tradition of her antebellum oratory, and the issue of women's part in the work of racial Reconstruction is suspended until the concluding paragraph. Relying once again on the Ciceronian *style périodique*, Harper grounded her argument in a clear definition of the political problem to be solved and its elucidation by reference to historical examples rather than personal experience.

In the opening sentence Harper defined "the great problem to be solved by the American people" as the question of "whether or not there is strength enough in democracy, virtue enough in our civilization, and power enough in our religion" to bring about the racial reconstruction of the nation (219). For Harper the answer lay not so much in the effectiveness of such abstractions or in any concrete measures taken by political parties but rather in the ability of African Americans to "do for ourselves" (219). Still adhering to her antebellum Unitarian philosophy and acutely aware of the importance of influencing public opinion, Harper asserted the development of "character" to be the primary mechanism both for achieving racial uplift within the black community and for turning "the world's dread laugh into admiring recognition" (219). Yet the ability to build character is only possible through a comprehensive understanding of history and thus, as in her antebellum speeches, Harper proceeded to pass in review the history of the African diaspora in the West, from the era of the international slave trade, through British emancipation, American slavery and abolitionism, and the Civil War, to the present condition of "freedom," which, however, must be qualified given the fact of white mob violence.

Arguing for the necessity of eradicating such violence, Harper once again invoked the framework of "humanity," insisting that to be a truly great civilization America must match its material prosperity with "a keener and deeper, broader and tenderer sense of justice—a sense of humanity" (220). Yet as in many of her antebellum speeches, Harper reinforced her humanitarian argument with a materialist one, insisting that it was to the nation's advantage to create an effective and productive black work force: "As a matter of political economy it is better to have the colored race a living force animated and strengthened by self-reliance and self-respect, than a stagnant mass, degraded and self-condemned" (221). To conclude her speech Harper shifted to a consideration of women's work in this task of national Reconstruction. Yet, perhaps because of the audience she was addressing, Harper refused to locate women's work in the economic arena but rather placed it in the more traditionally feminine sphere of the "inner life" (221). It is in a later speech to a Women's Congress in 1878 that Harper would bring together the twin issues of the political economy of the nation and the work of black women.

THE DISCOURSE OF SOCIAL ECONOMY:
REMOND, HARPER, AND CARY

Even before the end of the Civil War, black women revealed their determination to move beyond both local racial uplift programs and the national antislavery movement to participate in the work of national institutions that focused on broad questions of social and political economy. The increased participation of black women in such associations made available to them new forms of discourse through which to analyze these broader issues. At times these women still faced difficulties in gaining the acceptance of their male counterparts. If Harper had been able to address the 1864 National Convention of Colored Men held in Syracuse without controversy, a similar convention held in Washington, D.C., in 1869 acrimoniously revived the issue of the admission of women. It was left to Cary's old nemesis, I. C. Weir, to come to women's defense, arguing that to exclude them "would be too much like the actions of the occupants of the White House, who had excluded the colored race for two hundred years."[41] In addressing socioeconomic issues, black women exhibited concern not only for the "brave" but for all of their race; like the black male leadership, they confronted the vexed questions of the relation of labor to capital and the place of African Americans within the political economy of the nation.

As early as 1861, Sarah Parker Remond had read a paper at the National Association for the Promotion of Social Science held in Dublin. Although Remond's lecture consisted of a traditional indictment of the slave system and the federal government's collusion with it, it is significant that it was delivered at a meeting concerned with the application of disciplines in the social sciences to an analysis of social and economic organization. Remond's paper was placed under the rubric of "social economy," defined as a "department . . . embrac[ing] all those branches of inquiry concerning the conditions of industrial success, whether of nations or individuals, and the relations of labour and capital."[42] In 1864, finally, in the waning days of the Civil War but some few years before her despairing abandonment of her country, Remond published for a British audience the report of the secretary of war's committee of inquiry recommending the establishment of a temporary Freedmen's Bureau.

In the mid-1870s Harper attended an international Women's Congress at which she delivered a paper entitled "Coloured Women of America."[43] Subsequently published in the January 15, 1878 issue of the *Englishwoman's Review* in conjunction with other papers commenting on the Married Women's Property Act, the condition of women prisoners, and women's salaries, Harper's paper is indicative of her increased desire to utilize the discourse of social economy to articulate the special needs of black women as well as those of African Americans generally. Although the second half of Harper's speech focuses on black women's benevolent activities within the community as well as their intellectual and professional achievements carried out "in higher walks of life" (273)—singling out Forten and Cary for special praise—, the first half is particularly interesting for its analysis of the economic conditions and possibilities of black women in the Reconstruction South. Deviating once again from the tradition of her antebellum rhetoric, Harper in this speech abandoned the Ciceronian *style périodique* and the rhetorical mode of argumentation by reference to past historical example in order to offer terse factual statements concerning the present economic condition of black women based on personal observation and buttressed by the force of enumeration. In so doing, Harper repeatedly, and most often favorably, contrasted black women's work to that of black men: "The women as a class are quite equal to the men in energy and executive ability" (271); "in some cases the coloured woman is the mainstay of the family" (272); "in the city they are more industrious than the men" (273).

Yet despite its specific praise of black women's work, Harper's speech fully illustrates the tremendous difficulties facing the African-American leadership in its efforts to conceptualize a model of black economic empowerment. In Harper's speech blacks are represented as existing on the margins of a capitalist economy and possessing little leverage for entering it. As the women of the community are well aware, the cornerstone for empowerment lies in education: "In fact I find by close observation, that the mothers are the levers which move in education" (271). For the present, economic security is to be found not in urban employment but in land ownership, and specifically in the production of the old slave crop, cotton. Well aware of the vagaries of the international cotton market, however, Harper stressed the necessity of women's auxiliary labor to supplement the family's income and advance black economic autonomy. Thus, in example after example Harper offered evidence of the continued importance of the antebellum tradition of domestic economy, in which black women's in-house production of such items as cakes and preserved fruit and involvement in truck gardening contribute to the family's sustenance. The success of this economic model is perhaps best illustrated by a Mrs. Hill, who cultivates cotton on her five-acre farm, but "considering the low price of cotton and unfavourable seasons" also wisely "makes her garden [and] raises poultry" by means of which she "saves something every year," and thus can "keep a surplus in the bank" (272).

Unaddressed in the speech, however, is the question of how to expand and secure the economic base of the black family. In an earlier letter to William Still dated July 5, 1871, Harper had in fact conceptualized the possibilities of black entrepreneurship achieved through a meshing of domestic collaboration and capitalist enterprise, or what she termed "labor organized upon a new basis." In her letter Harper narrated the history of a former slave, Robert Montgomery, who had contracted several thousand acres of land from a former plantation owner in order to undertake the "experiment of a colored man both trading and farming on an extensive scale." Shifting from subsistence farming to the commercial production of cotton, Montgomery brought together his entire family, and other members of the community as well, to plant and grow cotton cooperatively, irrespective of traditional gender and generational roles. His daughters are employed as bookkeepers and storekeepers, his son "attends to the planting interest," and his wife farms cotton with "a number of orphan children employed," "every hand of his family [thus] adding its quota to the success of this experiment." Able to sell the cotton on the market at a time when cotton prices were still high, the Montgomery family firm has successfully amassed "between three and four hundred thousand dollars in a year."[44]

Of all the women discussed in this book, it is Mary Ann Shadd Cary who best exemplifies the Reconstruction efforts of black women to enter the public space of national institutions and make use of their discourses. Not only did Cary affiliate with the NWSA, but she was also an active member of the black press throughout the 1870s, attended the Colored National Labor Convention in December 1869, helped found a labor organization for black women in 1880, the Colored Women's Progressive Franchise Association, and, finally, gained admission to Howard Law school, where she received her bachelor of laws in May 1883. Yet much of Cary's work with these national institutions was marred at some level by the subordinate position assigned her by their all-male hierarchies as well as by the indifference and even contempt that she frequently encountered.

Cary's postbellum involvement with the black press is noteworthy for its accommodation to Frederick Douglass's leadership. Having taken up residence in Washington, D.C., and no longer the editor of her own newspaper, Cary associated herself with Douglass's *New National Era*, suppressing whatever political differences might still have existed between them. In 1871 she agreed to undertake a Southern subscription tour for the newspaper and thereafter wrote occasional articles for it. Douglass himself was fulsome in his public praise of Cary's newspaper career: "We, perhaps, regard this lady with all the more admiration because she was the first woman of our race in this country who had the nerve to enter upon the duties and labors of journalism. Until Mrs. Cary, we could not point to one colored lady among us who in this way vindicated the mental dignity and capacity of colored women. . . . Thanks to Mrs. Cary this darkness is broken, if only by a single ray" (*NNE*, July 13, 1871). But the rather formal tone of a private letter to Cary, alluding to her compensation for her forthcoming tour and offering suggestions on the best method for obtaining subscriptions, clearly indicates Douglass's sense of her status as an employee rather than an equal.

Douglass's advice to Cary in this letter was that she promote the *New National Era* as a national rather than a local paper: "Make editors of local papers see that the 'Era' does not interfere with their circulation. Theirs are local. The 'Era' national."[45] In this comment Douglass pointedly underscored the significance of a national newspaper whose goal would be to imagine community among African Americans. For her part Cary was convinced that African-American women recognized the need for such a national organ but often did not have the means to support it. In a letter to the *Era* early in her Southern tour, Cary noted that "many thousands of colored women I here find anxious to learn about the requirements and duties of the prospective positions. . . . Among the most decided expressions of approbation I have heard for the national organ—the New National Era—are from them; and except that they do not always hold a share in the purse-strings, I could have rolled up additional subscriptions in no mean number" (*NNE*, Aug. 10, 1871).

Indeed, the ability of black women to use the mechanism of the press to imagine community on a national scale remained virtually impossible in the 1870s. In the draft of an article located in the Moorland-Spingarn collection and entitled "The last day of the 43 Congress," Cary hailed the newfound "power of the concentrated national press" and women's place in it: "At the extreme limits of every other legitimate pursuit the gentler sex has halted and hesitated, or at most, plead to enter in deprecating protest: 'We would not seek admission but that we must have our daily bread'. In this unique department of letters and labor she begs not place, but is confessedly an equal;—an honored member of the guild." But in another draft Cary used the ironic and distancing medium of fiction to detail the real lack of power facing women operating in the public sphere of the newspaper world. In a fifteen-page narrative, highly Dickensian in its humorous tone, Cary fictionally recreated the atmosphere of the Capitol during the last days of the Forty-third Congress. The sketch depicts two newspaperwomen who together make up "the little firm of Kate and I" and who must stand up to a "potential lion of the press" seeking to buy their articles at a ridiculously low price. In defending the worth of their work, the women applaud their collaborators, those "lady itemizers" whose job it is to collect news items for them—"too retiring to face the world, yet they must have bread you know, and they do an immense amount of interviewing behind their vails [*sic*]." The newspaper world is thus represented as belonging to that male public sphere into which women must still negotiate entrance and in which their work remains undervalued.

If Cary faced difficulties gaining full acceptance into the national institution of the black press, she found that similar exclusions obtained in other organizations as well, in particular those concerned with labor issues. Yet despite the indifference of the 1869 Colored National Labor Convention to the participation of women and to "Woman's Labor," Cary turned her intellectual energies increasingly in the 1870s to an analysis of black labor. In a series of article drafts, she tentatively groped her way toward an articulation of the place that African Americans presently held, and might one day hope to hold, in the political economy of the nation. The Negro, she noted, is "regarded as out of the national concern." For although he is observable everywhere—"radiated in happy defiance of mathematics, physics or of Economic laws, from the Nation's Capitol massed at the South, to be again zig-zagged through every state and territory"—his economic marginality has incurred his invisibility. Emphasizing racial and ethnic difference by pitting African Americans against other nonwhite populations, Cary asserted that black invisibility was even greater than that of such border groups as "wild Indians and Mexican Greasers," whose presence is at least made visible through "amusing and relaxing literature": "The Greaser or Indian on the border thus becomes to be better known in his tribal and class relation, than the colored servant behind the chair of the Cabinet officer."

Seeking to analyze the social process that has thrust the Negro "out of the national concern," Cary named white mob violence, rationalized as the need to "suppress 'negro outlaws,'" as one obvious factor. But rather than lay blame outside the black community, Cary sought instead to answer the questions: "What are the colored people doing to elevate themselves? How are they doing the work and, what should be done for them?" Although formulated in secular rhetoric, Cary's analyses largely reiterate those made by David Walker in the late 1820s. Like Walker, Cary blamed the black community for its lack of unity: "The negro alone of all these American natives rejects unification as a social or other basis." In the postbellum period this lack of unity has been exacerbated by several factors: deepening class divisions; petty jealousies and corruption that have hampered the effectiveness of the political elite; a "morbid fearful self-hood" that has inhibited blacks from striking out together "into the illimitable field of enterprise and active national life"; and, finally, the loss of a belief in "clanship or kinship" so that "there is no co-operative point at which they can meet and devise and plan for the sucess of the family or social compact." It is African Americans' lack of historical consciousness that, according to Cary, has been both the cause and the result of such social phenomena.

In these same drafts Cary offered solutions that remained almost exclusively within the antebellum tradition of racial uplift: improved education, temperance, moral responsibility to self and neighbor. It was in her involvement with the National Colored Labor Union, however, that Cary sought to gain entrance into the male public sphere of economic agitation. In 1869 Cary attended a national labor convention in Washington, D.C., called to address the problems facing the working class in the aftermath of the Civil War. Noting the growing indifference of the Republican Party to issues of labor, the members of the convention insisted on the need for black and white laborers to assert a commonality of interest and, more specifically, for black labor to organize so that it might "effect a union with laborers without regard to color."[46] The convention vehemently rejected racial discrimination that might exclude "colored men and apprentices from the right to labor in any department of industry or workshops" (11), claiming any form of exclusion to be "suicidal," "for it arrays against the classes represented by it all other laboring classes which ought to be rather allied in the closest union, and avoid these dissensions and divisions which in the past have given wealth the advantage over labor" (20). Initially arguing the case for the interdependence of labor and capital—"that we do not regard capital as the natural enemy of labor; that each is dependent on the other for its existence" (11)—the convention nonetheless concluded by recognizing the degree to which capital controls labor: "Here we ha[ve] the spectacle of labor not simply struggling with capital, but capital sitting in *judgment* upon labor and controlling it at will" (33).

To correct such inequities, the convention emphasized both the political need for blacks to obtain the franchise in order to control their own economic destinies and the social need to obtain a better education in order to increase their employment opportunities. To achieve economic autonomy, the convention recommended the dismantling of the planters' land monopoly and the acquisition of homesteads for the freed people in the South and the creation of cooperative workshops for urban workers in the North. To encourage black control of credit, it proposed the formation of savings banks and loan associations.

Yet at no time in the debates did the convention address in any detail the specific problems facing black women workers; in fact, a delegate from Georgia expressed the sentiment that "as to women's rights, he hoped it would be confined north of the Ohio River" (13). As chair of the Committee on Female Suffrage, Cary was well placed to correct this omission of women's needs. Praising the individual actions of women of the elite who were currently agitating for the elective franchise and other rights for women, Cary's committee nonetheless stressed the primary importance of female "associations." Associations are necessary, its report maintained, first of all to energize black women, "lifting them up from the plane of indifference, frivolity, and dependence" (22); secondly, to provide mutual benevolent aid; thirdly, and perhaps most importantly, to protect black women in service and domestic jobs in which they presently work "without system or organization" (21). Such an emphasis on female association finds its ultimate expression in Cary's formation of the Colored Women's Progressive Franchise Association in 1880. Association is seen as the avenue to economic power, as Cary proposed in the draft of a statement of purpose that through it women would work cooperatively to found a banking institution, cooperative stores, a printing establishment, and a local directory and labor bureau that would enroll their names for perusal by prospective employers. On a still grander scale, Cary envisioned the creation of a newspaper "which conducted by colored women shall set forth the capability of their class" and a joint stock company controlled by women but enabling "poor persons to get a start in business of either sex."

Indeed, Cary's interest in political and social economy and her belief in the power of association were not confined to a desire to help black women alone. In a two-part article entitled "Trade for Our Boys" published in the March 21 and April 11, 1872 issues of the *New National Era*, Cary decried the climate of racism that made opportunities in trade impossible for "our boys." Once again sounding the theme of black disunity and the need to find "a co-operative point," she insisted that it was the obligation of the black leadership—male and female—to oppose job discrimination: "Indifference on the part of leading colored men, and the deathlike silence of colored women, contribute to it. . . . Our women must speak out; the boys must have trades" (March 21, 1872). Cary's demands here converge quite exactly with the call for "civil associations" made by Aunt Jane and Jenny in Harper's fictional sketches. To achieve these goals Cary asked her readership not to forget that all African Americans are ultimately bound together by "class ties, and a common interest" (April 11, 1872). What is needed, ultimately, is the creation of a black public space much like the antebellum black church in which common social, economic, and political interests may be articulated to both elite and mass audiences: "I know we have . . . conferences and . . . conventions. . . . But the people know comparatively little about them or their resolutions. We want then, an arousing of the people, and the pulpit must help in the work. We have no theatres, beer-gardens, opera, nor grand lecture amphitheatres, wherein such questions may be discussed, reshapen, dramatized, made vital issues" (March 21, 1872).

In 1883 Cary, who had been forced to leave Howard Law School in the 1870s when it refused to grant degrees to women, received her bachelor of laws after having presented a thesis on corporations. The notes taken for the writing of her thesis are remarkable for the manner in which they demonstrate Cary's determination to force her way into the institution of the law, manipulate its discourses, and implicitly consider how those associations called "corporations" might help in the creation of a black public space that could advance the common interest of African Americans and lead to their empowerment. Cary noted how corporations, initially conceived as public, were enterprises established in perpetuity to unite national and individual interests. Municipal corporations in ancient Rome and Greece, for example, were designed for the mutual protection of the cities' populations. Over time, societies introduced private corporations, understood by Cary in much the same way that Gramsci would later formulate his concept of civil society. Whether formed to meet the requirements of commerce, trade, learning, banking, or manufacturing, these entities sought to regulate human affairs while serving the interests of the people; for taken together, they "make up the atom of good, in Society," working against the oppressive force of the central state: "This necessity of corporations, as a corrective of abuses, and an element of social progress, must in all cases be the condition precedent of their creation."

This book has traced the search of the "brave" from approximately 1830 to 1880 in order to locate and define those forms of social and cultural activism in which black women engaged first within their local communities and then increasingly on the national level. Indeed, toward the end of the century black women's national organizations such as the National Association of Colored Women were established as yet another mechanism through which the "brave" could work toward racial uplift and the integration of African-American men and women within the political economy of the nation. The following one hundred years have demonstrated that solutions to the problems that confronted these nineteenth-century women have still not been found. As yet, no answer has been provided to the question of the place to be occupied by African Americans within the political economy of the nation; racism still dominates the attitudes of many white Americans toward blacks, and, in the face of such continued racism, blacks today often find themselves torn between integrationist impulses on the one hand and the quest for community empowerment and control on the other. Neither have answers been offered to the question of what constitutes black "nationality" or culture. Although black cultural forms are commodified and widely circulated on the marketplace as expressions of an authentic blackness, these can be neither essentialized or totalized. The black community remains deeply heterogeneous, marked by differences of gender, class, sexuality, region, and resistant to the homogenizing forces of racial essentialism and authenticity.

Despite these continued uncertainties, I have sought to write a narrative of faith (and perhaps of hope) rather than one of despair in my insistence on the necessity of recovering and appreciating our cultural past. I would like to think of culture as a space that allows for the formation of identity, gives shape and meaning to our lives, and offers us a place in the world. To analyze our culture in history invites us, then, to trace our collective racial identities and experiences—however diverse and complex these might be—over time. And it suggests to us that our traditions are not static but are susceptible of being reworked, encouraging us to stake out our positionalities and claim our agency as historical subjects.

Notes

Chapter 1

1. Olive Gilbert and Frances Titus, *Narrative of Sojourner Truth* (Boston: Published for the Author, 1878), 250.

2. Since both Mary Ann Shadd Cary and Frances Ellen Watkins Harper published under both their maiden and married names in the antebellum period, I refer to them as Shadd Cary and Watkins Harper. In discussing their postbellum activities in chapter 8, I simply use their married names, Cary and Harper.

For a recent study of the role of black men in nineteenth-century black cultural nationalism, see Sterling Stuckey, *Slave Culture: Nationalist Theory and the Foundations of Black America* (New York: Oxford University Press, 1987).

3. Abdul R. JanMohamed and David Lloyd, "Introduction," *Cultural Critique* 6 (1986): 8.

4. N. F. Mossell, *The Work of the Afro-American Woman* (Philadelphia: George S. Ferguson Co., 1894), 64–66.

5. Michel Foucault, *The Archaeology of Knowledge* (London: Tavistock, 1972), 27.

6. Donna Haraway, "Situated Knowledges: The Science Question in Feminism and the Privilege of Partial Perspective," *Feminist Studies* 14 (Fall 1988): 575, 581.

7. The phrase derives, of course, from the title of the 1982 book edited by Gloria T. Hull, Patricia Bell Scott, and Barbara Smith (Old Westbury, N.Y.: Feminist Press).

8. Nancy A. Hewitt, "Compounding Differences," *Feminist Studies* 18 (Summer 1992): 318.

9. bell hooks, "Choosing the Margin as a Space of Radical Openness," in *Yearning: Race, Gender, and Cultural Politics* (Boston: South End Press, 1990), 151. See also William L. Andrews, *To Tell a Free Story* (Urbana: University of Illinois Press, 1986), 167–204, for a discussion of the "uses of marginality" by ex-slave narrators.

10. Quoted in Bill Ashcroft, Gareth Griffiths, and Helen Tiffin, *The Empire Writes Back* (London: Routledge, 1989), 34. For discussions of "internal colonization," see Robert Blauner, "Internal Colonialism and Ghetto Revolt," in *Black Society in the New World,* ed. Richard Frucht (New York: Random House, 1971), 365–81, and Gayatri Spivak, "Who Claims Alterity?" in *Remaking History*, ed. Barbara Kruger and Phil Mariani (Seattle: Bay Press, 1989), 274, 278.

11. Edward Said, "Yeats and Decolonization," in *Remaking History*, ed. Barbara Kruger and Phil Mariani (Seattle: Bay Press, 1989), 10–11, 13.

12. Michel Foucault, *Discipline and Punish: The Birth of the Prison*, trans. Alan Sheridan (New York: Vintage Books, 1979), 195–228.

13. Biddy Martin and Chandra Talpade Mohanty, "Feminist Politics: What's Home Got to Do with It?" in *Feminist Studies/Critical Studies*, ed. Teresa de Lauretis (Bloomington: Indiana University Press, 1986), 195.

14. My use of these terms is an amplification of the vocabulary employed by Margaret S. Boone, "The Uses of Traditional Concepts in the Development of New Urban Roles: Cuban Women in the United States," in *A World of Women*, ed. Erika Bourguignon (New York: Praeger, 1980), 235–69.

15. Gary Nash, *Forging Freedom: The Formation of Philadelphia's Black Community, 1720–1840* (Cambridge, Mass.: Harvard University Press, 1988), 145–54, 248–53, 260–67; and James Oliver Horton, "Freedom's Yoke: Gender Conventions among Antebellum Free Blacks," *Feminist Studies* 12 (Spring 1986): esp. 69–72.

16. Nash, *Forging Freedom*, 222.

17. Peter Stallybrass and Allon White, *The Politics and Poetics of Transgression* (Ithaca, N.Y.: Cornell University Press, 1986), 27.

18. Nash, *Forging Freedom*, 222; for a full discussion of the continued presence of Africanisms in the antebellum North, see Stuckey, *Slave Culture;* and William D. Piersen, *Black Yankees: The Development of an Afro–American Subculture in Eighteenth–Century New England* (Amherst: University of Massachusetts Press, 1988).

19. Nash, *Forging Freedom*, 216–17, 250–53.

20. Leonard Curry, *The Free Black in Urban America, 1800–1850* (Chicago: University of Chicago Press, 1981), 196–215.

21. James Oliver Horton and Lois E. Horton, *Black Bostonians: Family Life and Community Struggle in the Antebellum North* (New York: Holmes and Meier, 1979), 28–31.

22. Carol V. R. George, *Segregated Sabbaths: Richard Allen and the Emergence of Independent Black Churches, 1760–1840* (New York: Oxford University Press, 1973).

23. Howard H. Bell, *A Survey of the Negro Convention Movement, 1830–1861* (New York: Arno Press, 1969). On the American Moral Reform Society, see Julie Winch, *Philadelphia's Black Elite: Activism, Accommodation, and the Struggle for Autonomy, 1787–1848* (Philadelphia: Temple University Press, 1988), 108–29.

24. For an extensive discussion of black abolitionism, see Benjamin Quarles, *Black Abolitionists* (New York: Oxford University Press, 1969).

25. Alexis de Tocqueville, *Democracy in America*, 2 vols. (1835–40; New York: Vintage Books, 1945), 2:109–28; Antonio Gramsci, *Selections from Cultural Writings*, ed. David Forgacs and Geoffrey Nowell–Smith (Cambridge, Mass.: Harvard University Press, 1985), 20–23; Walter L. Adamson, *Hegemony and Revolution* (Berkeley: University of California Press, 1980), 215–22; Benedict Anderson, *Imagined Communities: Reflections on the Origin and Spread of Nationalism* (London: Verso, 1991), chap. 3; ibid., 6–7.

26. See Frederick Cooper, "Elevating the Race: The Social Thought of Black Leaders, 1827–50," *American Quarterly* 24 (December 1972): 604–25.

27. Frantz Fanon, *The Wretched of the Earth*, trans. Constance Farrington (New York: Grove Press, 1968), 200, 197.

28. Frances Ellen Watkins, "The Colored People in America," in *Poems on Miscellaneous Subjects* (Philadelphia: Merrihew & Thompson, 1857), 53.

29. W. E. B. Du Bois, *The Souls of Black Folk* (1903; New York: New American Library, 1969), 84, 86.

30. Fanon, *The Wretched of the Earth*, 233.

31. Maria Stewart, *Meditations from the Pen of Mrs. Maria W. Stewart* (Washington, D.C., 1879), 68, 28, 32, 68.

32. Hester Hastings, *Man and Beast in French Thought of the Eighteenth Century* (Baltimore: Johns Hopkins University Press, 1936), 111.

33. *North Star,* March 23, 1849.

34. I paraphrase here the discussion of colonial discourse from Homi K. Bhabha, "Signs Taken for Wonders: Questions of Ambivalence and Authority under a Tree Outside Delhi, May 1817," *Critical Inquiry* 12 (Autumn 1985): 154–56.

35. Ibid., 154, 160, 156.

36. I paraphrase here the discussion of the function of silences in postcolonial texts in Ashcroft, Griffiths, and Tiffin, *The Empire Writes Back,* 54–55.

37. Henry Louis Gates Jr., *The Signifying Monkey: A Theory of Afro–American Literary Criticism* (New York: Oxford University Press, 1988), 51.

38. For more extensive discussions of these points, see Linda K. Kerber, "Separate Spheres, Female Worlds, Woman's Place: The Rhetoric of Women's History," *Journal of American History* 75 (1988): 9–39; Joan Kelly, "The Social Relation of the Sexes," in *Women, History, and Theory* (Chicago: University of Chicago Press, 1984), 1–18; Elizabeth Fox-Genovese, *Within the Plantation Household* (Chapel Hill: University of North Carolina Press, 1988), 37–99.

39. Curry, *The Free Black in Urban America,* 8–12.

40. Mina Davis Caulfield, "Imperialism, the Family, and Cultures of Resistance," *Socialist Revolution* 2 (1974): 74.

41. Dorothy Sterling, *We Are Your Sisters: Black Women in the Nineteenth Century* (New York: Norton, 1984), 129.

42. See also Dorothy B. Porter, "The Organized Educational Activities of Negro Literary Societies, 1828–1846," *Journal of Negro Education* 5 (October 1936): 556–66; and Sterling, *We Are Your Sisters,* chaps. 9–11.

43. Sarah P. Remond, "Sarah P. Remond," in *Our Exemplars, Poor and Rich; or Biographical Sketches of Men and Women,* ed. Matthew Davenport Hill (London: Cassell, Petter, and Galpin, 1861), 281.

44. M. Stewart, *Meditations,* 67.

45. For other discussions of the exclusion of black women from organizations of the male elite in the antebellum period, see Horton, "Freedom's Yoke," 51–76; and Winch, *Philadelphia's Black Elite,* 121.

46. See Michelle Zimbalist Rosaldo, "Woman, Culture, and Society: A Theoretical Overview," in *Woman, Culture, and Society,* ed. Michelle Zimbalist Rosaldo and Louise Lamphere (Stanford, Calif.: Stanford University Press, 1974), 28–30, for the use of the terms "ascribed" and "achieved" in anthropological discourse.

47. Victor Turner, *The Ritual Process: Structure and Antistructure* (Ithaca, N.Y.: Cornell University Press, 1977), 44–45, 126–28.

48. For a more extensive discussion of white women orators in the antebellum period, see Lillian O'Connor, *Pioneer Women Orators: Rhetoric in the Ante–Bellum Reform Movement* (New York: Columbia University Press, 1954).

49. Ann Boylan, "Benevolence and Antislavery Activity among African American Women in New York and Boston, 1820–1840," in *The Abolitionist Sisterhood: Antislavery and Women's Political Culture,* ed. John Van Horne and Jean Fagan Yellin (Ithaca, N.Y.: Cornell University Press, 1994), 120.

50. Mary Ann Shadd, "The Humbug of Reform," *Provincial Freeman,* May 27, 1854.

51. I paraphrase here the discussions of Barbara Welter, "The Cult of True Womanhood: 1820–1860," *American Quarterly* 18 (Spring 1966): 152; and Karen Halttunen, *Confidence Men and Painted Women* (New Haven, Conn.: Yale University Press, 1982), 71–91, 97.

52. For a discussion of European perceptions of the black female body, see Sander L. Gilman, "Black Bodies, White Bodies: Toward an Iconography of Female Sexuality in Late Nineteenth–Century Art, Medicine, and Literature," *Critical Inquiry* 12 (Autumn 1985): 204–42.

53. Frederick Law Olmsted, *A Journey in the Seaboard Slave States* (1856; New York: Negro Universities Press, 1968), 432, 386–87.

54. Frances Anne Kemble, *Journal of a Residence on a Georgian Plantation in 1838–1839*, ed. John A. Scott (Athens: University of Georgia Press, 1984), 293; *The Negroes and Anglo-Africans as Freedmen and Soldiers*, ed. Sarah Parker Remond (London: Victoria Press, 1864), 12; Olmsted, *Journey in the Seaboard Slave States*, 388.

55. For a discussion of the female grotesque, see Mary Russo, "Female Grotesques: Carnival and Theory," in *Feminist Studies/Critical Studies*, ed. Teresa de Lauretis (Bloomington: Indiana University Press, 1986), 213–29.

56. Zilpha Elaw, *Memoirs of the Life, Religious Experience, Ministerial Travels, and Labours of Mrs. Elaw*, in *Sisters of the Spirit*, ed. William L. Andrews (Bloomington: Indiana University Press, 1986), 147.

57. Julia Kristeva, *Powers of Horror: An Essay on Abjection*, trans. Leon S. Roudiez (New York: Columbia University Press, 1982), 10.

58. Elaine Scarry, *The Body in Pain: The Making and Unmaking of the World* (New York: Oxford University Press, 1985), 233–34, 219.

59. Kristeva, *Powers of Horror*, 120, 23.

60. Elaw, *Memoirs*, 91.

61. Quoted in William Still, *The Underground Railroad* (Philadelphia: Porter and Coates, 1872), 772. White women speakers such as Frances Wright were equally vulnerable to the charge of masculinization.

62. The issue of Africanisms in nineteenth–century African–American cultural life is extremely complex and, to a certain extent, must remain speculative. Historians of slavery have determined that kidnapped slaves came generally from West African and Central African tribes. Although the tribes undoubtedly had their own specific cultural forms, Sterling Stuckey has suggested that the experiences of the Middle Passage and of slavery must be seen as "incubators of slave unity across cultural lines, cruelly revealing irreducible links from one ethnic group to the other"; furthermore: "What we know of slave culture in the South, and of that of blacks in the North during and following slavery, indicates that black culture was national in scope, the principal forms of cultural expression being essentially the same. This is attributable mainly to the similarity of the African regions from which blacks were taken and enslaved in North America, and to the patterns of culture shared more generally in Central and West Africa" (Stuckey, *Slave Culture*, 3, 82).

Chapter 2

1. My discussion of Sojourner Truth relies on the 1878 edition. All references to this edition are included parenthetically in the text. For a discussion of the minor changes made by Titus to Gilbert's portion of the *Narrative*, see Carleton Mabee, *Sojourner Truth: Slave, Prophet, Legend* (New York: New York University Press, 1993), 203.

2. Margaret Washington, "Introduction," *Narrative of Sojourner Truth* (New York: Vintage Books, 1993), xviii–xx.

3. Nash, *Forging Freedom*, 146.

4. Nancy Woloch, *Women and the American Experience* (New York: Knopf, 1984), 172.

5. On this point see also Mabee, *Sojourner Truth,* 98. For a comprehensive history of Truth's relationship to communitarian experiments, see Wendy E. Chmielewski, "Sojourner Truth: Utopian Vision and Search for Community, 1797–1883," in *Women in Spiritual and Communitarian Societies in the United States,* ed. Wendy E. Chmielewski, Louis J. Kern, and Marlyn Klee-Hartzell (Syracuse, N.Y.: Syracuse University Press, 1993), 21–37.

6. For a discussion of the influence of African familial structures on the African–American family, see Niara Sudarkasa, "Interpreting the African Heritage in Afro–American Family Organization," in *Black Families,* ed. Harriette Pipes McAdoo (Beverly Hills, Calif.: Sage, 1988), esp. 40–44.

7. Alice Eaton McBee, *From Utopia to Florence* (Northampton, Mass.: Smith College, 1947), 20, 47, 44.

8. Charles A. Sheffeld, *The History of Florence, Massachusetts* (Florence: The Editor, 1895), 88.

9. Victor Turner, "Liminal to Liminoid, in Play, Flow, and Ritual: An Essay in Comparative Symbology," *Rice University Studies* 60 (1974): 82.

10. Quoted in Esther Terry, "Sojourner Truth: The Person Behind the Libyan Sibyl," *Massachusetts Review* 26 (Summer–Autumn, 1985): 442.

11. Nell Irvin Painter, "Sojourner Truth in Life and Memory: Writing the Biography of an American Exotic," *Gender & History* 2 (Spring 1990): 10.

12. See Mabee, *Sojourner Truth,* chap. 5.

13. William L. Stone, *Matthias and His Impostures* (New York: Harper and Brothers, 1835), 193; Gilbert Vale, *Fanaticism; Its Sources and Influence, Illustrated by the Simple Narrative of Isabella, in the Case of Matthias* (New York: G. Vale, 1835), 82.

14. John Wideman, "Frame and Dialect: The Evolution of the Black Voice in American Literature," *American Poetry Review* (September/October 1976): 35, 36.

15. Philippe Lejeune, *On Autobiography,* ed. Paul John Eakin, trans. Katherine Leary (Minneapolis: University of Minnesota Press, 1989), 196, 185.

16. Peggy Kamuf, *A Derrida Reader: Between the Blinds* (New York: Columbia University Press, 1991), 107.

17. Lejeune, *On Autobiography,* 189, 207–11.

18. Mabee, *Sojourner Truth,* 202–3.

19. Dan Schiller, *Objectivity and the News* (Philadelphia: University of Pennsylvania Press, 1981), 6–11.

20. Washington, "Introduction," xxix–xxxiii.

21. Hugh Blair, *Lectures on Rhetoric and Belles–Lettres,* 2 vols. (London: W. Strahan, T. Cadell, 1783), 1: 287, 281, 274, 283.

22. Jean Fagan Yellin, *Women and Sisters: The Antislavery Feminists in American Culture* (New Haven, Conn.: Yale University Press, 1989), 84.

23. Henry James, *William Wetmore Story and His Friends,* 2 vols. (Boston: Houghton Mifflin, 1903), 2:71, 77.

24. See also Painter for comments about how Stowe depicts Truth as exotic and as an entertainer ("Sojourner Truth in Life and Memory," 9–10).

25. Schiller, *Objectivity and the News,* 88–95.

26. Robert Taft, *Photography and the American Scene* (New York: Dover, 1964), 143.

27. Walter Benjamin, "The Work of Art in an Age of Mechanical Reproduction," in *Illuminations,* ed. Hannah Arendt, trans. Harry Zohn (New York: Harcourt, Brace, and World, 1968), 232.

28. Taft, *Photography and the American Scene,* 149–50.

29. Letter to Oliver Johnson, *National Anti–Slavery Standard,* February 13, 1864;

letter to Mary Gale, dated February 25, 1864, Sojourner Truth Papers, Manuscript Division, Library of Congress.

30. My comments on photography here owe much to discussions by Roland Barthes, *Image/Text/Music,* trans. Stephen Heath (New York: Hill and Wang, 1977); idem, *Camera Lucida: Reflections on Photography,* trans. Richard Howard (New York: Hill and Wang, 1981); John Berger and Jean Mohr, *Another Way of Telling* (New York: Pantheon Books, 1982); and Susan Sontag, *On Photography* (New York: Farrar, Straus and Giroux, 1977).

31. See Kathleen Collins, "Shadow and Substance: Sojourner Truth," *History of Photography* 7 (July–September 1983): 183–205, for the best and most comprehensive discussion of Truth's photographs to date.

32. Elizabeth Cady Stanton, Susan B. Anthony, and Matilda Joslyn Gage, *History of Woman Suffrage,* 6 vols. (Rochester, N.Y.: Fowler and Wells, 1881–1922), 1:115.

33. Washington, "Introduction," xxiv–xxix; and Gloria I. Joseph, "Sojourner Truth: Archetypal Black Feminist," in *Wild Women in the Whirlwind: Afra–American Culture and the Contemporary Literary Renaissance,* ed. Joanne Braxton and Andrée Nicola McLaughlin (New Brunswick, N.J.: Rutgers University Press, 1990), 38–40 .

34. James Gronniosaw, *A Narrative of the Most Remarkable Particulars in the Life of James Albert Ukawsaw Gronniosaw* (Leeds: Davies and Booth, 1814), 7.

35. Lawrence W. Levine, *Black Culture and Black Consciousness* (New York: Oxford University Press, 1978), 58; Washington, "Introduction," xxvi–xxviii; Levine, *Black Culture and Black Consciousness,* 66, 158.

36. Lejeune, *On Autobiography,* 204.

37. Levine, *Black Culture and Black Consciousness,* 66.

38. Kristeva, *Powers of Horror,* 23.

39. Turner, *Ritual Process,* 109–10.

40. See also Jeffrey Stewart's comment that Truth laid a "claim to being the moral conscience of the nation" ("Introduction," *Narrative of Sojourner Truth* [New York: Oxford University Press, 1991], xxxviii).

41. For other rhetorical analyses of Truth's speeches, see Janey Weinhold Montgomery, *A Comparative Analysis of the Rhetoric of Two Negro Women Orators: Sojourner Truth and Frances E. Watkins Harper* (Hays: Fort Hays Kansas State College, 1969); and Karlyn Kohrs Campbell, "Style and Content in the Rhetoric of Early Afro–American Feminists," *Quarterly Journal of Speech* 72 (November 1986): 434–36.

42. Kenneth Cmiel, *Democratic Eloquence: The Fight over Popular Speech in Nineteenth–Century America* (New York: Morrow, 1990), 57–73.

43. Levine, *Black Culture and Black Consciousness,* 66, 158; and Walter Ong, *Orality and Literacy* (London: Methuen, 1982), 32.

44. Ong, *Orality and Literacy,* 67–68, 34.

45. Mabee, *Sojourner Truth,* 229–30; for a discussion of the alternation of song and speech, see Eileen Southern, *The Music of Black Americans,* 2d ed. (New York: Norton, 1983), 19.

46. Sojourner Truth Papers, Manuscript Division, Library of Congress.

47. Deirdre La Pin, "Narrative as Precedent in Yoruba Oral Tradition," in *Oral Traditional Literature,* ed. John Miles Foley (Columbus, Ohio: Slavica Publishers, 1981), 349.

48. On call-and-response, see Southern, *Music of Black Americans,* 19; on the function of proverbs in oral cultures, see Viv Edwards and Thomas J. Sienkewicz, *Oral Cultures Past and Present: Rappin' and Homer* (Cambridge, Mass.: Basil Blackwell, 1991), 168–72.

49. Piersen, *Black Yankees,* 107–13.

50. Sojourner Truth Papers, Manuscript Division, Library of Congress.

51. Fred Tomkins, *Jewels in Ebony* (London: 1866?), 6.

52. Werner Sollors, *Beyond Ethnicity: Consent and Descent in American Culture* (New York: Oxford University Press, 1986), 241–47.

53. Angelina Grimké, *Appeal to the Christian Women of the South* (New York: Antislavery Society, 1836); idem, *Appeal to the Women of the Nominally Free States* (New York: W. S. Dorr, Printer, 1837); Sarah Grimké, *Letters on the Equality of the Sexes and the Condition of Woman* (Boston: I. Knapp, 1838).

54. For the 1851 and 1853 speeches, respectively, see Stanton, Anthony, and Gage, *History of Woman Suffrage*, 1:115–17 and 1:567–68. Future page references to the speeches are included parenthetically within the text. For Mabee's analysis, see chap. 6 and n. 15. For a reprint of the *Anti-Slavery Bugle* version of the 1851 speech, see Mabee, *Sojourner Truth*, 81–82; Washington, 117–18; I. Stewart, "Introduction," xxxiii.

55. Yellin, *Women and Sisters*, 81.

56. Levine, *Black Culture and Black Consciousness*, 92.

57. For a discussion of this use of the figure of Esther, see Yellin, *Women and Sisters*, 33, 40–41.

58. See Monica Schuler, *"Alas, Alas, Kongo": A Social History of Indentured African Immigration into Jamaica, 1841–1865* (Baltimore: Johns Hopkins University Press, 1980), 70–80.

Chapter 3

1. Maria W. Stewart, *Meditations from the Pen of Mrs. Maria W. Stewart* (Washington, D.C., 1879), 3. All future references are to this edition unless otherwise indicated and are included parenthetically within the text.

2. For a fuller discussion of Stewart's life, see Marilyn Richardson, "Introduction," *Maria W. Stewart, America's First Black Woman Political Writer* (Bloomington: Indiana University Press, 1987), 3–7.

3. Willard B. Gatewood, *Aristocrats of Color: The Black Elite 1880–1920* (Bloomington: Indiana University Press, 1990), 276.

4. My discussion of the meditation as a genre is endebted to the essay on meditation in the *New Catholic Encyclopedia*, 17 vols., ed. at the Catholic University of America, (Palatine, Ill.: J. Heraty, 1981), 11:676, 673; 9:620.

5. Edwards and Sienkewicz, *Oral Cultures Past and Present*, 6–11.

6. *New Catholic Encyclopedia*, 11:675.

7. Southern, *Music of Black Americans*, 35.

8. Robert Alter, "Psalms," in *The Literary Guide to the Bible*," ed. Robert Alter and Frank Kermode (Cambridge, Mass.: Harvard University Press, 1987), 246–51, 258–61.

9. *New Catholic Encyclopedia*, 11:676.

10. Mircea Eliade, *The Sacred and the Profane: The Nature of Religion*, trans. Willard R. Trask (New York: Harcourt, Brace, & World, 1959), 172–79.

11. Horton and Horton, *Black Bostonians*, 40–42.

12. Keith D. Miller, "Composing Martin Luther King, Jr.," *PMLA* 105 (January 1990): 77–79, 78.

13. Richardson, "Introduction," 12.

14. For a fuller discussion of Walker's life, see Charles M. Wiltse, "Introduction," *David Walker's Appeal in Four Articles; Together with a Preamble, to the Coloured Citizens of the World* (1829; New York: Hill and Wang, 1965), vii–xii. All page references to the *Appeal* are to this edition and will be included parenthetically within the text.

15. Wilson J. Moses, *Black Messiahs and Uncle Toms: Social and Literary Manipulations of a Religious Myth* (University Park: Pennsylvania State University Press, 1982), 38–47.

16. Sacvan Bercovitch, *The American Jeremiad* (Madison: University of Wisconsin Press, 1978), 3–33.

17. Thomas Jefferson, *Notes on the State of Virginia*, in *Writings*, ed. Merrill D. Peterson (New York: Viking Press, 1984), 263–71.

18. Woloch, *Women and the American Experience*, 167.

19. Maria W. Stewart, *Productions of Mrs. Maria W. Stewart* (Boston: Published by Friends of Freedom and Virtue, 1835), 4.

20. Porter, "Organized Educational Activities," 569, 559.

21. For a general discussion of Freemasonry in antebellum America, see Mark C. Carnes, *Secret Ritual and Manhood in Victorian America* (New Haven, Conn.: Yale University Press, 1989). For a discussion of Prince Hall Freemasonry, see William A. Muraskin, *Middle–Class Blacks in a White Society* (Berkeley: University of California Press, 1975).

22. Frank Kermode, "Introduction to the New Testament," and "Matthew," in *The Literary Guide to the Bible*, 377, 388.

23. Richardson, "Introduction," 26.

24. Niara Sudarkasa, "Female Employment and Family Organization in West Africa," in *New Research on Women and Sex Roles*, ed. Dorothy McGuigan (Ann Arbor: University of Michigan Press, 1976), 53.

25. For discussions of sanctification, see Andrews, "Introduction," *Sisters of the Spirit*, 15; Sue E. Houchins, "Introduction," *Spiritual Narratives* (New York: Oxford University Press, 1988), xxxiv; and Frances Smith Foster, *Written by Herself: Literary Production by African American Women, 1746–1892* (Bloomington: Indiana University Press, 1993), 61–62.

26. Jarena Lee, *Religious Experience and Journal of Mrs. Jarena Lee* (Philadelphia: Printed and Published for the Author, 1849), 3, 97. Since this 1849 edition of Lee's autobiography reproduces with no significant changes her 1836 text, *The Life and Religious Experience of Jarena Lee* (pp. 3–20, 97–98), all page references will be to the 1849 edition and will be placed parenthetically within the text.

27. See also David W. Wills, "Womanhood and Domesticity in the A.M.E. Tradition: The Influence of Daniel Alexander Payne," in *Black Apostles at Home and Abroad*, ed. David W. Wills and Richard Newman (Boston: G. K. Hall, 1982), 138.

28. Daniel A. Payne, *History of the African Methodist Episcopal Church* (Nashville: A.M.E. Sunday School Union, 1891), 269, 237. See also Wills, "Womanhood and Domesticity," 138.

29. Andrews, "Introduction," 14–15; Foster, *Written by Herself*, 58.

30. See also Andrews, "Introduction," 12.

31. Houchins, "Introduction," xl–xli.

32. Carroll Smith-Rosenberg, "The Cross and the Pedestal," in *Disorderly Conduct* (New York: Oxford University Press, 1985), 129–64; Alice Rossi, ed., *The Feminist Papers from Adams to de Beauvoir* (New York: Columbia University Press, 1973), 241–74. Foster has noted, however, that "even camp meetings carefully adhered to certain protcol [*sic*]. For example, physical accommodations were usually racially segregated and certain activities or services were dominated by whites and others by blacks" (*Written by Herself*, 67).

33. Luce Irigaray, *Speculum of the Other Woman*, trans. Gillian C. Gill (Ithaca, N.Y.: Cornell University Press, 1985), 191–202.

34. Nellie Y. McKay notes that Lee wrote to give "herself voice and authority within the established religious community" ("Nineteenth-Century Black Women's Spiritual

Autobiographies: Religious Faith and Self-Empowerment," in *Interpreting Women's Lives: Feminist Theory and Personal Narratives,* ed. The Personal Narratives Group [Bloomington: Indiana University Press, 1989], 145).

35. Joanne Braxton notes that "Lee's inner voice sets up a tension between her inner self and external religious authority" (*Black Women Writing Autobiography: A Tradition within a Tradition* [Philadelphia: Temple University Press, 1989], 58).

36. Payne, *History,* 190.

37. Braxton, *Black Women Writing Autobiography,* 54; Foster, *Written by Herself,* 59–63.

38. Jualynne Dodson, "Nineteenth-Century A.M.E. Preaching Women," in *Women in New Worlds,* ed. Hilah F. Thomas and Rosemary Skinner Keller (Nashville: Abingdon, 1981), 277.

39. Houchins, "Introduction," xxxvii–xxxviii.

40. Lydia Maria Child, *Letters from New York* (New York: C. S. Francis, 1845), 73–82. All page references to the letter will be placed parenthetically within the text.

41. For a more extensive discussion of the conventions of spiritual autobiography, see George A. Starr, *Defoe and Spiritual Autobiography* (Princeton, N.J.: Princeton University Press, 1965).

42. Richard Allen, *The Life, Experience and Gospel Labors of the Rt. Rev. Richard Allen* (Philadelphia: Martin and Boden, 1833).

43. Eliade, *The Sacred and the Profane,* 68, 70, 69, 63.

44. Margaret Washington Creel, *"A Peculiar People": Slave Religion and Community-Culture among the Gullahs* (New York: New York University Press, 1988), 82, 86.

45. See also Braxton, *Black Women Writing Autobiography,* 54.

46. Foster suggests that Lee's narrative has affinities with the African tradition of the praise song as well as with the Western genre of spiritual autobiography (*Written by Herself,* 63).

47. Piersen, *Black Yankees,* 75.

48. For the African origins of animalisms, see Newbell Niles Puckett, *Folk Beliefs of the Southern Negro* (New York: Dover, 1969), 35; for the dog as an omen of death, see ibid., 478–79, Eli Shepard, "Superstitions of the Negro," in *The Negro and His Foklore,* ed. Bruce Jackson (Austin: University of Texas Press, 1967), 248; for the description of the Jack-o'-lantern, see Puckett, *Folk Beliefs of the Southern Negro,* 135.

49. Shepard, "Superstitions of the Negro," 247–48; and Puckett, *Folk Beliefs of the Southern Negro,* 542.

50. See McKay for an analysis of the two women's different modes of narration, ("Nineteenth-Century Black Women's Spiritual Autobiographies," 149).

Chapter 4

1. In addition to their location in various archives, most of the newspaper articles I cite in this chapter are available in the microfilmed edition of *The Black Abolitionist Papers,* ed. C. Peter Ripley, Roy E. Finkenbine, Michael F. Hembree, and Donald Yacovone. References to the newspaper source will be placed parenthetically within the text.

2. John F. Sears, *Sacred Places: American Tourist Attractions in the Nineteenth Century* (New York: Oxford University Press, 1989), 87–99.

3. William C. Spengemann, *The Adventurous Muse: The Poetics of American Fiction, 1789–1900* (New Haven, Conn.: Yale University Press, 1977), 65–67.

4. Mary G. Mason, "Travel as Metaphor and Reality in Afro-American Women's

Autobiography, 1850–1972," *Black American Literary Forum* 24 (Summer 1990): 339.

5. Nancy Prince, *A Narrative of the Life and Travels of Mrs. Nancy Prince* (Boston: Published for the Author, 1850), 7, 14. Unless otherwise noted, all further references are to this edition and will be placed parenthetically within the text.

6. Mary Louise Pratt, "Scratches on the Face of the Country; or What Mr. Barrow Saw in the Land of the Bushmen," *Critical Inquiry* 12 (Autumn 1985): 119–43.

7. Nancy Prince, *The West Indies* (Boston: Dow and Jackson, 1841), 4. All further pages references will be placed within the text.

8. James Clifford, "On Ethnographic Authority," *Representations* 1 (Spring 1983): 124–30.

9. For a discussion of British missionaries in Jamaica, see Catherine Hall, "Missionary Stories: Gender and Ethnicity in England in the 1830s and 1840s," in *Cultural Studies*, ed. Lawrence Grossberg, Cary Nelson, and Paula A. Treichler (New York: Routledge, 1992), 251–52.

10. James M. Phillippo, *Jamaica: Its Past and Present State* (London: John Snow, 1843), 122, vii, 244.

11. Nancy Prince, *A Narrative of the Life and Travels of Mrs. Nancy Prince*, in *Collected Black Women's Narratives*, ed. Anthony G. Barthelemy (New York: Oxford University Press, 1988), preface. All page references to this reprint of the 1853 edition will be placed within the text.

12. Barthelemy also notes Prince's resistance to self–exposure ("Introduction," xxxiii, xxxv). For other comments on the economic oppression facing Prince, see Braxton, *Black Women Writing Autobiography*, 51; and Hazel V. Carby, *Reconstructing Womanhood: The Emergence of the Afro-American Woman Novelist* (New York: Oxford University Press, 1987), 41.

13. Sudarkasa, "African Heritage," 37–53.

14. See also Barthelemy's comment on narrative absence in relation to Prince's marriage ("Introduction," xxxviii–xxxix) and Braxton's rejection of the idea that "part of the resulting discontinuity of the *Narrative* is caused by the marriage. Yet this notion is not confirmed by the narrator's voice, which seeks to overcome the confines and limitations of physical abuse and overwork, as well as psychological anxiety about her racial and sexual difference and her perceived cultural isolation," (*Black Women Writing Autobiography*, 51).

15. According to Allison Blakely, Nero Prince was one of the organizers and first officers of Boston's Prince Hall Grand Lodge. A skilled cook, he went to Russia in 1810, became a butler for one of Russia's noble families, and sometime after 1812 started to work for the czar (*Russia and the Negro: Blacks in Russian History and Thought* [Washington, D.C.: Howard University Press, 1986], 16–18).

16. Pavel Svin'in, *Picturesque United States of America, 1811, 1812, 1813, Being a Memoir on Paul Svin'in*, ed. Avrahm Yarmolinsky (New York: W. E. Rudge, 1930), 6, 20–21.

17. Allison Blakely, "The Negro in Imperial Russia: A Preliminary Sketch," *Journal of Negro History* 61 (October 1976): 353.

18. Zephaniah Swift, *An Oration on Domestic Slavery* (Hartford, Conn.: Hudson and Goodwin, 1781), 15; Creel, *"A Peculiar People,"* 318.

19. For a discussion of maroonage as an African–American trope, see Houston A. Baker Jr., *Modernism and the Harlem Renaissance* (Chicago: University of Chicago Press, 1987), 76–80.

20. For an account of the Woman's Rights Convention, see Stanton, Anthony, and

Gage, *History of Woman Suffrage*, 2:384; the *Woman's Era* article is reprinted in Sterling, *We Are Your Sisters*, 222; Barthelemy, "Introduction," xxxviii.

21. Jim Bearden and Linda Butler, *Shadd: The Life and Times of Mary Shadd Cary* (Toronto: New Canada Publications, 1977), 12–21.

22. Quarles, *Black Abolitionists*, 20–25, 33; Bell, *Negro Convention Movement*, 16; Quarles, *Black Abolitionists*, 149.

23. *Proceedings of the Colored National Convention, Held at Cleveland, Ohio, on Wednesday, September 6, 1848* (Rochester, N.Y.: North Star Office, 1848), 5, 6, 11–12, 17.

24. *Proceedings of the Black State Conventions*, 2 vols., ed. Philip S. Foner and George E. Walker (Philadelphia: Temple University Press, 1979–80), 1:227, 2:91; *Proceedings of the National Emigration Convention of Colored People; Held at Cleveland, Ohio, 24–26 August, 1854* (Pittsburgh, 1854), 26.

25. William Wells Brown, *The Rising Son; or, The Antecedents and Advancement of the Colored Race* (1874; New York: Negro Universities Press, 1970), 539.

26. Blair, *Lectures on Rhetoric*, 2:54, 50; Cmiel, *Democratic Eloquence*, 57–73; Lawrence Buell, *New England Literary Culture from Revolution through Renaissance* (Cambridge: Cambridge University Press, 1986), 142–65.

27. Brown, *The Rising Son*, 540.

28. Mary Ann Shadd Cary Papers, Manuscript Division, Moorland-Spingarn Research Center.

29. Thomas R. Hietala, *Manifest Design: Anxious Aggrandizement in Late Jacksonian America* (Ithaca, N.Y.: Cornell University Press, 1985), 107–8.

30. Mary A. Shadd, *A Plea for Emigration; or, Notes of Canada West* (Detroit: George W. Pattison, 1852), 39.

31. William Wells Brown, "The Colored People of Canada," in *The Black Abolitionist Papers*, 5 vols., ed. C. Peter Ripley, Roy E. Finkenbine, Michael F. Hembree, and Donald Yacovone (Chapel Hill: University of North Carolina Press, 1988–92), 2:461–97.

32. M. M. Bakhtin, *The Dialogic Imagination*, ed. Michael Holquist, trans. Cary Emerson and Michael Holquist (Austin: University of Texas Press, 1981), 365.

33. Osborne P. Anderson, *A Voice from Harper's Ferry: A Narrative of Events at Harper's Ferry* (Boston: Printed for the Author, 1861), 8.

34. For a more extensive discussion of the earlier emigration debates see Winch, *Philadelphia's Black Elite*, 26–69.

35. See *Proceedings of the North American Convention*, in *The Black Abolitionist Papers*, 2:149–57; and *Minutes and Proceedings of the General Convention for the Improvement of the Colored Inhabitants of Canada* (Windsor: Bibb and Holly, 1853).

36. *Arguments, Pro and Con, on the Call for a National Emigration Convention* (Detroit: George E. Pomeroy, 1854), 9, 8.

37. J. Theodore Holly, "Thoughts on Hayti," *Anglo African Magazine* 1 (November 1859): 364–65.

38. Martin R. Delany, "The Political Destiny of the Colored Race," in *The Ideological Origins of Black Nationalism*, ed. Sterling Stuckey (Boston: Beacon Press, 1972), 203. See also Stuckey, *Slave Culture*, 226–31, for a discussion of Delany's theories of black nationalism.

39. Martin R. Delany, *Official Report of the Niger Valley Exploring Party* (New York: T. Hamilton, 1863), 77. For comprehensive discussions of African emigration schemes in the 1850s, see Floyd Miller, *The Search for a Black Nationality: Black Emigration and Colonization, 1787–1863* (Urbana: University of Illinois Press, 1975); and Cyril E. Griffith, *The African Dream: Martin R. Delany and the Emergence of Pan-African Thought* (University Park: Pennsylvania State University Press, 1975).

40. Delany, *Official Report*, 112, 43.

41. Ibid., 118.

42. Alexander Crummell, *The Future of Africa* (1862; rpt. New York: Greenwood Press, 1969), 46–47.

43. T. J. Bowen, *Central Africa: Adventures and Missionary Labours in Several Countries in the Interior of Africa from 1849 to 1856* (1857; rpt. London: Frank Cass, 1968), 304–5.

44. Delany, *Official Report*, 85, 83; Bowen, *Central Africa*, 296.

Chapter 5

1. Quoted in Still, *Underground Railroad*, 758.

2. "Address by William Watkins, Jacob M. Moore, and Jacob C. White, Sr.," in *The Black Abolitionist Papers*, 3:189–94.

3. Daniel A. Payne, *Recollections of Seventy Years* (1888, New York: Arno Press, 1968), 305.

4. Still, *Underground Railroad*, 758; *Provincial Freeman*, March 7, 1857.

5. Still, *Underground Railroad*, 758, 764.

6. For brief biographies of William Watkins and William J. Watkins, see *The Black Abolitionist Papers*, 3:96–97, 4:155.

7. William Watkins letter to William Lloyd Garrison, in *The Black Abolitionist Papers*, 3:92; William J. Watkins, "The Reformer," in *The Black Abolitionist Papers*, 4:212.

8. In addition to their location in various archives, most of the newspaper articles I cite in this chapter are available in the microfilmed edition of *The Black Abolitionist Papers*, ed. C. Peter Ripley, Roy E. Finkenbine, Michael F. Hembree, and Donald Yacovone. References to the newspaper source will be placed parenthetically within the text.

9. Greenwood, quoted in Still, *Underground Railroad*, 779; Brown, *The Rising Son*, 525; Phebe A. Hanaford, *Daughters of America, or, Women of the Century* (Augusta, Maine: True and Co., 1883), 326; Monroe A. Majors, *Noted Negro Women: Their Triumphs and Activities* (Chicago: Donohue and Henneberry, 1893), 26.

10. Rosalyn M. Story, *And So I Sing: African–American Divas of Opera and Concert* (New York: Warner Books, 1990), 23; Arthur R. LaBrew, *Elizabeth Taylor Greenfield: The Black Swan* (Detroit: Arthur LaBrew, 1969), 76, 79, 48, 79, 56, 59; Story, *And So I Sing*, 25.

11. Paul de Man, "The Rhetoric of Blindness," in *Blindness and Insight: Essays in the Rhetoric of Contemporary Criticism* (New York: Oxford University Press, 1971), 123–30.

12. Lawrence Buell, "Introduction," *Selected Poems of Henry Wadsworth Longfellow* (New York: Penguin, 1988), xii.

13. Joan R. Sherman, *Invisible Poets: Afro–Americans of the Nineteenth Century* (Urbana: University of Illinois Press, 1974), 65; and Maryemma Graham, "Frances Ellen Watkins Harper," *Dictionary of Literary Biography*, ed. Trudier Harris and Thadious M. Davis (Detroit: Bruccoli Clark, 1986), 50:166.

14. For a discussion of experimental activity in Unitarianism, see Anne C. Rose, *Transcendentalism as a Social Movement, 1830–1850* (New Haven, Conn.: Yale University Press, 1981), 2; on the spoken word, see Daniel W. Howe, *The Unitarian Conscience: Harvard Moral Philosophy, 1805–1861* (Cambridge, Mass.: Harvard University Press, 1970), 161.

15. Howe, *The Unitarian Conscience*, 194–97.

16. J. Saunders Redding, *To Make a Poet Black* (1939; College Park, Md.: McGrath, 1968), 40, 44.

17. Philip Fisher, *Hard Facts: Setting and Form in the American Novel* (New York: Oxford University Press, 1985), 94–95, 98. For a discussion of sentimentality as a bodied form, see Shirley Samuels, "Introduction," *The Culture of Sentiment: Race, Gender, and Sentimentality in Nineteenth-Century America* ed. Shirley Samuels (New York: Oxford University Press, 1992), 3–5.

18. Frances Ellen Watkins, *Poems on Miscellaneous Subjects* (Boston: J. B. Yerrinton & Son, 1854; enlarged, Philadelphia: Merrihew & Thompson, 1857). All future references are to the 1857 edition and are included parenthetically in the text.

19. Buell, "Introduction" *Selected Poems of Henry Wadsworth Longfellow*, xii, xi.

20. Frances Smith Foster, *A Brighter Coming Day: A Frances Ellen Watkins Harper Reader* (New York: The Feminist Press at the City University of New York, 1990), 31; Maryemma Graham, "Introduction," *Complete Poems of Frances E. W. Harper* (New York: Oxford University Press, 1988), xliii; Patricia Liggins Hill, "'Let Me Make the Songs for the People': A Study of Frances Watkins Harper's Poetry," *Black American Literature Forum* 15 (Summer 1981): 60.

21. Quoted in Donald Davie, *English Hymnology in the Eighteenth Century* (Los Angeles: William Andrews Clark Memorial Library, UCLA, 1980), 10.

22. Foster, *A Brighter Coming Day*, 30–31.

23. Blair, *Lectures on Rhetoric*, 2:115.

24. See Buell, *New England Literary Culture*, 143–65.

25. William Lloyd Garrison, "Preface," *Narrative of the Life of Frederick Douglass* (1845; New York: Anchor Books, 1973), xv.

26. Blair, *Lectures on Rhetoric*, 2:106.

27. *Black Abolitionist Papers*, 3:97; 4:155.

28. Buell, *New England Literary Culture*, 153–54; Cmiel, *Democratic Eloquence*, 71.

29. See Dorothy Burnett Porter, "The Remonds of Salem, Massachusetts: A Nineteenth-Century Family Revisited," *Proceedings of the American Antiquarian Society* 95 (October 1985): 262–65, 272–74.

30. *Black Abolitionist Papers*, 3:318; quoted in Ruth Bogin, "Sarah Parker Remond: Black Abolitionist from Salem," *Essex Institute Historical Collections* 110 (April 1974): 126.

31. Remond, "Sarah P. Remond," in Hill, *Our Exemplars, Poor and Rich*, 285. All further page references to this autobiographical narrative will be placed in this text. Letter to Abby Foster quoted in Sterling, *We Are Your Sisters*, 176.

32. *History of Woman Suffrage*, 1:668.

33. Letter published in the *Liberator*, Nov. 19, 1858.

34. Blair, *Lectures on Rhetoric*, 2:75, 76, 81, 83.

35. See David Ayerst, *The Manchester Guardian, Biography of a Newspaper* (Ithaca, N.Y.: Cornell University Press, 1971), 173–74; and Lucy Brown, *Victorian News and Newspapers* (Oxford: Clarendon Press, 1985), 102–3.

36. Christina Crosby, *The Ends of History: Victorians and the "Woman Question"* (New York: Routledge, 1991), 97, 106.

37. Sarah P. Remond, "The Negroes in the United States of America," *Journal of Negro History* 27 (April 1942): 218.

38. Ronald Blackett, *Building an Antislavery Wall: Black Americans in the Atlantic Abolitionist Movement, 1830–1860* (Ithaca, N.Y.: Cornell University Press, 1989), 196.

Chapter 6

1. "Prospectus," *Colored American Magazine,* September 1900: n.p.
2. Bakhtin, *The Dialogic Imagination,* 370, 67–68.
3. William L. Andrews, "The Novelization of Voice in Early African American Narrative," *PMLA* 105 (January 1990): 29.
4. Frederick Douglass, "The Heroic Slave," in *The Life and Writings of Frederick Douglass,* ed. Philip Foner, 5 vols. (New York: International, 1975), 5:474.
5. "Prospectus," n.p.
6. Regarding this shift from autobiography to fiction in the 1850s, see Andrews, "Novelization," 23–34; and Richard Yarborough, "The First-Person in Afro-American Fiction," in *Afro-American Literary Studies in the 1990s,* ed. Houston A. Baker Jr. and Patricia Redmond (Chicago: University of Chicago Press, 1989), 105–21.
7. Paul Smith, *Discerning the Subject* (Minneapolis: University of Minnesota Press, 1988), 105.
8. For book-length studies of these points see, for example, Frances Smith Foster, *Witnessing Slavery: The Development of Ante–Bellum Slave Narratives* (Westport, Conn.: Greenwood Press, 1979); and Andrews, *To Tell a Free Story.* Even doxological slave narratives contained, of course, seeds of "freedom" and techniques of resistance; for example, the many silences—refusals to speak—in Douglass's 1845 *Narrative.*
9. Andrews, "Novelization," 26.
10. Gerald Graff, "Literature as Assertions," in *American Criticism in the Poststructuralist Age,* ed. Ira Konigsberg (Ann Arbor: University of Michigan Press, 1981), 146.
11. Frank L. Mott, *Golden Multitudes: The Story of Best Sellers in the United States* (New York: Macmillan, 1947), 122; Nina Baym, *Novels, Readers, and Reviewers: Responses to Fiction in Antebellum America* (Ithaca, N.Y.: Cornell University Press, 1984), 31.
12. Frank J. Webb, *The Garies and Their Friends* (1857; New York: Arno Press, 1969), 7.
13. "Apology," *Anglo–African Magazine* 1 (January 1859): 3.
14. Quoted in Harriet Jacobs, *Incidents in the Life of a Slave Girl,* ed. and introd. Jean Fagan Yellin (1861; Cambridge, Mass.: Harvard University Press, 1987), 233. All references to Jacobs's correspondence, narrative, and to Yellin's introduction are to this edition and are placed within the text.
15. *Anglo–African Magazine* 1 (January 1859): 20; quoted in Floyd J. Miller, "Introduction," in Martin R. Delany, *Blake; or, the Huts of America* (1859–62; Boston: Beacon Press, 1970), xi.
16. See also Andrews's comments on fictionalization in slave narratives in the last chapter of *To Tell a Free Story.*
17. Harriet E. Wilson, *Our Nig; Or, Sketches from the Life of a Free Black,* ed. Henry Louis Gates Jr. (1859; New York: Random House, 1983), preface. All references to the narrative and to Gates's introduction are to this edition and are placed within the text.
18. See Sterling, *We Are Your Sisters,* 83.
19. See also Gates's introduction in which he suggests that the narrative shifts in *Our Nig* "point to the complexities and tensions of basing fictional events upon the lived experiences of an author" (xxxvii).
20. I adapt the phrase from Lejeune's discussion of collaboration in the autobiographical writings of "those who do not write" (*On Autobiography,* 189).
21. Karen Sánchez-Eppler, "Bodily Bonds: The Intersecting Rhetorics of Feminism and Abolition," *Representations* 24 (Fall 1988): 28–59.

22. Nina Baym, *Woman's Fiction: A Guide to Novels by and about Women in America, 1820–1870* (Ithaca, N.Y.: Cornell University Press, 1978), 25–26.

23. See Sánchez-Eppler, and Hortense J. Spillers, "Notes on an Alternative Model—Neither/Nor," in *The Difference Within: Feminism and Critical Theory*, ed. Elizabeth Meese and Alice Parker (Philadelphia: John Benjamins, 1989), 165–87.

24. See Eugene D. Genovese, *The Political Economy of Slavery: Studies in the Economy and Society of the Slave South*, 2d ed. (Middletown, Conn.: Wesleyan University Press, 1989), 16–31.

25. Lauren Berlant, "The Female Woman: Fanny Fern and the Form of Sentiment," in *The Culture of Sentiment: Race, Gender, and Sentimentality in Nineteenth-Century America* (New York: Oxford University Press, 1992), 270; Gillian Brown, *Domestic Individualism: Imagining Self in Nineteenth–Century America* (Berkeley: University of California Press, 1990), 1–3; Richard Brodhead, *Cultures of Letters: Scenes of Reading and Writing in Nineteenth-Century America* (Chicago: University of Chicago Press, 1993), 18.

26. For other discussions of how Jacobs revises sentimental ideology, see Yellin's introduction to *Incidents in the Life of a Slave Girl*, xiii–xxxiv; Carby, *Reconstructing Womanhood*, 40–61; and Valerie Smith, *Self–Discovery and Authority in Afro–American Narrative* (Cambridge, Mass.: Harvard University Press, 1987), 28–43.

27. See, for example, Carby, *Reconstructing Womanhood*, 58–59.

28. For an analysis of Freud and hysteria, see Hélène Cixous and Catherine Clément, *The Newly Born Woman*, trans. Betsy Wing (Minneapolis: University of Minnesota Press, 1986, 3–57.

29. Houston A. Baker Jr., *Blues, Ideology, and Afro–American Literature: A Vernacular Theory* (Chicago: University of Chicago Press, 1984), 51–54.

30. Frances Smith Foster, "Parents and Children in Autobiography by Southern Afro–American Writers," in *Home Ground: Southern Autobiography*, ed. Bill J. Berry (Columbia: University of Missouri Press, 1991), 102–6; and Sarah Way Sherman, "Moral Experience in Harriet Jacobs's *Incidents in the Life of a Slave Girl*," *NWSA Journal* 2 (Spring 1990): 177–80.

31. William Wells Brown, *Clotel; or the President's Daughter*, ed. William Edward Farrison (1853; New York: Carol Publishing Co., 1969), 243.

32. Franny Nudelman, "Harriet Jacobs and the Sentimental Politics of Female Suffering," *ELH* 59 (Winter 1992): 956, 957.

33. V. Smith, *Self-Discovery and Authority in Afro-American Narrative*, 43.

34. Albert J. Raboteau, *Slave Religion: The "Invisible Institution" in the Antebellum South* (New York: Oxford University Press, 1978), 230–31.

35. "The Nat Turner Insurrection," *Anglo-African Magazine* 1 (December 1859): 386.

36. Barbara A. White, "'Our Nig' and the She–Devil: New Information about Harriet Wilson and the 'Bellmont' Family," *American Literature* 65 (March 1993): 19–52.

37. Sharon V. Salinger, *"To Serve Well and Faithfully": Labor and Indentured Servants in Pennsylvania, 1682–1800* (Cambridge: Cambridge University Press, 1987), 3, 10, 103–12.

38. Karla F. C. Holloway has argued that Wilson's narrative is characterized by a form of monologism that reflects Frado's straitened social and economic circumstances. I would note, however, that this monologism is undercut by the the presence of multiple perspectives in the text ("Economies of Space: Markets and Marketability in *Our Nig* and *Iola Leroy*," in *The [Other] American Traditions: Nineteenth-Century Women Writers*, ed. Joyce W. Warren [New Brunswick, N.J.: Rutgers University Press, 1993], 127–31).

39. Robert C. Toll, *Blacking Up: The Minstrel Show in Nineteenth-Century America* (New York: Oxford University Press, 1974), 76–81; 137–45.

40. See Baym, *Woman's Fiction*, 37–38; and Gates, "Introduction," xli–xlii.

41. Carby, *Reconstructing Womanhood*, 44–45.

42. Gates, "Introduction," li.

43. On the picaresque as an early American novelistic genre, see Cathy N. Davidson, *Revolution and the Word: The Rise of the Novel in America* (New York: Oxford University Press, 1986), 151–78.

44. Carnes, *Secret Ritual and Manhood*, 32.

45. For a discussion of temperance ideology, see Barbara Leslie Epstein, *The Politics of Domesticity: Women, Evangelism and Temperance in Nineteenth-Century America* (Middletown, Conn.: Wesleyan University Press, 1981), 89–120.

46. Frances Ellen Watkins, "The Two Offers," *Anglo–African Magazine* 1 (September 1859): 288–91; (October 1859): 311–13; 289. All references are to this edition and are placed within the text.

47. *Anti–Slavery Bugle*, April 23, 1859.

Chapter 7

1. For a more detailed account of James Forten's life, see Ray Allen Billington, "Introduction," *The Journal of Charlotte L. Forten* (New York: Norton, 1981), 12–19; for a discussion of downward occupational mobility in antebellum Philadelphia, see Stuart Blumin, "Mobility and Change in Philadelphia," in *Nineteenth-Century Cities*, ed. Stephen Thernstrom and Richard Sennett (New Haven, Conn.: Yale University Press, 1969), 200–2.

2. Payne, *Recollections*, 51.

3. *The Journals of Charlotte Forten Grimké*, ed. Brenda Stevenson (New York: Oxford University Press, 1988), 92, 156. All further pages references to the *Journals* will be placed parenthetically within the text.

4. James Forten Jr., *An Address Delivered before the Ladies' Anti-Slavery Society of Philadelphia on the Evening of the 14th of April, 1836* (Philadelphia: Merrihew and Gunn, 1836), 5–6.

5. See also Stevenson, "Introduction," *Journals of Charlotte Forten Grimké*, 26.

6. For a short history of the *Home Journal*, see Frank L. Mott, *A History of American Magazines*, 5 vols. (Cambridge, Mass.: Harvard University Press, 1938–68), 2:349–55.

7. For the texts of "A Parting Hymn" and "The Angel's Visit," see William Wells Brown, *The Black Man, His Antecedents, His Genius, and His Achievements* (New York: T. Hamilton, 1863), 191, 196–99.

8. Payne, *Recollections*, 51; Mary Virginia Wood's album is located in the Francis J. Grimké Papers, Manuscript Division, Moorland–Spingarn Research Center.

9. See Gloria Oden, "The Black Putnams of Charlotte Forten's Journal," *Essex Institute Historical Collections* 126 (October 1990): 248.

10. M. H. Abrams, "The Correspondent Breeze: A Romantic Metaphor," in *The Correspondent Breeze*, ed. M. H. Abrams (New York: Norton, 1984), 25–43.

11. Margo Culley, "'I Look at Me': Self as Subject in the Diaries of American Women," *Women's Studies Quarterly* 3/4 (1989): 20.

12. Jane H. Hunter, "Inscribing the Self in the Heart of the Family: Diaries and Girlhood in Late-Victorian America," *American Quarterly* 44 (March 1992): 51–61.

13. See Braxton, *Black Women Writing Autobiography*, 85.

14. I paraphrase and quote here from Ann Douglas, *The Feminization of American Culture* (New York: Avon, 1978), 255.

15. For a discussion of the elm as a New England literary emblem, see Buell, *New England Literary Culture*, 306–7.

16. For a discussion of the picturesque, see David Miller, *Dark Eden: The Swamp in Nineteenth-Century American Culture* (Cambridge: Cambridge University Press, 1989), 134–35.

17. Alan Liu, *Wordsworth: The Sense of History* (Stanford, Calif.: Stanford University Press, 1989), 61–99, 117.

18. M. H. Abrams, "Structure and Style in the Greater Romantic Lyric," in *Romanticism and Consciousness: Essays in Criticism*, ed. Harold Bloom (New York: Norton, 1970), 225.

19. Quoted in Billington, "Introduction," 29.

20. For a fuller discussion of the Port Royal experiment, see Billington, "Introduction," 27–36; and especially Willie Lee Rose, *Rehearsal for Reconstruction: The Port Royal Experiment* (Indianapolis: Bobbs-Merrill, 1964).

21. For a discussion of the iconography of the swamp and the oak in nineteenth-century American art, see Miller, 6.

22. For a discussion of the shout, see Stuckey, *Slave Culture*, 27.

23. Laura Matilda Towne, *Letters and Diary of Laura Towne; Written from the Sea Islands of South Carolina, 1862–1884*, ed. Rupert Sargent Holland (New York: Negro Universities Press, 1969), 11, 87, 178.

24. Quoted in Rose, *Rehearsal for Reconstruction*, 161.

25. See also Ray Allen Billington, "Charlotte L. Forten Grimké," in *Notable American Women, 1607–1950*, 3 vols., ed. Edward T. James (Cambridge, Mass.: Harvard University Press, 1971), 2:96.

26. Charlotte L. Forten, "Life on the Sea Islands," in *Two Black Teachers during the Civil War*, ed. James M. McPherson (New York: Arno Press, 1969), 67. All further page references to the article will be placed parenthetically within the text.

Chapter 8

1. Eric Foner, *Reconstruction: America's Unfinished Revolution, 1863–1877* (New York: Harper and Row, 1988), 77. My comments on Reconstruction are endebted to Foner's much lengthier discussion.

2. Stanton, Anthony, and Gage, *History of Woman Suffrage*, 2:391.

3. DuBois, *Souls of Black Folk*, 76, 78.

4. Quoted in Still, *Underground Railroad*, 772.

5. Quoted in Sterling, *We Are Your Sisters*, 284–85.

6. Martin and Mohanty, "Feminist Politics," 196, 195.

7. Quoted in Sterling, *We Are Your Sisters*, 402.

8. Quoted in Still, *Underground Railroad*, 768, 772.

9. Quoted in ibid., 775.

10. Quoted in ibid., 767.

11. Quoted in Sterling, *We Are Your Sisters*, 402.

12. For a full account of these western emigration movements, see Nell Painter, *Exodusters: Black Migration to Kansas after Reconstruction* (Lawrence, Kans.: University Press of Kansas, 1986), esp. chaps. 6–10.

13. The text of this speech is reprinted by Titus in her portion of the *Narrative*. It may

also be found in Montgomery, *Comparative Analysis*, 101–3. All page references are to Titus's *Narrative* and are placed within the text.

14. Frances Titus, "Appendix," *Narrative of Sojourner Truth* (Battle Creek, Mich.: [Adventist] Review and Herald, 1884), 18–19.

15. Mary Ann Shadd Cary Papers, Manuscript Division, Moorland-Spingarn Research Center.

16. Brodhead, *Cultures of Letters*, 77–89, 122–33.

17. M. Graham, "Introduction" xliii.

18. For a discussion of the early American epic, see John McWilliams, *The American Epic: Transforming a Genre* (Cambridge: Cambridge University Press, 1989), 15–59; on *Leaves of Grass* as a "lyric-epic," see James E. Miller Jr., *The American Quest for a Supreme Fiction: Whitman's Legacy in the Personal Epic* (Chicago: University of Chicago Press, 1979), 25–31.

19. "Moses: A Story of the Nile," in Foster, *A Brighter Coming Day*, 156. All page references are to this edition and are placed within the text; *Anglo-African Magazine* 1 (May 1859): 160.

20. See also Foster, *Written by Herself*, 136–37.

21. See also ibid., 139.

22. Sterling Brown, "On Dialect Usage," in *The Slave's Narrative*, ed. Charles T. Davis and Henry Louis Gates Jr. (New York: Oxford University Press, 1985), 37; Wideman, "Frame and Dialect," 35.

23. "The Deliverance," in Foster, *A Brighter Coming Day*, 201–2.

24. "Lines to Hon. Thaddeus Stevens," in *Poems* (Philadelphia: Merrihew and Thompson, 1871), 4. All page references are to this edition and are placed within the text.

25. Lawson A. Scruggs, *Women of Distinction: Remarkable in Works and Invincible in Character* (Raleigh: L. A. Scruggs, 1893), 196.

26. Majors, *Noted Negro Women*, 214.

27. Charlotte Forten, "Charles Sumner," in *The Life and Writings of the Grimké Family*, 2 vols., ed. Anna J. Cooper (privately printed, 1951), 2:24. With the exception of Forten's May 1872 article on Whittier published in *Scribner's* and her June 1874 *Christian Register* letters, all of her writings discussed here are collected in this volume. Page references are placed within the text.

28. Susan Stewart, *On Longing: Narratives of the Miniature, the Gigantic, the Souvenir, the Collection* (Baltimore: Johns Hopkins University Press, 1984), 151–66.

29. Friedrich Nietzsche, *The Birth of Tragedy and the Case of Wagner*, trans. Walter Kaufmann (New York: Vintage Books, 1967), 35.

30. Robert W. Rydell, *All the World's a Fair: Visions of Empire at American International Expositions, 1876–1916* (Chicago: University of Chicago Press, 1984), 10–37.

31. Remy Saisselin, *The Bourgeois and the Bibelot* (New Brunswick, N.J.: Rutgers University Press, 1984), 62–74.

32. Douglas, *Feminization of American Culture*, 249–56.

33. On allegory, see J. Hillis Miller, "The Two Allegories," in *Allegory, Myth, and Symbol*, ed. Morton W. Bloomfield (Cambridge, Mass.: Harvard University Press, 1981), 357; on the Victorian language of flowers, see Michael Waters, *The Garden in Victorian Literature* (London: Scolar Press, 1988), 117–25.

34. "The Mission of the Flowers," in Foster, *A Brighter Coming Day*, 232.

35. See also Paula Giddings, *When and Where I Enter: The Impact of Black Women on Race and Sex in America* (New York: Bantam Books, 1984), 75.

36. Mary Ann Shadd Cary Papers, Manuscript Division, Moorland-Spingarn Re-

search Center. Unless otherwise noted, all quotations from and references to Cary's article and thesis drafts will be from this collection.

37. Stanton, Anthony, and Gage, *History of Woman Suffrage*, 3:73.

38. For the full text of these three speeches, see *Proceedings of the First Anniversary of the American Equal Rights Association, Held at the Church of the Puritans, New York, May 9 and 10, 1867* (New York: Robert J. Johnston, printer, 1867). All page references are placed within the text.

39. For the text of this speech, see the *Proceedings of the Eleventh Woman's Rights Convention Held at the Church of the Puritans, New York, May 10, 1866* (New York: Robert J. Johnston, printer, 1866). All page references are placed within the text. It is significant that this speech, which severely criticizes the conduct of white women, was omitted from *The History of Woman Suffrage*.

40. For the text of this speech, see Foster, *A Brighter Coming Day*, 219–22. All page references are placed within the text.

41. *Proceedings of the National Convention of the Colored Men of America, held in Washington D.C. on January 13, 14, 15, and 16, 1869* (Washington D.C., 1869), 12.

42. *Transactions of the National Association for the Promotion of Social Science*, ed. George W. Hastings (London, 1862), xi.

43. For the text of this speech, see Foster, *A Brighter Coming Day*, 271–75. All page references are placed within the text.

44. Quoted in Still, *Underground Railroad*, 774.

45. Mary Ann Shadd Cary Papers, Manuscript Division, Moorland-Spingarn Research Center.

46. *Proceedings of the National Labor Convention* (Washington D.C., 1869), 4. All page references are placed within the text.

Selected Bibliography

Articles and Books

Abrams, M. H. "Structure and Style in the Greater Romantic Lyric." In *Romanticism and Consciousness: Essays in Criticism,* edited by Harold L. Bloom, 201–29. New York: Norton, 1970.

———, ed. *The Correspondent Breeze: Essays on English Romanticism.* New York: Norton, 1984.

Adamson, Walter L. *Hegemony and Revolution: A Study of Antonio Gramsci's Political and Cultural Theory.* Berkeley: University of California Press, 1980.

Allen, Richard. *The Life, Experience and Gospel Labors of the Rt. Rev. Richard Allen.* Philadelphia: Martin and Boden, 1833.

Alter, Robert, "Psalms." In *The Literary Guide to the Bible,* edited by Robert Alter and Frank Kermode, 244–62. Cambridge, Mass.: Harvard University Press, 1987.

Anderson, Benedict. *Imagined Communities: Reflections on the Origin and Spread of Nationalism.* London: Verso, 1991.

Anderson, Osborne P. *A Voice from Harper's Ferry: A Narrative of Events at Harper's Ferry.* Boston: Printed for the Author, 1861.

Andrews, William L. "The Novelization of Voice in Early African American Narrative." *PMLA* 105 (January 1990): 23–34.

———. *To Tell a Free Story: The First Century of Afro-American Autobiography, 1769–1865.* Urbana: University of Illinois Press, 1986.

———, ed. *Sisters of the Spirit.* Bloomington: Indiana University Press. 1986.

Arguments, Pro and Con, on the Call for a National Emigration Convention. Detroit: George E. Pomeroy, 1854.

Ashcroft, Bill, Gareth Griffiths, and Helen Tiffin. *The Empire Writes Back: Theory and Practice in Post-colonial Literatures.* London: Routledge, 1989.

Ayerst, David. *The Manchester Guardian: Biography of a Newspaper.* Ithaca, N.Y.: Cornell University Press, 1971.

Baker, Houston A., Jr. *Blues, Ideology, and Afro-American Literature: A Vernacular Theory.* Chicago: University of Chicago Press, 1984.

———. *Modernism and the Harlem Renaissance.* Chicago: University of Chicago Press, 1987.

Bakhtin, M. M. *The Dialogic Imagination: Four Essays.* Edited by Michael Holquist. Translated by Caryl Emerson and Michael Holquist. Austin: University of Texas Press, 1981.

259

Barthes, Roland. *Camera Lucida: Reflections on Photography*. Translated by Richard Howard. New York: Hill and Wang, 1981.

———. *Image/Music/Text*. Translated by Stephen Heath. New York: Hill and Wang, 1977.

Baym, Nina. *Novels, Readers, and Reviewers: Responses to Fiction in Antebellum America*. Ithaca, N.Y.: Cornell University Press, 1984.

———. *Woman's Fiction: A Guide to Novels by and about Women in America, 1820–1870*. Ithaca, N.Y.: Cornell University Press, 1978.

Bearden, Jim, and Linda Butler. *Shadd: The Life and Times of Mary Shadd Cary*. Toronto: New Canada Publications, 1977.

Bell, Howard H. *A Survey of the Negro Convention Movement, 1830–1861*. New York: Arno Press, 1969.

Benjamin, Walter. *Illuminations*. Edited by Hannah Arendt. Translated by Harry Zohn. New York: Harcourt, Brace, and World, 1968.

Bercovitch, Sacvan. *The American Jeremiad*. Madison: University of Wisconsin Press, 1978.

Berger, John, and Jean Mohr. *Another Way of Telling*. New York: Pantheon, 1982.

Berlant, Lauren. "The Female Woman: Fanny Fern and the Form of Sentiment." In *The Culture of Sentiment: Race, Gender, and Sentimentality in Nineteenth-Century America*, edited by Shirley Samuels, 265–81. New York: Oxford University Press, 1992.

Bhabha, Homi K. "Signs Taken for Wonders: Questions of Ambivalence and Authority under a Tree outside Delhi, May 1817." *Critical Inquiry* 12 (Autumn 1985): 144–65.

Billington, Ray A. "Introduction." In *The Journal of Charlotte L. Forten: A Free Negro in the Slave Era*, 7–41. New York: Norton, 1981.

Blackett, Ronald. *Building an Antislavery Wall: Black Americans in the Atlantic Abolitionist Movement, 1830–1860*. Ithaca, N.Y.: Cornell University Press, 1989.

Blair, Hugh. *Lectures on Rhetoric and Belles-Lettres*. 2 vols. London: W. Strahan, T. Cadell, 1783.

Blakely, Allison. "The Negro in Imperial Russia: A Preliminary Sketch." *Journal of Negro History* 61 (October 1976): 351–61.

———. *Russia and the Negro: Blacks in Russian History and Thought*. Washington, D.C.: Howard University Press, 1986.

Blauner, Robert. "Internal Colonialism and Ghetto Revolt." In *Black Society in the New World*, edited by Richard Frucht, 365–81. New York: Random House, 1971.

Blumin, Stuart. "Mobility and Change in Philadelphia." In *Nineteenth-Century Cities*, edited by Stephen Thernstrom and Richard Sennett, 165–208. New Haven, Conn.: Yale University Press, 1969.

Bogin, Ruth. "Sarah Parker Remond: Black Abolitionist from Salem." *Essex Institute Historical Collections* 110 (April 1974): 120–50.

Boone, Margaret S. "The Uses of Traditional Concepts in the Development of New Urban Roles: Cuban Women in the United States." In *A World of Women: Anthropological Studies of Women in the Societies of the World*, edited by Erika A. Bourguignon, 235–69. New York: Praeger, 1980.

Bowen, T. J. *Central Africa: Adventures and Missionary Labours in Several Countries in the Interior of Africa from 1849 to 1856*. London: Frank Cass, 1968.

Boylan, Ann. "Benevolence and Antislavery Activity among African-American Women in New York and Boston, 1820–1840." In *The Abolitionist Sisterhood*, edited by Jean

Fagan Yellin and John Van Horne, 119–38. Ithaca, N.Y.: Cornell University Press, 1994.

Braxton, Joanne M. *Black Women Writing Autobiography: A Tradition within a Tradition.* Philadelphia: Temple University Press, 1989.

Brodhead, Richard H. *Cultures of Letters: Scenes of Reading and Writing in Nineteenth-Century America.* Chicago: University of Chicago Press, 1993.

Brown, Gillian. *Domestic Individualism: Imagining Self in Nineteenth-Century America.* Berkeley: University of California Press, 1990.

Brown, Lucy. *Victorian News and Newspapers.* Oxford: Clarendon Press, 1985.

Brown, Sterling. "On Dialect Usage." In *The Slave's Narrative,* edited by Charles T. Davis and Henry Louis Gates Jr., 37–39. New York: Oxford University Press, 1985.

Brown, William Wells. *The Black Man, His Antecedents, His Genius, and His Achievements.* New York: T. Hamilton, 1863.

———. *Clotel; or the President's Daughter* [1853]. Edited by William E. Farrison. New York: Carol Publishing, 1969.

———. *The Rising Son; or The Antecedents and Advancement of the Colored Race.* [1874]. New York: Negro Universities Press, 1970.

Buell, Lawrence. *New England Literary Culture from Revolution through Renaissance.* Cambridge: Cambridge University Press, 1986.

———. *Selected Poems of Henry Wadsworth Longfellow.* New York: Penguin, 1988.

Campbell, Karlyn Kohrs. "Style and Content in the Rhetoric of Early Afro-American Feminists." *Quarterly Journal of Speech* 72 (November 1986): 434–45.

Carby, Hazel V. *Reconstructing Womanhood: The Emergence of the Afro-American Woman Novelist.* New York: Oxford University Press, 1987.

Carnes, Mark C. *Secret Ritual and Manhood in Victorian America.* New Haven, Conn.: Yale University Press, 1989.

Cary, Mary A. Shadd. *A Plea for Emigration; or, Notes of Canada West.* Detroit: George W. Pattison, 1852.

Caulfield, Mina Davis. "Imperialism, the Family, and Cultures of Resistance." *Socialist Revolution* 2 (1974): 67–86.

Child, Lydia Maria. *Letters from New York.* New York: C. S. Francis, 1845.

Chmielewski, Wendy E. "Sojourner Truth: Utopian Vision and Search for Community, 1797–1883." In *Women in Spiritual and Communitarian Societies in the United States,* edited by Wendy E. Chmielewski, Louis J. Kern, and Marlyn Klee-Hartzell, 21–37. Syracuse, N.Y.: Syracuse University Press, 1993.

Cixous, Hélène and Catherine Clément. *The Newly Born Woman.* Translated by Betsy Wing. Minneapolis: University of Minnesota Press, 1986.

Clifford, James. "On Ethnographic Authority." *Representations* 1 (Spring 1983): 118–46.

Cmiel, Kenneth. *Democratic Eloquence: The Fight over Popular Speech in Nineteenth-Century America.* New York: Morrow, 1990.

Collins, Kathleen. "Shadow and Substance: Sojourner Truth." *History of Photography* 7 (July–September 1983): 183–205.

Cooper, Anna J., ed. *The Life and Writings of the Grimké Family.* 2 vols. Privately printed, 1951.

Cooper, Frederick. "Elevating the Race: The Social Thought of Black Leaders, 1827–50." *American Quarterly* 24 (December 1972): 604–25.

Creel, Margaret Washington. *"A Peculiar People": Slave Religion and Community-Culture among the Gullahs.* New York: New York University Press, 1988.

Crosby, Christina. *The Ends of History: Victorians and the "Woman Question."* New York: Routledge, 1991.

Crummell, Alexander. *The Future of Africa.* [1862]. New York: Greenwood Press, 1969.

Culley, Margo. "'I Look at Me': Self as Subject in the Diaries of American Women." *Women's Studies Quarterly* 3/4 (1989): 15–22.

Curry, Leonard. *The Free Black in Urban America, 1800–1850: The Shadow of the Dream.* Chicago: University of Chicago Press, 1981.

Davidson, Cathy N. *Revolution and the Word: The Rise of the Novel in America.* New York: Oxford University Press, 1986.

Davie, Donald. *English Hymnology in the Eighteenth Century.* Los Angeles: William Andrews Clark Memorial Library, UCLA, 1980.

Delany, Martin R. *Blake; or, the Huts of America.* [1859–62]. Edited by Floyd J. Miller. Boston: Beacon Press, 1970.

———. *Official Report of the Niger Valley Exploring Party.* New York: T. Hamilton, 1863.

———. "The Political Destiny of the Colored Race." In *The Ideological Origins of Black Nationalism,* edited by Sterling Stuckey, 195–236. Boston: Beacon Press, 1972.

De Man, Paul. *Blindness and Insight: Essays in the Rhetoric of Contemporary Criticism.* New York: Oxford University Press, 1971.

Dodson, Jualynne. "Nineteenth-Century A.M.E. Preaching Women: Cutting Edge of Women's Inclusion in Church Polity." In *Women in New Worlds: Historical Perspectives on the Wesleyan Tradition,* edited by Hilah F. Thomas and Rosemary S. Keller, 276–89. Nashville: Abingdon, 1981.

Douglas, Ann. *The Feminization of American Culture.* New York: Avon, 1978.

Douglass, Frederick. "The Heroic Slave." In *The Life and Writings of Frederick Douglass,* 5 vols. edited by Philip S. Foner, 5:473–505. New York: International, 1975.

———. *Narrative of the Life of Frederick Douglass; An American Slave.* [1845]. New York: Anchor Books, 1973.

Du Bois, W. E. B. *The Souls of Black Folk.* [1903]. New York: New American Library, 1969.

Edwards, Viv, and Thomas J. Sienkewicz. *Oral Cultures Past and Present: Rappin' and Homer.* Cambridge, Mass.: Basil Blackwell, 1991.

Elaw, Zilpha. *Memoirs of the Life, Religious Experience, Ministerial Travels, and Labours of Mrs. Elaw.* In *Sisters of the Spirit: Three Black Women's Autobiographies of the Nineteenth Century,* edited by William L. Andrews, 49–160. Bloomington: Indiana University Press, 1986.

Eliade, Mircea. *The Sacred and the Profane: The Nature of Religion.* Translated by Willard R. Trask. New York: Harcourt, Brace, and World, 1959.

Epstein, Barbara L. *The Politics of Domesticity: Women, Evangelism and Temperance in Nineteenth-Century America.* Middletown, Conn.: Wesleyan University Press, 1981.

Fanon, Frantz. *The Wretched of the Earth.* Translated by Constance Farrington. New York: Grove Press, 1968.

Fisher, Philip. *Hard Facts: Setting and Form in the American Novel.* New York: Oxford University Press, 1985.

Foner, Eric. *Reconstruction: America's Unfinished Revolution, 1863–1877.* New York: Harper and Row, 1988.

Foner, Philip S., and George E. Walker, eds. *Proceedings of the Black State Conventions 1840–1865.* 2 vols. Philadelphia: Temple University Press, 1979–80.

Forten, Charlotte L. *The Journals of Charlotte Forten Grimké.* Edited by Brenda Stevenson. New York: Oxford University Press, 1988.

————. "Life on the Sea Islands." [1864]. In *Two Black Teachers during the Civil War*, edited by James M. McPherson, 67–86. New York: Arno Press, 1969.

Forten, James, Jr. *An Address Delivered before the Ladies' Anti-Slavery Society of Philadelphia on the Evening of the 14th of April, 1836*. Philadelphia: Merrihew and Gunn, 1836.

Foster, Frances Smith. "Parents and Children in Autobiography by Southern Afro-American Writers." In *Home Ground: Southern Autobiography*, edited by Bill J. Berry, 98–109. Columbia: University of Missouri Press, 1991.

————. *Witnessing Slavery: The Development of Ante-Bellum Slave Narratives*. Westport, Conn.: Greenwood Press, 1979.

————. *Written by Herself: Literary Production by African American Women, 1746–1892*. Bloomington: Indiana University Press, 1993.

————, ed. *A Brighter Coming Day: A Frances Ellen Watkins Harper Reader*. New York: The Feminist Press at the City University of New York, 1990.

Foucault, Michel. *The Archaeology of Knowledge*. Translated by A. M. Sheridan Smith. London: Travistock, 1972.

————. *Discipline and Punish: The Birth of the Prison*. Translated by Alan Sheridan. New York: Vintage Books, 1979.

Fox-Genovese, Elizabeth. *Within the Plantation Household: Black and White Women of the Old South*. Chapel Hill: University of North Carolina Press, 1988.

Gates, Henry Louis, Jr. *The Signifying Monkey: A Theory of Afro-American Literary Criticism*. New York: Oxford University Press, 1988.

Gatewood, Willard B. *Aristocrats of Color: The Black Elite, 1880–1920*. Bloomington: Indiana University Press, 1990.

Genovese, Eugene D. *The Political Economy of Slavery: Studies in the Economy and Society of the Slave South*. 2d ed. Middletown, Conn.: Wesleyan University Press, 1989.

George, Carol V. R. *Segregated Sabbaths: Richard Allen and the Emergence of Independent Black Churches 1760–1840*. New York: Oxford University Press, 1973.

Giddings, Paula. *When and Where I Enter: The Impact of Black Women on Race and Sex in America*. New York: Bantam, 1984.

Gilbert, Olive, and Frances Titus. *Narrative of Sojourner Truth*. Boston: Published for the Author, 1878.

————. *Narrative of Sojourner Truth*. Battle Creek, Mich.: (Adventist) Review and Herald, 1884.

Gilman, Sander L. "Black Bodies, White Bodies: Toward an Iconography of Female Sexuality in Late Nineteenth-Century Art, Medicine, and Literature." *Critical Inquiry* 12 (Autumn 1985): 204–42.

Graff, Gerald. "Literature as Assertions." In *American Criticism in the Poststructuralist Age*, edited by Ira Konigsberg, 135–61. Ann Arbor: University of Michigan Press, 1981.

Graham, Maryemma. "Introduction." In *Complete Poems of Frances E. W. Harper*, edited by Maryemma Graham. New York: Oxford University Press, 1988.

Gramsci, Antonio. *Selections from Cultural Writings*. Edited by David Forgacs and Geoffrey Nowell-Smith. Cambridge, Mass.: Harvard University Press, 1985.

Griffith, Cyril E. *The African Dream: Martin R. Delany and the Emergence of Pan-African Thought*. University Park: Pennsylvania State University Press, 1975.

Grimké, Angelina. *Appeal to the Christian Women of the South*. New York: Anti-Slavery Society, 1836.

————. *Appeal to the Women of the Nominally Free States*. New York: W. S. Dorr, printer, 1837.

Grimké, Sarah M. *Letters on the Equality of the Sexes and the Condition of Woman: Addressed to Mary S. Parker, President of the Boston Female Anti-Slavery Society.* Boston: I. Knapp, 1838.

Gronniosaw, James. *A Narrative of the Most Remarkable Particulars in the Life of James Albert Ukasaw Gronniosaw.* Leeds: Davies and Booth, 1814.

Hall, Catherine. "Missionary Stories: Gender and Ethnicity in England in the 1830s and 1840s." In *Cultural Studies,* edited by Lawrence Grossberg, Cary Nelson, and Paula A. Treichler, 240–76. New York: Routledge, 1992.

Halttunen, Karen. *Confidence Men and Painted Women: A Study of Middle-Class Culture in America, 1830–1870.* New Haven, Conn.: Yale University Press, 1982.

Hanaford, Phebe A. *Daughters of America, or, Women of the Century.* Augusta, Maine: True and Co., 1883.

Haraway, Donna. "Situated Knowledges: The Science Question in Feminism and the Privilege of Partial Perspective." *Feminist Studies* 14 (Fall 1988): 575–600.

Harper, Frances E. W. "Fancy Etchings." *Christian Recorder,* February 20, 1873.

———. "Fancy Etchings." *Christian Recorder,* April 23, 1873.

———. "Fancy Sketches." *Christian Recorder,* January 15, 1874.

———. *Minnie's Sacrifice. Christian Recorder,* March 20, 1869–September 25, 1869.

———. "Opening the Gates." *Christian Recorder,* October 28, 1871.

———. *Poems.* Philadelphia: Merrihew and Thompson, 1871.

———. *Poems on Miscellaneous Subjects.* Boston: J. B. Yerrinton and Son, 1854. Enlarged, Philadelphia: Merrihew and Thompson, 1857.

———. *Sowing and Reaping. Christian Recorder,* August 10, 1876–February 8, 1877.

———. "The Two Offers." *Anglo-African Magazine* 1 (September 1859): 288–91; (October 1859): 311–13.

Harris, Trudier, and Thadious M. Davis. *Dictionary of Literary Biography.* Vol. 50. Detroit: Bruccoli Clark, 1986.

Hastings, George W. *Transactions of the National Association for the Promotion of Social Science.* London, 1862.

Hastings, Hester. *Man and Beast in French Thought of the Eighteenth Century.* Baltimore: Johns Hopkins University Press, 1936.

Hewitt, Nancy A. "Compounding Differences." *Feminist Studies* 18 (Summer 1992): 313–26.

Hietala, Thomas R. *Manifest Design: Anxious Aggrandizement in Late Jacksonian America.* Ithaca, N.Y.: Cornell University Press, 1985.

Hill, Patricia L. "'Let Me Make the Songs for the People': A Study of Frances Watkins Harper's Poetry." *Black American Literature Forum* 15 (Summer 1981): 60–65.

Holloway, Karla F. C. "Economies of Space: Markets and Marketability in *Our Nig* and *Iola Leroy.*" In *The (Other) American Traditions: Nineteenth-Century Women Writers,* edited by Joyce W. Warren, 126–40. New Brunswick, N.J.: Rutgers University Press, 1993.

Holly, J. Theodore. "Thoughts on Hayti." *Anglo-African Magazine* 1 (November 1859): 363–67.

hooks, bell. *Yearning: Race, Gender, and Cultural Politics.* Boston: South End Press, 1990.

Horton, James O. "Freedom's Yoke: Gender Conventions among Antebellum Free Blacks." *Feminist Studies* 12 (Spring 1986): 51–76.

Horton, James O., and Lois E. Horton, *Black Bostonians: Family Life and Community Struggle in the Antebellum North.* New York: Holmes and Meier, 1979.

Houchins, Sue E. "Introduction." In *Spiritual Narratives,* xxix–xliv. New York: Oxford University Press, 1988.

Howe, Daniel W. *The Unitarian Conscience: Harvard Moral Philosophy, 1805–1861.* Cambridge, Mass.: Harvard University Press, 1970.

Hull, Gloria T., Patricia B. Scott, and Barbara Smith, eds. *All the Women Are White, All the Blacks Are Men, But Some of Us Are Brave: Black Women's Studies.* Old Westbury, N.Y.: Feminist Press, 1982.

Hunter, Jane H. "Inscribing the Self in the Heart of the Family: Diaries and Girlhood in Late-Victorian America." *American Quarterly* 44 (March 1992): 51–81.

Irigaray, Luce. *Speculum of the Other Woman.* Translated by Gillian C. Gill. Ithaca, N.Y.: Cornell University Press, 1985.

Jacobs, Harriet A. *Incidents in the Life of a Slave Girl.* [1861]. Edited by Jean Fagan Yellin. Cambridge, Mass.: Harvard University Press, 1987.

James, Edward T., ed. *Notable American Women, 1607–1950: A Biographical Dictionary.* 3 vols. Cambridge, Mass.: Harvard University Press, 1971.

James, Henry. *William Wetmore Story and His Friends; From Letters, Diaries, and Recollections.* 2 vols. Boston: Houghton Mifflin, 1903.

JanMohamed, Abdul R., and David Lloyd. "Introduction." *Cultural Critique* 6 (1986): 5–12.

Jefferson, Thomas. *Notes on the State of Virginia.* In *Writings*, edited by Merrill D. Peterson. New York: Viking Press, 1984.

Joseph, Gloria I. "Sojourner Truth: Archetypal Black Feminist." In *Wild Women in the Whirlwind: Afra-American Culture and the Contemporary Literary Renaissance*, edited by Joanne M. Braxton and Andrée N. McLaughlin, 35–47. New Brunswick, N.J.: Rutgers University Press, 1990.

Kamuf, Peggy, ed. *A Derrida Reader: Between the Blinds.* New York: Columbia University Press, 1991.

Kelly, Joan. *Women, History and Theory.* Chicago: University of Chicago Press, 1984.

Kemble, Frances Anne. *Journal of a Residence on a Georgian Plantation in 1838–1839.* Edited by John A. Scott. Athens: University of Georgia Press, 1984.

Kerber, Linda K. "Separate Spheres, Female Worlds, Woman's Place: The Rhetoric of Women's History." *Journal of American History* 75 (1988): 9–39.

Kermode, Frank. "Introduction to the New Testament." In *The Literary Guide to the Bible*, edited by Robert Alter and Frank Kermode, 375–86. Cambridge, Mass.: Harvard University Press, 1987.

———. "Matthew." In *The Literary Guide to the Bible*, edited by Robert Alter and Frank Kermode, 387–401. Cambridge, Mass.: Harvard University Press, 1987.

Kristeva, Julia. *Powers of Horror: An Essay on Abjection.* Translated by Leon S. Roudiez. New York: Columbia University Press, 1982.

La Pin, Deirdre. "Narrative as Precedent in Yoruba Oral Tradition." In *Oral Traditional Literature: A Festschrift for Albert Bates Lord*, edited by John M. Foley, 347–74. Columbus, Ohio: Slavica Publishers, 1981.

LaBrew, Arthur R. *Elizabeth Taylor Greenfield: The Black Swan.* Detroit: Arthur LaBrew, 1969.

Lee, Jarena. *Religious Experience and Journal of Mrs. Jarena Lee.* Philadelphia: Printed and Published for the Author, 1849.

Lejeune, Philippe. *On Autobiography.* Edited by Paul J. Eakin. Translated by Katherine Leary. Minneapolis: University of Minnesota Press, 1989.

Levine, Lawrence W. *Black Culture and Black Consciousness: Afro-American Folk Thought from Slavery to Freedom.* New York: Oxford University Press, 1978.

Liu, Alan. *Wordsworth: The Sense of History.* Stanford, Calif.: Stanford University Press, 1989.

Mabee, Carleton. *Sojourner Truth: Slave, Prophet, Legend.* With Susan Mabee Newhouse. New York: New York University Press, 1993.

Majors, Monroe A. *Noted Negro Women: Their Triumphs and Activities.* Chicago: Donohue and Henneberry, 1893.

Martin, Biddy, and Chandra T. Mohanty. "Feminist Politics: What's Home Got to Do with It?" In *Feminist Studies/Critical Studies,* edited by Teresa de Lauretis, 191–212. Bloomington: Indiana University Press, 1986.

Mason, Mary G. "Travel as Metaphor and Reality in Afro-American Women's Autobiography, 1850–1972." *Black American Literary Forum* 24 (Summer 1990): 337–56.

McBee, Alice Eaton. *From Utopia to Florence: The Story of a Transcendentalist Community in Northampton, Mass., 1830–1852.* Northampton, Mass.: Smith College, 1947.

McKay, Nellie Y. "Nineteenth-Century Black Women's Spiritual Autobiographies: Religious Faith and Self-Empowerment." In *Interpreting Women's Lives: Feminist Theory and Personal Narratives,* edited by The Personal Narratives Group, 139–54. Bloomington: Indiana University Press, 1989.

McWilliams, John P. *The American Epic: Transforming a Genre, 1770–1860.* Cambridge: Cambridge University Press, 1989.

Miller, David C. *Dark Eden: The Swamp in Nineteenth-Century American Culture.* Cambridge. Cambridge University Press, 1989.

Miller, Floyd J. *The Search for a Black Nationality: Black Emigration and Colonization, 1787–1863.* Urbana: University of Illinois Press, 1975.

Miller, J. Hillis. "The Two Allegories." In *Allegory, Myth, and Symbol,* edited by Morton W. Bloomfield, 355–70. Cambridge, Mass.: Harvard University Press, 1981.

Miller, James E., Jr. *The American Quest for a Supreme Fiction: Whitman's Legacy in the Personal Epic.* Chicago: University of Chicago Press, 1979.

Miller, Keith D. "Composing Martin Luther King, Jr." *PMLA* 105 (January 1990): 70–82.

Minutes and Proceedings of the General Convention for the Improvement of the Colored Inhabitants of Canada. Windsor: Bibb and Holly, 1853.

Montgomery, Janey W. *A Comparative Analysis of the Rhetoric of Two Negro Women Orators: Sojourner Truth and Frances E. Watkins Harper.* Hays: Fort Hays Kansas State College, 1969.

Moses, Wilson J. *Black Messiahs and Uncle Toms: Social and Literary Manipulations of a Religious Myth.* University Park: Pennsylvania State University Press, 1982.

Mossell, N. F. *The Work of the Afro-American Woman.* Philadelphia: George S. Ferguson Co., 1894.

Mott, Frank L. *Golden Multitudes: The Story of Best Sellers in the United States.* New York: Macmillan, 1947.

———. *A History of American Magazines.* 5 vols. Cambridge, Mass.: Harvard University Press, 1938–68.

Muraskin, William A. *Middle-Class Blacks in a White Society: Prince Hall Freemasonry in America.* Berkeley: University of California Press, 1975.

Nash, Gary B. *Forging Freedom: The Formation of Philadelphia's Black Community, 1720–1840.* Cambridge, Mass.: Harvard University Press, 1988.

New Catholic Encyclopedia. 17 vols. Edited by the Catholic University of America. Palatine, Ill.: J. Heraty, 1981.

Nietzsche, Friedrich. *The Birth of Tragedy and the Case of Wagner.* Translated by Walter Kaufmann. New York: Vintage Books, 1967.

Nudelman, Franny. "Harriet Jacobs and the Sentimental Politics of Female Suffering." *ELH* 59 (Winter 1992): 939–64.

O'Connor, Lillian. *Pioneer Women Orators: Rhetoric in the Ante-Bellum Reform Movement.* New York: Columbia University Press, 1954.

Oden, Gloria. "The Black Putnams of Charlotte Forten's Journal." *Essex Institute Historical Collections* 126 (October 1990): 237–53.

Olmsted, Frederick Law. *A Journey in the Seaboard Slave States, With Remarks on Their Economy.* [1856]. New York: Negro Universities Press, 1968.

Ong, Walter. *Orality and Literacy: The Technologizing of the Word.* London: Methuen, 1982.

Painter, Nell Irvin. *Exodusters: Black Migration to Kansas after Reconstruction.* Lawrence: University Press of Kansas, 1986.

———. "Sojourner Truth in Life and Memory: Writing the Biography of an American Exotic." *Gender & History* 2 (Spring 1990): 3–16.

Payne, Daniel A. *History of the African Methodist Episcopal Church.* Nashville: A.M.E. Sunday School Union, 1891.

———. *Recollections of Seventy Years.* [1888]. New York: Arno Press, 1968.

Peterson, Carla L. "Capitalism Black (Under)development, and the Production of the African-American Novel in the 1850s." *American Literary History* 4 (Winter 1992): 559–83.

———. "'Doers of the Word': Theorizing African-American Women Writers in the Antebellum North." In *The (Other) American Traditions: Nineteenth-Century American Women Writers,* edited by Joyce W. Warren, 183–202. New Brunswick, N.J.: Rutgers University Press, 1993.

Phillippo, James M. *Jamaica: Its Past and Present State.* London: J. Snow, 1843.

Piersen, William D. *Black Yankees: The Development of an Afro-American Subculture in Eighteenth-Century New England.* Amherst: University of Massachusetts Press, 1988.

Porter, Dorothy B. "The Organized Educational Activities of Negro Literary Societies, 1828–1846." *Journal of Negro Education* 5 (October 1936): 555–76.

———. "The Remonds of Salem, Massachusetts: A Nineteenth-Century Family Revisited." *Proceedings of the American Antiquarian Society* 95 (October 1985): 259–95.

Pratt, Mary Louise. "Scratches on the Face of the Country; or What Mr. Barrow Saw in the Land of the Bushmen." *Critical Inquiry* 12 (Autumn 1985): 119–43.

Prince, Nancy G. *A Narrative of the Life and Travels of Mrs. Nancy Prince.* Boston: Published for the Author, 1850.

———. *A Narrative of the Life and Travels of Mrs. Nancy Prince.* [1853]. In *Collected Black Women's Narratives,* edited by Anthony G. Barthelemy, 3–89. New York: Oxford University Press, 1988.

———. *The West Indies: Being a Description of the Islands.* Boston: Dow and Jackson, 1841.

Proceedings of the Colored National Convention, Held at Cleveland, Ohio, on Wednesday, September 6, 1848. Rochester, N.Y.: North Star Office, 1848.

Proceedings of the General Convention for the Improvement of Colored Inhabitants of Canada. Windsor: Bibb and Holly, 1853.

Proceedings of the National Convention of the Colored Men of America, held in Washington D.C. on January 13, 14, 15, and 16, 1869. Washington, D.C., 1869.

Proceedings of the National Emigration Convention of Colored People; Held at Cleveland, Ohio, 24–26 August, 1854. Pittsburgh, 1854.

Proceedings of the National Labor Convention. Washington, D.C., 1869.

Proceedings of the Eleventh Woman's Rights Convention Held at the Church of the Puritans, New York, May 10, 1866. New York: Robert J. Johnston, printer, 1866.

Proceedings of the First Anniversary of the American Equal Rights Association, Held at the Church of the Puritans, New York, May 9 and 10, 1867. New York: Robert J. Johnston, printer, 1867.

Puckett, Newbell N. *Folk Beliefs of the Southern Negro.* [1926] New York: Dover, 1969.

Quarles, Benjamin. *Black Abolitionists.* New York: Oxford University Press, 1969.

Raboteau, Albert J. *Slave Religion: The "Invisible Institution" in the Antebellum South.* New York: Oxford University Press, 1978.

Redding, J. Saunders. *To Make a Poet Black.* [1939]. College Park, Md.: McGrath, 1968.

Remond, Sarah Parker. "The Negroes in the United States of America." *Journal of Negro History* 27 (April 1942): 216–18.

———. "Sarah P. Remond." In *Our Exemplars, Poor and Rich; or Biographical Sketches of Men and Women,* edited by Matthew Davenport Hill, 276–86. London: Cassell, Petter, and Galpin, 1861.

———, ed. *The Negroes and Anglo-Africans as Freedman and Soldiers.* London: Victoria Press, 1864.

Richardson, Marilyn, ed. *Maria W. Stewart, America's First Black Woman Political Writer: Essays and Speeches.* Bloomington: Indiana University Press, 1987.

Ripley, C. Peter, Roy E. Finkenbine, Michael F. Hembree, and Donald Yacovone, eds. *The Black Abolitionist Papers.* 5 vols. Chapel Hill: University of North Carolina Press, 1988–92.

Rosaldo, Michelle Z. "Woman, Culture, and Society: A Theoretical Overview." In *Woman, Culture, and Society,* edited by Michelle Z. Rosaldo and Louise Lamphere, 17–42. Stanford, Calif.: Stanford University Press, 1974.

Rose, Anne C. *Transcendentalism as a Social Movement, 1830–1850.* New Haven, Conn.: Yale University Press, 1981.

Rose, Willie Lee. *Rehearsal for Reconstruction: The Port Royal Experiment.* Indianapolis: Bobbs-Merrill, 1964.

Rossi, Alice S., ed. *The Feminist Papers from Adams to de Beauvoir.* New York: Columbia University Press, 1973.

Russo, Mary. "Female Grotesques: Carnival and Theory." In *Feminist Studies/Critical Studies,* edited by Teresa de Lauretis, 213–29. Bloomington: Indiana University Press, 1986.

Rydell, Robert W. *All the World's a Fair: Visions of Empire at American International Expositions, 1876–1916.* Chicago: University of Chicago Press, 1984.

Said, Edward. "Yeats and Decolonization." In *Remaking History,* edited by Barbara Kruger and Phil Mariani, 3–29. Seattle: Bay Press, 1989.

Saisselin, Remy G. *The Bourgeois and the Bibelot.* New Brunswick, N.J.: Rutgers University Press, 1984.

Salinger, Sharon V. *"To Serve Well and Faithfully": Labor and Indentured Servants in Pennsylvania, 1682–1800.* Cambridge: Cambridge University Press, 1987.

Samuels, Shirley. "Introduction." In *The Culture of Sentiment: Race, Gender, and Sentimentality in Nineteenth-Century America,* edited by Shirley Samuels, 3–8. New York: Oxford University Press, 1992.

Sánchez-Eppler, Karen. "Bodily Bonds: The Intersecting Rhetorics of Feminism and Abolition." *Representations* 24 (Fall 1988): 28–59.

Scarry, Elaine. *The Body in Pain: The Making and Unmaking of the World.* New York: Oxford University Press, 1985.

Schiller, Dan. *Objectivity and the News: The Public and the Rise of Commerical Journalism.* Philadelphia: University of Pennsylvania Press, 1981.

Schuler, Monica. *"Alas, Alas, Kongo": A Social History of Indentured African Immigration into Jamaica, 1841–1865*. Baltimore: Johns Hopkins University Press, 1980.

Scruggs, Lawson A. *Women of Distinction: Remarkable in Works and Invincible in Character*. Raleigh: L. A. Scruggs, 1893.

Sears, John F. *Sacred Places: American Tourist Attractions in the Nineteenth Century*. New York: Oxford University Press, 1989.

Sheffeld, Charles A. *The History of Florence, Massachusetts*. Florence: The Editor, 1895.

Shepard, Eli. "Superstitions of the Negro." In *The Negro and His Folklore in Nineteenth-Century Periodicals*, edited by Bruce Jackson, 247–53. Austin: University of Texas Press, 1967.

Sherman, Joan R. *Invisible Poets: Afro-Americans of the Nineteenth Century*. Urbana: University of Illinois Press, 1974.

Sherman, Sarah W. "Moral Experience in Harriet Jacobs's *Incidents in the Life of a Slave Girl*." *NWSA Journal* 2 (Spring 1990): 167–85.

Smith, Paul. *Discerning the Subject*. Minneapolis: University of Minnesota Press, 1988.

Smith, Valerie. *Self-Discovery and Authority in Afro-American Narrative*. Cambridge, Mass.: Harvard University Press, 1987.

Smith-Rosenberg, Carroll. *Disorderly Conduct: Visions of Gender in Victorian America*. New York: Oxford University Press, 1985.

Sollors, Werner. *Beyond Ethnicity: Consent and Descent in American Culture*. New York: Oxford University Press, 1986.

Sontag, Susan. *On Photography*. New York: Farrar, Straus and Giroux, 1977.

Southern, Eileen. *The Music of Black Americans: A History*. New York: Norton, 1983.

Spengemann, William C. *The Adventurous Muse: The Poetics of American Fiction, 1789–1900*. New Haven, Conn.: Yale University Press, 1977.

Spillers, Hortense J. "Notes on an Alternative Model—Neither/Nor." In *The Difference Within: Feminism and Critical Theory*, edited by Elizabeth Meese and Alice Parker, 165–87. Philadelphia: John Benjamins, 1989.

Spivak, Gayatri C. "Who Claims Alterity?" In *Remaking History*, edited by Barbara Kruger and Phil Mariani, 269–92. Seattle: Bay Press, 1989.

Stallybrass, Peter, and Allon White. *The Politics and Poetics of Transgression*. Ithaca, N.Y.: Cornell University Press, 1986.

Stanton, Elizabeth Cady, Susan B. Anthony, and Matilda Joslyn Gage, eds. *History of Woman Suffrage*. 6 vols. New York: Fowler and Wells, 1881–1922.

Starr, George A. *Defoe and Spiritual Autobiography*. Princeton, N.J.: Princeton University Press, 1965.

Sterling, Dorothy. *We Are Your Sisters: Black Women in the Nineteenth Century*. New York: Norton, 1984.

Stewart, Jeffrey. "Introduction." In *Narrative of Sojourner Truth*, xxx–xlvii. New York: Oxford University Press, 1991.

Stewart, Maria. *Meditations from the Pen of Mrs. Maria W. Stewart*. Washington, D.C., 1879.

———. *Productions of Mrs. Maria W. Stewart*. Boston: Published by Friends of Freedom and Virtue, 1835.

Stewart, Susan. *On Longing: Narratives of the Miniature, the Gigantic, the Souvenir, the Collection*. Baltimore: Johns Hopkins University Press, 1984.

Still, William. *The Underground Railroad*. Philadelphia: Porter and Coates, 1872.

Stone, William L. *Matthias and His Impostures, Or, The Progress of Fanaticism Illustrated in the Extraordinary Case of Robert Matthews, and Some of His Forerunners and Disciples*. New York: Harper and Brothers, 1835.

Story, Rosalyn M. *And So I Sing: African-American Divas of Opera and Concert.* New York: Warner Books, 1990.

Stuckey, Sterling. *Slave Culture: Nationalist Theory and the Foundations of Black America.* New York: Oxford University Press, 1987.

Sudarkasa, Niara. "Female Employment and Family Organization in West Africa." In *New Research on Women and Sex Roles at the University of Michigan,* edited by Dorothy G. McGuigan, 48–63. Ann Arbor: University of Michigan Press, 1976.

———. "Interpreting the African Heritage in Afro-American Family Organization." In *Black Families,* edited by Harriette P. McAdoo, 37–53. Beverly Hills, Calif.: Sage, 1988.

Svin'in, Pavel. *Picturesque United States of America, 1811, 1812, 1813, Being a Memoir on Pavel Svin'in,* edited by Avrahm Yarmolinsky. New York: W. E. Rudge, 1930.

Swift, Zephaniah. *An Oration on Domestic Slavery.* Hartford, Conn.: Hudson and Goodwin, 1781.

Taft, Robert, *Photography and the American Scene: A Social History, 1839–1889.* New York: Dover, 1964.

Terry, Esther. "Sojourner Truth: The Person Behind the Libyan Sibyl." *Massachusetts Review* 26 (Summer–Autumn 1985): 425–44.

Tocqueville, Alexis de. *Democracy in America.* 2 vols. [1835–40]. New York: Vintage Books, 1945.

Toll, Robert C. *Blacking Up: The Minstrel Show in Nineteenth-Century America.* New York: Oxford University Press, 1974.

Tomkins, Fred. *Jewels in Ebony.* London, 1866?

Towne, Laura Matilda. *Letters and Diary of Laura M. Towne; Written from the Sea Islands of South Carolina, 1862–1884,* edited by Rupert S. Holland. New York: Negro Universities Press, 1969.

Turner, Victor. "Liminal to Liminoid, in Play, Flow, and Ritual: An Essay in Comparative Symbology." *Rice University Studies* 60 (1974): 53–92.

———. *The Ritual Process: Structure and Antistructure.* Ithaca, N.Y.: Cornell University Press, 1977.

Vale, Gilbert, *Fanaticism; Its Sources and Influence, Illustrated by the Simple Narrative of Isabella, in the Case of Matthias.* New York: G. Vale, 1835.

Walker, David. *David Walker's Appeal in Four Articles; Together with a Preamble, to the Coloured Citizens of the World.* [1829]. Edited by Charles M. Wiltse. New York: Hill and Wang, 1965.

Washington, Margaret. "Introduction." In *Narrative of Sojourner Truth,* edited by Margaret Washington, ix–xxxiii. New York: Vintage Books, 1993.

Waters, Michael. *The Garden in Victorian Literature.* London: Scolar Press, 1988.

Webb, Frank J. *The Garies and Their Friends.* [1857]. New York: Arno press, 1969.

Welter, Barbara. "The Cult of True Womanhood: 1820–1860." *American Quarterly* 18 (Spring 1966): 151–74.

White, Barbara A. "'Our Nig' and the She-Devil: New Information about Harriet Wilson and the 'Bellmont' Family." *American Literature* 65 (March 1993): 19–52.

Wideman, John. "Frame and Dialect: The Evolution of the Black Voice in American Literature." *American Poetry Review* (September/October 1976): 34–37.

Wills, David W. "Womanhood and Domesticity in the A.M.E. Tradition: The Influence of Daniel Alexander Payne." In *Black Apostles at Home and Abroad: Afro-Americans and the Christian Mission from the Revolution to Reconstruction,* edited by David W. Wills and Richard Newman, 133–46. Boston: G. K. Hall, 1982.

Wilson, Harriet E. *Our Nig; Or, Sketches from the Life of a Free Black.* [1859]. Edited by Henry Louis Gates Jr. New York: Random House, 1983.

Winch, Julie. *Philadelphia's Black Elite: Activism, Accommodation, and the Struggle for Autonomy, 1787–1848.* Philadelphia: Temple University Press, 1988.

Woloch, Nancy. *Women and the American Experience.* New York: Knopf, 1984.

Yarborough, Richard. "The First-Person in Afro-American Fiction." In *Afro-American Literary Studies in the 1990s,* edited by Houston A. Baker Jr. and Patricia Redmond, 105–21. Chicago: University of Chicago Press, 1989.

Yellin, Jean Fagan. *Women and Sisters: The Antislavery Feminists in American Culture.* New Haven, Conn.: Yale University Press, 1989.

Newspaper and Periodical Source

The Black Abolitionist Papers, Microfilm, 17 reels. New York: Microfilming Coporation of America, 1981–83; Ann Arbor, Michigan: University Microfilms.

Newspapers and Periodicals

Anglo-African Magazine (New York). Abbr.: *AAM.*
Anti-Slavery Advocate (London). Abbr.: *ASA.*
Anti-Slavery Bugle (Salem, Ohio). Abbr.: *ASB.*
Atlantic Monthly.
Christian Recorder (Philadelphia). Abbr.: *CR.*
Christian Register (Boston).
Colored American Magazine (Boston).
Commonwealth (Boston).
Frederick Douglass' Paper (Rochester, New York).
Freedmen's Record (Boston). Abbr.: *FR.*
Freedom's Journal (New York)
Liberator (Boston). Abbr.: *Lib.*
National Anti-Slavery Standard (New York). Abbr.: *NASS.*
New National Era (Washington, D.C.). Abbr.: *NNE.*
North Star (Rochester, N.Y.).
Provincial Freeman (Canada). Abbr.: *PF.*
Scribner's Monthly.
Weekly Anglo-African (New York). Abbr.: *WAA.*
Warrington Standard. Abbr.: *WStandard*
Warrington Times. Abbr.: *WTimes*

Manuscript Collections

Manuscript Division, Moorland-Spingarn Research Center, Howard University. Washington, D.C.
  Mary Ann Shadd Cary Papers
  Francis J. Grimké Papers
Manuscript Division, Library of Congress. Washington, D.C.
  Sojourner Truth Papers

Index

Abolitionist movement. *See* Antislavery movement

"Aesthetics of restraint," 124, 128, 183

Africa: African-American women in, 115, 116; emigration to, 110, 111–18, 204–5; as home place, 7–8, 12; Kumina or "African dance" of, 54–55; missionaries in, 115; Prince on, 94, 96; religious beliefs from, 45, 206; social life in, 26–27; Stewart on, 13, 71, 72–73; women in, 72–73, 115–16

Afric-American Female Intelligence Society, 63, 67–68, 72

African-American women: in Africa, 115, 116; body of, exposed by dominant culture, 18, 20–22, 46–47, 81; and care for their bodies, 16; domestic sphere of, 15–16, 198; economic conditions of, during Reconstruction, 231–32, 236; and emigration movement, 112; in ethnic community sphere, 16; friendships with black men of the elite, 17; illnesses of, 21; and liminality, 17–23; limitations on activities of, in ethnic public sphere, 16–17, 22, 57, 58–59, 99, 100–102, 121; local associations of, 19; marginality of, 6–7, 18; missionary work by, 115; national organizations of, 19, 23, 199, 244, 237; in national public sphere, 16; participation in black state and national conventions, 100–102, 230–31, 235–36; public speaking by, 18, 21–22; purpose of writing of, 22; racial anxiety of upper-class women, 136–37; during Reconstruction, 198–99; relationship of self to self and Other in writing by, 23; sexu-

ality of, 20, 30, 33; and social economy, 230–37; social spheres of, 14–17; Stewart on, 66–67; tragic mulatta figure, 141, 154–56, 165–66, 174; Truth's redefinition of, 50–55; in Walker's *Appeal*, 65; and women's rights movement, 224–30. *See also* Body; Sexuality; Women's rights movement; and *specific women*

African Americans: and agrarian philosophy of Shadd Cary, 50, 105–6, 108–9, 118; and agriculture, 232; and the Bible, 56, 60–63; as bourgeoisie, 198; Canadian emigration of, 99, 100, 102, 104–6, 110; community sphere of, 8–10, 159; domestic sphere of, 9, 15–16, 72–73; education of, 85–86, 189–90, 199–201, 232; elite class of, 8–10, 11–13, 17, 18; and emigration movement, 110, 111–18; employment of, 9–10, 50, 94–95, 201, 232; empowerment of black men, 65–66, 173–74, 226; ethnic public sphere of, 10–11, 16–17, 100–102; families and domestic networks of, 10, 15–16, 200–201; literary production of, 11–14; living arrangements of, 10; marriage of, 200; and national sphere, 11, 16–17, 18–19, 100–102; need for unification of black community, 234–36; and "Negro nationality," 112–14, 117–18; place of, during Reconstruction, 202–8; place of, in antebellum North, 7–11; and racial uplift ideology, 11–12; and Reconstruction, 197–99; religion of, 9, 56, 58; social spheres of, 8, 72–73; and Southern homesteads, 202–4; subaltern class of, 9; in urban areas, 7–11;

course of, 46, 49, 205–6; escape to freedom by, 26; and Freedmen's Bureau, 199,
200; Gage's description of, 38, 42, 44,
194; Gage's reconstruction of "A'n't I a
Woman" speech, 51–54; Gilbert's and
Titus's ethnobiographies of, 23, 25–33,
39, 40, 45–46, 52, 76, 81, 200, 204; illiteracy of, 24–25, 29–30; as itinerant
preacher, 18, 28; and longing for community, 26–28, 45; marriage and children of,
25–26; in national public sphere, 16; in
New York City, 26; and newspapers, 44–
45; photographs of, 40–44, 76; public
speaking of, 46–55, 122, 132, 225–28; on
racial issues, 49–50; during Reconstruction, 199, 200, 204–6; relationships with
white reformers, 24–25, 29, 39; religious
beliefs of, 45, 206; self-description of, as
sign, 39, 46; self-naming as, 27, 28; separation from black social activists, 24, 29;
signatures collected by, in "Book of Life,"
39–40; as slave, 25–26, 54, 55; speech
characteristics and voice of, 22, 29, 46–
49; Stowe's description of, 33–34, 35, 38,
42, 44, 47; in subaltern class, 9; travel of,
28; visibility and invisibility of, 29; and
western lands for African Americans, 27,
202–4; and women's rights, 29, 50–55,
199, 224, 225–28; written record surrounding, 24–39
Tubman, Harriet, 24
Turner, Nat, 164, 170
Turner, Victor, 17, 28–29

Unitarianism, 124–25, 129, 132, 230

Vale, Gilbert, 30
Vesey, Denmark, 170
Voice merging, 62–63
Voice of the Fugitive, 103

Walker, David, 17, 27, 57, 63–67, 70, 212,
235; *Appeal to the Coloured Citizens of the
World*, 57, 64–66, 68, 69, 71
Ward, Samuel Ringgold, 106
Washington, Madison, 170
Washington, Margaret, 25, 33, 45
Watkins, Frances Ellen. *See* Harper, Frances
Ellen Watkins
Watkins, William, 9, 17, 120–21, 133, 135

Watkins, William J., 113, 116, 117, 120–21, 133,
135
Watts, Isaac, 60–61, 129
Wear, I. C. *See* Weir [Wear], I. C.
Webb, Frank J., 176; *The Garies and Their
Friends*, 146, 150, 173–75, 176
Webster, Daniel, 143
Weekly Anglo-African, 11, 117, 151, 163
Weir [Wear], I. C., 102, 231
Western migration, 204–6
Wheatley, Phillis, 176, 179
White, Allon, 9, 14
White, Barbara, 165
White racism: African-American resistance
to, 9; Forten on, 185; Forten's responses
to, 216, 217–18; of Northern traders,
204; Remond on, 143–44; Stewart on,
69–70
White women: constraints on British women in
public sphere, 137–38; Angelina Grimké's
antislavery appeal to, 51; and Sarah
Grimké on equality of women; indifference of, 229; public lecturing by, 18;
public sphere of, 66–67; and Shadd Cary,
118; and "slavery of sex," 51; Stewart on
achievements of European women, 71–72;
suffrage movement of, 198, 199; true
womanhood cult and, 20, 50–51; Truth's
relationship with, 24–25, 29, 39, 226;
Truth's women's rights speeches to, 50–
51, 225–28. *See also specific women*
Whitfield, J. M., 111, 112–13
Whittier, John Greenleaf, 185, 186, 189–90,
216, 219
Wideman, John, 31, 212–13
Willis, Nathaniel, 156, 187
Wilson, Harriet: biographical information on,
165; birth year of, 165; compared with
Prince, 97; financial needs of, and publication, 150; marriage of, 165; self and
Other in fiction of, 23; son of, 165. *Our
Nig*: authenticating documents in, 152;
author's preface to, 152; autobiographical
mode of, 94, 152–53, 252n19; ending of,
169; monologism of, 253n38; pseudonym
present in, 152, 169; publication date of,
146; publisher of, 150; refusal to compromise with white abolitionism in, 154; and
sentimentality, 168–69; sexuality in, 166,
167–68; summary of, 165–69; third-

About the Author

Carla L. Peterson is Professor of English and Comparative Literature at the University of Maryland, College Park. Her previous publications include *The Determined Reader: Gender and Culture in the Novel from Napoleon to Victoria* (1986).